Studies in the History of Educational Theory
VOLUME I

Studies in the History of Educational Theory

by

G. H. Bantock

Emeritus Professor of Education, University of Leicester

VOLUME I

ARTIFICE AND NATURE, 1350–1765

London

GEORGE ALLEN & UNWIN

Boston   Sydney

First published in 1980

GEORGE ALLEN & UNWIN LTD
40 Museum Street, London WC1A 1LU

© George Allen & Unwin (Publishers) Ltd, 1980

British Library Cataloguing in Publication Data

Bantock, Geoffrey Herman
   Studies in the history of educational theory.
   Vol. 1: Artifice and nature, 1350–1765
   1. Education – Philosophy – History
   I. Title
   370.1   LA21   79-41411

   ISBN 0-04-370092-6

Typeset in 10 on 11 point Imprint by Bedford Typesetters Ltd
Printed and bound in Great Britain by
William Clowes (Beccles) Limited, Beccles and London

Contents

ERRATUM

Chapter 10, page 215, line 9:
for 'behavioural problems could be
   solved'
read 'behavioural problems could
   not be solved'.

Acknowledgements

I am extremely grateful to the Leverhulme Trust for the award of an Emeritus Fellowship and a grant towards the cost of producing the book. I am also, as ever, grateful to my wife for helping to prepare the manuscript, reading and commenting on the text and producing the index.

Quotations from Castiglione and Montaigne are reprinted by permission of Penguin Books Ltd.

Introduction

I have always thought of educational theory as essentially prescriptive by nature, concerned to draw on such understanding of pupil, social environment and historical circumstance as may seem relevant with a view to pedagogic action. Put another way, it is systematic thought about how to educate people; to emphasise 'systematic' enables one to cut out mere ebullitions of opinion, and 'how' is intended to emphasise content rather than methodology.

'Content', and hence prescription, is what I am personally chiefly interested in. At various times during the last 2000 years books have appeared setting out, in the required systematic way, arguing coherently and drawing on relevant knowledge and understanding, their author's views on what ought to be passed on to the younger generation. These books have tended to proliferate when a change in the current norms has been thought desirable. Thus the medieval period is largely free from this sort of theorising,[1] but during the time of the Renaissance and again in the seventeenth century there is a fair diffusion of advice; this is because both the humanists and the Baconian scientists wished to recommend a new content for transmission to the young. In both cases this was accompanied by expressions of distaste for what was currently being offered.

There was a time when the examination of some of these works formed a very crucial part of the study of Education; and a course on so-called 'great educators', for instance, formed part of the initiation of most, if not all, intending teachers. In recent years, perhaps partly because of the proliferation of seemingly relevant knowledge in the field of Education as a result of the development of the social sciences, and partly because of the unpopularity of such courses among students, they have largely been abandoned. When there is so much that comes piping hot from the educational presses, even when it is not necessarily the product of minds of any very great distinction, why bother about the old fogies even if some of them, at least, were men of parts?

Let me begin an attempt to provide some answers to that question by defining a little more closely the nature of the theorist's prescription. As formal education inevitably involves value decisions it would seem that the omnipresent desire was to recommend the transmission of that part of the adult culture – in the restricted qualitative sense of that word – which was thought to be especially valuable and suitable for transmission to the young. Clearly, then, the recommended curriculum was subject to psychological limitations; but beyond that it represented an interesting indication, sustained by relevant arguments, as to what aspects of contemporary culture people of some sophistication considered to be of special importance. When I speak of 'curriculum' I do not use the word in its present limited sense of time-tabled subjects, but of the whole range of recommendations, whether of morals, manners or specific intellectual or artistic disciplines. Picked out in this way these recommendations are particularly revealing about the relative emphasis given to, say, manners rather than knowledge, or what specific kinds of knowledge were considered important and even why, in any identified historical period. Of course it is not possible to go on from there to extrapolate about the culture as a whole for often these theorists, as I have implied, are pioneers in recommending certain shifts of attention – which might imply a reasonably widespread dissatisfaction with present practices, but a lack of consensus within the society in its entirety. It is, however, possible to recognise growing points which later frequently harden into orthodoxies.

What I am arguing, of course, is that these books should be regarded as important documents in the delineation of intellectual and cultural history; they constitute a digest of adult cognitive, affective and moral cultivation thought to be of such importance that it should form the core of the next generation's understanding and behaviour. Clearly there must be reservations about their *representative* nature and their likely impact on the society as a whole. I have already suggested that initially at least they often betoken a minority view even among that minority which, at certain historical periods, was concerned with formal education at all. But by the time intellectual movements become sufficiently formalised and defined to make them viable for transmission they must already have achieved at least a limited currency and representative quality. In any case, this book is not concerned greatly with practice, though clearly the theorists chosen have all in some degree been effective if only in the long run.

As such these works have the intrinsic interest which attaches to all historical phenomena . . . and perhaps especially to something which so intimately reveals a different mental geography. Perhaps, indeed, the first task is to attempt to chart this mental map as carefully as possible, a difficult feat of the historical imagination. It requires the near impossible, the attempt to escape from the categories of our own thinking to enter upon a very different categorisation, a different set of priorities and a different set of emphases. By the time we get to the seventeenth and eighteenth centuries we begin at least to have the illusion that we are approaching the home country; the signposts – 'reason', 'understanding', 'evidence', 'discovery', 'method' – are beginning to have a familiar look about them; and this has its own significance and interest.

But in the two or three hundred years before then, we inhabited a somewhat different environment which may be identified initially as concerned with 'Words' rather than with 'Things' – or so at least the seventeenth and eighteenth centuries never ceased to imply, for with monotonous regularity they stressed the need to consider 'Things', not 'Words', and from that it is a fair extrapolation that in earlier theorising 'Words' in some way or other had played a predominating part.

So it proves; and the transition from one to the other is marked by an evolution in subject–object relationships and by the replacement of the quite different set of concepts in terms of which the humanists (for so the wielders of words were called) had deployed their educational recommendations. 'Words' were spoken, 'Things' were seen – or at least started out by being seen; the former imply a less differentiated world, the latter an increase in analytic objectivity. In the one case the world ('nature') was conceived of as functioning analogously to human beings, sharing in fundamental orientation their purposiveness, in the other 'nature' became indifferent to human aspirations and worked according to its own internal necessity. 'Words' implied a world of close intermeshed human relationships and hence placed communication at the centre of its educational structure, 'things' necessitated a degree of detachment in order to see them as organised in terms other than human ones, and in the process fostered a degree of individual autonomy and personality differentiation. The profound psychic change – evolved, of course, over long periods – is naturally reflected in the very different fundamental concepts in terms of which the humanists and their 'scientific' successors discussed their educational recommendations. Not only was the difference marked in alternative curricular recommendations but in the whole structure of procedures and psychological orientations intended to implement the two prescriptions. 'Reason' is common to both – but would not incorrectly be thought to refer to appreciably different forms of reasoning in the two cases. In the humanist camp suggestions of freedom or autonomy would be inhibited (though by no means totally excluded) by the centrality of the concept of 'imitation'; 'evidence' ('substance') would be derived not from observation but memory – and so on. Indeed, in only one major respect can it be said that the two sets of recommendations share a common feature – both are the subject of conscious articulation.

It is this feature which must justify my commencement with the Renaissance. Medieval education was little subjected to speculation or suggested revision. It emerged, in general, out of the classical tradition and ecclesiastical need. Medieval thought was highly contentious and in many respects intensely alive; but its foundation in religion secured its position in fundamentals. It needed a reorientation from the divine to the human (*studia humanitatis*) and a consequent shift of emphasis from logic as the instrument of theological argumentation to rhetoric as the tool of a human persuasiveness to encourage the emergence of a supporting theory to the implied reconstruction. The appearance of a revised recommendation is itself symptomatic of the application of critical thought to human affairs and implies an initial involvement of the renaissance mind with the conscious processes of artifice. Thought is no longer directed solely to the reconciliation of human speculation (of whatever kind) with revelation; tentatively it takes its first steps in the autonomous direction of life itself.

These educational articulations are the subject of this book. It is not intended to provide a sort of Cook's Tour of theorists, neatly encapsulated in brief summaries of their views on teacher, pupil and content but to choose those which seem to have a particular significance and interest developmentally or intrinsically and to comment in detail on such of their views as seem relevant to intellectual history and the understanding of its implications which form a major theme. Their notions of what should be taught are therefore central and one needs to ask what their recommendations were and what they implied in the contemporary structure of cultural learning. The humanists, for instance, suggested attention to rhetoric. What, in contemporary terms, did the stress on rhetoric betoken? Clearly it implied speech – the orator – and such writing as it involved was careful not to forget its affiliation with the spoken word – writing was a kind of speech to Castiglione's courtier. So initially one enters a world where the spoken still has a certain priority over the written and before the printed had helped reorient the whole psychic structure of the human individual. Not only speech, however, but persuasive speech – speech highly wrought in structure for a political or suasive purpose. Hence the training in the articulation of the argument and the employment of the 'commonplaces' and the 'figures' derived from classical sources. So one is led to the models and 'amplifications' also derived from classical times – the 'places' from whence derived the content – and the specific role and implications of 'imitation'. Notions of 'imitation' are so opposed to current stresses on 'creativity' and 'originality' that its role in what is clearly a very different psychic make-up deserves fuller investigation. What was imitated and how did it differ – if at all – from copying? Part of the humanist training involved the study of classical texts. What use in discourse was made of them, how did this study differ from that of medieval times, and what was implied by some of the recommended techniques and exercises, for instance that of Ascham's double translation? (Underlying the whole movement was an acceptance of artifice as a necessary spur to 'nature' – a recurrent pair of antithetical concepts which gives the book its title.)

These, of course, are simply a small selection of questions which may be asked in an attempt to reconstruct the different psychic make-up of the renaissance humanist. It has its own intrinsic interest, like all attempts at historical reconstruction; but its significance may be allowed to go beyond this. The artefacts – paintings, sculptings, buildings and writings – of the Renaissance constitute some of the most glorious and permanent additions to our cultural wealth. How did it come about that a system of education so apparently derivative produced a civilisation so rich in achievement and in the profoundest sense, original? We happen to know that the greatest literary genius the world has perhaps ever known underwent a grammar school education of the sort implied by this account; we happen to know that he deployed the reading he had done and the literary techniques he had mastered to great effect in his plays. Modern scholarship has reconstructed in precise detail what was almost certainly offered to him by his schoolmaster and demonstrated with equivalent details its deployment in the plays he has left behind him. It is impossible to dismiss the education as irrelevant or think of him as an untutored genius: Shakespeare underwent a particular sort of training and its incidence is everywhere apparent, built in to the substance of his theatrical rhetoric. A firm linkage must be made between the education he received and the plays he wrote. Though, as I have said, this book is not primarily concerned with the way in which the theorists' prescriptions are put into practice, an opportunity to gauge the incidence of a particular recommendation is too great to miss.

In the period of nearly 400 years which have elapsed since he wrote we have evolved a very different cultural orientation and a much altered set of psychic priorities and purposes. All civilisations, however, suffer from the unexamined accepted self-evidence of their assumptions; and the 'creative' success (I introduce the modern approved word deliberately) of a fundamentally different articulation must surely do nothing but good in drawing attention to an unanticipated but possible parochialism in our current acceptances. I am far from suggesting any crude imposition of a set of priorities derived from a very different cultural configuration in circumstances greatly altered from those prevailing when they appeared applicable; but I see no reason why current prejudices and conventionalities should not benefit from the reassessments mooted and indeed, to the conscientious and receptive mind, enforced. Viewed in the perspective of human history and human achievement, there is in fact nothing self-evidently 'right' or permanent about current preoccupation with, say, 'autonomy', 'freedom' and the like; for they, too, are revealed, in these studies, as the outcome of a specific orientation of the human spirit, an orientation which, like the previous incarnation, has bestowed immense benefit on mankind but for which, again as in the previous incarnation, a price has been exacted.

So the study of educational theory as a facet of intellectual and cultural history should prove intrinsically interesting and at the same time not without a certain profit for those with minds open enough to sense that past achievements have not always proved inferior to contemporary ones and that previous conditions of high accomplishment may conceivably have more than an historical interest. Educational theory has been neglected partly because the richness of its affiliations has been neglected. The most hackneyed curriculum recommendation, methodological injunction or psychological observation may summon up a whole configuration of thought or affective processes historically significant and by their very difference intellectually provocative. Nothing is more serious in contemporary educational theorising in its various guises, philosophical, sociological and psychological, than the neglect of the historical dimension, as I have constantly urged. We are all the children of memory as well of our own time and we absorb from our earliest training and experience concepts and affects loaded with historical significance. How is it possible to discuss anything like education which is essentially concerned with the transmission of the known and given, the habits of thought and behaviour already *in situ* – even the feigned novelty of 'problem solving' requires a grasp of the context within which the problem makes sense – without attention to historical considerations? Nowhere are the essential intellectual conditions within which any system of schooling must operate clarified more succinctly or more fundamentally than in the work of the historical theorists. Progressive education, for instance, would have gained immeasurably from a study of some of its basic principles in Rousseau – where a careful analysis would have assisted an assessment of the strengths and weaknesses of the recommendations; and attention to previous criticisms made by Rousseau's contemporaries would have established the whole progressive movement on a much more reliable and less naïve basis. By neglecting its history and its origins in a particular phase of cultural history progressivism has failed to protect even what is sound in its doctrines, so that in country after country – Russia, the USA, and now increasingly in this country – it has invited rejection, and the strengths as well as the sentimentalities of the movement are in danger of being eclipsed.

It is right and proper that cultural history should be seen as integrally linked with social processes – deeply affected by institutional life and the whole structure of society. Indeed 'affected' itself, by implying two self-contained entities rubbing off on one another, imperfectly suggests the close integration of our institutional and structural life and the culture which in a measure could be regarded as a manifestation of what is basically an inter-active process. Though I have to a degree suggested here linkages with wider political and social processes I have not made them the main focus of my attention. One has to stop somewhere, otherwise the whole work becomes unwieldy. In any case, thought manifests a degree of autonomy – it is about the world, even if from a specific social viewpoint. Only Durkheim (whom, I am ashamed to say, I had not read until the first draft of this book was completed) seems to make some attempt to see educational theory in its cultural context;[2] and Durkheim, though predictably brilliant and lucid in exposition, is now out of date – he is, in any case, totally inadequate on the Renaissance and concerned specifically with the Gallic scene. The usual approach tends to be either philosophical – as is the case in very different ways with John Adams and Professor Kingsley Price – or social and political, as is the case with William Boyd and Professor James Bowen. In my own exposition I have had to rely on the work of many other scholars – and I hope due acknowledgement is made of this fact, for this is a work of inter-pretation rather than, in the strict sense, one of scholarship. In the last thirty years the whole historiography of our intellectual life has undergone a transformation as historians have patiently attempted imaginative projec-tions into very different categories of thought and feeling. In my efforts to clarify and interpret what lies behind some of these often very baldly stated pedagogic recommendations I have made full use of these efforts. I hope that, in return, I may encourage other scholars to pay attention to what, in this country at least, has recently been a very neglected field of study. If I can only convince a few people that there is something there to be looked at – and something potentially of considerable cultural richness, indicative of important movements of thought – then I shall have succeeded in my aim. No man can hope to encompass the range of thought implied in an educational curriculum satisfactorily. To encourage others to probe further – if only in correction of my own shortcomings – would help to open up a significant and revealing area of historical study.

This book, then, does not pretend to cover all the theorists who wrote within the stated period – hence the series title '*Studies* in', etc.; nor does it set out to discuss all aspects of even those theorists included. Its themes relate primarily to the interplay of notions of 'nature' and 'artifice' (which is so historically revealing) and to the curricular and behavioural objectives implicit in the recommendations, with close attention to their significance within the wider culture. During the process of historical change 'imitation' gives way to gradually evolving notions of cognitive independence, attention to 'words' is replaced by attention to 'things'. These altered perspectives are symptomatic of a fundamental reorientation of the human mind in its mode of functioning and in its relations to the external world. In this volume the story is taken to the point when the efforts of mind in search of autonomy have sufficiently succeeded in the process of disengagement from any historical affiliations as to have revealed the beginnings of a serious identity crisis which lies behind much post-Rousseau theorising. Humanist replaced scholastic but the quarrel remained, as it were, identifiably within the family; even the earlier 'empirics', Comenius and Locke, retained important historical affiliations. But Rousseau's attempt to abstract the young Emile from his historical culture – doomed in a sense to failure though it was – posed in a new and dramatic fashion the problem of what he was to *become*. From then on, theorising proliferates and a plurality of models gradually emerge for attention. These will form the subject of the next volume.

Every effort has been made to integrate the various and developing themes of the book into the different chapters; at the same time, the studies of the individual theorists are intended to be read separately, if so desired. This means that a small amount of repetition has been necessary so as to allow what has been primarily planned as a continuity to sustain also a certain self-contained quality; but these repetitions have been reduced to the minimum necessary for intelligibility. References, as far as possible, are given to the most easily available editions.

NOTES

1 Not entirely free, however. There was, for instance, the theorising of Hrabanus Maurus (*c.* 776–836), Hugh of Victor (*c.* 1096–1141) and John of Salisbury (*c.* 1110–80); the last, indeed, provided a very early example of a humanist orientation. Good brief accounts of these writers will be found in J. Bowen, *A History of Western Education*, Vol. II (London, Methuen, 1975).

2 I refer, of course, to Durkheim's *The Evolution of Educational Thought* which has recently been translated by Peter Collins and published by Routledge (1977). This is made up of a course of lectures given by Durkheim in 1904–5, related specifically to the formation and development of secondary education in France. The work is immensely readable; but its scientific orientation perhaps makes Durkheim unsympathetic to the primarily literary and artistic interests of the Renaissance, cf. his remark 'art by definition moves in the realm of the unreal and the imaginary' (p. 207). This did, in fact, constitute an important issue in renaissance literary theory – and Durkheim seems unaware of the controversy and of the possibility of other points of view which were particularly strong during the renaissance period. Again, the aristocratic orientation of the Renaissance offends against his 'democratic' sentiments.

PART ONE

The Humanists: 'Words'

CHAPTER 1

'A Chattering Flock':
the Humanist Experience

I

During the fourteenth and fifteenth centuries a group of Italian intellectuals advocated a changed image of the educated man and an altered purpose for education from that which had prevailed in previous times. They included men like Pietro Paulo Vergerius (1349–1420), author of *De Ingenuis Moribus* (*The Education of the Noble Man*) and one of the first of the new educational theorists, Guarino da Verona (1374–1460), who settled in Verona as a Master of Rhetoric, Vittorino da Feltre (1378–1446) who taught in Padua and later, at the request of the Duke of Mantua, established one of the first great schools of the Renaissance, Leonardo Bruni d'Arezzo (1370–1444), former Papal Secretary, who became Chancellor of Florence and historian of the Florentine people, and Aeneas Sylvius Piccolomini, who became Pope Pius II and died in 1464. All of them wrote on education and helped to initiate a revolution in content which focused attention on the *studia humanitatis*[1] (thus earning for themselves the name of humanists) and rhetoric in place of the theological and logical concerns of the scholastics who for so long had dominated much of European education. It is true that the scholastics had not been as ubiquitous in Italy, where the rhetorical tradition was stronger, as they were in the European countries north of the Alps. Nevertheless the humanists, though increasingly well placed in the state bureaucracies of the small Italian principalities and republics, attracted some criticism even in the country where conditions were most favourable to them. A Florentine patrician with literary interests, Cino Rinucci, dismissed those in his own city as a 'chattering flock',[2] ridiculed their concern with the niceties of language and defended scholastic pursuits. What was the quarrel all about?

II

The pre-industrial and especially the pre-print world made the arts of communication central aspects of its educational curriculum. As I am speaking in this respect of a period stretching from classical times until at least the end of the Renaissance it would be surprising if there was unanimity during that length of time as to how exactly these arts were to be defined.

Grammar – the broad structural aspects of language, in this case Latin – certainly laid the foundations, but the status of the two major more advanced linguistic disciplines – logic, with which dialectic was usually but not invariably associated, and rhetoric – was more in doubt. Between them they constituted the medieval and renaissance *trivium* – the arts of Words which provided the content of the basic curriculum. (The *quadrivium* – arithmetic, geometry, astronomy and music – was usually reserved for higher education; the *trivium* was undertaken in at least some measure at school.) Occasionally the definitions of these two more advanced basic studies would suggest that some degree of integration between them was possible and indeed desirable; but, in general, they were regarded as distinct fields of discourse, with definably different functions even though the sheer complexity of human communication did on occasion necessitate a degree of overlap and, indeed, interaction. (Altogether they made up the seven liberal arts.)

Both logic and rhetoric claimed to deal with 'reality'. Logic was the tool of the schoolmen. 'Scholasticism', indeed, refers to the method rather than the content of medieval philosophy; it constituted 'a method of discovering and illustrating philosophical truth by means of a dialectic based on Aristotelian logic'.[3] A major characteristic of the method was the use of disputation by means of which questions were posed and arguments deployed, often through the agency of the logical device of the syllogism. Initially in the scholastic period philosophy was very closely bound to theology, and was employed largely for the purpose of reconciling, by rational means, philosophical postulates with the truths of revelation. Gradually philosophy gained its independence and became an autonomous discipline without any necessary reference to theology. Nevertheless, the general character of scholastic thought remained tied to divine truth and Christian ethics, regarding itself as being, in an explanatory and apologetic capacity, the means by which the reality of divine revelations could be sustained by reason. Methodologically, however, the scholastic approach became increasingly arid; it remained dependent on authoritative texts, employing devices such as deduction and inference to establish the truth of statements concerned with a transcendental reality with which, for instance, it sought to reconcile relevant facts of empirical behaviour. Its discourse was adapted to convince men of intellectual calibre and scholastic training and had little popular appeal. Scholastic logic, indeed, which continued in the hands of the schoolmen to form a rival discipline to the rhetoric of the humanists, was marked by deference to authority manifest in a limited number of texts, an increasingly stiff and highly formalised methodology and a particular concern for the logical methods of Aristotle. It was the intellectual instrument of an ecclesiological civilisation which helped to sustain a hierarchical, God-given social structure.

Rhetoric, the object of humanist study, was much more popularly oriented:

Rhetoric was . . . regarded as the theory behind the statements intended for the populace. Since the populace consisted of laymen, or of people not learned in the subject being treated by a speaker or a writer, and since the speaker or writer by his very office was to some extent a master of the real technicalities of his subject, rhetoric was regarded as the theory of communication between the learned and the lay world, or between expert and layman.[4]

Its highest purpose was to persuade contemporaries to moral truths with a view to the harmonious and fruitful conduct of civic life. As a technique it was influenced greatly by Cicero, though of course it was modified and added to by numerous subsequent advocates of the 'art'. It involved an analytic approach which examined the intended discourse from the point of view of invention (the process of discovering valid arguments and material to render a case plausible), arrangement (the structuring of a discourse), style, delivery and memory. ('Style' and 'delivery' are broadly self-explanatory within the persuasive framework which constituted the *raison d'être* of rhetoric. The role of 'memory' will be discussed later.) Aristotle defined rhetoric as the art of 'discovering in the particular case what are the available means of persuasion'.

But the dilemma the humanists faced was the extent to which rhetoric was to be involved simply with techniques of persuasion (following the Greek Sophists) or was to concern itself with matters of content drawn from a study of philosophy (by which they meant moral philosophy) and human learning. Clearly, discourse could be directed to bad ends; it needed refining, therefore, by knowledge and moral purpose and insight. Yet as its appeal was intended to be popular, limits were placed by the capacity of the audience to comprehend ethical positions, an understanding of which often needed an ability to transcend mere opinion or customary belief. Cicero had found himself in the same dilemma; his opening affirmation in the *De Inventione*, that wisdom without eloquence was of little use in civic life, though eloquence separate from wisdom was often of great harm,[5] was frequently quoted by later writers. Yet philosophy spoke only to the expert – a restricted audience.

On the one hand, then, the humanists were committed to the persuasions of eloquence; on the other the more sensitive of them realised that eloquence, in needing to speak a persuasive popular language, might involve falsities and untruths.

In general the solution they adopted was similar to that of Cicero and Quintilian. They stressed the importance of philosophy and knowledge, but on occasions accepted a somewhat more relaxed ethical stance than in their hearts they knew to be justified. Essentially, however, they remained moralists with that knowledgeable concern for reality in social and political relations that moralists at best demonstrate; they sought the learned orator (*doctus orator*) who had acquired moral insight on a basis of cultivation. Thus Leonardo Bruni in *De Studiis et Literis* (*On Study and Letters*) in repudiating the aridity of contemporary scholasticism is at pains to stress the need for 'true learning':

For true learning has almost died away among us. True learning, I say: not a mere acquaintance with that vulgar, threadbare, jargon which satisfies those who devote themselves to Theology, but sound learning

in its proper and legitimate sense, viz. the knowledge of realities –
Facts and Principles – united to a perfect familiarity with Letters and
the art of expression.[6]

Truth, 'realities', then, were the pursuits of the humanists as well as of their
rivals.

Yet those 'realities' were comprised of very different components. The
scholastics were little concerned with empirical fact; they subordinated close
observation to the need to reconcile behaviour with a divine teleology. The
humanists were increasingly immersed in the world of a purely human
experience; they became more neglectful in the elaboration of metaphysical
explanations.

Both logic and rhetoric, however – and especially rhetoric – made extensive
use of what were called 'commonplaces' – *loci communes, topoi*. The doctrine
of the 'places' has an extensive role to play in all ancient, medieval and
renaissance discourse. 'Places' were sources of arguments and forms of
persuasion – pigeon-holes in the memory, as it were – which would provide
material for an oration. They were storehouses of traditional and classical
sayings, aphorisms, stylistic devices ('figures'), images, which could be
drawn on to support or embellish an argument for the purposes of persuasion,
usually heavily moralistic in content and, where rhetoric was concerned,
intended to add erudition, elegance and distinction to discourse. Books of
these sayings, methodically arranged, abounded during the period of the
Renaissance; used unimaginatively they became clichés, witnessing the
intense reliance on past models, stylistic devices and moral comments which
informed the renaissance mind; and 'invention' which, to the modern mind,
implies the creation of something new, mainly implied the searching out and
recall of suitable commonplaces for the subject in hand. 'Invention . . . as the
Renaissance man conceived it, was the key which opened the wisdom of the
past that it might be applied to contemporary experience.'[7] Prominent later
humanists like Erasmus published collections of these *Adagia* for use and
schoolboys spent long hours paraphrasing and committing suitable passages
and extracts to memory, to be deployed on suitable occasions in 'themes'
written by the children. (The 'commonplaces' could also refer to the headings
or categories (e.g. genus, species, cause, etc.) 'common' to a number of
subjects.)

It has been suggested by Professor Ong that

> Since logic and rhetoric correspond to the basic polarity in life repre-
> sented in other ways by contemplation . . . and action, or intellect and
> will, and since logic and rhetoric have come into being not in the hollows
> of men's minds but in the density of history, it is quite possible to
> analyse almost anything in Western culture (and perhaps in all cultures)
> in terms of its relationship to the logical and rhetorical poles.[8]

Clearly, then, the disputation concerning the relative merits of rhetoric and
logic is of much more than academic interest – indeed it strikes at some of

the deepest political, social and cultural movements of the age. This educational revision, then, reflects a considerable reorientation of the human spirit; and after some initial exposition of the humanists' educational theories it will be necessary to relate them to much broader social and cultural movements.

But some preliminary words of warning are necessary. Though the humanists with their 'new learning' become the focus of attention, it must be remembered that the scholastics continued to exercise their logical skills, especially in the universities, until well into the seventeenth century.[9] Furthermore, as already hinted (and the matter must now be emphasised), the relationship between rhetorician and scholastic was not always as antagonistic as the formulaic polarisation of their approaches would seem to suggest. Often, of course, like Bruni, the humanists expressed only contempt for their 'logic-chopping' rivals. But Coluccio Salutati, a very prominent early humanist, on occasions adopted scholastic procedures of argument and composition and maintained friendly relationships with individual scholastics. After all, both were concerned with argument in some form; it would be surprising if there was not at times a degree of interaction; and this interaction grew in the later renaissance period, especially after the Ramists, in the later sixteenth century, detached 'invention' from rhetoric and considered it a part of logic, leaving only elocution and pronunciation as specifically characterising 'rhetoric'. Again, the first great humanist creative writer, Petrarch, sometimes wrote (in the medieval manner) as if truth was to be found only in the recesses of intellect, and not in public utterance, for he pointed out that the crowd 'is not able to see anything with the mind: it judges all things according to the testimony of its eyes. It is the task of a higher spirit to recall his mind from his senses, and to remove his thoughts from the common practice.' This is to encourage the contemplative outlook of the middle ages rather than the more active social spirit of the humanist: 'Truly then, *unless we care more about what we seem than about what we are*, the applause of the foolish crowd will not please us so much as truth in silence' (my italics).[10] Finally, in the later neo-Platonic phase of the Renaissance (in the latter part of the fifteenth century) there was a certain reversion to more contemplative ideas, partly because the Medicis now held political power in a state (Florence) formerly devoted to republican political idealism; even then, however, it is relevant to remember that the Platonic Academy flourished in the closest connection with Cosimo and Lorenzo de Medici and hence maintained humanistic links with the centres of political power. 'Humanism', after all, is a complex concept containing within it numerous strands; all I can be concerned with here is its general orientation, which was to action rather than contemplation; and with this broad indication of their standpoint in mind, let us first consider, in general terms, who these humanists were.

III

It must not be thought that the humanists used their rhetorical skills in democratic assemblies of entire civic populations though they did seek an extended audience of citizens through their writings. Manifest earliest in Italy they served in general in the bureaucracies of the city states, either as advisers to their princes or in the service of the republican oligarchies. They were the heirs to a strong Italian rhetorical tradition associated with the concern in the schools with *ars dictaminis*, or *dictandi*, the art of letter-writing. Changing social requirements implicit in the development of the city state had created increasingly a demand for lawyers, notaries, administrators, ambassadors, merchants and the like; and here, at least, the clerical monopoly of education was broken quite early. The first reference to a lay teacher in Italy appears in 1130.[11] By the fourteenth century the secular school had become general and grammar schools common. Here the pupils acquired the art of rhetorical expression, which had implications for writing as well as speech:[12]

> This emphasis upon the *ars dictandi*, with its ideal of a formal verbal expression, its stress upon a highly stylised rhetorical expression and its store of *topoi* or commonplaces, was one of the most important features in the promotion of Italian culture of the age. Its influence can be discerned in all medieval literature, but it is particularly prominent in Italian. Its strong hold from childhood on the pupils of the grammar schools explains not only the rhetorical character of writing in the age . . . but also the highly rhetorical character of the Italian language . . .[13]

There was, of course, a close connection between rhetoric and law; and the greatest centre of legal study in medieval Europe, at the University of Bologna, had developed out of a school of rhetoric. Three of the most important of the earlier humanists, Salutati, Bruni and Poggio, were all trained as notaries and originally came of comparatively humble backgrounds. They managed to break into the city's elite because they exercised their pens in the service of the state; they wrote much else besides, but their prime function was that of legally trained administrators, using their skills in the diplomatic and legal service of their society.

Such lowly origins were, on the whole, not usual, though a number of humanists did in fact begin their careers as teachers of rhetoric or in the service of private commercial enterprises. Yet in Florence, an important centre for humanists, the large majority, as Dr Lauro Martines has shown in *The Social World of the Florentine Humanists*, were identified with 'power, place and good breeding'. They all belonged originally, or came to belong, to the ruling class. Economically they can be assigned to the upper and upper middle classes; many originated from old families of distinction; they all married well. They defined, in fact, before the onset of the Medicis the political ideology of the dominant oligarchy. Even though humanism, as it developed, was by no means always associated with quasi-democratic regimes, in its earlier phases it was closely associated with republicanism and civic liberty and in Florence at least there was the closest communication between the humanists and the affairs of the republic; even under the Medicis, as already indicated, they remained close to the centres of power. Those humanists who taught or wrote on education – those with whom we shall be most concerned – taught and advised the sons and daughters of the socially and politically prominent. It has been suggested that at this time 'the aim of a humanist education . . . was to embellish the leisure and fortify the virtue of that approximately 2 per cent of the population of the Italian City States who controlled the levers of political and economic power',[14] even though the humanists represented a point of view which was gradually diffused ever more widely. What, then, as educationists did they advocate?

IV

They believed that man was a creature peculiarly gifted with a capacity for, and a love of, learning. In this they subscribed to the Aristotelian view, expressed in the *Metaphysics*, that 'by nature every man desires to know things' – a view which in itself bore witness to the increased interest in *humanitas* and its mundane characteristics. As Battista Guarino, son of Guarino da Verona and writing probably with his father's direct connivance, put it in *De Ordine Docendi et Studendi* (1459) (*Concerning the Methodology of Studies*):

> To each species of creatures has been allotted a peculiar and instinctive gift. To horses galloping, to birds flying, comes naturally. To man only is given the desire to learn. Hence what the Greeks called *Paideia* we call '*studia humanitatis*'. For learning and training in Virtue are peculiar to man; therefore our forefathers called them '*humanitas*', the pursuits, the activities proper to mankind.[15]

Hence 'The educator . . . is generally entitled to assume a native bent towards mental activity on the part of his charge'; to develop such a 'native bent', however, 'methodical training and experience' were necessary. The stages of development were 'nature, training, practice'.[16] Art (as artifice) was central to the humanists' approach. 'In the pursuit of learning . . . order and method are the secret of progress', Battista Guarino considered;[17] and Vergerius spoke of the need for 'every art' to 'be employed to bring [boys] under control and attract them to grave studies'; especially did 'children of modest powers' need to have their 'natural defects . . . supplied by art'.[18]

Nature, in the sense of those characteristics with which a person was born, was to be recognised by the teacher in his concern for the specific bent of individual children. 'The choice of studies will depend to some extent upon the character of individual minds.'[19] But in all cases original endowment was to be fostered and transcended – the aim was excellence in defined studies, not self-expression. The prevailing image was one of moulding – 'the disposition moulded whilst it is susceptible and the mind trained whilst it is retentive'.[20] For instance, in the development of style, that seemingly most individual form of expression, as in more important matters we may not take usage to be merely the practice of the majority, as Quintilian warns us. Eloquence, like wisdom, like nobleness of life, is a gift of the minority. The usage of the commonalty degrades Latin . . . So we must look for a higher standard for our usage, and we shall find it. For as in Conduct we agree to take as our norm the customary motive and action of *good* men, so by usage in style we mean only such as are exhibited in the uniform practice of scholars and men of education.[21]

'Authoritative usage', then, was the criterion – and the principle of imitation when evoked was advocated only with reference to the best models, for 'the search for models or patterns constituted one of the most conspicuous features of renaissance humanism'.[22] Who provided the best models?

Professor Kristeller defines the central core of the humanists' disciplines, the *studia humanitatis*, in these terms:

a cycle of studies that included grammar, rhetoric, history and moral philosophy, and involved the study of the ancient Greek and Latin authors. The best known, and probably the earliest document is the library canon composed by Nicholas V as a young man; and the same text also makes it clear that theology, jurisprudence, medicine, mathematics, and the philosophical disciplines of logic, physics, and metaphysics were not included among the humanities.[23]

It must be emphasised that individual humanists were by no means ignorant of aspects of the curriculum which are explicitly excluded from this account:

There were humanists who were also artists like Alberti, theologians like Erasmus and Melanchthon, jurists like Alciato or Cujas, physicians like Vesalius, or metaphysicians like Vives.[24]

But undoubtedly the core of the humanist educational and cultural endeavour lay in a revised and more sophisticated attention to the authors of classical Rome and Greece. The humanists collected classical artefacts – sculptures and coins, for instance. They examined classical ruins. But above all, they strove to discover new manuscripts from the classical periods and to purify philologically those which were already in circulation. Thus Vergerius defines humanist studies, in the classical manner, as '*liberal* which are worthy of a free man' and as productive of that 'moral worth and fame' which constitutes the aim of a 'lofty nature'. His major emphasis is on the Art of Letters, defined as history, moral philosophy and eloquence; while not denying that learning might prove an additional weapon in the hands of the cruel and corrupt, 'To a man of virtuous instincts knowledge is a help and an adornment' – a help in that a man of affairs needs 'to speak and write with elegance', an adornment in that it prevents loneliness, diverts from cares and provides inspiration and a key to the secrets of Nature. Manner is as important as matter: 'I do not think that thought without style will be likely to attract much notice or secure a sure survival.'[25] 'Style', of course, implied rhetoric and eloquence, by which we 'bring conviction to differing minds'. Likewise Aeneas Sylvius Piccolomini, later Pius II, in his book *De Liberorum Educatione* (*Concerning the Education of Children*), also emphasises the crucial importance of philosophy and letters, for 'Literature is our guide to the true meaning of the past, to a right estimate of the present, to a sound forecast of the future';[26] and philosophy (by which he implied moral philosophy) constituted the ultimate source of wisdom. He too stresses the role of Eloquence with its attendant disciplines: grammar to order the expression of speech, dialectic to give it point, rhetoric to illustrate it and (moral) philosophy to perfect it. Grammar involved good speech, the arts of prose composition and the writing of letters.

Thus it is emphasised that content must be 'ennobling', worthy of a good man; at the same time, a major stress in these studies is on the quality and elegance of the discourse, as would be expected in view of the rhetorical bias of the humanists; they were proposing a revolution that was essentially stylistic. Thus Battista Guarino in his *De Ordine Docendi et Studendi* emphasises, as his title would suggest, the method of teaching the classical authors in order to secure the maximum elegance and accuracy through an acquaintanceship with the best authorities. The study of metrical form is recommended because it helps 'insensibly [to] mould our taste'.[27] Bruni ties together inextricably 'breadth of learning and grace of style',[28] and recommends the harmonies and rhythms of poetry on the ground that such features are especially relevant to the nature – and nurture – of the soul; he stresses the role of oratory in providing a store of elegant or striking expressions, wealth of vocabulary, an easy-flowing style, verve and force. Vittorino da Feltre taught that refinement of utterance must be accompanied by dignity of mien and carriage, as an indication of elegance of manners. The classics had never lost an important place in the education of the middle ages – for utilitarian purposes at least. What the humanist educators peculiarly added was a new grace and refinement of utterance derived from their practice, and a new insight into the very essence of the classical experience. And such education they regarded as an important propaedeutic to professional studies – law and medicine, for example – as well as existing in its own right. There was every reason why a professional should acquire the style of a gentleman. And indeed it must never be forgotten that, despite its social implications, its engagement with the life of politics and the business of the state, the fundamental engagement of humanist education was with the liberalisation of the mind. It was to provide, in the classical sense, a liberal education; and it was a mind freed from the contingencies of local events by contact with the classical experience – even linguistically it was Latin (latterly Greek and even some Hebrew were added) and not the vernacular which was to be studied – which was then to be redeployed in the service of republic or prince. 'I study much that I may be an educated man, but more that I may be good and free. The one makes one feel right, and the other makes one live rightly', wrote Vergerius.[29] And a humanist training, it was explicitly formulated, was also intended as 'an adornment of leisure'.

Some of the humanists found room for physical exercises, 'for where an active frame is conjoined to a vigorous intellect a true education will aim at the efficient training of both – the Reason, that it may wisely control, the Body that it may promptly obey';[30] furthermore the social position of many of the pupils demanded attention, to some extent in the chivalric tradition, to martial exercises – the art of the sword – and the principles of generalship. More fundamentally, however, the stress of the humanists was to persuade to the equal relevance for those of political standing of 'that other great discipline of mind and character, Literature' and the art of expression: 'To be able to speak and write with elegance is no slight advantage in negotiation, whether in public or private concerns.'[31] Their work was to transform the intellectual standing of the secular elite. Eloquence, sustained by knowledge, was Power. The ultimate aim was *vir virtutis* as a social force, seeking honour as a truly manly man.

V

The very appearance of these admittedly brief studies in educational theory points to an important reassessment of the human position; and the new orientation was, in fact, to penetrate many aspects of life – philosophical, political, artistic, involving changed attitudes to the nature of man and of the cosmos, to space and time. It is clear that medieval learning was conceived of as meeting relatively unchanging needs and was therefore the subject of little educational controversy. In England, for instance, 'the place of schools within the . . . ecclesiastical system was taken for granted, and hardly any conscious effort was made to keep them under control'. The authorities, 'untroubled by heresy until the 1380's, seem to have taken the orthodoxy of the school curriculum for granted and to have been complacent about its quality'.[32]

But this revival of interest in the general theory of education of a kind that had not occurred to any appreciable extent between the times of Augustine and Aquinas necessitated a departure from the customary, a differentiation of social role which implied a certain degree of atomisation. The gradual articulation of a new educational ideal after a long period of quiescence in itself implies an alternative model for the individual, a new identity. The first support, then, for any proposition concerning a developing individual differentiation during the Renaissance is manifest in the very act of recommending change at all. Any heterodoxy implies some breakdown of dominant group norms; and heterodoxy in education, whose function is normally essentially a conservative one, implies a fairly fundamental break with tribal *mores*. What is being advocated constitutes almost inevitably some basic shift in the very norms themselves. In Italy, it is true, as indicated, that there had been a long rhetorical tradition; but the nature of the humanists' rhetorical interests differed very considerably from those of their medieval forebears.[33]

But initially the extent of the heresy is likely to be somewhat circumscribed.

One can only discover from the 'individuality' of the humanist undertaking a comparatively slow diffusion of a new individual identity in the society at large. The humanists themselves in the period of the early Renaissance were relatively few in number; and even their 'individuality' – a word which carries strong atomistic overtones – was limited by the facts that they were rooted, usually, in a particular social context, manifest much of their putative individuality in their fierce civic pride, and fulfilled, in the Italian city state, specific social functions.[34] First and foremost they were citizens, though citizens whose minds had been 'liberalised' by contact with the classics. This is not the private individuality of which the characteristic artistic form was to be found in the novel with opportunities for individual psychological subtleties; but the more public individuality, manifest in the exoteric spectacle of the theatre. The stage was to renaissance 'individuality' what the novel became for romantic inwardness. Renaissance man wished to flaunt himself before an audience; his romantic successor recognised his own uniqueness and accepted, even gloried in, isolation and loneliness. (Rousseau's repudiation of the Citizen as an educational aim marked the end of the renaissance ideal; for that ideal was rooted in a specifically socialised culture – that of the essentially communal experience of the Roman and Hellenistic past.)

Nor must the persistence of scholasticism and all it implied in ecclesiastical organisation be underrated. Yet the general view that the passage from medieval to renaissance outlooks can in general be defined in terms of a change from a theocentric to an increasingly anthropocentric concern is clearly broadly true. Indeed, in a recent book, Professor Ullmann has argued that the humanists represented a radically different conception of man which had its origins in the gradual secularisation of the state in the later middle ages and which, in its concern for the 'natural', unregenerate human being constituted a profoundly significant departure from the traditional image of man regenerated through baptism which had characterised the ecclesiological society of the earlier period. In Professor Ullmann's view, a profound, if gradual, political reorientation preceded the cultural evolution with which we shall be most concerned. The original impulse for a revivified classicism had come from the desire of an increasingly secular society to unearth images, *exempla*, of social and political conduct which might guide the newly developing national or independent states: the classics were thus consulted for 'topical and practical reasons, simply in order to study natural man before his baptismal rebirth had changed him and to learn from the lessons which antiquity had provided for governing the citizen's State'.[35] The Carolingian renaissance of the eighth century had inaugurated the ecclesiastically oriented rule of the Christian middle ages and had exercised 'an unparalleled and fructifying influence on all branches of learning and scholarship'; in the same way, the new politicisation which accompanied the gradually emerging secular state had profound cultural as well as political repercussions: '*Humanitas* and *Christianitas* came to be the ideological poles upon which the new world outlook was to rest.'[36] At first the secular ideal of moral virtue derived from the classics coexisted with the Christian – up to the sixteenth century these were regarded as complementary rather than hostile. But an increasingly secular emphasis can be inferred from changes which gradually affected, for instance, the renaissance doctrine of wisdom (*sapientia*). From being a virtue dependent on the interventions of grace in the Augustinian tradition it gradually came to be conceived of purely as an attribute of the 'natural' man. It becomes 'secularised in its source, in its object, and in its end' – its source 'no longer God but man or nature', its object 'living man' and the 'factual rules' governing their relationships, and its end 'mundane happiness and a good and successful life'.[37]

One of the main contributory factors to the new secular ideology was the study, in Italy, of Roman law which was to provide a source of lay juris-prudence with which to confront ecclesiastical law on increasingly equal terms: 'What . . . Roman law, its study, and its application in the public field did was to set in motion the process of secularisation on the governmental level.'[38] The links between law and rhetoric are obvious enough; the pre-eminence of Italy in this process of secularisation has already been touched upon and is confirmed by Professor Ullmann's findings. What is new and interesting in his thesis, however, is the insistence on a social and political reorientation preceding the cultural and educational; and in so far as educa-tion tends always to reflect social movements rather than to initiate them, the educational revolution with which we are more specifically concerned receives its first really convincing explanation. Gradually, of course, with the development of the relevant studies, what had started as thoroughly practical exercises came to take on a life of their own: 'What had been merely relative, because useful to politics became progressively detached from the original point of reference and assumed autonomous character.'[39] And indeed, it is, in general, true that the humanist educationists, though perfectly aware, as we have seen, of the highly practical and social implications of these recom-mendations, laid stress on their liberal as well as their social benefits.

Untidy though historical developments are, then, a gradually changed orientation, despite hesitations and temporary reversals (as in the revived religiosity of the Reformation), is unmistakable. Professor Kristeller admits that 'there is at least a core of truth in the view that Renaissance thought was more "human" and more secular, although not necessarily less religious, than medieval thought';[40] and though he is right to urge that any such identification of changed orientation should be hedged round with reservations, some shift in focus can be unmistakably identified in the higher consciousness of the age.

To begin with, changes in epistemology in the later middle ages – the re-emergence of nominalism – focused attention on the particular rather than the universal. This move had to some extent been prepared for by St Thomas Aquinas' insistence '*nihil est in intellectu, nisi prius fuerit in sensu*' (the mind cannot perceive anything which has not previously been apprehended by the senses). Thus the world was a 'real' place and no longer a mere shadow and symbol of the true one: 'Grace does not destroy nature, it perfects her.' Thus the natural world was becoming a datum in the apprehension of 'reality', not something to be dismissed simply as shadowing the 'real', transcendental world. Aquinas' epistemology was a moderate realist one, between that of

Plato and the nominalists. The way, indeed, was being prepared for William of Occam and a more thorough-going nominalism; and the significance of this move is admirably summarised by Dr H. B. Parkes:

> The movement of medieval thought from realism to nominalism reflected the more general movement of Western society toward individualistic and rationalistic attitudes. Realism gave support to the belief in the reality of the Church and other organic bodies and in the authority they claimed over their individual members; it also implied that the classes into which feudal society was divided were more real than their individual members. The gradual development of nominalism in the later Middle Ages reflected both the decline in ecclesiastical authority and the rise of economic and social individualism; and by breaking down the whole medieval conception of the universe as a hierarchical order, that development prepared the way for a completely new cosmology in which the basic reality was not God but matter in motion.[41]

The process was a long one – but a start had already been made in the middle ages.

This change in political and philosophical perspective was accompanied by one in ideas of human perfectibility, when Hellenistic–Christian conceptions began to give way to more modest notions more humanly oriented, involving 'the deliberate intervention of . . . fellow man':

> The teleological concept of perfection, for which to be perfect is to attain some remote end, has been replaced by an aesthetic concept, for which to be perfect is to possess a harmoniously developed moral character, a character which men can, in principle, be so educated as to possess here and now.[42]

The older metaphysical yearnings of union with the One, of attaining a vision of God or of the Form of the Good, yield to a more mundane process of moral development arising out of the daily practice of morality; reason in pursuit of moral virtue becomes more important than intellect in contemplative pursuit of metaphysical truth. The urge towards union with God and the interventions of Grace were to be replaced by forms of social enlightenment of which one of the foremost was education: the early civic humanists

> extolled the active life, as contrasted with either the purely contemplative or the mixed life, and identified it with the 'civically good' life of free, enterprising, community-minded citizens. Theirs was essentially a city-centred view of life, reminding us of the etymological origins of such words as 'urbane' and 'civilized'. They totally rejected that ideal of retirement which Epicurus had advocated and monasticism had carried into practice. In many ways, indeed, their attitude represented a resurgence of the ideals of ancient Athens, the Periclean City-State.[43]

Thus a faith in education and the importance of the schoolmaster was being ventilated which has lasted until our own day as, increasingly, during the centuries, men have turned their attention from metaphysical visions to social processes, from dependence on Grace to a reliance on their own efforts to shape their destiny. Augustinian notions of original depravity give way to more optimistic assessments of human nature. Other indications of a re-adjusted vision abound as the highly educated increasingly turned their attention from the cosmic drama implicit in Christian ritual to the 'theatre of the world'. The process – let it be once more emphasised – is protracted and involved: it neither begins in the Renaissance, nor, clearly, has it totally ended today – that is a measure of the complexity which the historian per-force must register in a formulaic abstraction.[44] The humanists nearly always paid overt respect to religion. Many did much more. Though their emphasis was on literary skill, historical and philological scholarship and moral wisdom, so that their thought was in essence the handmaiden of *studia humanitatis*, not of theology, and their main contributions to classical scholarship and, in the fields of conduct, to moral philosophy, the humanist movement must not, as Professor Kristeller points out, be regarded as a harbinger of the Enlighten-ment nor of nineteenth-century Liberalism:

> The often expressed view that theology was by definition scholastic and that humanism had no relevance to it is in need of serious qualifications. After the middle of the fifteenth century, many theologians in history and elsewhere had a humanist training . . . The humanist contribution to patristic scholarship is largely ignored, but it is extensive and im-portant . . . The whole attitude of the Reformation period towards the sources of Christianity, that is, the tendency to go back beyond the Scholastics and their dialectic to the Bible and to the church fathers who still belong to the period of classical antiquity reflects a fundamentally humanistic attitude.

Certainly fifteenth-century Italy produced a large religious and theological literature thoroughly imbued with humanist learning.[45]

Yet there was a general tendency towards the intellectual formulation of various social processes – hitherto regarded as largely customary – in politics, education, artistic activity and the like. In Italy the oligarchies, the princes and tyrants increasingly sought to carve out their own destinies, assisted (as in the case of Machiavelli's *Prince*) by the intellectual formulation of the social and political problems they faced. As Burkhardt pointed out, for instance, the Condottieri attempted to found independent dynasties of their own: 'Facts and the actual relations of things apart from traditional estimates, are alone regarded; talent and audacity win the great prizes.'[46] Personal merit counted increasingly, the ability of a man to direct his destiny apart from traditional role allocations: in the same way, the state was the product of human decision – a work of artifice – not feudal tradition. Whatever refine-ments to the Burkhardtian theses may have been introduced in the intervening century since his book was first published, the picture of a society in which,

for instance, commercialisation permitted a new scope for individual enterprise and the general social condition of a country divided into small, often
warring, states, gave opportunity for the carving out of a personal destiny,
remains broadly true. Furthermore, the somewhat later emergence, in other
parts of Europe, of a nascent nationalism provided further scope for a gradual
political secularisation. The Citizen, the third estate, was gradually making
his presence felt north of the Alps as he had done earlier in Italy.

So this notion of man as the arbiter of his own destiny, as making something through his powers of reason, his capacity for the intellectual formulation, the theoretical articulation of what formerly had been largely instinctive
or habitual, comes to play an increasing part in the renaissance outlook. In
this, of course, it was influenced, as in so much else, by classical models. To
Cicero 'art', derived from Greek precedent, implied those theoretical systems
which, transcending specialist knowledge of detail, provided guiding principles in the exercise of some sophisticated discipline. Thus, for instance, he
complains that Roman law is not yet an 'art' because it lacks systematic
form. His conception of 'art' has affinities with the Greek notion of *techne*,
which involved a set of principles intended to have some practical outcome,
the practice of a sophisticated skill based not on routine experience but general
rules and theoretical knowledge. It involved, therefore, notions of 'making' –
artifice – and would be applied to professions like medicine and to educating
the young – wherever, indeed, theoretical understanding was essential as a
propaedeutic to action. Whenever the words 'art', 'artifice' or 'artificial' are
used in a renaissance context, this derivation must be remembered. At the
same time, it must also be remembered that there were what would be
regarded as 'arts' in our own times (for instance, painting) which in the early
renaissance period had not yet acquired the necessary theoretical basis to
rank as anything other than as crafts – though in fact painting did acquire
'respectability' as a liberal art supported by theory during the renaissance
period. (Science itself, as we shall see, becomes an 'art' in these terms as it
gradually evolves a means of clarifying its developing 'loose' empiricism by
the theoretical underpinning of mathematics and a quantitative methodology.)

In the later Platonic phase of the Renaissance, too, stress was laid on man's
intellectual freedom. Men like Ficino and Giannozzo Manetti (1396–1459)
emphasised his dignity and praised him for his arts and skills and secular
knowledge. Pico della Mirandola insisted, in the later fifteenth century, on
man's liberty to choose his own nature among many potentialities:

> Man's excellence is realised only when he chooses the higher forms of
> moral and intellectual life that are open to him, and this excellence
> belongs to his given nature only in so far as this nature includes among
> its potentialities those higher forms of life.[47]

Given this choice, however, the 'natural' man 'by art, by hard work, by
self-cultivation and self-formation' can bring to fruition the seeds of wisdom
that Nature has planted in him and the wise man becomes the end and perfection of the natural man. 'The wise man is the natural man reduplicated

by art, the fruit, end and wisdom of the natural man . . . Wisdom is innate in the natural man and brought to mature perfection in him' – such was the renaissance culture hero defined by Bovillus in his *Liber de Sapienta* published in 1511, one who can achieve perfection by his own efforts: 'The angel is perfected by nature; man is perfected by art.'[48] 'Art' was the training of nature – and thus a central concept in renaissance theorising.

In other words, the ground was being prepared for a very crucial and important development with profound educational implications. Man was not only being reformulated as importantly a new sort of rational, learning creature: but also that learning, directed by the excellence of its chosen models, constituted the terms in which he achieved his freedom to guide his own destiny and attain, at its highest, his own perfection unassisted by Grace. The orientation of the sophisticated was no longer to contemplation and silence, but to expression and action. The notion of man as artificer, exercising his cultural and political arts in time, characterised a movement which resulted 'in the tremendous expansion of secular culture and learning which it brought about in the area of literature, historiography and moral thought'. The active procedures of the orator, the grammarian and the historian replace the more static approach of the logician, philosopher and philosophical theologian. Active persuasion succeeds the more passive task of the analytical harmonisation of given and revealed texts, will replaces intellect.[49]

Thus renaissance humanism in its historical development (and it must be remembered that it was a phenomenon stretching over 250 years) responded to a certain dissatisfaction with the way in which personal and political values were structured by the transcendent values of Christianity: the world of fact and behaviour, the actual conditions of human and historical order were beginning to seem at odds with the distant and remote defining power of theological and religious imposition. Certainly the attempt persisted to reconcile 'the actual, existential nature of man and the conception and vision of man on which Christianity was premised'.[50] But while it is true that the humanists realised the misery of man's estate as much as they appreciated his potential for action and the exercise of will (this must be stressed, for it constituted an important and perhaps neglected strand in renaissance thought), the gradually predominating effect is one of the new power of man in 'shaping and imposing his will on the world, falling into greater savagery, and soaring beyond the angels'.[51] Intellect is no longer to harmonise the given but, at the disposal of the will, to engender new forms. A passage from Cicero, of which Giannozzo Manetti, Florentine citizen-humanist and author of *De Dignitate et Excellentia Hominis*, seems to have been aware, though he does not directly quote it, defines the new orientation: 'Then, too, the human race has dominion over all the products of the earth – in short we set about the fashioning of another nature, as it were, within the bounds and precincts of the one we have.' The 'fashioning of another nature' – the phrase could hardly be happier in its implication of a new creative *élan* within a world (of nature) which increasingly was being regarded as the special province of man, specifically provided for his delectation.[52] What Manetti in his book does, in fact, is to bring into 'sharper focus and more explicit statement the dynamic and volitional conception of human activism – moral, artistic, technical, civilisational and political . . . Man's dignity lies not in his high status and capacities but in how he utilised them in active functioning'.[53] What was developed in renaissance Italy was

> a vision of man as master of the world through the power of his psychic endowment, both of intellect and will teamed together as an operative, inventive, industrious faculty within the individual, and linked socially with other individuals in given cities, engaged in the construction of civilisation both as a physical aedificatory entity and as a culture sustaining itself through the arts, liberal disciplines and sciences. Men as individuals and as members of a community might take pride in their high god-like dignity that these achievements betokened . . . fittingly consummated in their ultimate heavenly fruition of their Creator – God in whose image they so insistently repeated they themselves were created.[54]

Furthermore, the new empiricism, the new concern for man's existential condition fostered, too, a concern for individual natures: a controversy over the relative worth of birth and talent arose which forecast a new degree of social mobility following the more static, hieratic class divisions of the ecclesiastical age. In Bruni's *Laudatio* it was looked on as matter for congratulation that the service of the state offered a career open to talents:

> The hope of winning public honours and ascending is the same for all, provided they possess industry and natural gifts and lead a serious-minded and respected way of life: for our commonwealth requires *virtus* and *probitas* in its citizens. Whoever has these qualifications is thought to be of sufficiently noble birth to participate in the government of the republic.[55]

This notion that talent and industry and not birth were the signs of true nobility was the theme of Buonaccorso da Montemagna's *Disputatio de Nobilitate*. And here it is culture and learning which make it possible for the lowly born to attain true nobility of spirit, provided they deploy this learning for the good of the commonwealth by participation in public life. Nature extends a similar chance to high and lowly born according to the use they make of their lives. 'In this most excellent task of humanity nobody can accuse Nature that she has not been generous.'[56] And this was a book which was widely diffused beyond Italy and translated into a number of European languages, including English, during the years 1459–60.

And so an alternative identity was being evolved by the humanists, and the nature of that identity was to be profoundly significant for the future. Oriented to social action rather than to contemplation, it revealed a revised belief in the power of words, of rhetoric, to persuade. At the same time, as the more acute of the humanists realised, words as power could constitute a threat as well as an opportunity. Used for purposes of persuasion to action they were open to equivocation; they could hide as well as reveal, or could be turned to evil purposes. The arguments of logic to some extent could be checked according to the rules. But there are no such checks on the persuasions of rhetoric; and this accounts for the concern, noted above, which the humanists showed for moral philosophy. Some of the earlier humanists uttered frequent warnings against falsification through over-zealous appeals to sentiment: 'Swim through the sea of eloquence in such a way that you don't desert truth', urged Salutati in 1400; he even warned against the possible excesses of rhetoric:

> For whatever we say is made up of words and things. And the worth of things is such, that a weighty and knowledgeable utterance even without any adornment of language must be preferred to the most elegant and ornate style.[57]

'By learning', proclaimed Bruni, 'I understand . . . the fitting and honourable kind which joins literary skill with the knowledge of things'.[58] 'Things', of course, is not intended to refer to material objects but 'affairs', objective assessments of situations illumined by moral insights. If the aim of eloquence was 'to control the notions of the mind', the integrity of the speaker was of fundamental importance. Hence the humanists' praise for consistency; and hence Petrarch's warning quoted above against caring more for what 'we seem than about what we are' takes on a new resonance.[59] 'Seeming' constitutes a major dilemma for the new educational ideal; it involves the temptations implicit in the psychic mobility of the new individualism, the opportunity to assume roles other than the traditional and the relatively fixed.

VI

The source of both the humanists' rhetorical and moral insight, then, was to be sought in a 'revival' of classical antiquity; they were profoundly historically oriented. To a degree, classical antiquity required no such 'revival' for in fact interest in it had never passed away: Latin had remained the language of the learned all through the middle ages, and there had been a previous 'revival' of attention to the classics in the eleventh and twelfth centuries. But the nature of the renewed interest varied in a significant way from that of the previous time. In the earlier period the focus of attention had been on the new knowledge, specifically in the fields of law, medicine, logic and natural philosophy, which could be culled from the ancient authors. This revived attention was not without its influence on the style of later medieval Latin: the contemporaries of Abelard knew far more about classical literature than did the contemporaries of Alcuin. But the influence was general and to some extent spasmodic, rather like the development of political humanism itself; it did not penetrate to the core of the writer's consciousness. The work of John of Salisbury will, in the words of Dr R. R. Bolgar, point to the difference between the revival of the twelfth century and the renaissance approach:

John's work is typical. He is the medieval classicist as we find him outside the strictly professional fields. His classical knowledge is not narrow, but it is fragmentary and it influences his view of the world from the outside, modifying his opinions here and there, widening his experience but not as yet providing the kernel of his thought. When the Renaissance Humanists eventually decided to write classical Latin and nothing but classical Latin, they forced themselves by so doing to arrange their experience in the categories common to their classical models, with the result that they entered a new world which gradually became their own to such an extent as to transform even their daily thinking in the vernaculars. The absence of this linguistic rigour in the imitation of the Middle Ages meant that the ancient categories of thought were not wholeheartedly adopted.[60]

The concepts we use, the linguistic conventions we employ, the very syntax of our utterance at once structure and are structured by the world of reality we encounter and cognise – and that reality, and the categories in terms of which we discuss it are, in part at least, the creation of the historical language in which we record it: there is a close relationship between percept and concept. The effect of the close stylistic imitation which constituted the classicism of the humanists was to produce 'men whose worlds of thought and expression stood recognisably nearer to Cicero's than to the traditionally educated average of their day'.[61] Teachers are recommended by Leonardo Bruni to attend to more than the general structure of the writings they are to expound; close scrutiny of the minutiae of style – words, tropes, figures and ornaments of every kind – is to lead to an assimilation in the minutest form of the classical experience.

How that experience and the concepts and expressions in which it was contained structured – among other things – the critical reactions of the humanists to the world around them – in this case to the criticism of contemporary paintings – has been admirably demonstrated by Dr Baxandall:

> In 1300 a man could not think as tightly in [Latin] words as he could by 1500; the difference is measurable in categories and constructions lost and found. To retrieve these facilities, to re-possess the concepts involved not just in words like *decus* and *decor* but in a mood like the Latin subjunctive – concepts often not transferable with any available in languages then current – was much more than a grammarian's *tour de force*; it implied a reorganisation of consciousness on a more complex level.[62]

Again 'experience was being re-categorised – through systems of words dividing it up in new ways – and so re-organised'.[63] And Dr Baxandall goes on to explore the specific words used in art criticism and their possible effects on practice, as well as the pattern of the neo-classical sentence ('The periodic sentence is the basic art form of the early humanists') and demonstrate their effects, not only on art criticism, but on what the humanists themselves actually *saw*. For – as was criticised by the later opposition – 'they let *verba* influence *res* to an extraordinary degree'.[64] When a man has learned a particular language, it organises, for him, the sort of attention he can bring even to visual stimulants:

> People who have trained themselves in the labels *decor* and *decus* will approach a painting by Giotto with a predisposition to look for, distinguish, and recall qualities different from someone equipped with the terms *maniera*, *misura*, and *aria*. A person given to categories like *supersplendere* or *deiformitas*, of course, will attend differently again.[65]

It is even possible that the expectations of the humanists reflected back on what the painters – to whom the patrons, among whom humanists were to be found, called the tune to an extent difficult to appreciate today – saw it as their task to provide. After all, painting became an art – and arts demanded intellectual skills established by practice. Alberti's *De Pictura* indicates the way in which by 'treating the art of Giotto as if it were a periodic sentence by Cicero or Leonardo Bruni' he was able 'to put painting through an astonishingly firm functional analysis'.[66]

All this implies something highly wrought – a closely textured experience controlled by thought as that thought is schematised in verbal concepts; and indeed once more we encounter the notion of art – of artifice, a making – as lying at the centre of the renaissance experience as a matter of personal intervention in and imposition on, the historical process. It is a theme which is clearly highly relevant to education – the 'moulding' of the younger generation. And during this period the part played by words – language – is crucial.

Yet as one assesses the cultural significance of this classical revival, one is faced with a paradox. What at first sight would seem to enforce the production of something essentially derivative, arising out of the assimilation both of the linguistic minutiae and the stereotyped content of the classical past (the 'commonplaces' of the training in rhetoric indicated earlier), in actuality produced a burst of artistic creativity almost unparalleled in the history of mankind. Certainly there were those who copied slavishly – and earned the contempt of their fellow humanists such as Erasmus who mocked them in his *Ciceronianus*; but every system of education has its failures. There were others, manifestly the products of this apparently oppressive regimen, whose creative use of language astonished and continues to astonish the world. The man who, more than any other in the world's history, has explored the sheer range and heterogeniety of human kind – he lacks only the religious dimension, though he has too distinguished a mind to be irreligious – was the product of this education the humanists advocated and slowly imposed. (It came much later, of course, in England than in Italy.) It can with the utmost confidence be asserted that Shakespeare could never have written as he did apart from his rhetorical training, for modern scholarship has reconstructed the sources – many of them the commonplaces – of his greatest verbal triumphs. Thus we have the paradox that this educational regimen (oppressive by modern standards) produced the extraordinary facility and effortlessness of creativity.

What, then, did the training in rhetoric provide Shakespeare with? Briefly, an incredible range of verbal facility, 'effortlessness' capable of being geared to the complexities, nuances and minutiae of meaning in their full cognitive-emotive significance. What marks the miracle of Shakespeare was this store-house of phrase, word, sentence and period capable of being deployed in a hundred different tones and emotional colourings, an astonishing ubiquity of characterisation high and low to whom speech is geared with an almost supernatural surety of touch. He arrived just in time – barely a hundred years before the 'mathematical plainness' began to take over and the language game lost some of its amplitude and richness.

And so we have the profound paradox that revival did not necessitate sub-jugation by the past but a rebirth of fecundity and plenitude – and that this creativity would never have occurred had it not been fed by this assimilation in all its minute detail. The notion of 'imitatio' involved the closest attention to previous models – as Ascham's technique of double translation makes clear; but at the same time this close imitation was intended to foster a degree of internalisation that paradoxically made the scholar free to deploy his linguistic resources in ways which permitted a flexibility creative of a new and refined utterance. The paradox of the situation has been well spelt out by T. W. Baldwin: 'the paradox, which Shakespeare shares with his age. Shakespeare never originated anything; literary types, verse forms, plots etc. etc. And yet he is one of the most original authors who has ever lived'.[67]

VII

This implied divarication between revival and rebirth constituted one of the fundamental tensions of the age: on the one hand there was its appeal to history, its sense of a renewal, its apparent orientation to the past, to a tradi-tion, the customary. At the same time, more clearly than ever before this 'revival' came to recognise the inescapable 'otherness' of historical circum-stance:[68] hence the philological interests of the humanists – their determination to grasp what exactly the classical writers were saying and thus implicitly to accept their identity in time as manifesting something other than contemporary experience. Now a recognition of the 'otherness' of others is to some extent the offshoot of a developing self-identity; and this self-identity, as has been made clear, increasingly involved the subjection of social processes to re-flection and calculation, intellectual formulation – 'the state as a work of art', as Burkhardt put it. The implied contrast between the earlier medieval political outlook where custom did indeed largely reign, and that of the renaissance citizen is spelt out by Professor J. G. A. Pocock: 'It can be argued that the ideal of the citizen implied a totally different conceptualization of the modes of political knowledge and action from that implicit in the scholastic-customary framework.'[69] Within the latter, the scope for individual decision making was limited to those comparatively rare problems where neither custom nor tradition provided a ready-made answer. A citizen, however,

> constantly involved with his fellows in the making of public decisions, must possess an intellectual armory which takes him beyond the perception of hierarchy and tradition, and gives him cause to rely on his and his fellows' power to understand and respond to what is happening to them. A customary community in one corner of an eternal order is not a republic of citizens . . . The citizen must have a theory of knowledge which allows great latitude for public decisions upon public events.[70]

The attitude of the humanists helped to create such an 'intellectual armory' as would place a new emphasis on conscious decision making ('art'). Their approach to history was selective, placing an emphasis on particular periods as being of peculiar value as *exempla*, instead of accepting and appealing simply to the total development as customary and judging in accordance with precedent. The whole 'bias of humanism . . . was toward viewing life in terms of particular actions at particular times'; this was because the humanist, as rhetorician, regarded 'truth as uttered rather than perceived, [and] became interested in the moments and occasions on which – the contexts in which – the speech-acts embodying it had been performed'. For instance, the scholastic abstracted from Aristotle the universal principles to be found there, the humanists regarded his work as that of a specific individual in a specific context: 'the effect of the humanist technique was to exalt philology, the attempt to find out what the documents actually contained, what the words actually meant, what the philosopher, orator, historian, or poet had actually said . . .' The consequences of this approach were considerable; the more men became conscious of the difference in time dividing them from a writer long dead, the more conscious they became of the 'temporal, social, and historical circumstances in which he had expressed his thought and which, in shaping the language and the content of it, had shaped the thought itself'. The implication was that 'the humanist rhetoricians were converting the intellectual life into a conversation between men in time'.[71] Another way of putting it would be that they were becoming increasingly aware of identity – their own and other people's – and hence of difference as well as similarity:

> The idea of direct conversation with antiquity is a key concept in all forms of humanism . . . The conversation with the ancients which results in knowledge is affiliated with the conversation among citizens which results in decision and law . . . If man as intellectual animal is defined as 'humanist', while man as political animal is defined as 'citizen', both acts of knowledge and acts of decision are agreed upon by living men, located in time and employing the intellectual resources possessed by beings so located. [And] such intellectual acts . . . are fixed by both humanists and citizens at the very center of the picture and call for intellectual powers considerably greater than the simple prudence.[72]

The humanist, in fact, by his concern for *vita activa*, had a commitment to participation in human life in particular and concrete detail. He became increasingly conscious of his position in time and the relationship of his times to other people's – hence the development of a specific historical consciousness and the stress he placed on history in his educational recommendations. Hence too he develops an ability to transcend his historical dependence on the classics – and to deploy them creatively as 'experience' on which to build something fresh and new. Both in history and in painting a new sense of perspective enabled men to realise their subject matter in time and space with a new complexity which revitalised their age; hence the importance of the particular educational stress on the value of history.

VIII

So the developing lesson of the Renaissance was that man was, increasingly, to create himself within a given social environment through art and artifice; the offsprings of learning (involving the past) and experience, of control and accomplishment. Joshua Reynolds defended the great style of the high Renaissance as being 'artificial in the highest degree', and presupposing 'in the spectators a cultivated and prepared artificial state of mind'. This view was broadly supported by a nearer contemporary, Vasari, who found in the works of Michaelangelo the culmination of a long process during which Nature had been both followed and subdued in the higher interests of art. In the earlier stages of the fifteenth century 'Nature had been the century's goal, Nature ordered and regulated. It had tried to incorporate truth into art, curbing fantasy often in the interests of science, knowledge and experience . . . But the faults of the fifteenth century partly came from being too simply natural.'[73] Instead, with a developing confidence, finish, assurance, manifestations of 'grazia' (grace) came to be the marks of the ultimate triumph of art over nature – who, having made her contribution (as native 'genius' or even 'inspiration') was to be overtaken in the supreme achievements of an essentially artful art. And so a theme – the relationship of artifice to *nature* – was adumbrated which evokes the central concern of any educative process conceived of as involving some transformation of an original datum through cultivation and culture.

In his 'Study of the History of Ideas', which forms the first chapter of *The Great Chain of Being*, Arthur Lovejoy assigns to the historian of ideas 'an enquiry which may be called philosophical semantics – a study of the sacred words and phrases' and adds: 'The word "nature", it need hardly be said, is the most extraordinary example of this, and the most pregnant subject for the investigations of philosophical semantics.'[74]

The word is indeed used in a wide variety of senses. In the renaissance period Nature (*natura naturans*) was regarded as a creative and regulative power which operated through the physical phenomena of the world and could be said to constitute their immediate cause. Its use in this sense evolved a teleological cosmology and hence was often closely related to or even identified with the Divine; and thus its usage became inescapably normative. What Nature provided or ordered represented a standard: the law of Nature or 'Natural law', for instance, constituted an ideal against which human law could measure itself; it could be appealed to in order to demonstrate the injustice of man-made regulative law. 'Nature', however, could also be used – and during the sixteenth and seventeenth centuries increasingly was – to refer to the physical phenomena of the world – the world of plants and animals, for instance, that part of the phenomenal world not subject to man's cultivation or artifice – things as they now are or have become (*natura naturata*).[75] To copy nature, then, in its most literal sense simply implied the exact representation of features of the external world. One tendency during the late renaissance and post-renaissance period was to abstract nature from its regulative and creative implications, with their associations with the divine, and regard it as something neutral and objective, functioning according to laws and principles quite independent of man and even of God except as Creator and First Mover. In this sense, as that part of empirical nature untouched by the interference of man, the neutral scene of his subsequent endeavours, it comes to be assimilated to the notion of the primitive, that which has not been ordered or interfered with by civilisation, pre-lapsarian *possibly* (but not necessarily). To those who dislike the current order of society (with what man has created) such a primeval setting also comes to take on overtones of the desirable and hence once again to assume normative implications. The nearer a state of nature unspoilt by man's interference the more acceptable; 'nature' provided better what in general the Renaissance assigned to 'nurture', 'art' or artifice. After all, the fact that God was Creator and First Mover afforded Nature even in this sense with a vestigial contact with divinity – a contact, of course, which disappears with the development of secularisation.

An example of what is meant is to be found in Erasmus' *Praise of Folly* – though with the ironic intent usually inseparable from Folly's parody of a humanist oration:

> by far the happiest men are those who have no traffic at all with any of the sciences and follow nature for their only guide . . . Nature hates any counterfeit, and everything turns out to be happier when it's unspoilt by artifice. Well then, can't you see that of all the rest of living creatures the happiest in life are those which have least to do with any scientific training and have nature alone for a teacher? Bees do not even have all natural instincts, yet they are the happiest and most marvellous of insects . . . to be desired is the life of flies and little birds who live for the moment solely by natural instinct . . .[76]

The preferential reference to the lives of the sub-human world clarifies what is intended by 'nature' here – the sentient world untouched by human consciousness or interference as the norm by which to measure the discontents of man. Erasmus explicitly overturns the normal renaissance preference for 'artifice' for his own ironic purposes. Such sentiments go

34

strongly counter to his own recommendations elsewhere in his writings. There thus comes to be an uneasy relationship between usages which are essentially normative and those which are neutral: and normatively nature can be assimilated either to the divine, as the highest, or to the primitive, the simplest.

A further complication is introduced by the fact that though nature was to many Christians something essentially good, though not perfect, because it was God's handiwork and therefore had this close relationship with its Divine Author, there were others who considered nature as man's habitat after his disgrace and expulsion from Paradise; hence its association with the depraved and the Satanic. Thus the divine order of Grace was thought to be separate from and indeed opposed to that of nature. The humanists in general contributed to the rehabilitation of nature and the scientists, by the seventeenth century, carried the process even further in order to protect their attempts to probe the secrets of nature. Nevertheless, used evaluatively, the word often conveys a certain ambiguity: Milton, for instance, in the seventeenth century can still speak of Nature's 'guilty front'. In general, however, the usage becomes increasingly favourable with the passage of time; and the two senses, good and bad, had in any case coexisted even in medieval times.

Then the word is used to refer to those features which constitute the essential defining characteristics of a being or object – those essential qualities which give it its fundamental character. Thus we speak of the 'nature' of man – either in general terms or of an individual specifically; and in both these ways the word is extensively used in educational theory. Ideally the word should here be used neutrally; but often it has normative overtones. If it is said that man by nature cannot fly unaided, the statement is strictly factual and unexceptionable; and there are a number of similar features of man – and of individual men – which must be accepted as fact. But if it is said that man is by nature good, then it is not subject to scientific evaluation, and the statement becomes unmistakably normative in implication. Even if it is asserted that by nature man is a learning creature, the context *may* imply a normative intent, a desire to promote a particular view of man: this is how, for his purposes, the speaker wants to persuade you to see man's potential. Furthermore, to speak of a 'nature' which itself is the creation of a divine nature is to encourage the assimilation of the normative attributes of the divinity to the potentialities of the created, as part of their intrinsic structure rather than dependent on the external interventions of Grace. Attempts, then, to define the essential characteristics of a being may well be covertly normative under the guise of a neutral factuality; to define man as a learning (rather than, say, as an aggressive, being) may be to formulate a covert value-judgement. Historically, for instance, it could constitute a blow aimed against the chivalric tradition (with its emphasis on physical rather than mental attributes), and find support in its putative correspondence with divine intent. Any developmental concept of potentiality put forward as characterising man is likely to prove normative in this way; and so again an ambiguity is introduced into the usage of the word.

Further complications are involved in the use of the concept of naturalness. It is a word which, no doubt because of its associations with the concept of nature in its normative sense, carries with it a general aura of approval in our society – and sometimes, indeed, in the renaissance period. 'Naturalness' is today often contrasted explicitly or implicitly with artificiality, to the detriment of the latter. In general, however, as we have seen, the Renaissance was more appreciative of the virtues of artifice. It implied 'that which displayed art or skill' – and the Renaissance valued the highly wrought. Thus the literary theorist George Puttenham conceived of art as 'a certain order of rules prescribed by reason, and fathered by experience'. 'Artificial' was to him a word of praise, when applied to those 'activities' which needed 'study and discipline or exercise' for their perfection – as 'to dance by measures, to sing by note, to play on the lute, and such like . . . because they be not correctly known or done, but by rules and precepts or teaching of schoolmasters'. During this period, indeed, 'to imitate the excellentest artificiality of the most renowned work-masters that antiquity affordeth' was the ideal which many sought to achieve; and Thomas Nashe thought nothing more 'odious . . . than the artless tongue of a tedious dolt', though he was quick to point to the importance of experience: 'Endeavour to add unto art experience: experience is more profitable void of art than art which hath not experience.'[77] And indeed, as we shall see, in so far as the arts worked on 'nature' with its ambiguous status, at once neutral object and normative power, a characteristic dilemma of the Renaissance was whether the highest products of art were not themselves in some sense 'natural'. But the elucidation of this puzzle must be postponed until the consideration of Castiglione's *Courtier*.

So in any use of 'nature' or its derivatives, one needs constantly to be on one's guard against possible evaluative (normative or even pejorative) implications. Nor is it sufficient simply to be on one's guard. If the word is used approvingly, with clear normative overtones, it is always necessary to ask what it is that is being approved of, for this very often differs from writer to writer. When Erasmus enjoins us to 'follow nature' in educating the young, he means that 'nature' has provided a potential for learning which then needs to be actualised by human intervention and training. When Rousseau employs precisely the same imperative he considers that 'nature' has made men good in a way which can only be spoilt by human intervention. Thus precisely the same injunction is used to bolster, on the one hand, a very definite and forceful human intervention, and on the other hand, a policy of non-interference: 'Do not save time, but lose it', argued Rousseau; for Erasmus there was not a moment to be lost. An appeal to 'nature' by a theorist may well disguise the evocation of an alternative ethic to the prevailing norm. Thus its use needs to be considered in detail in relation to individual theorists.

IX

The humanists, then, define man as a learning animal, and thus reveal their normative bias. They express their evaluative concerns in their desire to transform the initially given through a process of selective acculturation – they stress, even, as we have seen, the *best* models. Their 'best' is manifest in their curriculum and the specific choices within it they emphasise (for example, not only classical literature but especially Cicero). Thus man's original nature (potential) is transformed through culture (in the selective sense): as Erasmus was to put it, '*Homines non nascuntur sed finguntur*' (Men are not born but made). Hence their images of 'moulding', 'fashioning', and their stress on 'art'. Man's 'nature' provides the potential; his 'art' actualises it. Roger Ascham sums up the situation when he urges that 'to the goodness of nature be joined the wisdom of the teacher'.[78]

What they hoped to achieve can be variously described, in accordance with the usage of the term, as the realisation or the transcendence of nature. If 'nature' is regarded as the normative, regulative principle defined above (*natura naturans*), then 'realisation' is appropriate; if it implies simply the phenomenal world (which, though the setting of much that was good, nevertheless remains necessarily imperfect), or, worse, the scene of man's shame and depravity, the alternative usage is implied. What is crucial for my purposes, however, is the recognition of a formative, regulative power through education – essentially, this exercise of art. Only by 'art' can man be 'made' either to surpass or (according to implication) realise 'nature'. In general it can be said that during the later renaissance period most writers would have agreed with Alberti that 'it is rarely granted even to Nature herself to produce anything absolutely perfect in every part'. Thus man's ultimate aim in practice was, whilst respecting what nature had provided, to exercise, in his search for perfection, a formative power which would involve a transcendence of the raw materials of the 'nature' that was offered. Hence the usual position during this period is that culture both accepts what nature provides and seeks to transcend her. Renaissance educators, true to their Ciceronian heritage, are in general not given to primitivism – apart from the perennial appeal exercised by classical pastoral. It is somewhat later that the many primitivistic strains in classicism begin to receive a sympathetic hearing.

In another sense the humanists were increasingly concerned, as noted above, with the 'natural' world – here as opposed to the transcendental. While still accepting man's final other-worldly resting place, they lay increasing emphasis on 'natural' as opposed to 'supernatural' means to salvation. If 'moral activism, heavenly destiny and the dignity of man are closely linked in humanist thought', as Professor Trinkaus asserts, the heavenly destiny is to be achieved through the moral activism as much as through supernatural grace. The world was no longer to be renounced but to provide the scene of man's endeavours: the balance St Thomas had kept between a classical ideal of natural perfection (conceived of as realisable in time) and a Christian ideal of world renunciation and union with God was being weighted, it will be clear from the foregoing, in the direction of the 'natural' world manifest in non-human phenomena, human culture and, increasingly, the interplay between them.

More and more, indeed, the 'natural' world (initially *natura naturata*) lost most of its lingering associations with the satanic. As Arthur Lovejoy has pointed out, in his *Great Chain of Being*, there were extant during the later medieval and renaissance periods two ultimately irreconcilable views of the divine nature manifest in two different principles of the Good. One was the Idea of the Good, God as the 'apotheosis of unity, self-sufficiency and quietude', which men were to seek in the 'way up'; the other the Idea of Goodness – the principle of Plenitude which emphasised God as the source of 'divinity, self-transcendence, and fecundity'.[79]

> The one programme demanded a withdrawal from all 'attachment to creatures' and culminated in the ecstatic contemplation of the indivisible Divine Essence; the other, if it had been formulated, would have summoned man to participate, in some finite measure, in the creative passion of God, to collaborate consciously in the processes by which the diversity of things, the fullness of the universe, is achieved. It would have found the beatific vision in the disinterested joy of beholding the splendour of the creation or of curiously tracing out the detail of its infinite variety; it would have placed the active life above the contemplative; and it would, perhaps, have conceived of the activity of the creative artist, who at once loves, imitates, and augments the 'orderly variousness' of the sensible world, as the mode of human life most like the divine.[80]

On the whole, as Lovejoy points out, the earlier medieval period chose the former; but the latter position, though dormant, did not disappear – and it became dominant as a justification for the artistic creativity of the Renaissance. As Giordano Bruno puts it, '. . . the gods take pleasure in the multiform representation of multiform things, in the multiform fruits of all talents, for they have as great pleasure in all the things that are, and in all representations that are made of them, as in taking care that they be and giving order and permission that they be made'.[81] This principle of Plenitude, then, also reinforces the notions of the goodness of 'nature' conceived of as the fullness of creation; existence in nature is a good, 'i.e. that the addition of concrete actualities to universals, the translation of supersensible possibilities into sensible realities, means an increase, not a loss, of value; that, indeed, the very essence of the good consists in the maximal actualisation of variety, and that the world of temporal and sensible experience is thus good, and the supreme manifestation of the divine'.[82]

Thus was prepared a welcoming attitude of benevolence both to the natural world as embodying the plenitude of God's creativity, the sum of his fecundity and to human artistic achievement which reinforced through man's activity and energy – the person who had been created 'in our [i.e. the divine] image and likeness' – the principle of fullness through an analogous manifestation of creativity. The analogy extended even to the forms created. Thus human artefacts like buildings were intended to reflect, in their mathematical proportions, the forms and harmonies of the natural world which in their turn correlated with the pure forms of absolute mathematics characterising the intelligible world. In this way the natural world manifested an excellence as the visible counterpart of the unseen world graspable by intellect alone; and at the same time human culture was further encouraged to regard the natural world in a benevolent light. To summarise, human culture was seen as both friendly to and yet going beyond 'nature'; nature, in so far as it retained elements of imperfection, offered itself simultaneously to be rejected, accepted in its fecundity and transcended by its own supreme manifestation, man.

X

Certainly man became increasingly aware of the importance of sense experience, the education of the senses through their apprehension of natural 'forms'. Indeed, in 1449 a renaissance playwright wrote as follows:

> The Eye is called the first of all the gates
> Through which the Intellect may learn and taste.
> The Ear is second, with the attentive word
> That arms and nourishes the Mind.[83]

And indeed, any account of the renaissance world which aimed to reveal its implications for education would be incomplete without some reference to manifestations of the observable which are fraught with increasingly important consequences for later renaissance theorists like Vives.

So far the emphasis has been on man's 'making' in the social and political spheres – and a humanist education, directed at the social and political elite, has stressed the ear (words) rather than the eye in the world of experience. But the humanists themselves were not exclusively verbal in their outlook – I have emphasised above their concern for classical artefacts as well as classical language. Furthermore they became increasingly aware of the physical appearance of their cities, as their fostering of grandiose architectural schemes bore witness. A prominent humanist, Leo Battista Alberti, considered architecture as essentially a civic activity, the one most closely connected to the practical needs of man and one most sustaining of that civic pride which so exercised the humanist ideology – through its power of defence against attack and the sheer splendour of its design. He speaks of the arts as other humanists spoke of education: they are 'learnt by reason and method; they are mastered by practice'.[84] There was a close analogy, in broad procedure, between making a building and making a man – indeed it was not customary in the Renaissance to individualise the approach to the specific arts. Hence theories about the creation of works of painting, sculpture or achitecture have their relevance for the educationist. The sheer practicality of the Renaissance must not be overlooked.

Furthermore some of the earlier humanists (Vergerius and Vittorino, for instance) placed great emphasis on the inclusion of geometry and aspects of mathematics and mechanics in their curricula; even Aeneas Sylvius, who allows geometry only a place in the earlier stages of a boy's education, recommends it because it 'quickens alike the perceptive faculty and the reasoning powers'.[85] And it must be remembered that what Aeneas Sylvius calls 'the perceptive faculty' had always been the main educative agency of the commonalty: hence changes in the cognitive style of painting and sculpture, for instance, reveal further aspects of renaissance culture and education and contain within themselves an incipient tribute to the authority of 'things' which were to exercise post-renaissance educationists of the seventeenth century.

Thus much medieval painting and sculpture had been metaphysical in the sense that the manifest images were intended to relate to a transcendental truth. Medieval artists in general – at least those concerned with sacred objects – 'were not out to create a convincing likeness of nature or to make beautiful things – they wanted to convey to their brothers in the faith the content and the message of the sacred story'.[86] In the church's view, the purposes of images were threefold: John of Genoa's late thirteenth-century *Catholicon* summarised them in this way:

> Know that there were three reasons for the institution of images in churches. *First*, for the instruction of simple people, because they are instructed by them as if by books. *Second*, so that the mystery of the incarnation and the examples of the Saints may be the more active in our memory through being presented daily to our eyes. *Third*, to excite feelings of devotion, these being aroused more effectively by things seen than by things heard.[87]

Religious paintings, in fact, constituted the bible of the illiterates; and hence at that time the artist was in general 'not concerned with an imitation of natural forms, but rather with the arrangement of traditional sacred symbols'.[88] Thus the 'arrangement' followed a different logic from that of later times: it reflected a metaphysical hierarchy rather than a naturalistic vision, and its use of space was tailored accordingly. Painting and sculpture constituted a sign language rather than a representation of what, for several centuries, we were to come to regard as 'reality'. Furthermore, all medieval sculpture had been 'applied' sculpture, not free-standing, for free-standing sculptings were regarded as idols.

But gradually the 'cognitive style' alters. Gothic sculptors no longer remained content with purely symmetrical arrangements of draperies; they begin to recapture the lost classical art of letting the body show through, though their aim is still primarily religious; the message matters more than the medium. Also, the 'revival of the free-standing, self sufficient statue was the first achievement of Early Renaissance Art, an achievement that signals a radical unmedieval image of man'; for 'the free-standing statue was a primary symbol of that classical humanity whose modern heirs the Florentines of Leonardo Bruni's time had declared themselves to be'.[89] The Italian painters developed a similar naturalism, and on their canvases deployed space in an entirely new way, no longer reflecting simply the old metaphysical structure but translating the flat surface into an appearance of three-dimensional form and relating the subjects in terms of an internal dramatic structure rather than an external pattern. The device of perspective with its geometrical implications emphasised the standpoint of the individual observer from a fixed position. It constituted that 'rationalisation of sight' which one historian considers to have been 'the most important thing that happened in the Renaissance'. Certainly, by making possible 'the measurement of dimensions and distances in exact and constant terms' it had implications for later scientific advances.[90] It also introduced the notion of the relativity of viewpoint, as it came to be accepted that reality could be considered from a variety of angles and this incipiently raised the issue as to what was 'real' – a question with most important implications for the epistemology of the seventeenth century. In this it was encouraged by rhetorical practice which, in debate and argument, fostered a plurality of perspectives.

The part played by Giotto in these developments is notorious and hardly needs elaboration. 'Painting, for him, is more than a substitute for the written word. We seem to witness the real event as if it were enacted on a stage.'[91] Painting, indeed, comes to be localised and particularised increasingly in the post-Giotto era and such manifestations as portrait painting begin to appear. As an educative device – in the wider sense – pictorial representation was defended by that early humanist already mentioned, the Chancellor of Florence, Colucci Salutati: partly on the grounds that the nature of the understanding was analogous to that of the ancient Romans' feelings about their religious images, but also on those, already rehearsed, that 'one enters into understanding and knowledge of spiritual things through the medium of sensible things', a sentiment which might well have recommended itself to St Thomas Aquinas and was therefore pervasive among the intellectuals – scholastic and humanist – of the times. And though in considering the humanists we are concerned with a limited minority, while initially pictures and images constituted the bible of the ignorant, there is a profound significance in the fact that, from very different viewpoints, intellectuals and populace were beginning to share a common world of sense-experience. True, the intellectuals relied primarily on the power of words, and their emphasis was on books and letters. But inevitably they participated in a highly visual culture. As indicated above, they were keen collectors of visual artefacts, sculptings, architectural remains – which further shaped their apprehension of current building programmes – and smaller objects like coins, with their impressed portraits of the emperors, intaglios, cameos and the like.[92] Then, they formed part of that enhanced lay patronage for art – no longer primarily religious – which characterised the period; and contemporary painters themselves employed a visual language of gesture (for instance) which related to the sign language of orators, preachers, 'skilled visual performers with a codified range of gesticulation'.[93] There were links, too, with the gestures of drama and dancing, and both Alberti's treatise on painting and Guglielmo Ebreo's treatise on dancing 'shared a preoccupation with physical movements as a reflex of mental movements' and were 'expressive of psychological relationships'.[94] The new pictorial style constituted the visual counterpart to the rhetorical emphasis of the new learning.

All this is cognate to any attempt to chart the mental geography, the newly conceived sense of reality of a renaissance Italian with humanist interests. If 'drawing' does not rank high in the humanists' educational priorities until later, this does not mean that, in so imagistic a culture, visualisation did not play an important part in their psychic make-up. The objections to drawing were largely intellectual and social (it ranked initially, as noted earlier, as a manual rather than a liberal art because it lacked a set of theoretical principles). But humanist education was intended to produce an essentially dramatic, active life, the man of affairs treading the world's stage – the active citizen directing and administering the affairs of state: such a world is visual as well as oral, and the image of himself produced by humanist education implied visual as well as oral effects. These visual elements of the culture constituted part of the new common reality, a new 'naturalism'; a concern for the phenomenal world which was to play an important part in the developing cosmology. But of course it was in line with the humanist preoccupation with making, 'moulding', shaping and fashioning, a world where reason was to play a conspicuous part, through the realisation of geometrical form and mathematical harmony. Perspective was based on primarily scientific principles which facilitated the translation of three-dimensional space into two-dimensional form. A similar mathematical concern characterised humanist architecture. Thus, for instance, a new centralised plan for the construction of churches replaced the traditional Latin Cross plan with its long nave, transept and choir. The reason lay

> in the new scientific approach to nature which is the glory of Italian fifteenth-century artists. It was the artists, headed by Alberti and Leonardo, who had a notable share in consolidating and popularizing the mathematical interpretation of all matter. They found and elaborated correlations between the visible and intelligible world which were as foreign to the mystic theology as to the Aristotelian scholasticism of the Middle Ages. Architecture was regarded by them as a mathematical science which worked with spatial units: parts of that universal space for the scientific interpretation of which they had discovered the key in the laws of perspective. Thus they were made to believe that they could re-create the universally valid ratios and expose them pure and absolute, as close to abstract geometry as possible. And they were convinced that universal harmony could not reveal itself entirely unless it were realized in space through architecture conceived in the service of religion.[95]

As both painting and architecture became 'respectable' and liberal arts, because progressively based on intellectual and not simply manual skills, there was an astonishing and quite rapid increase in the artist's status during this period – from craftsman to the habitués of courts and princes. All this helped to make the visible phenomenal world increasingly 'respectable' and constituted an important aspect of that worldly 'experience' to which educationists increasingly appealed – in the world of observable phenomena.

XI

One fascinating area in which eye and ear combined was in the art of memory
– for memory was a crucial mental attribute for the early rhetorician before
the era of print made memorising less important. Memory, it will be recalled,
constituted one of the major focal points of rhetorical education.[96] For a
long time, an important source for the art of memory – the *Ad Herennium* –
was thought to have been written by Cicero and was therefore received with
particular reverence by later medieval and early humanist scholars; even
the establishment by later humanist philologists that the *Ad Herennium* was
not written by Cicero did not altogether weaken enthusiasm for the art – and
it was avidly taken up by the neo-Platonists.[97] What was the classical art of
memory which was revived in the later medieval and renaissance periods –
and how did it link eye and ear through remembered speech?

It involved a complex process by which natural memory was to be improved by artificial memory. Artificial memory could help in memorising
both things and words. In both cases the process involved the creation of
inner 'places' (*loci*) in which 'images' (*imagines*) reminiscent of what was to
be remembered were deposited. By travelling in imagination through the
'loci', deposited in right order, the images would bring to mind the points
(incidents, people, words) to be remembered. This in brief was the basic
system.

What were the inner 'places' or 'loci'? Usually, these were architectural
in form – a room, a house, an inter-columnar space; later – significantly – a
theatre: in fact any space enclosed with niches or architectural features of
various kinds where the 'imagines' could be 'placed' – and which could be
used over and over again for that purpose. The 'imagines' could be confined
to images which would remind of notions, arguments, 'things' and their
order in the speech – or they might be extended to include the words, a
process, of course, which was much more complicated. The images in general
should be striking, active and dramatic, so as to stimulate the memory by
their affective force, and remind by some association with the point to be
remembered: 'We all know how, when groping in memory for a word or a
name, some quite absurd and random association, something which has
"stuck" in the memory, will help us to dredge it up. The classical art is
systematizing that process.'[98] This constitutes the classical art in essence –
those who want a longer account are urged to consult Dr Yates's fascinating
account. As we shall see, some modifications were introduced in the medieval
period; but first it is necessary to draw attention to some important features
of the basic classical account.

First of all it implies a capacity, under training, for the development of an
intense capacity for internal visualisation. The placing of the 'imagines' in
the 'loci' implied some sort of architectural sense of spatial discrimination,
which may have been of considerable importance in the classical and renaissance period. The visual structure, too, emphasised and reinforced the mental
one. It constituted a method, a sense of ordering, which certainly played a
vital part in the development of the European consciousness and had its

profound implications for the development of method of the later renaissance period and the seventeenth century. Furthermore, it encouraged the translation of both 'res' and 'verba' – of concepts as well as 'things' – into concrete objects. St Thomas Aquinas, long ago, had urged that 'it is natural to man to reach the *intelligibilia* through the *sensibilia* because all our knowledge has its beginning in sense'. This was a strand of thought which the Renaissance, with its developing sense of visualisation, was to emphasise – especially as the 'corporeal similitudes' became gradually more 'real' than the 'intelligibilia' through the development of nominalism. The encouragement the art of memory, revived by the scholastics, gave to the translation of abstracts into concrete form carried on well into the seventeenth century, as this quotation from Bacon indicates:

> Emblems [i.e. *imagines*] bring down intellectual to sensible things; for what is sensible always strikes the memory stronger, and sooner impresses itself than the intellectual . . . And therefore it is easier to retain the image of a sportsman hunting the hare, of an apothecary ranging his boxes, an orator making a speech, a boy repeating verses, or a player acting his part, than the corresponding notions of invention, disposition, elocution, memory, action.[99]

The classical art of memory underwent some important amplifications and modifications during the later renaissance period. But a clearer indication of its ultimate intention – with vast and important cultural implications – could hardly be given than in this Baconian pronouncement.

It will be noted, too, that Bacon employs the word 'emblem'. Emblems, in the later neo-Platonic phase of the Renaissance, carried on the tradition of the visual symbolisation of abstract entities, with the further neo-Platonic addition that such forms of representation were thought somehow to partake of the very essence of the idea itself. The new national monarchs 'deliberately developed complicated personal imagery in decorating not only their palaces and public buildings but even the most menial items of everyday life – book bindings, fabrics, silver, glass and dress';[100] and this visual emphasis was translated into court spectacles, progresses, masques, and so on.

If, then, the medieval orientation was to 'discover things unseen that are hidden beneath the shadow of things natural', the revival of the classical art of memory in the late medieval period, with its carefully structured *loci* and *imagines agentes* may well have contributed to that growing concern for the 'exact representation of the field of vision',[101] in itself a symptom of a greater concern for the reality of appearances in the world of nature, and the natural study of form, which marked the artistic reorientation of the Renaissance, and characterised the socialised world of the humanists. At the very moment when 'words' structured experience in the minds of educationists, an alternative and strictly contemporaneous approach prepared the way for the pre-eminence of the observable – as 'things' – which was to constitute the next revolution in educational theorising – as mind directly confronted world without the intervention of classical 'letters'.

XII

Let me now summarise some of the basic features of humanist educational theory. It is essentially moral and social in orientation – and moral implies not only right conduct but elegant and refined behaviour. This morality is oriented to conduct in a society rather than regarded as a means to the contemplation of a transcendental deity. Christian feeling, true, is not only respected but encouraged; inevitably, however, the pride in individual achievement – *fama* and *virtu* – the stress on will through persuasion rather than on the outcome of intellect working in terms of logic, introduced a very specific hint of secularisation. The basis of humanist writing, even, is speech – and speech exists specifically in a social context. The morality is that of the classical and patristic experience as represented by its finest orators, historians and poets – Cicero, Virgil – who provide a standard of behaviour, and, as vital, of elegance of style. The studies are intended to be liberal, and to provide an essential basis for further professional study. Above all, humanism is based on the notion of imitation – of the best models – and provides an initiation into an essentially masculine, classicised world defined in persuasive utterance, linked with the rational decision making which constituted the life of the Greek and Roman citizens, and infused with Christian sentiment.

On the day on which I write this, a leading article in the *Times Higher Educational Supplement* is headed 'Research: corruption lies in preferring rhetoric to reality'. But of course this book is involved in a period when 'rhetoric' at its best *was* the reality and our psychic understanding must be correspondingly readjusted to the implications of an oral age – which persisted for quite a time even after the development of print in the 1450s. The old fixed categories – social in feudalism and ecclesiastical authority, intellectual through logic – were being superseded by a new dynamism of social interaction and a limited degree of mobility, first in Italy and a little later north of the Alps, based on a speech-oriented discourse employed specifically for persuasive purposes and linked to government. As the hieratic gestures of medieval painting dissolved into the more naturalistic poses of Giotto or Masaccio, so the new humanly oriented culture based on the dynamic expression of classical experience – a literature rather than a biblical text or the abstractions of Aristotelian metaphysics and logic – gradually, hesitantly but inescapably implied a new human dynamic; a dynamic which accepted more fully the *plenitude* of nature and made it subject for artifice – those arts which were 'natural' to the human being. In the earlier humanistic period, *studia humanitatis* had not degenerated into mere verbal elegance; language was the means by which experience was transmitted across the centuries; and philological studies were not arid but a means of making precise just what was meant by what was being said and thus establishing the 'otherness' of earlier peoples in time. Thus the study of literature was a means to an end, that of the enlargement of mind in true education. Guarini, in a letter to the mayor of Bologna, urged that the muses, and they alone, were a preparation for a life of politics: he considered *litterae* the cause of the development of all civilised energy, (moral) philosophy, grammar the key to living

45

meaning. To come into contact with the great of classical antiquity was to be reborn to a higher understanding.

'*Natura sine disciplina caeca*' (Nature without discipline is blind); the need was for consistent application and a 'burning will', as Alberti advised, in order to create what Cicero had called 'a second nature'. But this new 'nature' demanded form. Rhetoric provided its own stylistic structure and, in the hands of the best humanists, its own moral order derived from historical models. History itself evolved a form which recognised the 'otherness' of the past. Visual education through painting, sculpture and architecture achieved a new naturalistic objectivity through the developments of geometrical and mathematical forms which evolved as perspective in painting, rational planning in architecture and naturalistic, free standing poses in sculpture. Here is forecast the scientific, mathematical and technical triumphs of later centuries; the gradual objectification of human experience. The development of educational theorising itself – among other forms of theorising – constitutes an element in that process of objectification – a power of abstracting oneself from the customary and projecting a new social identity. Thus the Renaissance was marked by a degree of individualisation of character matched by a growing autonomy of field.

The social implications of the humanists are of considerable importance. Where the aristocracy were concerned it marked a gradual change from a warrior to a scribe culture – learning became an essential element in the equipment of the new administrative state officers of the developing national societies. In the changeover the participants did not wholly abandon their aggressiveness. Nothing comes over more clearly in the Renaissance than the fact that culture is a weapon – of a less mortal kind than the siege engine or the lance – but still a means of triumphing over rivals. The collection of masterpieces is often a disguised form of aggression and ego satisfaction, building (in England, for instance, of the country house) a form of display. Furthermore language has once more come to be linked with politics and rhetoric can become a form of assault – Hamlet was not alone in realising that it was possible to *speak* daggers. It is not surprising that the study of Latin in the renaissance period has been described as a form of puberty rite.[102] It constituted the gateway to a new personal identity and it stressed the ritualistic importance of learning and education in the new forms of aristocratic life.

And so, too, are implied the themes of this book: Man as artificer, preparing for the making of 'a second nature' through education: the various 'forms' implied by curricular prescription, identifiable first in 'words' and then, in a later period, as 'things': the interplay of mind and cultural form issuing in a gradually evolving personal identity increasingly finding its home in the 'natural' world. These are three of the great themes that a study of educational theory offers the intellectual and cultural historian at the gateway of the modern world. They imply a gradually increasing sense of personal autonomy necessitating a developing pluralism of educational prescription which constitutes the eighteenth-century Enlightenment's legacy – sharply manifest in the confusions of Rousseau – to the nineteenth and twentieth centuries, and which poses its own problems for that interplay of artifice and nature which is the great theme of any theoretical consideration of education.

NOTES

1 Humane studies, in general, were those which enabled man to lift himself above the lower, unreflective, menial world of physical labour and hence turned him into a reflective human being as distinct from the animals or those condemned to a menial life of physical toil. The word 'humanist' was used to describe a group of educational reformers who persisted over at least two-and-a-half centuries and therefore hides a number of varying curricular emphases, as will become apparent in the text. It always carries with it the classical implication of human cultivation, *paideia*, refinement in both matter and manner. As Cicero puts it, 'We are all called men, but only those of us are men who have been civilised by the studies proper to culture' (*propriis humanitatis artibus*). In general they constituted studies (like history, philosophy, literature) which reflected on human beings and their behaviour.
2 cf. G. Holmes, *The Florentine Enlightenment* (London, Weidenfeld & Nicolson, 1969), p. 1.
3 D. Knowles, *The Evolution of Medieval Thought* (London, Longman, 1962), p. 87.
4 W. S. Howells, *Logic and Rhetoric in England (1500-1700)* (Princeton, NJ, Princeton University Press, 1956), pp. 3-4.
5 Quoted J. E. Seigel, *Rhetoric and Philosophy in Renaissance Humanism* (Princeton, NJ, Princeton University Press, 1968), p. 6.
6 W. H. Woodward, *Vittorino da Feltre and Other Humanist Educators* (New York, Teachers College Press, Columbia University, 1963), pp. 123-4.
7 J. M. Lechner, *Renaissance Concepts of the Commonplaces* (New York, Pageant Press, 1962), p. 70. At the same time, there were indications that the word was beginning to be used in its modern sense, e.g. Sidney speaks of how 'Invention, Nature's Child, fled step-dame Study's blows' ('Astrophel and Stella', Sonnet 1). This relates to the ambiguities implicit in the notion of 'imitation'.
8 W. J. Ong, *Rhetoric, Romance and Technology* (Ithaca, NY, Cornell University Press, 1971), p. 7.
9 There was a revival of interest in scholasticism at the end of the sixteenth century; cf. H. Kenney, *Scholars and Gentlemen* (London, Faber, 1970), ch. V.
10 Seigel, op. cit., p. 45.
11 cf. J. Larner, *Culture and Society in Italy 1290-1420* (London, Batsford, 1972), p. 188.
12 'From antiquity through the Renaissance and to the beginnings of romanticism under all teaching about the art of verbal expression there lies the more or less dominant supposition that the paradigm of all expression is the oration' (Ong, *Rhetoric*, p. 3).
13 Larner, op. cit., p. 192.
14 Foreword by E. E. Rice to Woodward, *Vittorino da Feltre*, p. x.
15 Quoted Woodward, *Vittorino da Feltre*, p. 177.
16 A. S. Piccolomini, *De Liberorum Educatione* (1450) in Woodward, *Vittorino da Feltre*, p. 136.
17 B. Guarino, *De Ordine Docendi et Studendi* (1459) in Woodward, *Vittorino da Feltre*, pp. 175-6.
18 P. P. Vergerius, *De Ingenuis Moribus* (1404) in Woodward, *Vittorino da Feltre*, p. 102.
19 ibid., p. 109.
20 ibid., p. 96.
21 Piccolomini, op. cit. in Woodward, *Vittorino da Feltre*, p. 148.

22 Walter Ullmann, *Medieval Foundations of Renaissance Humanism* (London, Elek, 1977), p. 39.
23 P. O. Kristeller, 'Philosophy and humanism in renaissance perspective' in *The Renaissance Image of Man and the World*, ed. B. O'Kelly (Columbus, Ohio State University Press, 1966), p. 31.
24 ibid., p. 33.
25 Woodward, *Vittorino da Feltre*, pp. 104-5.
26 ibid., p. 141.
27 ibid., p. 165.
28 ibid., p. 133.
29 Quoted K. Charlton, *Education in Renaissance England* (London, Routledge & Kegan Paul, 1965), p. 39.
30 Vergerius in Woodward, *Vittorino da Feltre*, p. 112.
31 ibid., p. 104.
32 Nicholas Orme, *English Schools in the Middle Ages* (London, Methuen, 1973), p. 143.
33 cf. Seigel, op. cit.: 'Medieval Italian rhetoric was quite a different thing from the Ciceronian humanism of the Renaissance' (p. 205).
34 cf. Holmes, op. cit., especially chs 1 and 2.
35 Ullmann, op. cit., p. 113. Professor Ullmann uses the phrase 'natural man' to imply those who had not been potentially regenerated through baptism.
36 ibid., p. 10.
37 E. F. Rice, *The Renaissance Idea of Wisdom* (Cambridge, Mass., Harvard University Press, 1958), p. 177.
38 Ullmann, op. cit., p. 37.
39 ibid., p. 169.
40 P. O. Kristeller, *Renaissance Concepts of Man* (New York, Harper Torchbooks, 1972), p. 2.
41 H. B. Parkes, *The Divine Order* (London, Gollancz, 1970), p. 183. 'Realism', philosophically speaking, implied that it was the universal that was 'real'. Nominalists, however, believed that reality resided in the particular.
42 J. A. Passmore, *The Perfectibility of Man* (London, Duckworth, 1972), p. 153.
43 ibid., p. 150.
44 For instance, the conflict between the Augustinian belief in the sinfulness of man's nature and the Pelagian heresy that sin was not inherent in men's natures rumbled on during the whole of the medieval period.
45 P. O. Kristeller, 'The impact of early Italian humanism on thought and learning', reprinted in *Developments in the Early Renaissance*, ed. B. S. Levy (New York, State University of New York Press, 1972), pp. 138-40.
46 J. Burckhardt, *The Civilisation of the Renaissance in Italy* (London, Phaidon, 1944), p. 9.
47 Kristeller, *Renaissance Concepts of Man*, p. 14.
48 Rice, op. cit., pp. 120-1.
49 Another way of putting it would be to assert that man was acquiring an increasing degree of 'psychic mobility' after the comparative fixities of a feudal and ecclesiastical hierarchical organisation.

It is interesting in this respect to note that in Thomas Wilson's *Rule of Reason* (published in England as late as 1551), 'judgment' (i.e. the arrangement of subject matter) precedes 'invention' (i.e. the systematic discovery of subject matter), in his description of the 'Art of Logique'. Professor Howells in his *Logic and Rhetoric in England (1500-1700)* comments on the seeming illogicality of this order of exposition in these terms:

> Wilson justifies himself for placing judgment before invention by saying that you have to know how to order an argument before you seek for it, and that anyway 'a reason is easier found than fashioned'. This attitude is a significant phenomenon in intellectual history. It really is a way of saying that subject matter presents fewer difficulties than organisation, so far as

composition is concerned. A society which takes such an attitude must be by implication a society that is satisfied with its traditional wisdom and knows where to find it. It must be a society that does not stress the virtues of an exhaustive examination of nature so much as the virtues of clarity of form. (p. 23).

His further comment that 'the great shift which recurred in men's thinking between 1500 and 1700 was in fact a shift from the preponderant emphasis upon traditional wisdom to the predominant emphasis upon new discoveries, and this shift is nowhere better illustrated than in the transition from Wilson's belief in the relative ease of discovery to the modern belief in its relative difficulty' (p. 124) is, of course, of profound interest for our theme. What it marks is a gradual willingness to think things out for oneself rather than fit them into an accepted scheme. Hardin Craig, for instance, in *The Enchanted Glass* comments on the abstract nature of much renaissance thought: 'The established method of thinking was to fit the particular objects of thought into their places in a pre-arranged scheme . . . [The mind of the Renaissance] was in the habit of adopting and applying generalisations made by others.' Against this there was a developing sense of the actualities of human behaviour, manifest in Machiavelli, and the need to observe and judge in relation to particularities of behaviour. Bacon, for instance, urged the need for a new ethic 'based upon the observation of life as it was lived then' (cf. Hardin Craig, op. cit., Oxford, Blackwell, 1950, pp. 201-3).

50 C. Trinkaus, '*In Our Image and Likeness*', Vol. 1 (London, Constable, 1970), p. 147.
51 ibid., p. 196.
52 Another way of putting it would be that implicit in the notion of *studia humaniora* as Erasmus described them. Medieval scholasticism had not distinguished between natural science and the humanities – both remained within the sphere of philosophy. But the Renaissance distinguished between nature and culture and defined the former in relation to the latter – i.e. nature as the whole world accessible to the senses, except for the records left by men (which constituted culture). 'Thus, while science endeavours / to transform the chaotic variety of natural phenomena into what may be called a cosmos of nature, the humanities endeavour to transform the chaotic variety of human records into what may be called a cosmos of culture' (E. Panofsky, *Meaning in the Visual Arts* (Harmondsworth, Penguin, 1970), p. 28.

The phrase about a 'second nature' was extensively used; thus Sidney speaks in *The Defence of Poetry* of the poet as 'Lifted up by the vigour of his own invention, he doth grow in effect into another nature, in making things either better than Nature bringeth forth, or, quite anew, forms such as were never in Nature.'
53 Trinkaus, op. cit., p. 248.
54 ibid., p. 276.
55 Quoted H. Baron, *The Crisis of the Early Italian Renaissance* (Princeton, NJ, Princeton University Press, 1966), p. 419.
56 Quoted ibid., p. 420.
57 Quoted Seigel, op. cit., p. 90.
58 ibid., p. 101.
59 cf. p. 14 above. Poggio Bracciolini (1380-1459), Chancellor of the Florentine Republic, was much exercised by the problems of deceit and fraudulent discourse in public life. cf. N. S. Struever, *The Language of History in the Renaissance* (Princeton, NJ, Princeton University Press, 1970), pp. 165-70.
60 R. R. Bolgar, *The Classical Heritage and its Beneficiaries* (Cambridge, Cambridge University Press, 1954), pp. 199-200.
61 ibid., p. 268.
62 M. Baxandall, *Giotto and the Orators* (London, Oxford University Press, 1971), p. 6.
63 M. Baxandall, *Painting and Experience in Fifteenth Century Italy* (London, Oxford University Press, 1972), p. 151.

64 Baxandall, *Giotto and the Orators*, p. 46.
65 ibid., p. 48.
66 ibid., p. 131.
67 cf. T. W. Baldwin, *William Shakspere's 'Small Latine and Lesse Greeke'*, 2 Vols (Urbana, University of Illinois Press, 1944).

The centrality of the notion of 'imitation' in the pedagogy of the humanists demands a more extended gloss. Perhaps two quotations will clarify what was involved. Ascham indicates how the master should deal with the boy's retranslation of the Englished version of the original Cicero:

> Tully would have used such a word, not this; Tully would have placed this word here, not there; would have used this case, this number, this person, this degree, this gender, he would have used this mood, this tense, this simple rather than this compound; this adverb here, not there, he would have ended the sentence with this verb, not with that noun or particle etc. (ed. L. V. Ryan, p. 15; see note 77 below).

Could anything more stereotyped or repressive be imagined? But Ascham insists that his aim is not a slavish following; what he looks for is the assimilation of a style which will enable the pupil to rival, not simply slavishly to copy, the best models. The gradual internalisation of the finest examples is to encourage the freedom of facility in elegant writing. The advice of another humanist, Vives, makes clear what is intended:

> Repeated practice is the best master for the attainment of good style, and the fashioner of speech. In the beginning use not only words taken from Latin authors, but also short sentences collected from them. They should be so aptly put together that for the most part they are another's. But little by little you will mix your own composition until the time when your stage of erudition has developed, *your writing can become all your own* (my italics).

'Here', as Professor Baldwin states, 'is the doctrine of imitation, so faithfully applied by 16th century schoolmasters' (op. cit., Vol. 1, p. 189). (Yet humanist Latin study was made relatively more attractive than medieval – cf. *A Fifteenth Century School Book*, ed. W. Nelson, London, Oxford University Press, 1956.) In his two massive volumes Professor Baldwin has documented the nature of humanist education as found in English grammar schools at the end of the sixteenth century and worked out in precise detail the influence of the classical texts and the books of rhetoric he studied on Shakespeare's actual writing. It strikes me that his work probably constitutes the most detailed record of the effect of an education ever made. Lest it be thought that the thesis maintained relies too heavily on evidence from one writer it is surely unlikely that, in a literature which is extensive for a small population – roughly a tenth of what it is today – and in which the rhetorical influence is ubiquitous, other writers have not been similarly stimulated by their rhetorical training. Furthermore, the ability of Elizabethan audiences to listen to complex verbal discourse is well documented. There is also the well-researched case of John Milton (cf. D. L. Clark, *John Milton at St. Paul's School*, New York, Columbia University Press, 1948; and H. F. Fletcher, *The Intellectual Development of John Milton*, Vol. 1: *From the Beginnings through Grammar School*, Urbana, University of Illinois Press, 1956). On Shakespeare cf. also Sister Miriam Joseph, *Shakespeare's Use of the Arts of Language* (New York, Columbia University Press, 1949).

The question of the effects of humanist education is discussed in Dr R. R. Bolgar's curiously equivocal essay reprinted in *The Changing Curriculum*, edited by the History of Education Society (London, Methuen, 1971). I disagree with parts of Dr Bolgar's essay which, to my mind, underplays the contribution of the schools. But, even he admits that the schools had a 'preparatory' role which guaranteed a 'minimum of literacy and intellectual interest', though he assigns the major contribution to 'self education'. I am not sure what more one could reasonably claim of any school education than that it should 'prepare' its pupils for future achievements.

68 'No medieval man could see the civilisation of antiquity as a phenomenon complete in itself and historically detached from the contemporary world; as far as I know, medieval Latin has no equivalent to the humanistic "*antiquitas*" or "*sacrosancta vetustas*". And just as it was impossible for the Middle Ages to elaborate a system of perspective based on the realisation of a fixed distance between the eye and the object, so it was equally impossible for this period to evolve an idea of historical disciplines based on the realisation of a fixed distance between the present and the classical past' (E. Panofsky, *Meaning in the Visual Arts*, Harmondsworth, Penguin, 1970, p. 26).

69 J. G. A. Pocock, *The Machiavellian Moment* (Princeton, NJ, Princeton University Press, 1973), p. 49.

70 ibid., pp. 49–50.

71 ibid., pp. 60–1.

72 ibid., p. 62.

73 Michael Levey, *High Renaissance* (Harmondsworth, Penguin, 1975), pp. 17–18.

74 A. O. Lovejoy, *The Great Chain of Being* (Cambridge, Mass., Harvard University Press, 1942), p. 14.

75 Thus Collingwood distinguishes '*natura naturata*, or the complex of natural changes and processes, from *natura naturans*, or the immanent force which animates and directs them' (R. G. Collingwood, *The Idea of Nature*, London, Oxford University Press, 1965, p. 94).

76 Erasmus, *Praise of Folly*, trans. B. Radice (Harmondsworth, Penguin, 1975), pp. 114–15.

77 This account owes much to Sister Miriam Joseph, op. cit., first chapter.

78 L. V. Ryan (ed.), *The Schoolmaster* (1570) by Roger Ascham (Ithaca, NY, Cornell University Press, 1967), p. 35.

79 Lovejoy, op. cit., pp. 82–3.

80 ibid., p. 84.

81 ibid., p. 86.

82 ibid., pp. 97–8.

83 From *Abraham and Isaac* (1449) by Feo Belcari of Florence, quoted Baxandall, *Painting and Experience*, p. 153. A. N. Whitehead considered that 'The rise of Naturalism in the later Middle Ages was the entry into the European mind of the final ingredient necessary for the rise of science' (*Science and the Modern World*, Cambridge, Cambridge University Press, 1933, p. 19).

84 Quoted Antony Blunt, *Artistic Theory in Italy 1450–1600* (London, Oxford University Press, 1962), p. 11.

85 Woodward, *Vittorino da Feltre*, p. 156.

86 E. H. Gombrich, *The Story of Art* (London, Phaidon, 1967), p. 115.

87 Quoted Baxandall, *Painting and Experience*, p. 41.

88 Gombrich, *Story*, p. 128.

89 'The image of man in renaissance art' by H. W. Janson, reprinted in *The Renaissance Image of Man and the World*, ed. B. O'Kelly, p. 82.

90 L. Reti (ed.), *The Unknown Leonardo* (London, Hutchinson, 1974), p. 22.

91 Gombrich, *Story*, pp. 146–7.

92 cf. R. Weiss, *The Renaissance Discovery of Classical Antiquity* (Oxford, Blackwell, 1973), *passim*.

93 Baxandall, *Painting and Experience*, p. 64.

94 ibid., p. 78.

95 R. Wittkower, *Architectural Principles in the Age of Humanism* (London, Academy Editions, 1973), p. 29.

96 cf. A. S. Piccolomini: 'we must . . . insist upon the overwhelming importance of Memory, which is in truth the first condition of capacity for letters. A boy should learn without effort, retain with accuracy, and reproduce easily. Rightly is memory called "the nursing mother of learning" ' (Woodward, *Vittorino da*

Feltre, p. 144). Similarly Ascham makes a good memory one of the seven characteristics of a child with a 'good wit' for learning.

97 It seems to have suffered an eclipse during the dark and earlier middle ages – and it was deprecated by a few later humanists like Erasmus (some of whom favoured repetition learning) as medieval and therefore barbaric – cf. Frances A. Yates, *The Art of Memory* (Harmondsworth, Penguin, 1969), pp. 131-4. My account clearly owes a great deal to her work.
98 Yates, *Memory*, p. 29.
99 Quoted, ibid., p. 358.
100 Roy Strong, *Splendour at Court* (London, Weidenfeld & Nicolson, 1973), p. 59.
101 cf. Holmes, op. cit., ch. 7.
102 cf. W. J. Ong, 'Latin language study as a renaissance puberty rite' in op. cit., ch.5.

CHAPTER 2

'Fashioned not Born': Erasmus

I

By the early sixteenth century 'political' humanism had already made considerable progress north of the Alps. The north Italian townships had just seen the significant emergence of the third estate, and certain regions of France and Germany had not been far behind. The diffusion of Roman law from Italy sustained a developing nationalism; growing interest in the vernaculars fostered a sense of national identity. The Crusades long ago had initiated a degree of social and cultural mobility, further encouraged by commercialism, urban development and the consequent evolution of a bourgeoisie as in Italy. The ground was being prepared for the emergence of 'cultural' humanism.

The later fifteenth century was marked by a large measure of dynastic consolidation in Spain, France and England. New forms of economic organisation implied a nascent capitalism, industrial expansion and the decline of the traditional commercial ethic. The modern state began to take shape in theory as well as in fact; the political development of the Italian city state provided a model for certain expectations of social change. Though the world of the city state was coming to an end, the politicisation of life it had implied fed into the statecraft and directed the relations between the new national entities north of the Alps and even, in some degree, into their internal arrangements. Culturally, the period was marked by an extension of interest, among ruling monarchs, in the accumulation of treasures of literature and learning; 'in the space of a hundred years the number of considerable libraries in Western Europe was at least doubled'.[1] The development of printing with movable type further encouraged the growth of a secular reading public; the diffusion of Italian arts and letters began to exercise a strong influence over the cultural life of the Western world even in countries as remote as Russia and Poland. Durer, for instance, manifested much the same close semi-scientific observation, which fed into his art, as had the Italian Leonardo; furthermore, the provision by the Italian humanists of a body of texts and translations of Greek science and philosophy further stimulated a developing observational interest. Nationalism, capitalism, science – all these features of the modern world were embryonically present in the Europe of Erasmus.

53

II

Yet the first of these Erasmus specifically rejected; by the other two he was largely untouched; only his cult of simplicity may have had indirect scientific implications though he did make extensive use of one developing technology, printing. He shared, rather, the historical perspectives of the Italian humanists – their sense of the social and political reality of the ancient world, their philological interests and their concern for the precise understanding of words. As with the best of the early humanists he sought the spirit of ancient writing rather than a slavish copying. Like them he saw the spirit of the ancient world as profoundly *educative*, and he was pre-eminently an educationist – 'an educator of educators' Bainton calls him.[2] Furthermore he shared their general distaste for the scholastics – learning and erudition were for action, not pure knowledge or contemplation. He was never really at home with Plato, despite his knowledge of Greek – 'philosophia' to him implied moral understanding rather than philosophical speculation – and thus he remained relatively untouched by later Italian developments in Florentine neo-Platonism. There is certainly some neo-Platonic influence in the *Enchiridion Militis Christiani* (*Handbook of the Militant Christian*) in his insistence on the importance of spiritual inwardness rather than outward ceremony – his English friends, Colet, Grocyn and Linacre had been affected by neo-Platonism and to some extent infected him. But other aspects of Florentine neo-Platonism – its concern for the occult, for instance – repelled him. Perhaps even more than the earlier humanists he sought to reconcile classicism and Christianity: but theological speculation as such was foreign to his nature. Like his forebears, he sought in his commentaries to uncover the real meaning of the gospels, and doctrinal matters were subordinated to the study of their implications for morality and social conduct. It was the practical wisdom of the Roman statesman-moralist and the morality of Christianity which appealed to him – the concrete actualities of conduct rather than the abstractions of medieval piety – and certainly not the mistiness of medieval mysticism. He too lacked the deeper Christian awareness of man's sinfulness; instead he tended to see man as good and attributed his deficiencies to circumstances and bad training. Deficient in any profound sense of evil he naturally failed to see the potential corruption implicit in certain aspects of the classics. Graeco-Roman culture, he considered, had made Christianity possible in the first place; the Christian fathers had approved of classical literature and doubtful passages could be explained away as allegory. Antiquity squared with his temperament and thought and provided a standard by which society as a whole could be elevated to a new plane. Here had been universality of government, law and peace. Hence he was blind to the implications of the new nationalism, and his own life was spent in many countries – whose vernaculars (e.g. English and Italian) he often refused to learn: 'he longs in his heart for a republic of enlightenment which knowing no country shall be co-terminous with humanity'.[3] When twice invited to become a citizen of Zurich he replied that he wished 'to be a citizen of the world, not of a single city'.

The practical orientation of his thought was, then, not consolidated through political experience. He represented, indeed, a high water mark of humanistic optimism concerning man's potential and remains a portent of a later, romantic stress on man's innate goodness. (It is interesting, indeed, that these 'studies of humanity' should produce, as almost exact contemporaries, Erasmus and Machiavelli.) Erasmus, indeed, has something of the remoteness from the actualities of human political conduct of the scholar. Historically he had come at a time when the old feudal order was disintegrating but the new national monarchies were not fully established. Hence he was able to preserve a certain independence, manifesting the new confidence of a comparatively free ranging scholarly intelligentsia restlessly wandering through Europe, maintaining contact with like-minded contemporaries as part of a new clerisy: 'Let others paint lions, eagles, and other creatures on their coats of arms. More true nobility is possessed by those who can ascribe on their shields all that they have achieved through the cultivation of the arts and sciences.'[4]

Professor Ullmann has pointed out how humanism, originally largely political, became diffused as a cultural phenomenon, detached from the need to meet specifically political questions and manifested 'in the study and cultivation of the means by which the essence of humanity was expressed'.[5] Though the political and social orientation of Erasmus still seems apparent, in effect it dissolves into a high-minded but ultimately sentimental affirmation of universal possibilities, ignoring the political realities of the developing nation states. He lacked the insight which close contact with the affairs of a specific country or the routines of administration might have given him. In this respect his career followed the later orthodox humanist preoccupation with editing and collecting. Although he had much contact with princes and the highest political writers (he actually wrote a book on the *Education of a Christian Prince*, a quasi political work on the role of rulers) he demonstrated a considerable distaste for aspects of the political life of his times. The centrifugal effects of Luther's revolt, for instance, dismayed him. His aspiration after a universal state remained a dream: though a good deal of what he actually wrote was intended to have considerable political implications it lacked the defined sense of political reality all too manifest in Machiavelli. He was, indeed, to some extent a rootless intellectual – the child of his works not of his father, as the French critic Professor Margolin puts it. (He was, in any case, illegitimate.) Hence perhaps his psychological emphasis, in his educational writings, on individual temperament rather than on social or hereditary influences – and his touching faith in education as such, a faith little borne out in human history except where a few are concerned.

And yet education did prove to be the one area where he did have a very definite and distinctive practical effect. His textbooks were used widely throughout Europe; in England, for instance, his ideas were directly relevant to the foundation of the first of the great humanist schools, St Paul's, and his textbooks were introduced as the concrete embodiment of his ideas. Thus he sent the *De Ratione Studii* to Dean Colet in 1511 and Colet replied inviting him to 'give use some aid, if it is only in teaching our masters'. Here, first in

St Paul's and then to some extent throughout the grammar schools of England, Erasmus' conception of language as arising out of imitation and practice rather than the learning of grammatical rules which had so characterised the medieval system triumphed. As Colet himself put it, 'men spake not latin, because such rules were made, but contrarywise, such rules were made because men spake such latin'.[6] So boys learned by rote only the basic minimum of grammatical rules and then read, wrote and spoke Latin, learning further rules as occasion required. In order to acquire a good style, Erasmus had urged, it was necessary to 'write, write and then write'; and the author of the most important grammar of the sixteenth century, Lily, placed a similar stress upon the imitation of good authors rather than on memorised rules.

So 'the curricula of English grammar schools are founded upon the authors designated by Erasmus, and the methods pursued in teaching them are those suggested by him. Further, the texts which Erasmus wrote for St Pauls and elsewhere became almost universally the grammar school texts of England.'[7] Of the texts, the *De Copia Verborum ac Rerum* was especially widespread and was, for instance, almost certainly used by Shakespeare. Through Erasmus' influence, ideas received the same emphasis as style, matter became as important as manner and reasoned and adaptive 'imitation' rather than closely copied 'imitation' the recommended approach. In both, imitation was fundamental – but Erasmus allowed for a greater flexibility of individual usage than did the later classical rhetoricians (such as Brinsley and Ascham), who emphasised the purity of the original and its reconstruction as far as possible. The 'originality' of Erasmus must not be exaggerated; 'inventio' still implied the finding of the 'commonplaces' in the body of Roman literature. It was simply that his emphasis on practice invited an important element of freedom that encouraged variations which went beyond slavish copying, ringing the changes in choice of word or sentiment (for instance) which must have encouraged the pliability of a Shakespeare, that most original of imitators.[8]

III

Yet stylistic purity remained one of his major aims. As a boy still at school he reacted against the 'barbaric' textbooks and teaching he encountered. He disliked their dialectical slant and reliance on doubtful etymologies and developed a distaste for the neologisms and syntactical peculiarities of medieval Latin. At the age of 18 he was asked to paraphrase Lorenzo Valla's *Elegantiae Linguae Latinae* for schools; thus he began a concern for the purification of the Latin tongue which lasted the rest of his life.

Style indeed he considered an outward manifestation of an inner spirit of harmonious and elegant utterance which was intended to exercise due influence on the relations between men. Erasmus had something of the attitude towards language that Plato had towards music – coarse and crude language he considered led to analogous behaviour. The reverse was also

true: 'The study of letters was to be an integral part of the art of friendship
. . .' *Antibarbarorum Liber*, a composition begun in the monastery, expresses
the idea more fully. 'Who was it, pray tell, who led those stony and boorish
men to a more human (*humaniorem*) life, a more gentle nature, and more
modest ways? Was it not letters? They mould our spirit, mitigate the emotions,
blunt untamed impulses, soothe and do not suffer our nature to be ferocious.'[9]
Though, as we shall see, he stressed the equal importance of 'things' (*res*)
and 'words' (*verba*) in his statement of educational aims, as a humanist he
was committed to verbal expression at least as much as to the scrutiny of
facts. In the context of our current emphasis on scientific fact Dr Bietenholz
is surely right to stress, in his *History and Biography in the Work of Erasmus
of Rotterdam*, that

> The humanist, first and last, is a rhetorician, a linguist. His professional
> devotion as well as skill is aligned to *verba*, not to *res*. His real *gesta*,
> deeds, are *verba*, the words and not the *res gestae*, the actions of historical
> significance. To achieve the mastery of verbal expression a humanist
> professes the *artes liberales* and among them *historia rerum gestarum*.
> Theoretical systems never much bothered Erasmus, but basically he
> seems to have considered history and poetry as two cognate subjects of
> learning, both ancillary to grammar or the advanced stage of grammar,
> rhetoric, which relies upon either for its material.[10]

As already noted, his conception of human nature was fundamentally –
until perhaps his last years – an optimistic one: 'Nature herself has placed
certain seeds of peace in our souls, by which we are borne towards love and
concord. For if we all studiously follow the impulses of nature, we are eager
for living together in companionship, we pursue friendships, we love near-
ness and the need . . . for others, and we rejoice in familiar society.'[11] Scholasticism implied dispute, discord, argument: it was based on logic and the sort
of argumentation that logical analysis led to. 'Humanitas' implied 'tran-
quillitas'. The education of 'humanitas' could reform society. The comparative ethical optimism of the Italian humanists was accentuated in Erasmus,
who saw in a process of simplification of style (which yet preserved elegance)
and of religious observance a more inclusive order, a more harmonious
community. Ceremonies in religious matters were as destructive of human
well-being as barbarous discourse, for they led to superstitious fear and dread
of offence against petty observances. In essence, Erasmus' belief involved the
libertas which arose out of the learning of *humanitas* and the observance of
simplicitas in matters of religion. As Dr James Tracy indicates, from the age
of 30 Erasmus was preoccupied with the same complex of questions: 'the
reform of education by a return to the classics, the reform of piety by a return
to the original meaning of scripture, and the moral amelioration of society
by means of these reforms in piety and education'.[12] In the pursuit of these
aims there are three concepts that are of fundamental importance in understanding what he is about – *humanitas*, *libertas* and *simplicitas*. It was in the
deployment of these ideas that he went in some degree beyond his Italian
forebears.

IV

The Augustinian tradition implicit in monastic training had necessitated rules and 'external' observances by which men became disciplined in the practice of virtue; the rules of colleges in medieval universities necessitated a similar submission to authority. Humanist educational theory (and theology) implied a more optimistic conception:

> Humanists found support for their optimism in the conception of human nature espoused by classical rhetoricians in the context of their profession. From philosophers the rhetoricians borrowed the notion that man had an inborn sense of what was right and wrong just as they had an inborn sense of the noble and the beautiful. This moral sense was to be developed by persuasion. A free man would resist whatever might be imposed on him by force, but it was in keeping with his dignity to be persuaded; this was the task of the orator.[13]

Erasmus learnt much from Quintilian's *Institutes*. Like Quintilian, like his Italian predecessors, he assumed an aptitude to learning as part of human nature – an aptitude that was common to all but specific in the way in which it manifested itself in each; it constituted that rationality which was the essential part of human endowment.

There was a good deal of controversy as to the role of emulation and competition – manifestations of a certain 'spiritedness', a desire for glory and achievement – as devices for bringing out ('e-ducare') a boy's 'potential'. Many humanists recommended such emulation as a spur. Vergerio had argued, for instance, that it was 'a mark of soundness in a boy's nature that he is spurred by a desire for praise'. Others like Lorenzo Valla thought such love of glory a cause of envy and discord. Erasmus considered that the true nobility of human nature was to be found in 'modesty' rather than 'spirit'. And it was in the complex qualities which surrounded 'modesty' – sincerity, well-mannered straightforwardness, friendliness and mildness – that Erasmus defined the characteristics of *humanitas*. 'Erasmus thus defined the good qualities of human nature somewhat differently than many of his humanist predecessors except for Valla.'[14]

These good qualities could be fostered by three means: the study of the great classical authors ('within these two literatures [those of Latin and Greek] is contained all the knowledge which we recognise as of vital importance to mankind'), the cultivation of eloquent speech and a pleasant atmosphere for learning. 'Only literature can calm our spirits; without literature we are not even men.'[15] Learning was to become a game rather than a labour (Erasmus himself never taught a class, though he did sometimes act as tutor). In these points he was at one with his predecessors. But his comparative distaste for 'spiritedness' and 'emulation' led him to emphasise the conversational aspects of discourse rather than the argumentative. The humanists in general had still preserved something of the scholastics' concern for argumentation, implicit in their oratorical aims. The scholastics had in mind the skill of a speculative philosopher while the humanists sought the persuasiveness of an ambassador or preacher. But Erasmus shows a distinct lack of interest in formal reasoning or the deployment of arguments: 'I am not unjust to philosophy, but she is only an adjunct to knowledge', he once said. Instead, he advocated an education in Latin that emphasised (after the manner of Petrarch) the familiar rather than the argumentative style. He maintained a careful distinction between familiar letters and oratory; and for the teaching of Latin he recommended the cultivation of a written style modelled on the relaxed interchange of conversation rather than the grandiloquence and formality of oratory. *Copia* (the notion of amplitude) summarises how he saw good style in its emphasis on variation and amplification of example, ease and lucidity of manner: 'nothing is more admirable or magnificent than discourse abounding in a certain rich *copia* of words or ideas, like a river of gold'. His own style was easy and fluid; he had a rapid manner of both speaking and writing and seldom rewrote or seriously altered what he had set down. His emphasis was on ordinary speech ('sermo') rather than 'contentio' and the formality of eloquence that went with it:

> Just as a concentration in education on formal logic produced a morose and quarrelsome temperament, so an emphasis on friendly conversation and self-expression would produce a peaceful and humane temperament. Training that allowed for spontaneous self-expression was linked to humanity, training that forced the mind into rigid channels was linked to moroseness. This pattern was fundamental to Erasmus' educational thought.[16]

His collection, *Adagia*, constituted an attempt to make the finest thoughts of the ancients available to as wide a public as possible with the aid of the printing press. They constituted, too, an attempt to convey abstract notions in concrete form. Just as *copia* was the first requirement of eloquence, so *exempla*, one of the main categories of *adagia*, held first place in the achievement of *copia*: they involved, too, metaphors, similes and other striking figures which assisted the process of persuasion through the concrete: 'His discussion of *copia* led in turn to a concentration on *exempla*. This whole development reflected his basic belief that moral persuasion, the only true education, took place in the context of *sermo* rather than *contentio*.' As Erasmus put it, 'Who does not know that the choicest riches and delights of discourse are contained in *sententiae*, metaphors, parables, paradigms, similes, images and other figures of the same kind.'[17] Ease of manner, delight, sometimes the stimulus of an unusual, conceivably obscure image to 'tickle the ignorant with a witty allusion' or 'rouse a nodding reader with its very obscurity' rather than perspicuity and logical clarity as the only virtues constituted the Erasmian concept of persuasive conversation: in this sense Erasmus still belonged to a world where it was thought that the task of the learned was not to discover new truths but to convey the known truths in a palatable and delightful way. In his concern, on occasions, for allegorical interpretation he showed his affinity both with his medieval and his classical forebears. 'It is beyond controversy among all who are learned in antiquity that allegory lies hidden beneath all figments of the ancient poets.'[18]

And so the new man was an elegant conversationalist rather than an arguer: the flow of conversation, persuasive, refined, copious and concrete replaced the contentiousness of the medieval dialectician – and even of the earlier humanist orator. The ideal was more consciously social and urbane though in an idealised way; and it was this distaste for controversy and argumentation that characterised his dislike of nationalism and local patriotism.

In another sphere Erasmus demonstrated a similar dislike of rigidity of form – and though not directly related to his educational views, it throws some reflected light on them. He reacted, in his religious life, against all 'ceremonies' – public or external acts of worship or penance. He preferred spiritual to material manifestations; for visible rituals benefited only those who strove beyond them to *invisibilia*. Ceremonies must be interiorised, made real through personal commitment – the outward form implied only nominal adherence and could foster superstition. Outward observances could mask the realities of the spiritual life, which should be manifest in the way in which it carried out its moral duties – in behaviour, in short:

> In his view a superstitious observance of ceremonies developed the same contentious and morose character fostered by an education based on dialectic. *Libertas* as a pattern of thought means that men are made violent and morose by rigid systems of training, and that the systems of training must be changed before men can be formed in a genuine *humanitas*. Erasmus seems to have disliked mandatory ceremonies even more than he disliked strict rules of logic or composition . . . Fixing a text by logic to a specific meaning bothered him, as did fixing outward expressions of piety to a specific time and manner of execution.

He allowed the need for ceremonies in the earlier stages of belief; and he did not believe in scandalising the untutored by a public show of indifference. But basically

> In his educational works he argued that *bonae litterae*, together with a method of instruction that allowed pupils to develop freely according to their inclinations, would foster *humanitas*. In his religious writings he argued that the study of the Scriptures, in an atmosphere of Christian *libertas*, would foster the imitation of Christ.[19]

There is thus a structured continuity manifest as between his educational and religious attitudes. He saw even the purpose of theology as persuasive rather than speculative: hence the usefulness of the figurative language of the scriptures; the fact that it spoke in images and allegories made it gentle and persuasive rather than rigid and violent.

In his later work he spelt out the full implications of Christian *simplicitas*. There is, indeed, a certain anti-aristocratic stance implicit in his cult of simplicity: for he believed that much of the violence which characterised

Christian society arose out of the cult of 'ceremonies' and the aristocratic (feudal) code of honour. Any rigidity – logical, ceremonial, aristocratic, even stylistic (his style became simpler and less complex with time) – earned his condemnation: 'What others do by fear of laws, do you from your hearts, and more perfectly than they, that you may declare yourselves free.'[20]

'A method of instruction that allowed pupils to develop freely according to their inclinations' – Dr Tracy's formula above has a very modern ring, which however, does considerable injustice to Erasmus' fundamental position on education; and a more detailed account of his specifically educational prescriptions, now their general orientation has been spelt out, must be given so that the precise limitations of that 'freely' may be judged, and their implications for 'nature'.

V

There are two major works on education – *De Ratione Studii* published in 1511 and *De Pueris Statim ac Liberaliter Instituendis* (1529). The former was concerned with the right method of instruction, the latter to argue that children should, from their earliest years, be trained in virtue and sound learning. This latter bases its arguments on certain views of nature which it will be necessary to examine closely.

Erasmus, indeed, uses the concept of 'Nature' extensively – especially in *De Pueris*. I would initially distinguish two uses: there is nature as *natura naturans*, the immanent force which directed 'natural' processes; and there is 'nature' in the sense of characteristic features by which a phenomenon is distinguished. Let us see how these two uses are interlinked.

Nature (*natura naturans*) applies as a largely benevolent force: and it is she who has created a human nature, in part analogous to that of the other animals (so that analogies drawn from the development of brute beasts still have their relevance to the upbringing of the young human) but also, of course, possessed of a very special set of characteristics which distinguishes the human from the non-human world, especially for instance a power of reasoning. What nature gives is, in general, oriented towards good – and the injunction to 'Follow Nature' in seeking to know how to behave plays a part in Erasmus' prescriptions.

Before we consider the implications of 'following Nature's teaching', it will be as well to clarify more precisely the 'nature' that Nature has implanted. It is, initially, admitted to be that of a 'rude, unformed creature, which it is your part to fashion so that it may become indeed a man'.[21] Education, training, practice, play a central role in Erasmus' theory, as they did in that of the Italian humanists. Several of his statements bear this out explicitly: '*Efficax res est natura, sed hanc vincit efficacior institutio*' and '*Educatio superat omnia*'[22] ('Nature is effective but instruction even more so' and 'Education overcomes all obstacles'). Nature has 'implanted' in man a potential for learning – and 'all living things strive to develop according to their proper nature' – conventional Aristotelianism. Men are capable of reason: 'Now it is the possession of Reason which constitutes a Man';[23] 'a man ignorant of Letters is no man at all'.[24] Man, then, has a 'mind apt for training'.[25]

Man, however, does not develop like the animals as a result of 'innate power or instinct' – but 'Providence in granting to man alone the privilege of reason has thrown the burden of development of the human being upon training' – 'Sound education is the condition of real wisdom' and this capacity for training constitutes a major aptitude which has been bestowed upon humanity.[26] '*Homines non nascuntur sed finguntur*' (Men are not born but fashioned) – this is fundamental to Erasmus' educational thought.

Erasmus illustrated his beliefs by means of a typically classical reference to the behaviour of the Spartan Lycurgus who demonstrated the difference in performance between two hounds, one well trained but inferior, the other of good mettle but undisciplined: the former proved more effective, because ' "Nature", he said, "may be strong, yet Education is more powerful still" '.[27] So 'if trees or wild beasts grow, men, believe me, are fashioned';[28] and Erasmus uses images of moulding and shaping: 'Handle the wax whilst it is soft, mould the clay whilst it is moist, dye the fleece before it gather stains.'[29] 'Nature, Training and Practice' are the three essential elements of his system:

> By *Nature*, I mean, partly, innate capacity for being trained, partly native bent towards excellence. By *Training*, I mean the skilled application of instruction and guidance. By *Practice*, the free exercise on our own part of that activity which has been implanted by Nature and is furthered by Training. Nature without skilled Training must be imperfect, and Practice without the method which Training supplies leads to hopeless confusion.[30]

'Innate capacity for being trained' we have already considered in general terms; its specific psychological components will be considered shortly. But for the moment we must consider the other aspect of Nature – 'nature bent towards excellence'.[31] Erasmus' view of human nature, as I have pointed out above, is basically optimistic; and this is so because he considers that Nature has provided a strong potential for good. As it is the '*proper* nature of man' (my italics) to live the life of reason, men rather than nature are to blame for shortcomings (Margolin explains that in Erasmus '*la nature n'est pas purement naturelle*'):[32]

> It is then certain that desire for excellence and aversion to folly come readily to man if only his nature, as yet empty of content, be from the outset filled with right activities. Yet we hear extravagant complaints 'how prone is child-nature to wrong, how hard to win to excellence'. But herein men accuse nature unjustly. Parents themselves are to blame in taking little heed for that which the child imbibes in his early years.[33]

Only rarely does Erasmus refer to the doctrine of original sin: 'But we may not forget that children are prone to follow the allurement of the senses rather than the rule of reason; to store up in mind what is trivial or bad rather than what is of enduring worth.'[34] This fact, he said, puzzled the ancients, but 'has its key in the Christian doctrine of Original Sin'.[35] Even then, he tends to blame bad education: 'True as this explanation is [of original sin], we are not to forget the part played by faulty training, particularly in the first and most impressionable stage.'[36] Constantly he points out the evil consequences of the neglect of education; he pleads for beginning at the earliest possible moment, and choosing wise, gentle perceptors who will make learning a pleasure – even play – rather than a task; he has harsh words for those pedagogues who ill treat and flog children or who are ignorant and debased in their manners. Nature may in general be benevolent; but her benevolence needs *instant* assistance from well-disposed human beings who, fully appreciating the potential she provides, seek to lead to good what still contains an element of ambivalence – the need for '*right* activities' (my italics). A child's nature is only the 'primitive endowment with which he is born';[37] and though 'as the instinct of the dog is to hunt, of the bird to fly, of the horse to gallop, so the natural bent of man is to philosophy and right conduct',[38] it is clearly necessary to further this' so strong . . . instinct' by a very specific intervention.

To this end, that Nature may be supplemented and furthered by education (experience alone is not enough) she has, according to Erasmus, provided the child with certain psychological characteristics. 'Nature' then has a psychological as well as an ontological significance. There are the capacities for memory, imitation and activity: 'nature has planted in the youngest child an ape-like instinct of imitation and a delight in activity'[39] – hence he can from birth be trained in conduct and from the time he can talk in letters. (Indeed, from these psychological and physiological characteristics Erasmus illegitimately derives the value decision that, among the aims of education, conduct should take priority over learning and the liberal arts.)[40] She also affords tenacity of purpose; 'Youth indeed lacks that sheer force which marks the bull, but on the other hand Nature has given it something of the tenacity and industry of the ant.'[41] The child likes play and endless activity – and here we are enjoined to 'Follow Nature' and 'so far as is possible take from the work of the school all that implies toilsomeness, and strive to give to learning the quality of freedom and of enjoyment'.[42]

There is, of course, a strong normative element in this concept of Nature: as a regulative principle Nature is equated with tendencies – psychological and ontological – to good: she provides a metaphysical 'nature' where the element of sin is much underplayed and a series of psychological and physiological traits aid the realisation in actuality of the metaphysically defined potential. The emphasis, however, is shifted from Nature to nurture in the realisation of this potential. Despite its ontological optimism, then, the responsibility of realising nature's gifts is placed unequivocally on man and the training he affords. He may follow nature, work with nature but the choices are his: there is no suggestion that development could be endogenous. Indeed, as indicated, the stress is on the earliest possible human intervention, and there is some discrepancy between Erasmus' emphasis on the benevolence of 'Nature' and his eagerness for early training which can only be resolved by suggesting that he considered training also as a 'natural' necessity demanded by the central place allocated to man's powers of reason and learning. Anyone who places such emphasis on acquired learning must see the necessity for a degree of formal acculturation.[43]

In addition to these general characteristics each individual is differently endowed: and Erasmus makes it plain that 'nature' has this further implication:

> the characteristic peculiar to each personality, which we may call *individuality*. Thus one child may show a native bent to Mathematics, another to Divinity, another to Rhetoric, or Poetry, another to war. So strongly disposed are certain types of mind to certain studies that they cannot be won to others; the very attempt in that direction sets up a positive repulsion.[44]

And so the master will be wise to observe such 'natural inclinations' early on, for children most easily learn according to the bent of their dispositions. On the question of different levels of aptitude Erasmus has little to say: at one time he seems to be of the opinion that, when the method was sound and teaching was accompanied by adequate practice, 'any discipline may ordinarily be acquired by the flexible intellect of man'.[45] On the other hand, he also believed that there were boys 'good only for the farm and manual toil'.[46] So 'individuality' implied different levels of ability as well as orientation of interest. Like the Italian humanists, however, Erasmus was writing for a small elite: the book was in fact addressed to William, Duke of Cleves, and was intended to give guidance on the education of the 'son lately born to you'.[47]

VI

Erasmus' aims were social, scholarly and religious: 'no man is born to himself, no man is born to idleness. Your children are begotten not to yourself alone but to your country: not to your country alone, but to God.'[48] Thus rebutting any notion that education should not start too early for fear that such early application might be harmful to health, Erasmus pointed out that: 'We are not concerned with developing athletes, but scholars and men competent to affairs.'[49] Knowledge (philosophy) would seem to be subordinate to conduct, to which 'learning and the liberal arts must prove themselves her hand maidens'; at the same time, immersion in affairs as such was not in itself sufficient to ensure right behaviour; knowledge (reviving memories of *doctus orator*) was an essential element in the moral life:

> They err, therefore, who affirm that wisdom is won by handling affairs and by contact with life, without aid from the teaching of philosophy. Tell me, can a man run his best in the dark? The precepts of philosophy

– which is knowledge applied to life – are, as it were, the eyes of the mind, and lighten us to the consciousness of what we may do and may not do. A long and manifold experience is, beyond doubt, of great profit, but only to such as by the wisdom of learning have acquired an intelligent and informed judgment. Besides, philosophy teaches us more in one year than our own individual experience can teach us in thirty, and its teaching carries none of the risks which the method of learning by experience of necessity brings with it.[50]

Doctors don't learn by experience to distinguish between poisons and healing drugs nor sailors to navigate as a result of shipwrecks, he argues. Experience, for its understanding, needs a mind trained to discriminate. Such statements are historically important, for they take a stance diametrically opposed to that of the later writers, who start from experience. Erasmus considered it necessary to prepare the mind to cope with experience; he did not assume a 'natural' capacity for discovery. In this sense, too, nature needed to be completed, whatever assistance she afforded in potential; actualisation belonged to culture, not to her. Furthermore, *liberal* knowledge was to precede professionalisation, and form its essential base. General culture was to precede the training of the lawyer, the doctor or the diplomat. Once more it is emphasised that the understanding (*ratio*) of the teacher was to shape the nature (*natura*) of the pupil: '*ratio facit hominem; ratio ducit naturam*'. Reason may be 'natural', then, but it needed to be actualised through training for nature to be fulfilled.

The suggested curriculum was highly selective. Erasmus, as we have seen, was antagonistic to the nationalistic aspirations of his age. Children were to be protected from local myths and legends:

the old wives' fairy rubbish such as most children are steeped in nowadays by nurses and serving women. Who can think without shame of the precious time and energy squandered in listening to ridiculous riddles, stories of dreams, of ghosts, witches, fairies, demons; of foolish tales drawn from popular annals; worthless, nay mischievous stuff of the kind which is poured into children in their nursery days?[51]

Instead they were to be taught to use the classical languages, 'to speak clearly and accurately':[52] 'Ability to speak is easily learned by use. Next come the arts of reading and writing, where the skill of the teacher can do much to lighten the monotony of learning.'[53] The teaching of the vernacular was unnecessary: 'The common tongue of the people may be left to be picked up in the ordinary intercourse of life',[54] a concession to 'experience' which indicates how little Erasmus valued the indigenous tongues. Instead he devotes much attention (more especially in *De Ratione Studii*) to the best method of inducting the child into his classical heritage. He begins – as might be anticipated – by distinguishing knowledge as falling into two divisions: 'the knowledge of truths and the knowledge of words' – '*rerum ac verborum*'; but 'if the former is first in importance the latter is acquired first in order of time'.[55] 'Res', of course, implied 'ideas', 'notions', not simply material objects:

> The study of facts is by Erasmus not differentiated into systematic branches of knowledge. Natural science, descriptions, travellers' tales, traditional lore, mathematics, astrology, geography, medical rules, tend to merge into one another, and are classed under the common term 'res'.[56]

But understanding was considered to be dependent on language; without words neither names nor descriptions made sense, nor could records be taken. Though the teacher might make use of natural phenomena for interest's sake, neither observation of the facts of nature nor even the study of artefacts could serve as a substitute for ancient authorities. Whenever he comes close to what might be termed 'real' studies, Erasmus takes up a literary attitude; for he recommends, not observation, but the study of certain authors: 'What can *men* learn from trees?' he asks, in the light of Bernard of Clairvaux' statement that 'trees and rocks will teach you what you can learn from no Master'. Facts come from literary sources not from nature: and indeed, Erasmus shares a common early humanist prejudice against scientific investigation. In the Golden Age men 'had too much piety to search out, with profane curiosity, the secrets of nature; to investigate the dimensions, notions and influences of the stars on the hidden courses of things; deeming it a sacrilege for mortal man to try to know more than is proper to his station'. (It constitutes an argument in Folly's celebration of 'natural instinct' in the Golden Age, a further indication of Erasmus' deprecation of notions of original sin.)[57]

Expression, indeed, is crucial in the understanding of truths:

> For ideas are only intelligible to us by means of the words which describe them; wherefore defective knowledge of language reacts upon our apprehension of the truths expressed. We often find that no one is so apt to lose himself in verbal arguments as the man who boasts that facts, not words, are the only things that interest him. This goes to prove that true education includes what is *best* in both kinds of knowledge . . .[58]

The word 'best' echoes throughout the little treatises. The method of language instruction is analogous to what today would be described as the direct method – not rule oriented but 'by daily intercourse with those accustomed to express themselves with *exactness and refinement*, and by the copious reading of the *best* authors' (my italics).[59] From the beginning the child is to be acquainted 'only with the best there is available'.[60] The Christian Prince is to read for improvement, not pleasure. Memory is to be cultivated so that precision can be aimed at. Writing requires some acquaintance with technicalities; exercises in composition need to draw on similes, allegories, terms of expression, etc. There is some emphasis on the use of models (the

66

best, naturally) for imitation. There is, after all, an *art* to be acquired – and Cicero and Quintilian are evoked for their advice: elegance as well as precision is required. But though rules are not to be neglected, the major emphasis – not surprising in view of the threefold injunction, Nature, Training and Practice – is on practice. The secret of style 'lies in the use of the pen; whatever the form, whether prose or verse, or whatever the theme, write, write and again write'.[61]

Directed, structured activity, then, is the keynote of Erasmian methodology. Progress is from the easier to the more difficult authors, from imitation to original composition; and the curriculum is geared to a specific, carefully evolved methodology. Content, at various ages, is controlled by psychological considerations: order is being introduced into learning:

> The time will now have come when the able teacher must select certain of the more necessary rules of accidence and syntax, and state them simply, arrange them in proper order and dictate them for entry in note-books. An author may now be attempted, but of the easiest sort; choose one likely to be helpful in composition and conversation.[62]

Detailed accounts of suitable authors are given and detailed instructions concerning pleasantness and attractiveness of presentation.

For the rest, subjects either relevant to classical studies (such as Geography, Archaeology, even Astrology, and above all History) or to the particular natural bent of the student (such as Music, Arithmetic or Geography) should also be studied: for 'nothing can be well accomplished *invita Minerva*' (without ability).[63] Erasmus deprecates medieval classical models, and he finds little to say in favour of logic: his own childhood, he complains, was tortured by logical subtleties which were neither true in fact nor sound in expression. Earlier, in the *De Ratione*, he had not demurred against some logic finding a place in the course; 'but I refuse to go beyond Aristotle and I prohibit the verbiage of the schools'.[64] 'Fixing a text by logic to a specific meaning bothered him',[65] let it be remembered. Finally, he rejected the medieval chivalric tradition as ardently as he did the scholastic. He had no real place for bodily training in his system: 'I would also denounce those who bring up their sons to a love of war. Straight from their mother's arms they are bidden to finger swords and shields, to thrust and strike.'[66]

VII

So it is pre-eminently a literary education, though one actively involved in transposing ancient learning to modern usage in the tradition of *doctus orator* – one not for bookishness alone but for affairs, though 'affairs' understood as the result of a prior bookish training, *verba* providing the conceptual development necessary for an understanding of *res* and guaranteed, indeed, a fundamentally 'liberal' orientation. It was not imitative in any slavish sense – in his *Ciceronianus* (1528) he ridicules those who blindly follow Cicero and pleads for a living Latin speech which, while adopting the spirit of the ancient, achieves its own personal flavour in line with the needs of the age. His practice was that of the great literary and pictorial artists of all time – an assimilation and redeployment of the virtues of the past made personal by the needs of the present and the integrity of the individual writer. '*Non enim sum Cicero; me tamen, ut opinor, exprimo*' (For I am not Cicero, therefore I should express myself). A self-conscious imitative style he considered the mark of a second-rate mind: it produced 'Apes of Cicero'.[67]

He admired, then, the concreteness, the actuality, the practical morality of the ancient world. It contrasted favourably in his mind with the *a priori*, abstract quality of medieval conceptions. In classical writing all was 'singularly actual, definite and realisable' – objective and descriptive, not mystic nor over analytic. And this experience was one that could be – needed to be – deployed to the reformation of the over-logical subtlety which made up the world of the 'schools' and the moral chaos which marked too much of the new, nationalistic Europe. 'Philosophia' involved the moral exhortations of a practical, classical people; the mystical like the demonic had little place in Erasmus' understanding of wisdom (*sapientia*).

This historical emphasis warrants a brief indication of Erasmus' view of history and its function. History constituted a form of truth and as such was welcomed as a formative influence; he, like other renaissance thinkers in a variety of contexts, draws on a theatrical analogy: *historia: theatrum mundi*. 'History, like the play on the stage, shapes the receptive faculties of its audience. The morals of the spectator will be impaired or improved according to the quality of the performance.'[68] But the controlling element derives from a point outside the earthly drama – Christ himself: as Erasmus wrote to Ammonius in 1531,

> far too long already the world has been in labour; when it will give birth to a child fit to live I do not know. So far the proemia [the first parts of the play] do not seem promising to me. But Christ is alive and directs the scenes of human affairs with his secret guidance. For the rest and until the *Choragus* will produce the catastrophe [final act] of the play (*fabula*) I must continue to act in this play of life . . .[69]

Erasmus had a great gift for understanding the historical ambience of the literary works he so frequently edited; he saw them as genuinely historical documents to be interpreted in relation to their age. But secular history needed to be completed by a history on a different plane – that of *historia sacra*. The individual act is but an image of eternal values. Ultimately Truth stemmed from revelation rather than historical investigation: the history of secular investigation provided but a parable of the eternal truth. In this he is perhaps still partly medieval.

Thus in drawing on historical *exempla* – a typical humanistic strategy of rhetorical persuasion – Erasmus had a very particular conception of the 'individuality' which underlay his choice of specific figures:

68

In examining Erasmus' biographies one must bear in mind that for all his skilful painting of individual features and shades of features his ultimate goal was to show the individual character *sub specie aeternitatis* . . . The individual, he thought, was centred upon an inner focal point, but the central point itself was a mirror, clear or cloudy, as may be the case, for the universal individuality of Christ.[70]

This points to a profound difference between humanist individualism and modern – for modern individualism is pluralistic and centrifugal; in the earlier conception the centripetal image of Christ controlled still, for Christian humanists like Erasmus, at least, the disruptive implications of romantic self-assertion which has marked our own times. Even the image of the theatre which we have seen playing so prominent a part in renaissance thinking implies a *structure* of relationships which holds the actors in some sort of unified coherence. The movement in Italian humanism towards an unfettered Promethean assertion was counterbalanced by a civic, integralist sense which was the message both of the Italian city state and of classical antiquity – 'the man of affairs' was the man of *civic* affairs. Erasmus had no such limited civic sense – he was, as we have seen, a 'citizen of the world', a vague enough concept as even the twentieth century has discovered. But his sense of 'individuality' was held in check by the focusing power of Christ. As Ernst Cassirer has pointed out, 'From the religious view-point, the individual is not the opposite of the universal, but rather its true fulfilment.'[71] The spiritual, universal content of humanity in terms of which individuals realise themselves is perceived in the Christian message.

His claim to be a citizen of the world received some support from his extensive use of the new printing presses which ensured the dissemination of his ideas rapidly throughout Europe. His *Colloquies* was the most popular 'reader' of the sixteenth and seventeenth centuries. He aimed to provide a model of human excellence through the proliferation of classical and patristic texts which he edited. His intimate association with publishers of note, such as the famous house of Froben in Basel, indicated his appreciation of the role of the new presses in disseminating sound learning to the ease and benefit of mankind.

Yet in contrast with other contemporary humanists like Castiglione and Sir Thomas Elyot his educational recommendations have a hint of remoteness about them. The earlier humanists and his courtier contemporaries, for all their liberal idealism, reveal a sense of context which is lacking in Erasmus. He may urge the instrumentality of his course of study, its intended social implications, yet he remains the most abstracted of the famous humanists. His universalism revealed his lack of sympathy with the social and political atomisation of his day which was increasingly providing the context within which the classical emphasis had to make sense. This was not a mistake made by either group of his fellow humanists whose recommendations are anchored firmly to the developing centres of power in the emerging absolutist monarchies and principalities.

Yet in many respects he exemplifies the characteristic humanist standpoint.

While perhaps more religiously inclined than the earlier Italian civic humanists, his cosmology is similarly teleologically oriented so that he sees 'nature'
in normative terms while stressing the need to actualise potentiality through
'art' – education. Nature, however genial in her provision, remains subordinate to nurture, culture. Erasmus shared the general humanist belief in
man's power of self-determination; man's achievement was intrinsic to his
moral efforts, and at a time when many still stressed the depravity of mankind
he did much to rehabilitate the 'natural' in man and his capacity to achieve
by the cultivation of his highest impulses through learning and education.
Erasmus contributed, too, to the moral rehabilitation of the classics against
possible attacks by Christian apologists, on the grounds that much of classical
literature accorded with the Christian spirit. He softens the oratorical and
combative spirit of the earlier humanists with a milder conversational persuasiveness, but he ceded nothing in his belief in the importance of *verba*
to any consideration of *res*. Hence instruction is to precede experience in his
educational methodology. There is perhaps a modification in the strong
renaissance urge towards achievement and creativity in his dislike of contentiousness and of ceremonies and rituals, a developing inwardness rather
than the public sense of the earlier humanists. The irony which plays so
pervasive a role in, say, the *Praise of Folly* better represents his muted tones
than the theatricality of some of his humanist contemporaries; he does speak
of the world as theatre but he occupies the role of participant spectator
rather than holds the stage himself. This may partly be explained by his
remoteness from any actual specific social role – and to the fact that he abandoned the chivalric, and hence the more theatrical, element in his educative
prescriptions which, for instance, his near contemporary Castiglione retained.
He stressed those scholarly aspects of humanism that had emerged out of its
political stage through its philosophical and historical emphasis rather than
an active participation in civic affairs. It is not that he did not attempt to
make his views known to the rulers of the day; but they were the interventions
of a publicist and scholar seeking to guide the general course of events rather
than those of someone who participated in the day to day commerce of
politics. Bainton's description of him as an 'educator of educators' success-
fully indicates the long-term implications of his interventions. Any movement towards individual autonomy is counterbalanced by an insistence on
the centrality of culture; 'freedom' is the outcome of art, the facility of
verbal mastery not the unrestrained outcome of primitive impulse, even
though it is right to consider individual bent in coming to educational decisions. Paradoxically, 'inwardness' was to result from 'formation' – it was
not a product of primitive nature.

I had completed this view of Erasmus before I encountered Professor
Norbert Elias's profoundly significant book *The Civilising Process* and was
interested to discover the extent to which he confirms on quite different
grounds my view of Erasmus as representing a 'developing inwardness' and
at the same time one springing from restraints rather than from 'natural' –
in the sense of primitive – impulse. Professor Elias examines Erasmus' short
work *De Civilitate Morum Puerilium* (*On Civility in Children*) which is con-

cerned with people's 'outward bodily propriety' in society – bodily carriage, gesture, dress, etc., as the expression of the man, of 'a well composed mind' – and sees in it features representative of a transitional society in which new models of behaviour are being diffused. These new models imply an increased awareness of the behaviour of others, a heightened human observation and stricter standards of individual restraint in one's relations with one's fellows. It represents 'a new standard of shame and repugnance which begins to form slowly in the secular upper class',[72] a degree of affective detachment as part of a general move towards the greater social isolation of the individual and a new conception of subject–object relationships. This is a theme of such importance for the development of educational theory and the changed orientation of its curricular recommendations that its appearance at this stage and in this affective guise is worth careful note. In terms of 'manners' it marks the development from medieval 'courtoisie' to renaissance 'civilité' and one of its major landmarks form the subject of the next chapter, Castiglione's *Courtier*. But it is representative also of a more general move towards the 'autonomy' of the individual manifest in intellectual terms in the new objectification of material objects already noted in the first chapter; there it is apparent in the development of perspective in painting, and subsequently may be consistently identified in the changed attitude to knowledge characterising the seventeenth- and eighteenth-century theorists. The new conception of social relationships implied in Erasmus' work, then, its emphasis on toleration and harmony, implying a certain detachment, not only supports notions of his own developing inwardness but alerts to possible future developments which will be confirmed in intellectual as well as in specifically social orientations and affective controls. A new structure is in process of emerging which will affect the total personality at both the emotional and intellectual levels. The rest of this book will spell out the details – details which must necessarily encompass regression as well as development, the persistence of earlier traits (for example, the medieval attitude to 'nature' and its basis in the analogical concept of the 'correspondence') as well as reorientations to a new objectified nature of mechanical necessity distinct from human volition and involvement. In the process 'autonomy' will be both threatened by the need for obedience to necessity and strengthened by the increased ability to control, a paradoxical situation which is only the latest of the paradoxes which characterise the situation of a being who is both part of and distinct from nature – and who, like Erasmus himself, is involved in the ever-present tension which exists between the potential of the 'natural' man (implying freedom from restraints) and the realisation that that freedom can only be realised through 'right activities' which necessitate moral choices and therefore direct human intervention through formal education.

NOTES

1 M. P. Gilmore, *The World of Humanism 1453–1517* (New York, Harper Torchbooks, 1962), p. 184.
2 cf. R. H. Bainton, *Erasmus of Christendom* (London, Collins Fontana Library, 1972).

3 W. H. Woodward, *Desiderius Erasmus Concerning the Aim and Method of Education* (New York, Teachers College Press, Columbia University, 1964), p. 35.

4 Quoted N. Elias, *The Civilising Process*, trans. E. Jephcott (Oxford, Blackwell, 1977), p. 74. R. Mandrou in his *From Humanism to Science 1480–1700* (Harmondsworth, Penguin, 1978) gives an interesting account of the emergence of this new intelligentsia.

5 W. Ullmann, *Medieval Foundations of Renaissance Humanism* (London, Elek, 1977), p. 201.

6 Quoted T. W. Baldwin, *William Shakspere's 'Small Latine and Less Greeke'* (Urbana, University of Illinois Press, 1944), Vol. II, p. 95.

7 ibid., p. 130.

8 cf. ibid., p. 194.

9 J. D. Tracy, *Erasmus: The Growth of a Mind* (Geneva, Librairie Droz, 1972), pp. 40–1.

10 P. G. Bietenholz, *History and Biography in the Work of Erasmus of Rotterdam* (Geneva, Librairie Droz, 1966), pp. 17–18.

11 Quoted Tracy, op. cit., pp. 42–3.

12 ibid., p. 10. The account that follows owes a good deal to Dr Tracy's analysis.

13 ibid., p. 62.

14 ibid., p. 67. It is interesting to note that Erasmus was not infrequently somewhat devious in his own relationships – and that he could be contentious.

15 Quoted ibid., p. 70.

16 ibid., pp. 75–7.

17 ibid., p. 78.

18 Quoted ibid., p. 81.

19 ibid., pp. 97–8. At the same time, of course, as noted above, he was deeply concerned about accuracy of meaning.

20 Quoted ibid., p. 169.

21 Woodward, *Erasmus*, p. 187.

22 ibid., p. 81.

23 ibid., p. 186.

24 ibid., p. 181.

25 ibid., p. 184.

26 ibid., pp. 183–4.

27 ibid., p. 184.

28 ibid., p. 186.

29 ibid., p. 187.

30 ibid., p. 191.

31 cf. also Erasmus' reference to 'a disposition and propensity deeply implanted in us for that which is good'.

32 cf. J. C. Margolin, *Erasmus: Declamatio de Pueris Statim ac Liberaliter Instituendis* (Geneva, Librarie Droz, 1966), p. 68.

33 Woodward, *Erasmus*, pp. 192–3.

34 ibid., p. 200.

35 In the *Enchiridion* the emphasis on original sin is perhaps a little stronger. But even in its fullest statement there is a certain optimism that 'by degrees' man can be transformed into a state of oneness with God.

36 Woodward, *Erasmus*, p. 200.

37 ibid., p. 194.

38 ibid., p. 190.

39 ibid., p. 198.

40 ibid., p. 198.

41 ibid., p. 217.

42 ibid., p. 217.

43 Thus Erasmus to some extent shares Rousseau's optimism concerning human nature, but because he values traditional learning he is inevitably forced to emphasise training to an extent that the Genevan with his much greater indifference to acculturation does not. See below, Ch. 12.

44 Woodward, *Erasmus*, p. 196.
45 ibid., p. 196.
46 ibid., p. 209.
47 ibid., p. 180.
48 ibid., p. 187.
49 ibid., p. 202.
50 ibid., pp. 191-2.
51 ibid., p. 214. This is historically interesting for it points to the extent to which the educated classes were withdrawing themselves from popular cultural pursuits (cf. P. Burke, *Popular Culture in Early Modern Europe*, London, Temple Smith, 1978, p. 29). Dr Burke dates the withdrawal of the 'upper classes' from the seventeenth and eighteenth centuries. Evidence from Erasmus, Castiglione and Elyot, the last two of whom stress the need to preserve some distance, for reasons of prestige, from the commonalty, would seem to suggest that the process was already well under way in the sixteenth century. Indeed, Dr Burke himself refers to the increasing self-consciousness of the nobility during the sixteenth century (p. 271).
52 Woodward, *Erasmus*, p. 199.
53 ibid., p. 215.
54 ibid., p. 201.
55 ibid., p. 162.
56 ibid., pp. 138-9.
57 cf. Erasmus, *Praise of Folly*, trans. B. Radice (Harmondsworth, Penguin, 1975), pp. 112-13 and n. 61.
58 ibid., p. 162.
59 ibid., p. 164.
60 ibid., p. 166.
61 ibid., p. 165.
62 ibid., p. 169.
63 ibid., p. 213.
64 ibid., p. 165.
65 Tracy, op. cit., p. 97.
66 Woodward, *Erasmus*, p. 189.
67 cf. the discussion of the notion of 'imitation' earlier, pp. 30-1 and Ch. 1, note 67.
68 cf. Bietenholz, op. cit., p. 26.
69 ibid., p. 27.
70 ibid., pp. 89 and 98.
71 E. Cassirer, *The Individual and the Cosmos in Renaissance Philosophy* (New York, Harper Torchbooks, 1964), p. 31.
72 Elias, op. cit., p. 135.

CHAPTER 3

'A Graceful and Nonchalant Spontaneity': Castiglione

I

By the middle of the fifteenth century there had been a change of direction in the development of Florentine intellectual life. The common diagnosis, which owes a good deal to Baron and Garin, is that political developments – the emergence of the princes as the predominant political forces in the peninsula – transformed the civic humanists into courtiers with a corresponding decline in political involvement and commitment. 'For the new prince forced everybody from active political life and transformed culture either into an elegant decoration of his court or into a desperate flight from the world.'[1] The explanation is surely an oversimplification and involves the projection of current 'liberal' prepossessions back into an inappropriate setting. Certainly, there were those in Florence, like Alamanno Rinuccini in his *De Libertate*, who regretted the Medici and their stranglehold over the city. But the princely courts were to afford different cultural possibilities and an alternative rhetoric: the achievements of the high Renaissance are not inferior to those of earlier times. The civilisation which produced Castiglione's *Courtier* in some respects was a more sophisticated one than that which encouraged the early humanists; and there is no reason to think that bureaucratic decision making was any less widely diffused in courts than it had been in oligarchies. Kings needed their ministers, their ambassadors, their local officials. Castiglione and Elyot were to show how they should be produced within a humanistic framework. The strengthening of the idea of monarchy, which accompanied the breakdown of feudal order and the growth of a more centralised system in the developing nation states, had helped to transform the court from a purely administrative unit to a cultural and political centre of incalculable importance for the life of Europe from the end of the medieval period to the end – at least – of the eighteenth century. Indeed, Dr Gervase Mathew in his book on *The Court of Richard II* considers that 'court life was a factor in the society of western Europe from the late fourteenth until the early twentieth century'.[2] The features that distinguished it, in his view, from the *Curia Regis* of the earlier medieval period included 'the presence of women of influence and standing', 'a strict ceremonial that merged into an elaborate etiquette', 'an intricate system of patronage', 'a tendency for courtiers to form distinct groupings' leading to court intrigues, an 'element of luxury' and perhaps above all 'the conception of fashion' which affected manners deeply and reflected the tastes of the king or prince.[3] 'Political' and 'cultural' humanism were, in some degree, to come together in the education of the courtier.

It must not be thought that the pre-twentieth-century courtier was necessarily a merely decorative figure. Power emanated from the king, and the courtier would have many of the functions of the modern minister or high civil servant. Castiglione himself, for instance, fulfilled for long periods ambassadorial functions. Written probably by 1514, though not published for a further fourteen years, *Il Cortegiano* deals with the select group who gathered at the court of Urbino at the beginning of the sixteenth century. All the characters who take part in the conversation were historical figures who could well have participated in such a discussion. The tone of the court had been set by the great Duke Federico da Montefeltro, whom Ficino had described as the pattern of a wise ruler and perfect man: for this Duke

> built on the rugged site of Urbino a palace which many believe to be the most beautiful in all Italy; and he furnished it so well and so appropriately that it seemed more like a city than a mere palace. For he adorned it not only with the usual objects, such as silver vases, wall-hangings of the richest cloth of gold, silk and other similar material, but also with countless antique statues of marble and bronze, with rare pictures, and with every kind of musical instrument; nor would he tolerate anything that was not most rare and outstanding. Then, at great cost, he collected a large number of the finest and rarest books, in Greek, Latin and Hebrew, all of which he adorned with gold and silver, believing that they were the crowning glory of his great palace.[4]

In this 'grammar school of courtesies', as W. B. Yeats later called it, Castiglione, whose mother was a Gonzaga and therefore belonged to Mantua, nevertheless spent twelve years of his early mature life (1504–16). By then Federico was dead, and had been succeeded by his ailing son Guidobaldo who, along with his wife Elizabetta, maintained his father's interest in learning and the cultivation of the arts and who, as the Venetian envoy described, 'with the help of the Duchess, who was as eager as her lord in welcoming and entertaining accomplished guests . . . collected a greater number of finer spirits than any Prince of his age, and held up to the world the model of an admirably regulated court'.[5]

The model of the courtier forms the subject of the four evenings' conversations that Castiglione purports to report in his book. The aim is explicitly Platonic: 'For (leaving aside any dispute about the Intelligible world and the Ideas) just as . . . there exists the Idea of the perfect Republic, of the perfect King and the perfect Orator, so there exists that of the perfect Courtier.'[6] Its ideas draw extensively on classical sources – especially Cicero. The method of exposition recalls the humanist (and ancient) rhetorical pedagogic tradition of posing questions and exploring answers through the consideration of opposing viewpoints.

75

II

Plato perhaps more than any other philosopher raises, for the Renaissance, questions relating to the nature of 'reality'. Certainly it is clear that the equivocation of appearance and reality profoundly exercised the times in terms significantly different from the purely philosophical conflict of the medieval realists and nominalists. Now it is related to the ambiguities of human behaviour in a social context: the implications of Petrarch's distinction between 'what we seem' and 'what we are' are becoming apparent.

The leading neo-Platonists were at great pains in their examination of man's nature to stress its indeterminate character – its freedom, its autonomous quality – while emphasising its power and importance. The leader of the Platonic Academy in Florence, Marsilio Ficino (1433–99), had as his central purpose the demonstration of the immortality and divinity of the human soul; and the major argument he deployed related to man as a creator of culture – the active changing and re-creating of the world of nature by means of art and industry:

> The other animals either live without art, or have each one single art to the use of which they do not turn by their own power but are dragged by a law of fate . . . On the contrary, men are the inventors of innumerable arts which they practise according to their decision. This is shown by the fact that individuals practise many arts, change, and become more expert by extensive exercise . . . Man at last imitates all the works of divine nature and perfects, corrects and modifies the works of lower nature.[7]

Ficino was much influenced by the evidences of man's creative capacity manifest in his own city of Florence:

> How marvellous the cultivation of the earth throughout the world. How stupendous the structures of buildings and cities. How ingenious his works of irrigation. He acts as the Vicar of God, since he inhabits all the elements and cultivates all, and, present on earth, he is not absent from the ether . . . Finally the use of speech and writing especially proper to man indicates a certain divinity of mind present in us which animals lack . . . Hence speech is granted to us for a certain more excellent task, namely as the interpreter of the mind, and herald and infinite messenger of infinite discoveries.[8]

Man's soul dominated his animal part, the body – and strove to become God: 'The entire striving of our soul is that it become God'; and one of the marks of this attempted self-deification was the instinct for ubiquity – politically in the state, culturally in his attempt to be 'everywhere' – 'He measures the earth and the heavens, and he sounds the hidden depths of Tartarus . . . He is content with no frontier. He yearns to command everywhere and to be praised everywhere. And so he strives to be, as God, everywhere.'[9] Here, indeed, is a Faustian image – a vision more metaphysical and cultural than ethical and social, as Professor Trinkaus points out: 'He assimilated those trends of fourteenth and fifteenth century humanist speculation about man and God and transformed them into a shape that the less political, more religious and more systematic sixteenth century could use.'[10] One might slightly amend this: less political in the republican sense, but serving a new political end in the apotheosis of monarchy; Castiglione himself compares the position of God in the universe to that of the king in the state; so we are beginning to move towards the time when Bossuet cried in the seventeenth century: 'Oh Kings, you are Gods on earth!' The elevation of the ruler to some extent, indeed, mirrored the elevation of man implicit in the neo-Platonist position. If the core of Platonic 'humanism' as opposed to the earlier civic humanism of men like Salutati, Valla, etc., lies in its metaphysical quality (as Kristeller suggests), then such views affected the specifically political role of kingship, conceiving of it as the highest human dignity in a system which elevated the human to the level almost of divinity.

Pico della Mirandola, a pupil of Ficino, in some respects extends the picture. The essence of human dignity he finds in its freedom – I have noted that briefly earlier. Pico believed that man when created had been assigned a share of all the gifts distributed to the other creatures – and hence contained the germs of all possibilities within himself. His task was to overcome the lower forms of life and elevate himself to God. Unlike Ficino, he does not assign to man a fixed place in the hierarchy but stresses his freedom to choose his own nature among his many potentialities. Man exists outside the conventional hierarchy of the Chain of Being and demonstrates a flexibility foreign even to Ficino. As Pico says, in his *Oratio de Hominis Dignitate*,

> At last the best of artisans ordained that that creature to whom He had been able to give nothing proper to himself should have joint possession of whatever had been peculiar to each of the different kinds of being . . . 'We have made thee neither of heaven nor of earth, neither mortal nor immortal, so that with freedom of choice and with honour, as though the maker and moulder of thyself, thou mayest fashion thyself in whatever shape thou shalt prefer . . . Thou shalt have the power, out of thy soul's judgment, to be reborn into the higher forms, which are divine.'[11]

'The maker and moulder of thyself', the opportunity to be 'reborn into the higher forms' – once more the implied stress is on effort and the transformation of the 'primitive' self. As Kristeller puts it:

> Man's dignity is not merely something that is given him with his birth, according to Pico, but rather something he has to attain and to realise through his own effort. What is given is merely the ability to strive toward this end. We assert our dignity as human beings not simply by being what we happen to be but by choosing the best among our potentialities, by cultivating reason rather than blind feeling.[12]

This emphasis on man's freedom to choose the role he seeks to play is, of course, educationally important in that it suggests a potential variety of role assumption. Man was an earthly image of God and shares, *in potentia*, God's subjectivity:

> This subjectivity comprised man's freedom to participate in the universe at whatever level and in whatever condition he chose. Man could debase himself to the pure materiality of the elements, vegetate with the flowers . . . indulge his senses with the animals . . . rise with reason to the spheres of the heavens, ascend beyond them to the super-celestial realm of the intelligences or the angels, by using his intellect. Here he would closely approach towards becoming akin to God himself.[13]

But the responsibility is man's; it is he who must hold the universe together in harmonious peace; and in a significant analogy Pico points to the punishment which awaits those who fail to live up to that dignity which is God's gift: 'It entirely exceeds every kind of madness that we should believe that it is permitted to anyone placed in some city, decorated with the highest honours, to sin against its prince, against the entire republic deserving so well of him without punishment . . .'[14]

So, man can transform nature – and his own nature. Subjectively and objectively he exercises a controlling hand. This pervasive platonising atmosphere clearly influenced Castiglione. As the translators of the letters of Marsilio Ficino urge,[15] he 'was . . . the first of many in European literature to portray Ficino's notion of a purely spiritual love between friends . . . as extending between members of the opposite sex'. The culmination of the courtier's education in its withdrawal from the material world to that of the super-celestial realm shows the unmistakable influence of the neo-Platonists.

III

The exposition is in dialogue form – the conversational mode need not surprise when it is considered how central good talk and conversation was to such a group of cultured and sophisticated people. As we have seen, conversation rather than formal oratory was Erasmus' ideal; and indeed, one of the important virtues of the ideal courtier lay in his ability to converse; as signor Gaspare puts it: 'in my opinion this is of considerable importance, seeing that at Court this is the chief occupation for most of the time . . .'[16] Humanist rhetoric is adapted to the needs of a small comparatively literate circle. Writing itself is regarded as a kind of speech: 'For it is my belief that writing is nothing other than a kind of speech which remains in being after it has been uttered, the representation as it were, or rather the very life of our words . . . the finest speech resembles the finest writing.'[17] Though there are admitted to be some differences between the two (writing preserves the words and the reader can afford them more attention) the consensus of the discussion continues to stress the close relationship between them – and it is even noted that the courtier 'has to make use of speech more often than of writing'.[18] However, literacy is certainly regarded as an essential attribute of the courtier, thus indicating his assimilation to the new state 'bureaucracy' and his need to play his part in the business of government, which demanded an elegant and sophisticated style. But the assimilation of literacy to speech reminds us that we are still in a predominantly oral age. Print, by the time *Il Cortegiano* was published in 1528, had already begun to make profound cultural alterations in the consciousness of the age – and as noted, Erasmus at least had grasped the significance of the change. But writing was, for long enough, to bear the rhetorical marks of the speech from which it emanated and whose models (until, indeed, the 'mathematical plainness' of the seventeenth century) dominated the form of the written word.[19]

The emphasis on conversation and speech reveals the intensely *social* character of the courtier. The virtues appropriate to the courtier having been declared, the conversation, on the second night, veers to a lengthy discussion as to how the courtier 'ought to use his good qualities'.[20] His purpose is to maximise his social effect; he plays the role which will enhance his prestige and influence: to these ends

> let him consider well whatever he does or says, the place where he does it, in whose presence, its timing, why he is doing it, his own age, his profession, the end he is aiming at, and the means that are suitable, and so bearing all these points in mind, let him prepare himself discreetly for all he wishes to do or say.[21]

There follows much worldly advice on how to shine in the best company and not let oneself down in front of one's inferiors. 'Bold and notable exploits' should be performed, where feasible, in front of the most eminent men and, if possible, before the prince himself. The courtier should dress appropriately and show himself before the spectacle has staled – an analogy with a 'great actor of the ancient world' who always insisted on speaking the first lines of a play is explicitly used. In sports he must give 'full consideration to the kind of audience present and to who his companions are; for it would be unbecoming for a gentleman to honour by his personal appearance some country show, where the spectators and participants were common people'.[22] Though one of the group indicates that 'In Lombardy we are not so fussy', the speaker insists on the courtier's maintaining a certain decorum – for instance, in front of a crowd 'he should maintain a certain dignity' when he is dancing. Only when masked is he allowed a degree of licence and even then he should strive to appear to advantage, for such masquerading 'enables the courtier to choose the role at which he feels himself best'.[23]

The process, then, is one of constant adaptation to the needs of the moment. Rules, it is asserted, can hardly be given; for

> whoever has to accommodate his behaviour to dealings with a considerable number of people must be guided by his own judgment and,

recognising the differences between one man and another, must change his style and method from day to day, according to the nature of those with whom he wants to converse.[24]

Such a development of social awareness, of the need on the one hand for politeness and attention to the claims of equals and on the other for the preservation of distance in dealings with inferiors, marks a further stage in that 'civilising process' identified by Professor Elias, with its implication of increased self-awareness and control of the emotions.

IV

With these injunctions we begin to approach the core of the book: for it is in the precise delineation – with its implications for the concept of 'natural-ness' – as to how this highly socialised and politicised personality is to operate that its formative educational influence resides. Something so chameleon-like implies a complex 'nature'. It implies, too, an accelerating degree of psychic mobility, albeit to a very specific end and in a closely defined context. We are now far from the fixities of early medieval social role attribution.

Indeed, a way of approaching this central interest of the book would be to recognise that already the modern reader is likely to have been antagonised – as indeed has the translator, Mr George Bull: 'It is hard, indeed, to think of any work more opposed to the spirit of the modern age. At an obvious level, its pre-occupation with social distinction and outward forms of polite be-haviour creates an intense atmosphere of artificiality and insincerity.'[25] The fundamental error – not to see that always and everywhere since the dawn of consciousness, man has been the creature of artifice not instinct – has already been adumbrated earlier. Man makes himself – the situation is clear in Erasmus and his humanist forebears, for man is forced to inhabit both the natural world and the moral world of culture; and hence he must come to terms with a symbolic world which both reflects and transcends through culture what has been given in nature (*natura naturata*). Indeed, man's perennial struggle is ultimately concerned with the precise concessions and assents he must make to the 'given' of nature and the extent to which he can shape his own destiny; and some *decision*, conscious or unconscious, must be taken on this problem. Thus artifice inescapably becomes a defining characteristic of human development. Into 'being oneself' some *conception* of that self must, of necessity, enter. 'Naturalness' as the thrush and the tiger are 'natural' is not possible to man.

It is true that Mr Bull precedes his accusation of 'artificiality and insin-cerity' by the word 'intense' – and it is arguable that, the point in the last paragraph conceded, it is a matter of degree. Here Mr Bull would be on stronger ground, for the extent of social conciliation can seem reprehensible. To translate the charge into a modern idiom, the 'other directedness' of the courtier offends against a developed sense of individualism, progenitor of modern notions of 'sincerity' and 'authenticity'. But there are mitigating circumstances, for not all advocacies of social orientation imply the same society. The assumption is that the courtier will be thrown among people of a sensitivity and cultivation equal to himself, that the 'game' will be played among those who are equally respect-worthy. Moreover, the ultimate purpose of this diplomatic role playing is the inculcation of virtue and the purging and purification of government – nothing less than the health of the whole state. The intention behind the role assumption is still the humanist purpose of social improvement.

Furthermore, in the fuller elaboration of the formation of the courtier it becomes clear that 'naturalness' is not eschewed; by a paradox 'naturalness' is the final product of artificiality, and the purpose behind the highly wrought socialisation based on imitation is in fact the achievement of a kind of freedom, autonomy. In fact an art that was to a high degree imitative was intended to provoke 'naturalness' – 'naturalness' which would seem to be its antithesis. Tacitly Castiglione accedes to Pico's stress on human freedom, though in terms significantly different from those ruling in our own society today. Partly, of course, such art arose out of a desire, inherited from the Greek view of a liberal education, to avoid any suggestion of a narrow expertise, any hint of professionalism.

'Imitation' certainly plays an important role in the formation of the courtier. The first hints come with the reference to the influence of the Duchess who, as a 'model of fine manners', inspired the whole court with a desire to 'imitate her personal way of behaviour'.[26] For whatever 'nature' has given can be improved by following the best models:

> Therefore anyone who wants to be a good pupil must not only do things well but must also make a constant effort to imitate and, if possible, exactly reproduce his master. And when he feels he has made some progress it is very profitable for him to observe different kinds of courtiers and . . . take various qualities now from one man and now from another.[27]

Castiglione, indeed, like all the humanists, is unequivocal in his appreciation of the need for education, art, in the achievement of his aims. It is true that the precise contribution of Nature (conceived of as those forces outside of human control) remains a matter of dispute among the participants. Count Lodovico da Canossa believes that the courtier should be drawn from a good family precisely because

> those who are most distinguished are of noble birth, because Nature has implanted in everything a hidden seed which has a certain way of influencing and passing on its own essential characteristics to all that grows from it, making it similar to itself. We see this not only in breeds of horses and other animals but also in trees . . .; and if they sometimes degenerate, the fault lies with the man who tends them.[28]

This notion of selective breeding is challenged by Gaspare Pallavicino. Admitting that men are not born equally endowed, he denies that such inequalities correlate with birth in specific strata of society:

> I fully concur with what you said about the happiness of those endowed at birth with all the perfections of mind and body; but this is seen among those of humble origins as well as those of noble birth, since Nature has no regard for these fine distinctions. On the contrary . . . the finest gifts of Nature are often found in persons of very humble family.[29]

The contestants agree that some are more 'naturally' endowed for courtiership than others; they agree that such 'natural' propensity is important – the courtier-to-be should 'receive from Nature not only talent and beauty of countenance and person but also that certain air and grace that makes him immediately pleasing'.[30] They both appeal to 'Nature' to support their arguments. They disagree as to whether nobility of birth is likely to produce better aspirants than effort applied to 'natural' talent; but they concur in recognising individual differences which make some 'naturally' more apt for courtiership and in the possibility that those 'not perfectly endowed by Nature can, through care and effort, polish and to a great extent correct their natural defects'.[31] Indeed, the emphasis on imitation comes from a request to be told how those who do not possess this 'natural God-given gift'[32] in which lies the essence of courtiership, grace, can acquire it in some measure:

> But regarding those who receive from Nature only so much as to make it possible for them to acquire grace through enterprise, application and effort, I should like to know by what art, teaching and method they can gain this grace, both in sport and recreation which you believe are so important, and in everything else they say or do.[33]

After asserting that 'it is almost proverbial that grace cannot be learned', Count Lodovico contradicts his own precept by indicating ways and means by which this essential quality can in some measure be acquired – through the 'best teachers' and by means of imitation.

For 'grace' is the essential quality – the book's thematic word, a word, moreover, which carries with it theological overtones. And the central core of gracious behaviour is something called 'sprezzatura', which is best translated as 'effortlessness'. This notion is crucial to the understanding of the book – and especially to the understanding of the *art* of courtiership: for the courtier has an end beyond himself, as the *teacher* of princes. The notion must, then, be carefully examined.

V

Briefly, it is the art which hides art. Grace is essential to the 'art' of the courtier – but its essence lies in its manifestation as an apparently 'natural' gift. Hence, in acquiring it every effort must be made to hide its 'artificial' nature. The Count defines this crucial element in a passage that must be quoted at some length.

> However, having already thought a great deal about how this grace is acquired, and leaving aside those who are endowed with it by their stars, I have discovered a universal rule which seems to apply more than any other in all human actions or words: namely, to steer away from affectation at all costs, as if it were a rough and dangerous reef, and (to use perhaps a novel word for it) to practise in all things a certain nonchalance which conceals all artistry and makes whatever one says or does seem uncontrived and effortless. I am sure that grace springs especially from this, since everyone knows how difficult it is to accomplish some unusual feat perfectly, and so facility in such things excites the greatest wonder; whereas . . . to labour at what one is doing . . . shows an extreme lack of grace . . . So we can truthfully say that true art is what does not seem to be art; and the most important thing is to conceal it, because if it is revealed this discredits a man completely and ruins his reputation.[34]

Only in this way can be achieved 'a graceful and nonchalant spontaneity'.

There are several interesting features of this account. The highest art is that which hides art – and achieves qualities like 'effortlessness', 'facility' and 'spontaneity', which imply a kind of freedom – 'positive' and not 'negative' freedom, 'freedom to' and not 'freedom from' and manifest as the characteristic humanist 'liberalisation'. Command of oneself and of situations arises not from any lack of discipline (nor freedom from restraints) but is in fact its finest flower. 'Naturalness' in these terms is something to be achieved, not simply something to be expressed; it is associated, in this sense, with actualisation rather than with original endowment or potentiality. There are, in fact, interesting analogies here with theories of painting, for 'facility' became a much sought after artistic trait – as, of course, also did 'grazia'. What is intended in both cases is that the qualities of mind and hand have been so internalised that they have become part of the personality structure; out of constraint comes freedom – the 'civilising process' carries its own sophisticated autonomy.

But an illustration of what the Count means has certain further implications:

> I remember once having read of certain outstanding orators of the ancient world who, among the other things they did, tried hard to make everyone believe that they were ignorant of letters; and, dissembling their knowledge, they made their speeches appear to have been composed very simply and according to the promptings of Nature and truth rather than effort and artifice. For if the people had known of their skills, they would have been frightened of being deceived.[35]

'Naturalness' and truth here are equated with a sort of assumed simplicity and ignorance consciously adopted for the purpose of deceiving, at least to the extent of concealing, for the purposes of persuasion, acquired skills. Here is revealed a potentiality for what the humanists had most feared – the use of their arts for the purpose of deceit. It is fair, I think, to protest that in Castiglione the whole argument exists within a framework which asserts that the aim of the art of courtly behaviour is virtuous conduct – virtue manifest in the guidance given by the courtier to his prince, to the tendering of which his whole training is adapted so that he can be as persuasive as possible.

Nevertheless the concept of 'simplicity' implies an equivocation; does it stem from what I must distinguish as an 'artificial' naturalness or a 'natural' naturalness – spontaneity as the offspring of art or of artlessness, the fully formed or the pre-formed, the sophisticated or the primitive. For in another context Castiglione seems to equate simplicity and naturalness, not with the art that hides art, but artlessness:

> How much more attractive than all the others is a pretty woman who is quite clearly wearing no make-up on her face . . . whose own colouring is natural and somewhat pale . . . who lets her unadorned hair fall casually and unarranged, and whose gestures are simple and natural, betraying no effort or anxiety to be beautiful. Such is the uncontrived simplicity which is most attractive to the eyes and minds of men, *who are always afraid of being tricked by art* (my italics).[36]

Here, then, would seem to be an '*uncontrived* simplicity', not the *contrived* simplicity of the orator. In the same speech by the Count he speaks of someone having hands 'which are delicate and fine' and being so 'more by Nature than through any effort or design'.

Yet there is even here a distinction to be made. Beautiful hands constitute natural attributes because they owe nothing to human intervention – they are so, as described, as a physical manifestation in which human culture can play no part. But not to wear make-up, like wearing make-up, *letting* the hair fall rather than pinning it up, involve human decisions – to wear or not to wear, to fall or not to fall.[37] Therefore even what I have termed 'natural' naturalness has to be distinguished into 'natural' naturalness – the hands, and 'artificial' 'natural' naturalness – the hair and the make-up, which hide an artifice behind a resolute show of naturalness.

The point of this somewhat exhaustive analysis is to reveal the extent to which the 'natural' is so often a human creation, a human artefact. Purely physical attributes can owe nothing to human intervention but the *posture* of the hair and the *care* of the face imply a human decision. The interest of this passage lies in the coexistence of two categories of artifice – the admittedly contrived which I have termed 'artificial naturalness' unashamedly and the covertly contrived which I have called 'artificial natural naturalness'. In the first case the notion of simplicity is associated with the highest form of human artifice; with the second it is bound up with notions of the primitive, the unsophisticated and the move in this direction in the midst of this highly sophisticated audience is significant and should be noted. These two notions of naturalness – the highly wrought and the primitive – exercise the most powerful influences on educational ideas over the next 250 years. But much more characteristic of the Renaissance is the 'artificial naturalness', the highly wrought simplicity, the actualisation of potentiality through an art which hides art – and this constitutes the essential element in the creation of the courtier, the high water mark of renaissance culture and civilisation, applied equally to the creation of pictures, poems – and men. Its key characteristic is *sprezzatura* – that 'natural' effortlessness which marks the furthest extreme to any suggestion of the primitive.

The great question mark that lies over the whole exercise relates to the framework, virtuous or otherwise, within which the role assumption takes place; and it was this equivocation which exercised the imagination of so many Elizabethan writers, as it had, at a cruder level, the medieval preacher. For so often, of course, artifice can hide corruption rather than clothe virtue. The problem endlessly fascinated Shakespeare, the major theme of whose work can perhaps be identified in terms of Petrarch's remark, quoted above, concerning the difference between 'what we seem' and 'what we are'. If we seem only to enhance what we are, all is well. 'Seems Madam, nay I know not seems', cries Hamlet to his mother – and who doubts at that moment his sincerity? But time and again in Shakespeare 'seeming' covers actuality – 'I am not what I am', exclaims Iago; 'Look like the innocent flower but be the serpent under't', enjoins Lady Macbeth. The threat of the courtier lies in Bassanio's assertion, 'Now may the outward shows be least themselves,/The world is still deceived with ornament.' The courtier, then, as defined in Castiglione, constitutes at once the high water mark of a secularised civilisation, the greatest creation of a purely humanistic culture – and offers the greatest threat to its integrity. The paradox he poses, in intellectual terms, constitutes a central focal point of educational theorising for the rest of this book. No theorist from now on ignores the promises and the threats – more promises, incidentally, than threats – of 'naturalness' in one or other of its guises. Put another way, as affect control increases as the result of a more sophisticated socialisation implicit in the development of civility, it can seek either transcendence into a new realm of learned autonomy or regress to an appropriate level of impulse release as protest against the inhibitions demanded. In terms of theorists examined in this book the idealised courtier of Castiglione stands at the opposite pole to the idealised pre-adolescent Emile of Rousseau.

I have emphasised that the courtier, having achieved this perfection of grace – its constituents we will examine shortly – becomes teacher. The elaborate assimilation of graciousness is intended to make his advice palatable:

> In my opinion . . . the end of the perfect courtier . . . is, by means of the accomplishments attributed to him by these gentlemen, so to win for himself the mind and favour of the prince he serves that he can and always will tell him the truth about all he needs to know . . . And, if he knows that his prince is of a mind to do something unworthy, he should be in a position to dare to oppose him, and make courteous use of the

favour his good qualities have won to remove every evil intention and persuade him to return to the path of virtue . . . Therefore I consider that just as music, festivities, games and other agreeable accomplishments are, so to speak, the flower of courtiership, so its real fruit is to encourage and help his prince to be virtuous and to deter him from evil.[38]

So there is a discussion on the extent to which virtues are 'natural' or can be taught. Signor Gaspare remarks that the virtues cannot be learned; 'rather, I think that the men who possess them have been given them by Nature and by God'. Signor Ottaviano repudiates this on the grounds that 'nothing can ever grow accustomed to what is naturally its opposite'; 'So if the virtues were . . . natural to us . . . we would never become accustomed to vice. Nor are the vices natural to us in this way, for then we could never be virtuous' – and it would be unjust to punish men by law for what is not their fault: 'So we see that the laws accept that the virtues can be learned, and this is certainly true; for we are born capable of acquiring virtues, and similarly vices . . .'[39] The potentiality for these virtues is admittedly rooted in our souls – but they often fail 'to develop unless helped by education':

Therefore, as with other arts and skills so also with the virtues it is necessary to have a master who by his teaching and precepts stirs and awakens the moral virtues whose seed is . . . buried in our souls and who, like a good farmer, cultivates and clears the way for them by removing the thorns and tares of our appetites which often so darken and choke our minds as not to let them flower or produce those splendid fruits which alone we should wish to see born in the human heart.[40]

For potentiality 'to pass to actuality' it cannot 'rely on Nature alone but needs the assistance of skilful practice and reason to purify and enlighten the soul'.[41] To the objection that men often do what they know to be wrong because their desires prove too strong, Ottaviano indicates that what such men have is only a vague understanding of evil and so allow emotion to conquer reason:

But if they enjoyed true knowledge there is no doubt that they would not fall into error. For reason is always overcome by desire because of ignorance, and true knowledge can never be defeated by the emotions; which originate in the body rather than the soul. And if the emotions are properly governed and controlled by reason then they become virtuous, and if otherwise, then vicious.[42]

Once again it is clear that while nature cannot be totally contravened, what she provides needs to be completed by human agency exercising a formative power. This of course is in line with what has been said above about 'art'. 'Art', furthermore, exists in terms of knowledge directing the rational powers of the mind to the exercise of temperance; for temperance is what moderates the emotions and makes them, not wholly quiescent but conducive to virtue – it is temperance that 'hands over to reason the sceptre of absolute power'. The element of affect control achieves explicit recognition.

So the specifically educational recommendations are clearly within the humanist tradition both in their acceptance of human self-regulation through reason and in many of the details of the curriculum by which this is to be achieved. Here Castiglione blends humanist recommendations with some of the traditional elements of chivalric training: '. . . the first and true profession of the courtier must be that of arms; and this above everything else I wish him to pursue vigorously',[43] urges Count Lodovico. Hence he is to 'demonstrate strength and lightness and suppleness and be good at all the physical exercises befitting a warrior'. So 'his first duty is to know how to handle expertly every kind of weapon, either on foot or mounted, to understand all their finer points, and to be especially well informed about all those weapons commonly used among gentlemen'.[44] He is to know how to wrestle, to be 'an accomplished and versatile horseman',[45] skilled in sports which are 're-lated to arms and demand a great deal of manly assertion',[46] able to play tennis, but ignoring acrobatics which were not considered appropriate for a gentleman. For once again, in physical exercises, the emphasis is on the ability to perform with grace and without affectation; chivalry dons its renaissance rather than its medieval guise: 'Let him laugh, jest, banter, romp and dance, though in a fashion that always reflects good sense and discretion, and let him say and do everything with grace.'[47] He was indeed to 'imbue with grace his movements, his gestures, his way of doing things and in short, his every action'.[48]

Equally central, however, is the stress on knowledge; in learning to speak and write the sense of what is said matters at least as much as the mode of expression: 'Because to divorce sense from words is like divorcing the soul from the body.'[49] So what the courtier 'requires in order to speak and write well . . . is knowledge, because the man who lacks knowledge and has nothing in his mind worth hearing has nothing worth writing or speaking'. While 'it is the words themselves which give an oration its greatness and magnificence',[50] and grace must inform the orator's movements, enunciation and expression, matter is as important as manner: and a prime source of 'matter' was to be found, in characteristic humanist theory, in literature: 'in addition to goodness, I believe that for all of us the true and principal adornment of the mind is letters'.[51] Even the French, who despised such matters, 'could easily be persuaded to [value learning] if they would listen to reason, since nothing is more naturally desired by men or more proper to them than knowledge'.[52] So the courtier is to be a 'more than average scholar',[53] at least in the humanities, and to have a knowledge of both Latin and Greek – in order to be able to follow the example of many of the most distinguished ancients.

The courtier's education, however, is broadened to include a range of artistic skills. He is to be a musician: 'the man who does not enjoy music can be sure there is no harmony in his soul'.[54] He should be able to draw and paint, despite their apparent unsuitability to a gentleman; there are classical precedents for painting being regarded as a liberal art; and skills of this kind have important utilitarian implications, for military purposes: 'thus a knowledge of the art gives one the facility to sketch towns, rivers, bridges, citadels, fortresses and similar things'.[55] Furthermore, to be able to imitate the handi-work of God in nature is deserving of the highest praise. Sculpting, too, is praised and the relative merits of sculpting and painting discussed.

So the courtier is to acquire a range of physical, intellectual and artistic skills: on to the training of the medieval knight are to be grafted the intellectual capacities of the classical orator and the new cultural adornments of the renaissance court, skills such as playing music, painting, made respectable by their development in theoretical and therefore intellectual content, and acceptable as liberal arts. These were the qualities which to the high Renaissance, had come to seem 'natural' to man; and all served to make the court a cultural as well as a political centre. Indeed, the two elements merged into one another; for what might be distinguished as cultural was intended to serve a political end by fostering in the courtier accomplishments which were designed to assist him in his virtuous attempt truly to advise and serve his prince, to the latter's greater glory.

VI

It is urged that neither Aristotle nor Plato 'would have scorned the name of perfect courtier'; and the conversations end with a lengthy discussion of the nature of Platonic love, for being in love had previously been identified as one of the characteristics of the courtier. Perfection in courtiership, however, would seem to be an attribute of age – and surely it would be unfitting for such a person to be in love? Pietro Bembo, however, urges that he could love 'in a way that would not only bring him no blame but earn him great praise and complete happiness, free of all vexations, which rarely if ever happens with younger men'.[56] Prompted by the Duchess (for she considers this as one of the most important endowments of the courtier) Bembo embarks on an analysis of 'what love is and what is the nature of the happiness that lovers experience . . .'[57] There follows a neo-Platonic analysis of the nature of love – the longing to possess beauty which is associated with goodness and which stems from spiritual contemplation, not that of the senses: 'Consequently its possession brings them nothing but good, since beauty is goodness and so the true love of beauty is good and holy and always benefits those in whose souls the bridle of reason restrains the iniquity of the senses; and this is something the old can do far more easily than the young.'[58] From contemplation of the single beauty, however, man can come to achieve a realisation of universal beauty. Even this stage of love, though, will not be perfect. Through contemplation it is possible to achieve an appreciation of the angelic beauty in which are to be discovered traces of God. And so love affords the soul the greatest happiness:

> For just as from the particular beauty of a single body it guides the soul
> to the universal beauty of all bodies, so, in the last stages of perfection,
> it guides the soul from the particular intellect to the universal intellect.

And from there, aflame with the sacred fire of true divine love, the soul flies to unite itself with the angelic nature, and it not only abandons the senses but no longer has need of reason itself. For, transformed into an angel, it understands all intelligible things and without any veil or cloud it gazes on the wide sea of pure divine beauty, which it receives into itself to enjoy the supreme happiness the senses cannot comprehend.[59]

Thus is the sensual abandoned and love leads the soul to unity with the highest. On this note of Platonic ecstasy, the conversation ends. In this way does the courtier manifest his highest nature.

The highest achievement of the courtier, then, was this form of Platonic love, for through it he corrected the falsity of the senses, achieved the transcendence of the passions and that union with the divine beauty which is also the highest form of goodness. In this way he would attain inward happiness and contentment and would thus free himself for the greater service of his prince; at the same time he can realise his highest nature through the apprehension of spiritual reality. It is not surprising to find that Castiglione takes a very different stand over matters of ceremony and ritual from that of his contemporaries, Erasmus and Vives. When, towards the end of his life, as papal nuncio in Spain, Alfonso Valdes, the Latin secretary to Charles V, wrote a pamphlet approving the sack of Rome in 1527 as a divine judgement on the corruption of the papacy – a pamphlet which incidentally was much approved by the followers of Erasmus – Castiglione replied, defending the church and the ancient rituals and criticising those who would take away the relics which 'seek by means of things seen, to raise the thoughts of man to the unseen': 'Even if these relics were false, the worshipper would not be an idolater, because whatever stirs devotion in the hearts of men, and leads them to pray to God with the faith that can work miracles, must of necessity be good.'[60] Thus did Castiglione at once defend the importance of rituals and at the same time maintain that loyalty to his master (in this case the Pope), which he considered an essential attribute of the ideal courtier.

VII

During the fifteenth and sixteenth centuries, the disintegration of the old feudal order produced a vastly expanded literature of etiquette manifesting an increasing formalisation of court functions and public spectacles intended to help legitimise new emerging secular hierarchies. Castiglione's *Courtier* proved the most sophisticated and one of the most widely read of this court-oriented literature. Rarely did a year go by in the sixteenth century without an edition or a translation of the work being published; and Roger Ascham considered that the book 'advisedly read and diligently followed but one year at home in England, would do a young gentleman more good, iwis, than three years' travel abroad spent in Italy'[61] which, coming from one who normally disapproved of things Italian, constituted no mean testimonial.

Yet we have noted that it has not had a good press in our age which makes a cult of 'sincerity'; and one of its latest critics, Dr Sydney Anglo, is clearly highly equivocal in his attitude to the book. While admitting that it 'became the pattern of the courtier and ultimately of the gentleman', a pattern which has 'only really been discarded within living memory, and not wholly with advantage', and granting it to be 'the most significant book in the history of courtly literature', he too seems repelled by what he terms its dilettantism and its 'sparkling superficiality'. As with Mr Bull, he finds its nonchalance too premeditated: 'This perfect courtier simply tries too hard to appear not to be trying.'[62] It is in effect the old accusation of artificiality and insincerity – manner surpassed matter 'in terms of honesty, reliability and loyalty'. The courtier's aim is 'to advance his career by ingratiating himself with authority'. Much the same indictment is to be found in Dr Javitch's *Poetry and Courtliness in Renaissance England*.

This seems to me unfair as I read the book – I find the stress on virtue and, in the Platonic outcome which Dr Anglo seems to ignore, on spirituality, goodness and beauty. In the literature relating to the Renaissance there is too great a tendency (the political bias is patent) to see early civic humanism as good, courtly humanism as bad; yet both existed on rhetoric, either as oratory or conversation, and both therefore are wedded to persuasion. Men are known to further their careers in popular assemblies as well as in courts; the earliest humanist, Petrarch, was as keenly aware of the dangers of 'seeming' in any context where words are master as are any of Castiglione's critics; it was a problem that must arise near any centre of power, republican or princely – or, for that matter, democratic.

But there is a deeper reason for defending Castiglione in that he frankly accepts the artifice implicit in any education. Men make themselves and others, for such is the logic of the human situation. In all willed activity – and education is essentially that – 'nature' (as original endowment) must be transcended and realised by art, and 'naturalness' itself as an aim inevitably becomes normative. It is part of the virtue of the *Courtier* that this is unmistakably revealed in its argument, for Castiglione consciously aims to achieve a 'naturalness' which is openly and admittedly 'artificial', and thus opens the way to a frank appraisal of the concept. It is his virtue to have elaborated one of the most highly sophisticated of educational models – and at the same time to have raised questions relating to the pursuit of 'naturalness' which illumine all future employment of the term. Once again it is necessary to insist that claims to 'naturalness' in opposition to a despised 'artificiality' often simply constitute a device for disseminating an alternative ethic – one, for instance, which makes concessions to the primitive.

Analysis of Castiglione's work may reveal something of the logic of the concept of 'naturalness'; but the book itself, of course, contains a highly idealised picture of the courtier and of court life. There was an extensive anti-court literature, drawing to some extent on attacks on parasites and flatterers in classical literature. One brief quotation may be allowed to sum up a widespread indictment of courtiers and court life:

Base sycophants, crumb-catching parasites
Obsequious knaves, which bend at every nod:
Insatiate harpies, gormandising kites,
Epicures, atheists, which adore no God
But your own bellies and your private gain
Got by your oily tongues bewitching train.[63]

Moralists, often, found court life not only corrupt but considered it necessarily so, implicit, as it were, in the logic of the courtier's position. The career of an actual courtier provides a deeper insight into the complexities of a courtier's position. Dr Stephen Greenblatt's study of *Sir Walter Raleigh* provides a sophisticated account of his subject – and, to some extent, of his subject's queen – as a man who had dramatised himself precisely in the manner implied by Castiglione's analysis, as he sought to adapt his role to what he himself called 'this stage-play world'; for Raleigh considered the 'theatre a central metaphor for man's life'.[64] Greenblatt brings out well the contradictions implicit in the metaphor of theatre with its threat of emptiness and unreality and yet its assertion of man's self-formative dignity and power to direct his own destiny; and he reveals in his complex study at once the falsities and yet the disciplined intelligence needed to fulfil a self-appointed role which is paradoxically imposed by the social conditions of the time (or for that matter, of any time, for those who would seek a political career) – 'the need to discover a viable relation between the cultivated individual and the source of power in the state'. Indeed, does not any form of social life impose an element of role playing – a *presentation* of self?[65] The corruptions of role playing have received extensive analysis in literature throughout the centuries; less attention has been paid to the egotism and selfishness equally reprehensible in the ethic of 'sincerity' to which our age is so much committed. Is the life-style of the flatterer and parasite more reprehensible than that of the urban guerilla simply because the latter can plead, in extenuation, a claim to 'authenticity'; and yet in the muddled ethics of our age the latter attracts in some circles, regrettably intellectual, a degree of sympathy which would be indignantly refused almost universally to the former.[66] If it could be recalled that men are responsible equally for the depredations of their 'sincerities' as they are for the corruptions of their ingratiations, that 'naturalness' can manifest itself as self-degrading as can 'artificiality', in that both are subject, willy-nilly, to the responsibilities of art in gestation – both involving inescapably an active *presentation* of self – something might be done to lessen the conviction that somehow the reductionism of our own times constitutes a stance morally superior in potential to the simulation of another age. Dirty jeans imply an image as much as fine clothes – it is simply that in one case the model is proletarian, in the other aristocratic.

What makes the *Courtier* something of a landmark in the history of European civilisation is the ubiquity of its artistic intent.[67] It marks the highest and most extended of the secular (as opposed to the Christian) attempts to transform the 'natural' man – in the more primitive sense – as a means of realising the totality of his potentiality, intellectual, artistic, moral and physical – *l'uomo universale, vir virtutis*. The ideal permeates every aspect of his physical and intellectual presence through the cultivation of learning, artistic accomplishment, virtue, bodily movement and physical courage, all contributing to that graciousness which informs the aristocratic ideal at its finest. It constitutes, of course, an essentially active ideal historically manifest in the evolution of the 'gentleman' who thus enters the European consciousness as having a specifically defined role which combined political service in the state hierarchy with wide cultural and artistic interests. It lacked the specific Christian virtues of charity and humility, but it was to play an important and often benevolent role in the increasingly secularised society of the later and post-renaissance periods. In its specifically English manifestation it is worth further consideration in the work of Sir Thomas Elyot; for it is to the evolution of the English gentleman that classical humanism made perhaps its finest and most lasting contribution.

NOTES

1 E. Garin, *Italian Humanism*, trans. P. Munz (Oxford, Blackwell, 1965), p. 78.
2 G. Mathew, *The Court of Richard II* (London, Murray, 1968), p. 1.
3 ibid., p. 1.
4 B. Castiglione, *The Book of the Courtier*, trans. G. Bull (Harmondsworth, Penguin, 1967), p. 41.
5 Quoted J. Cartwright, *Baldassare Castiglione: His Life and Letters* (London, Murray, 1908), Vol. I, pp. 84–5.
6 Castiglione, op. cit., pp. 35–6.
7 Quoted C. Trinkaus, '*In Our Image and Likeness*', Vol. 2 (London, Constable, 1970), p. 482.
8 ibid., pp. 483–5.
9 ibid., pp. 487–91.
10 ibid., p. 492.
11 Quoted E. Cassirer *et al.*, *The Renaissance Philosophy of Man* (Chicago, University of Chicago Press, 1948), pp. 224–5.
12 P. O. Kristeller, *Renaissance Concepts of Man* (New York, Harper Torchbooks, 1972), p. 21.
13 Trinkaus, op. cit., p. 506.
14 Quoted ibid., p. 522.
15 Published by Shepheard-Walwyn, 1975, p. 25.
16 Castiglione, op. cit., p. 139.
17 ibid., pp. 71–2.
18 ibid., p. 73.
19 Elizabethan prose and verse, for instance, carry on the tradition of ordered *speech*: and the rules of *rhetoric* dominated, in form and manner, the written word. Indeed, Father Ong has indicated his belief that until the modern technological age, Western culture was essentially a rhetorical culture and had its consequent effect on human thought structures – as we have noted in Chapter 1: 'human thought structures are tied in with verbalization and must fit available means of communication' (W. J. Ong, *Rhetoric, Romance and Technology*, Ithaca, NY, Cornell University Press, 1971). Though rhetoric represents will and action, it is usually manifest as a will of persuasiveness rather than of dogma. Perhaps the decline of dogma is related to the relative unpopularity, among the new aristocracy, of the certainties of logic and the greater popularity of persuasive talk and conversation.
20 Castiglione, op. cit., p. 112.
21 ibid., p. 115.

22 ibid., p. 117.
23 ibid., p. 119.
24 ibid., p. 124.
25 G. Bull, Introduction to Castiglione, op. cit., p. 15.
26 Castiglione, op. cit., p. 43.
27 ibid., p. 66.
28 ibid., p. 54.
29 ibid., p. 56.
30 ibid., p. 55.
31 ibid., p. 55.
32 ibid., p. 65.
33 ibid., p. 65.
34 ibid., p. 67.
35 ibid., p. 67.
36 ibid., pp. 86–7.
37 It may be argued that Mr Bull's translation of the original Italian – 'co i capelli à caso inoinati, et mal compositi' – stresses inadmissibly the consciousness behind the apparent neglect. But 'mal compositi' surely *does* imply alternative strategies of arrangement and bears witness to the inescapable element of consciousness behind the 'neglect'. One is reminded of the description by George Santayana of one of his female characters: 'she was perfectly unaffected – at least she affected nothing but being perfectly natural' (*The Last Puritan*). The whole speech of the Count makes it quite clear that, wittingly or unwittingly, he is speaking not even of some unselfconscious country girl but of court ladies who are self-consciously unself-conscious. Simone de Beauvoir acutely assesses the situation: 'the least sophisticated of women, once she is "dressed", does not present *herself* to observation, she is, like the picture or the statue, or the actor on the stage, an agent through whom is suggested someone not there – that is, the character she represents, but is not' (*The Second Sex*).
38 Castiglione, op. cit., pp. 284–5.
39 ibid., pp. 289–91.
40 ibid., p. 291. The role and nature of the virtues in renaissance Platonic thought is discussed in J. M. Major, *Sir Thomas Elyot and Renaissance Humanism* (Lincoln, University of Nebraska Press, 1964), pp. 241–61.
41 Castiglione, op. cit., p. 291.
42 ibid., p. 293.
43 ibid., p. 57.
44 ibid., p. 61.
45 ibid., p. 62.
46 ibid., p. 63.
47 ibid., p. 64. How very different is the unconstrained behaviour of the young Emile, cf. below, pp. 271–2.
48 ibid., p. 65.
49 ibid., p. 72.
50 ibid., p. 77.
51 ibid., p. 88.
52 ibid., p. 89.
53 ibid., p. 90.
54 ibid., p. 95.
55 ibid., p. 97.
56 ibid., p. 324.
57 ibid., pp. 324–5.
58 ibid., p. 327.
59 ibid., p. 340.
60 Quoted in Cartwright, op. cit. Vol. II, p. 403.
61 R. Ascham, *The Schoolmaster*, ed. L. V. Ryan (Ithaca, NY, Cornell University Press, 1967).

62 S. Anglo, 'The Courtier' in *The Courts of Europe*, ed. A. G. Dickens (London, Thomas & Hudson, 1977), pp. 42–4.
63 Quoted Anglo, op. cit., p. 33.
64 S. J. Greenblatt, *Sir Walter Raleigh: The Renaissance Man and his Roles* (New Haven, Conn., Yale University Press, 1973), p. 26.
65 cf. Irving Goffman, *The Presentation of Self in Everyday Life* (Harmondsworth, Penguin, 1969).
66 If this statement seems a trifle extreme, the reader is urged to look at Professor Duncan Williams's *Trousered Apes* (London, Churchill Press, 1971). cf., for instance, the quotation from Henry Miller: 'Either you are crazy, like the rest of civilised humanity, or you are sane and healthy like Buñuel. And if you are sane and healthy you are an anarchist and throw bombs' (p. 8).
67 The latest to draw attention to the vocabulary analogously applied to various human arts – education, painting, literature – is Dr Javitch (*Poetry and Courtliness in Renaissance England* (Princeton, NJ, Princeton University Press, 1978)), who points to similarities of expression and interest as between Castiglione's *Courtier* and George Puttenham's *The Arte of English Poesie*. I do not accept, however, the sharpness of the distinction Dr Javitch makes in his first chapter between the Orator of earlier humanism and the Courtier of its later phase, though changed social circumstances clearly implied some modifications in persuasive techniques.

CHAPTER 4

'The Governor': Sir Thomas Elyot

Sir Thomas Elyot's *Governor*, first published in 1531, reflects many aspects of Castiglione's *Courtier* translated into the less sophisticated, national setting of the Tudor monarchy. Within the narrower confines of the Italian city state the courtier served in the more immediate entourage of his master or performed on occasions ambassadorial functions; the 'governor' acted as his ruler's representative in the country at large. This afforded him a degree of independence and necessitated the exercise of power which explains the rather greater stress, in Elyot's analysis, on moral rather than cultural quali-fications, though, significantly, the latter receive an emphasis new in the administrative life of the country. But the basic pattern remains broadly true to the general humanist position – a new concern for knowledge leading to an eloquent virtue in action. 'The book became a handbook of ethics and education for the English ruling class.'[1] It was in any case written in the vernacular by a man who had had experience both at the level of local and central government. He had held office as a justice of the peace and sheriff; he had also for a short period been ambassador at the court of Charles V and was almost certainly a member of parliament. Much influenced by the work of both Erasmus and Sir Thomas More, the *Governor* nevertheless contained a distillation of much that he had derived from his own direct experience.

The Book named The Governor,[2] first published in 1531, begins with what Castiglione had taken largely for granted, a justification of monarchy and an analysis of the relevant social structure: 'A public weal is a body living, compact or made of sundry estates and degrees of men, which is disposed by the order of equity and governed by the rule and moderation of reason.'[3] Both the natural and the supernatural realms provide focal points for analysis by means of which the notions of order and hierarchy can be justified; for both on heaven and on earth hierarchy is said to constitute the 'natural' order – within the heavenly mansions, the body of man and the domain of nature (in the sense of the natural world of plants and animals): 'so that in every-thing is order, and without order may be nothing stable or permanent; and it may not be called order, except it do contain in it degrees, high and base, according to the merit or estimation of the thing that is ordered'.[4] Hence the justification of ranks in society – 'God giveth not to every man like gifts of grace, or of nature.'[5] Especially are men to be distinguished in terms of different levels of understanding:

Notwithstanding for as much as understanding is the most excellent gift that man can receive in his creation, whereby he doth approach most nigh unto the similitude of God, which understanding is the principal part of the soul . . . so in this world they which excel others in this influence of understanding . . . such ought to be set in a more high place than the residue . . . that by the beams of their excellent wit, showed through the glass of authority, other of inferior understanding may be directed to the way of virtue and commodious living.[6]

These arguments are deployed to justify the rule of 'one being' – the analogies of God in his heaven and the bee in his hive are employed as further justification; as are a number of comparisons from classical sources. (The relevant passages in Elyot are probably the origin of Ulysses' famous speech on order in Shakespeare's *Troilus and Cressida*, an indication of the approved currency of Elyot's remarks.) A new social hierarchy was in process of formation as substitution for the medieval feudal order.

The question then arose as to who was to be admitted to the elite of governors. The king required 'sundry mean authorities, as it were aiding him in the distribution of justice in sundry parts of a huge multitude; whereby his labours being levigate [lightened] and made more tolerable, he shall govern with the better advice, and consequently with a more perfect governance'.[7] They are to become the king's 'eyes, ears, hands and legs'.[8] Learning and virtue are considered to be basic requirements but Elyot expresses a distinct preference for recruitment from the ranks of those already eminent:

And except excellent virtue and learning do enable a man of the base estate of the commonalty to be thought of all men worthy to be so much advanced, else such governors would be chosen out of that estate of men which be called worshipful, if among them may be found a sufficient number, ornate with virtue and wisdom, meet for such purpose . . .[9]

This concession, grudging though it is, to the possibility of the lowly born providing suitable material for such responsibilities can be assigned to the influence of Plato's *Republic* where talent was a major criterion, a model never far from Elyot's mind; it may also have shown some appreciation of the developing element of social mobility which characterised the new monarchy of the Tudors. However, his preference for advancement from the ranks of the traditionally well endowed is explained on the grounds that those who own more should also have pre-eminence in administration; they are likely to be less corruptible, and more affable and acceptable to the people, who 'therewith the less grutch [complain] or be disobedient'.[10] Finally those in established positions have the resources necessary to secure the adequate 'bringing up of their children in learning and virtues'.[11] That said, Elyot turns to consider the proper training of such offspring in 'true nobility'.

Man is by nature prone to knowledge – the theme is by now a familiar one – though its seeds need to be cultivated by education. By such cultivation a man may achieve virtue and a knowledge of right action – such, in essence, is Elyot's view. He accepts the Platonic division of the three parts of the soul

– vegetative, sensitive and 'the part intellectual or of understanding'.[12] The last of these is the most noble and most characterises man, distinguishing him from the plants and the beasts:

It is the principal part of the soul which is occupied about the beginning or original causes of things that may fall into man's knowledge, and his office is, before that anything is attempted, to think, consider, and prepense [anticipate] . . . And therefore it is to be remembered that the office or duty of understanding precedeth the enterprise of acts . . .[13]

The nature of man justifies the stress on learning and 'doctrine'. For in physical development men are exceeded by trees, beasts, fishes and birds; but in 'cunning . . . man excelleth all other creatures in earth . . . What so perfectly expresseth a man as doctrine?'[14] Elyot has to overcome the prejudice felt by many of the nobility against what they consider to be the province of clerks: a major purpose of his work is to stress the importance of learning and its aptness to people who traditionally have tended to despise it: 'to a great gentleman it is a notable reproach to be well learned and to be called a great clerk; which name they account to be of so base estimation that they never have it in their mouths but when they speak anything in derision'.[15] Yet there is ample classical precedence for a princely interest in learning; and, as indicated, the importance of learning is rooted in the 'natural' capacities of man himself and in that part of him which specifically marks him off from the vegetative or sensitive beings.

Knowledge leads to virtue – a capacity for which also characterises mankind: 'The nature and condition of man, wherein he is less than God Almighty, and excelling notwithstanding all other creatures in earth, is called humanity; which is a general name to those virtues in whom seemeth to be a mutual concord and love in the nature of man.'[16] So his plea for the improvement of education arises from his belief that education develops man's innate capacity for knowledge which in turn makes him apt to virtue. And he derives these views from a metaphysical conception of the nature of man's 'soul' which owes a great deal to Plato and probably to neo-Platonists like Ficino.[17] Where virtue is concerned, the potential governor proceeds from natural virtue (gentleness, humanity, etc.) to moral virtues (justice, fortitude and temperance) and ends with the intellectual virtues – prudence, sapience and understanding. By progressing in this manner the governor fits himself for governance in his province and the counselling of his prince, which constitute his major purposes. For 'the end of all doctrine and study is good counsel'.[18]

What was the nature of the learning proposed and how did the upbringing proposed reflect other notions of the 'natural' explicit in the book? To take the second question first, Elyot employs a metaphor which, in several guises, is to reappear during the period covered by these two volumes – the horticultural analogy. In view of its later manifestations it is important to examine precisely how Elyot uses it. The emphasis is on the gardener (implying the educator) rather than, as later, on the plant: '. . . I will use the policy of a

wise and cunning gardener: who . . . will first search throughout his garden
where he can find the most mellow and fertile earth, and therein will he put
the seed of the herb to grow and be nourished . . .'[19] The gardener's attention
is central: he is to protect against weeds, water and nourish, and prevent
breakage of the shoots: 'Semblable order will I ensure in the forming the
gentle wits of noblemen's children.'[20] This, then, is a typically humanistic
teacher – directed education; indeed constant supervision is essential. Children are to be protected against evil companionship and 'to be kept diligently
from the hearing or seeing of any vice or evil tache'; steps are to be taken
positively 'to instil in them sweet manners and virtuous custom'.[21] These
steps are necessary because of the various individual natures of the children;
and a major task of the tutor is 'first to know the nature of his pupil',[22] and
this on two counts. First, 'in some children nature is more prone to vice than
to virtue' and they must therefore be assigned to a tutor 'in whom is approved
to be much gentleness, mixed with gravity',[23] one who can apply the necessary
correctives. (It is admitted, however, that others have a natural inclination
to goodness, in which case their natural propensity can be strengthened by
good instruction and example.)[24] But also it is important that education
should have regard to the individual potentialities of the learner: 'let us follow
our own proper natures, that though there be studies more grave and of
more importance, yet ought we to regard the studied whereto we be by our
own nature inclined'.[25] For Elyot has little truck with notions of equality,
as we have seen earlier,[26] and he shares the general renaissance view which
had come to recognise the importance of individual differences.

Education, then, is grounded in the 'nature' of the child, both metaphysical
and psychological; but as is implicit in the metaphor of the gardener, Elyot
considers, like all humanists, that nature needs to be assisted. Goodness, for
instance, 'seldom cometh only of nature, except it be wonderful excellent;
but by the diligent study of very philosophy . . . nature is thereto prepared
and helped'.[27] Elsewhere, in his *Knowledge which maketh a Wise Man*, Elyot
also impresses the importance of study: '[By] study of mind art is augmented;
like as contrarywise by sluggardy and idleness the said activity is appalled
and the wits consumed; whereby men be made unapt for the life which is
active or politic.'[28]

Elyot is clear that knowledge must precede experience: 'And therefore it
is to be remembered that the office or duty of understanding precedeth the
enterprise of acts, and is in the beginning of things.'[29] So a liberal education
must precede a more vocationally oriented concern for the law:

I think verily if children . . . were retained in the right study of very
philosophy until they passed the age of twenty-one years, and then set
to the laws of this realm . . . undoubtedly they should become men of so
excellent wisdom that throughout all the world should be found in no
common weal more noble counsellors.[30]

Education, then, brings knowledge; knowledge can be strengthened by experience and should issue in right action, the counselling of the prince and

the wise administration of responsibility. Public duty of one form or another is typically the aim of humanist education and Elyot is no exception. What, then, is to be taught to the fledgling 'governor', how is he to be formed? Though we shall need to consider this in some detail, it can be said straight away, as Professor Major points out, that 'the *Governor* is a "traditional" book, in the sense that it draws freely on the ideas, form, illustrative material, and even style of a whole series of books of similar kind which stretch back to antiquity'[31] an off-shoot of the 'mirror-for-princes' *genre*.

The earliest years are to be spent exclusively in the company of women.[32] Great care is to be taken in the choice of such people as nurses, for the influences of these early years are vital:[33] children are to be kept from any contact with vice through evil companionship. Positive steps are to be taken to teach them their letters and introduce them to Latin, albeit in an attractive and pleasant manner. The English spoken in the child's presence is to be 'clear, polite, perfectly and articulately pronounced'.[34] At the age of 7 the child is to be removed from the company of women and a tutor is to be assigned. To vary the labour of study the learning of music is to be encouraged and the playing of musical instruments, 'which moderately used and without diminution of honour, that is to say without wanton countenance and dissolute gesture, is not to be condemned'.[35] Music will serve for recreation; it has a deeper use in that the harmony of the music will reflect, for the child, the harmony of orders and degrees in the public weal he is learning to serve – an analogical argument which is further used to justify dancing. Painting and sculpting, too, are permitted largely because of their practical usefulness, provided the child is by nature so inclined. In all cases where the arts are concerned care is to be taken that the future governor does not lose caste in the eyes of his inferiors, 'the people forgetting reverence when they behold him in the similitude of a common servant or minstrel'.[36] Bacon's injunction that 'Every man of superior understanding in contact with inferiors wears a mask' receives strong support from sixteenth-century protagonists of elitist education. The stress on the need to keep up appearances and maintain dignity provides an interesting contrast with present-day concern for an unsophisticated 'naturalness' and 'sincerity' and, as we have seen, provides a major theme for sixteenth-century (and later) writings.[37] Furthermore Elyot lacks Castiglione's sense of aesthetic appreciation – he has an eye to practical usefulness and moral edification rather than aesthetic delight. Even the furnishings of a nobleman's house must assist in teaching moral lessons – the painting and tapestries 'containing histories, wherein is represented some monument of virtue'.[38]

So the place of the arts is practical rather than aesthetic; they will assist in learning other matters such as geometry, astronomy, and cosmography – 'In which studies I dare affirm a man shall more profit in one week by figures and charts well and perfectly made, than he shall by the only reading or hearing the rules of that science by the space of half a year . . .'[39] Practice rather than precept I have noted as a feature of Erasmus' methodology.

For the rest emphasis is placed on intellectual and physical development. Greek and Latin, Elyot agrees with Quintilian, should be learned together, the former from the age of 7, the latter from the earlier years. Again, the aim is largely moral – elegance is accompanied by 'much moral and politic wisdom'[40] in the relevant texts, and they will serve to advance virtue and discourage vice. Homer, to take an example, is strongly recommended for his encouragement of the warlike qualities as well as his 'incomparable wisdom, and instructions for politic governance of people'.[41] The child may be encouraged to make verses in imitation of Virgil and Homer, for did not 'the noble Augustus and almost all the old emperors [make] books in verses'.[42] Constantly one is aware of the characteristic humanist stress on imitation and the following of models. Poetry especially Elyot considered had a formative power – the poetry, of course, of classical antiquity: 'a man can be truly formed only if he learns to recognise the model of humanity in antiquity and makes it an active force by re-creating it in his own life'.[43] The stress, it will be obvious, is on the perfection of the individual though the orientation is to a social role. It is this strongly individualistic emphasis in the human concern for a social idea that, as Professor Caspari points out, 'distinguishes humanistic nationalism from the various diseased nationalisms of our own age. There is no way to Elyot's goal [and, one would add, the goal of the other humanists] except through the process of perfecting the single personality'.[44] As with Castiglione, a degree of autonomy and social responsibility are fused in a rich synthesis.

After grammatical understanding has been acquired and the approved poets allowed to work their effects, the child shall, at the age of 14, be introduced to the disciplines of the 'orator' – some logic, and the art of rhetoric, with the help of Cicero, Quintilian and Erasmus' *Copia*; 'words' again are crucial: 'The utility that a nobleman shall have by reading these orators is that when he shall hap to reason in counsel, or shall speak in a great audience or to strange ambassadors of great princes, he shall not be constrained to speak words sudden and disordered, but shall bestow them aptly and in their places.'[45] History – the study of which will be assisted by a prior introduction to cosmography – will again introduce the pupil to works of elegant writing and moral example. Then, three years later, comes the time for moral philosophy – the *Ethics* of Aristotle, the *De Officiis* of Cicero, and above all the works of Plato – 'those three books be almost sufficient to make a perfect and excellent governor'.[46] Biblical stories, the proverbs of Solomon and the books of Ecclesiastes, together with the historical sections, are also recommended. Content is as important as style – and in line with Cicero and Quintilian Elyot urges that knowledge as well as linguistic facility are fundamental to the orator's art: 'Wherefore inasmuch as in an orator is required to be a heap of all manner of learning, which of some is called the world of science, of other the circle of doctrine, which is in one word of Greek *Encyclopaedic*; therefore at this day may be found but a very few orators.'[47] So, 'Verily there may no man be an excellent poet nor orator unless he have part of all other doctrine, specially of noble philosophy'.[48] Hence, as pointed out above, the more vocational training in the laws should be preceded by this encyclopaedic liberal education which Elyot considers to be an essential propaedeutic. In this Elyot is in the best humanist tradition of *doctus orator*.

Learning, then, is fundamental to the education of a gentleman. But it must be supplemented by 'exercise' to adapt his body to 'hardness, strength, and agility'.[49] Though the renaissance stress on learning represented an important departure from the medieval knightly ideal, enough of the older need to provide for warfare remained to necessitate various kinds of physical training. Wrestling, running and swimming are recommended; it is necessary to learn to handle weapons and 'to ride surely and clean on a great horse and a rough, which undoubtedly . . . importeth a majesty and dread to inferior persons'.[50] Hawking and hunting are defended – partly as an imitation of battle; and one of the most interesting recommendations is the stress he places on dancing, for Socrates had not been 'ashamed to account dancing among the serious disciplines, for the commendable beauty, for the apt and proportionate moving, and for the crafty disposition and fashioning of the body'.[51] But there is more to dancing than this, and Elyot propounds an interesting analogy between the different figures and movements of the dance and various human characteristics. The dancing together of a man and woman, for instance, 'holding each other by the hand or arm . . . betokeneth concord', symbolising the harmonious joining together of the differing masculine and feminine traits. And Elyot continues through several chapters to point out how the various steps of the *basse danse* demonstrate the meaning of one of the main virtues, prudence, without a knowledge of which it is not possible to attain to the other virtues: 'And because that the study of virtue is tedious for the more part to them that do flourish in young years, I have devised how, in the form of dancing, now late used in this realm among gentlemen, the whole description of this virtue prudence may be found out and well perceived . . .'[52]

And so the young gentleman is not only exercised but receives his first lesson in the moral virtues. Much of the rest of the book is taken up with an account of these virtues and how they may be acquired. As Miss Kelso puts it, in her *Doctrine of the English Gentleman:*

In no respect did classical influence on the European ideal of the perfect man show itself more clearly than in transferring the emphasis from a belief in the virtues as innate and therefore more the possession of the well-born than the base-born to a belief in the necessity of education for the development of the virtues, a change due to the fuller recognition of the possible attainments of the individual through education rather than ancestry.[53]

Sir Thomas Elyot, it is clear, was not an original thinker. He reports much that is common to the humanists of his age – and much of that sprang from historical and classical literary examples. Experience comes from books as well as life; this justifies the stress on the prior importance of knowledge – for knowledge itself comes through books. True, 'as in hounds is a power or disposition to hunt . . . in the souls of men so is ingenerate a leme [gleam] of science, which with the mixture of a terrestrial substance is obfuscate or made dark; but where there is a perfect master prepared in time, then the brightness of the science appeareth polite and clear'.[54] Ruling, indeed, is an art to be learned.

Elyot's main task, then, is to set out the conditions under which the secular state should be governed and how to set about training the governors. I find Major's accusation that by contrast with More's *Utopia*, Elyot seems 'remote, abstract, theoretical', strange. Far from wishing to create a Utopia from nothing Elyot accepts the Tudor state as it is (though admittedly he does not examine very closely its faults – too dangerous an undertaking, no doubt), and seeks to fulfil a current social need by showing how its administrators can be trained. The situation was as described by Professor Lawrence Stone in his *Crisis of the Aristocracy*:

> What had happened was that the technical requirements for public service had altered. The demand for military expertise had slackened, and the demand for intellectual and organisational talents had increased. As the state bureaucracy grew and as the modern diplomacy took shape, the highest public offices went to those who had been trained to think clearly, could analyse a situation, draft a minute, know the technicalities of law, and speak a foreign language.[55]

It was to meet a precise social demand rather than to create a new society that Elyot wrote his book. True, he produced an idealised version of what was required; but its 'relevance' is unmistakable. The image of the elite ('With us', stated Thomas Starling, 'gentlemen study more to bring up good hounds than wise heirs') had to be altered – Elyot contributed to the process. Indeed, Major's point accords ill with his remark that 'Elyot's work was intended to be, in part at least, a kind of anti-Utopia, a defence of the traditional structure of English society against proposals that would sweep away that structure . . .'[56] It is precisely Elyot's appreciation of current social needs that gives his work its historical interest; its very unoriginality shows him to be working within a humanistic tradition which had its roots in a changing social situation, whether brought about by increasing urbanisation, the revival of trade and a money economy as in the Italian context[57] or an increasingly centralised nationalism as in the demands implied by the Tudor monarchy.

Furthermore, the secular trend of Elyot's thought seems to be unmistakable. Major urges that Elyot's 'viewpoint was fundamentally religious and Christian', a notion for which there is, in his view, 'abundant evidence'.[58] That Elyot worked within a Christian framework is undeniable; but his Christianity, like his classical learning to which he appeals much more frequently (especially, of course, to Plato), is oriented towards state service. We are certainly to render unto Caesar – the things of God play a lesser role except in so far as they encourage virtuous social action. Here, certainly, is no mystic: 'In vain were your long travail in study and learning, if actual experience did not show forth their fruits.'[59] The effect was to marry knowledge to action after the Platonic model of an elite of guardians trained through a rigorous education in relevant intellectual disciplines as the conditions of virtuous behaviour.

A knowledge of 'letters' had become more useful than a training in chivalry. By stressing the role of learning in the importance of knowledge, Elyot, despite his preference for the well-born, inevitably paved the way for a more open society, one where talent must play an increasing part. The immediate effect was to revitalise the aristocratic conception of society, but that aristocracy itself could no longer remain rigidly exclusive; it needed the intellectual strengthening that only the talented outsider could on occasions supply. Furthermore the 'Tudor humanists . . . established what was to remain the ruling motive of English classical study down to the days of the "Jowett mind" '.[60]

Elyot, though less genial in exposition than Castiglione, has something settled and solid about him, something representative and soberly enunciated. A tradition is in process of being established which is to last practically down to our own days, paradoxically at almost the same moment as the humanism which formed its central core was about to be undermined by other forces. In his analysis of the various virtues which go to make up the ethos of the new gentleman-rulers Elyot lays a stress on moral conduct and self-restraint which reveals a characteristic humanistic basis: 'They shall not think how much honour they receive, but how much care and burden.'[61] Their responsibilities are to entail 'a laborious office and travail' and they are to be inducted into a formidable list of the traditional classical virtues.

But as the new aristocracy evolved under the Tudors there began to be initial hints among humanist writers at insufficiencies in the classical experience. The classical formulation was about to meet the challenge of the new empiricism – the actualities of conduct and habitat to challenge the sufficiency of the classical world. Vives bluntly opts for the prior authority of 'things', Montaigne reveals the psychological disorientations of a rhetorically trained mind facing the ambiguities and ambivalences of personal experience. After all, quadrivial (i.e. 'scientific' and practical) subjects played a part in renaissance higher education[62] – and helped to strengthen the grasp on empirical actuality.

With the benefit of hindsight it is perhaps possible to detect some such developments in the humanly unstable equilibrium likely to be fostered by that attempted fusion of autonomy and social responsibility which formed the core of the humanist synthesis. 'Autonomy', the product of successful imitation ('successful' in that it transcended copying) of former or classical models, nevertheless has a potential for doubts as well as acceptances, evokes at least possibilities of self-questioning; 'social responsibility' widens awareness of other social groupings and activities and alerts to the actualities of behaviour, human or material. Vives and Montaigne, humanists though they are, already reveal the initial possibilities of a new orientation. Elyot himself, more practical and less idealistic than Castiglione, offers recommendations which lay themselves more open to an empirical checking. Is the world in fact ordered precisely as the humanist sees it partly at least through the eyes of a former civilisation? Does he really *know* what he thinks he knows?

NOTES

1 J. M. Major, *Sir Thomas Elyot and Renaissance Humanism* (Lincoln, University of Nebraska Press, 1964), p. 3.
2 Hereinafter referred to as *The Governor* (Everyman edition). Professor Lawrence Stone sees the book as the first representative of an extensive literature which put forward 'a modified, Anglicised version' of Castiglione's emphasis on the role of the court, a version in which 'prime stress was laid on service to the Prince in either the court or the country, and in which piety and virtue played a larger part' (L. Stone, *The Crisis of the Aristocracy 1558-1641*, London, Oxford University Press, 1965, p. 400).
3 *The Governor*, p. 1.
4 ibid., p. 3.
5 ibid., p. 4.
6 ibid., p. 4.
7 ibid., p. 13.
8 ibid., p. 13.
9 ibid., pp. 13-14.
10 ibid., p. 14.
11 ibid., p. 14.
12 ibid., p. 225.
13 ibid., pp. 225-6.
14 ibid., p. 43.
15 ibid., pp. 40-1.
16 ibid., pp. 120-1.
17 cf. Major, op. cit., p. 28.
18 *The Governor*, p. 238.
19 ibid., p. 15.
20 ibid., p. 15.
21 ibid., p. 16.
22 ibid., p. 20.
23 ibid., p. 19.
24 ibid., p. 28.
25 ibid., p. 52.
26 ibid., pp. 165-7. Ontologically men are equal but socially 'degree' is necessary.
27 ibid., p. 190.
28 Quoted Major, op. cit., p. 196. Professor Major points to some contradiction in Elyot's views on the acquiring of sapience or wisdom. Often he speaks as if this is a gift of grace from God, and thus undermines his ideas, stated elsewhere, on the importance of education. Major considers though that his 'real' view approximates to that of Erasmus and Vives, that man must put out some effort on his own part as well as accept the gift God gives him; thus the importance of education is reinstated.
29 *The Governor*, p. 226.
30 ibid., p. 52.
31 Major, op. cit., p. 43.
32 *The Governor*, p. 16.
33 ibid., p. 16.
34 ibid., p. 18.
35 ibid., p. 20.
36 ibid., p. 22.
37 'Naturalness' in the modern sense and 'sincerity' are perhaps only advocated in societies where no hierarchy exists to set an example or provide an alternative model for an 'assumed' personality. Thrown back on one's own resources what else is there except 'sincerity'? - which nevertheless paradoxically assumes much of its colouring from peer group pressures. To be cast back on the fluidity of one's own individuality constituted a problem that, for instance, Montaigne saw. There is no escape for human beings to *become* something.

38 Major, op. cit., provides an extended discussion of the point – pp. 62-7.
39 *The Governor*, p. 24.
40 ibid., p. 29.
41 ibid., p. 30.
42 ibid., p. 32.
43 F. Caspari, *Humanism and the Social Order in Tudor England* (New York, Teachers College Press, Columbia University, 1968), p. 170.
44 ibid., p. 173.
45 *The Governor*, p. 35.
46 ibid., p. 39.
47 ibid., p. 46.
48 ibid., p. 50.
49 ibid., p. 60.
50 ibid., p. 64.
51 ibid., p. 76.
52 ibid., p. 79.
53 R. Kelso, *Doctrine of the English Gentleman* (Urbana, University of Illinois Press, 1929), p. 108.
54 *The Governor*, p. 222.
55 Stone, op. cit., p. 673.
56 Major, op. cit., p. 109.
57 cf. W. K. Ferguson, 'The reinterpretation of the Renaissance' in *The Renaissance: Basic Interpretations*, ed. K. H. Dannenfeldt (United States of America, Heath, 1974), p. 211.
58 Major, op. cit., p. 55.
59 Elyot, *Image of Governance*, quoted Major, op. cit., p. 179.
60 D. Bush, quoted Caspari, op. cit., p. 97. In the nineteenth century, emphasis was also placed on its potential for training the mind.
61 *The Governor*, p. 97.
62 Hardin Craig, *The Enchanted Glass* (Oxford, Blackwell, 1950), p. 89.

CHAPTER 5

'A Knowledge of Nature': Vives

Vives lived from 1492 to 1540; socially, he belonged to the circle of Erasmus, though he was a somewhat younger man. There were, moreover, certain likenesses between the outlooks of the two; but Vives introduces an element which is quite foreign to his elder colleague and which distinguishes him as a portent of future developments.

Teleologically both Erasmus and Vives showed considerable similarities: both saw the ultimate purpose of life, as they saw that of education, as the achievement of God, and both made piety fundamental to their system. Their visions of God, too, revealed an analogous undogmatic quality; neither cared much for ceremonies or institutionalised religion. Both, too, emphasised the need for a practical, socially oriented morality, one of service to mankind: in this perhaps lay the essence of their humanism. But their psychological accounts as to how these ends were to be achieved differed considerably. In Erasmus, as we have seen, learning was essentially acculturation, the assimilation of judgement from the earliest possible moment through the development of language to the authority of the ancients; only thus was it possible to confront experience. Put it another way: in Erasmus culture needs to precede nature – nature here interpreted as the phenomenal world admitted through the senses – and the senses themselves play little part in his account of how man acquires understanding, for the processes of accul-turation and categorisation are assumed as part of the historical 'given' to which the young child must be assimilated. 'What can *men* learn from *trees*?' he had asked.

What Erasmus repudiated, Vives spells out in terms which enforce an awareness of the world of nature, the phenomenal world, as playing a de-fined part in the process of upbringing. Gifted with a mind, and born to live in society, man has developed various 'arts' which help to bring him to wisdom and piety. But the process by which those 'arts' have been discovered is the subject of a lengthy disquisition at the beginning of *De Tradendis Disciplinis*, book V. While Vives begins with the orthodox humanist view that learning peculiarly distinguishes the human:

> there is nothing in life more beautiful or more excellent than the culti-vation of mind through what we call the branches of learning (*disciplinae*), by means of which we separate ourselves from the way of life and customs of animals and are restored to humanity, and raised towards God Himself . . .[1]

he raises doubts about the authority of the ancients where certain branches
of learning are concerned. This is a matter of fundamental importance: no
longer are we told, as by Erasmus, that all that matters stems from the
ancient world: instead 'it is far more profitable to learning to form a critical
judgement on the writings of the great authors, than to merely acquiesce in
their authority, and to receive everything on trust from others . . .'[2] This
strikes a blow for autonomy in judgement which Montaigne was later to
endorse. Furthermore we are to acquire learning by direct confrontation
with nature herself: 'Nature is not yet so effete and exhausted as to be
unable to bring forth, in our times, results comparable with those of earlier
ages. She always remains equal to herself, and not rarely she comes forward
more strongly and powerful than in the past . . .'[3] The past certainly has
opened up opportunities through the 'comprehension of the different branches
of knowledge'. Furthermore the ancients do set a precedent for development
in that they too departed from the practices of their forebears: nevertheless

> It is . . . clear that, if we only apply our minds sufficiently, we can judge
> better over the whole round of life and nature than could Aristotle,
> Plato, or any of the ancients . . . Is it, then, to be forbidden to us to at
> least investigate, and to form our own opinions? . . . Truth stands open
> to all. It is not as yet taken possession of. Much of truth has been left
> for future generations to discover.[4]

The major manifestation of this openness lies in the process or method by
which truth is discovered through the development of the various 'arts'.
These are no longer made up of the revealed truths of Christian belief, nor
the admitted truths of classical authority in the manner appropriate to the
training of *doctus orator*; they arise out of the direct interaction of mind and
nature. And Vives traces, in evolutionary fashion, man's development
through necessities (food, shelter, laws) to conveniences, the contemplation,
at leisure, of 'this theatre in which man was placed by God'.[5] (As already
indicated, the goal was 'the desire to know God more truly – piety is of all
things the more necessary'.)[6] The development of these various arts was
furthered by a process of induction, the collection of 'general aspects of norms
to a definite end':

> In the beginning just one, then another experience, through wonder at
> its novelty, was noted down for use in life; from a number of separate
> experiments the mind fathered a universal law, which after it was
> further supported and confirmed by many experiments, was considered
> certain, and established. Then it was handed down to posterity.[7]

The point is that 'whatever is in the arts was in nature first, just as pearls are
in shells, or gems in the sand'.[8] Thus culture has evolved as a result of direct
contact between mind and nature, not as a result of a verbal assimilation
derived from a past civilisation. Vives quotes with approval Manilius' dictum
that 'Experience through various applications has made art' and adds that

'experiences are casual and uncertain unless they are ruled by reason', with an approving glance at Plato's dictum in the *Gorgias*: 'let experience bring forth the art, and let art rule experience'.[9] 'Art', in fact, is now the name given to those means of attaining 'a sure and predetermined end in which mind and experience play an integral and interactive part', and can be defined as 'a collection of universal rules brought together for the purpose of knowing, doing or producing something'.[10] The stress is no longer on imitation but on the direct confrontation of experience.

Once evolved out of experience it then becomes the function of the 'art' to teach so that its precepts may be applied to individual cases; for instance, medicine considers health in general and not that of a particular person; this latter must be the concern of the artificer, the one who is skilled in the art. Arts, thus, are for use, not studied for their own sakes: 'we do not learn arts and sciences for their own sakes, but for our good'.[11] Individual aptitudes ('a distinct type of natural mental ability') are fitted for the pursuit of different arts.

So mind has two functions – that of observing and that of applying the outcome of observation in judgement. It is socially oriented: 'We men are born for society, and cannot live thoroughly without it.'[12] As social beings, men's 'experience', on which mind works, can result from individual discovery, or spring from 'that obtained by others' throughout history. The arts which are the subject of education are manifestations of the cultivation of mind by these means; but whether the means arise out of direct contact or through the assimilation of the observations of others, the prior importance of experience is clearly assumed.

With a mind developed in these ways it is possible to proceed 'to those studies which escape every observation of the senses',[13] the spiritual questions. So knowledge is divided into that which derives from the senses (dietetics, medicine, etc.) and that which results from reflection (ethics, economics, politics, grammar, rhetoric, etc.) leading to practical wisdom, and to further speculation on sciences (geometry, arithmetic, etc.) which are useful to other branches of knowledge.

Now, of course, 'In furthering these studies Vives is clear about the value of books and culture: To books we must refer for knowledge in every subject.'[14] But even when he has protested that books and the experience of others play an essential part in that foreshortening of human experience which is essential in the current state of civilisation – for of course Vives sees that the young cannot recreate the process of acculturation which has already proceeded so far – and given directions by which the best books may be chosen as guides in the various fields of study, it is clear that his humanistic interests imply a radical change from those humanists who see in literary taste or rhetoric the keystones to the educational process. His bookishness is ultimately subordinate to experience: 'No other man of his generation had such a vivid conception of the pragmatic character of knowledge and of the importance of immediate sense perception as the source of every human experience.'[15]

So his basis was in nature rather than in culture – and this had implications for his curriculum. Though he realised that 'man is *taught* nothing by nature, but everything is evolved by instruction, by hard work, habit and diligence' (my italics),[16] nature, not culture, constituted the *ultimate* court of appeal; for 'There is no human mind, however silly and far removed from human instruction, which has not received from nature certain germs of all arts.'[17]

It is true that in Vives' scheme the study of languages precedes that of nature; but the reason for this priority is symptomatic: 'The boy should give his attention to learning Latin whilst as yet unfitted by the feebleness of his wits to the understanding of other branches of scientific knowledge, i.e. roughly from the seventh to the fifteenth year.'[18] Furthermore

> The educative value of a language is in proportion to its apt suitability for supplying names to things. Its eloquence consists in its variety and abundance of words and formulae; all of which should make it a pleasure to man to use. It should have the capacity to explain most aptly what they think. By its means much power of judgement should be developed.[19]

Hence the use of Latin: 'For that language, whose words should make clear the natures of things, would be the most perfect of all; such as it is probable was that original language in which Adam attached the name to things.'[20] The implication is that *verba* are subordinate to *res*: no longer is it eloquence and style which are *primarily* or even equally valued – it is the denotative use of language which motivates the priority assigned to linguistic studies. This is not to deny a value to copiousness, to mellifluousness, to all the qualities attached traditionally to oratory: but it is to shift the balance of the relationship between *verba* and *res* and to pre-empt the priority for *res*. The world, not language, is the source of experience.[21]

Languages, too, should include the vernacular – for which the traditional humanist (such as Erasmus) often had little time. Greek could be added. Significantly the teaching of poetry, while permitted, is in some degree devalued. It is 'not real life but a kind of painting'[22] (this is very reminiscent of Bacon); it is 'to be relegated "to the leisure hours of life". It is not to be consumed as if it were nourishment, but is to be treated as a spice.'[23] Homer is praised, however, for his depiction of the 'actuality of life'.[24] The elucidation of the phenomenal world is beginning to take priority over 'style' – this warm praise of 'actuality' constitutes a significant step away from the 'ornamentation' of the rhetorical tradition – and introduces alternative criteria for literary judgement. Furthermore the depreciation of poets (who 'add very little to knowledge of the arts, or to life, or indeed to language itself')[25] sounds a note to become increasingly familiar in the post-humanist period.

After the fifteenth year, when the study of languages is completed, we move to the 'higher studies'; and the purpose of the language studies is made abundantly clear: they are 'the gates of all sciences and arts':

> let those who study remember, that if nothing is added to their know-
> ledge by the study of the languages they have only arrived at the gates

of knowledge . . . no language is in itself worth the trouble of learning, if nothing is sought beyond the linguistic aspect. Rather let students gain as much of the language as will enable them to penetrate to those facts and ideas, which are contained in these languages, like beautiful and valuable things are locked up in treasuries.[26]

As further preparation, the study of logic as a means of testing the true and the false should be undertaken.

Now should follow 'a knowledge of nature'; and this must be confined to what will be useful: 'the contemplation of nature is unnecessary and even harmful unless it serves the useful arts of life, or raises us from a knowledge of His works to a knowledge, admiration and love of the Author of these works'.[27] These useful matters involve the 'origin and nature of plants and animals, and the reasons why, as well as the way in which, natural events happen'.[28] Easiest things first –

viz.; those things that are evident to the senses. There should be, in the first place, a general explanation, an exposition or, as it were, a picture of the whole of nature, of the heavens, the elements, and those things that are in the heavens, and in the elements, in fire, air, water and earth; so that a full representation and description of the whole earth is included in the picture.[29]

Here an initial expository text is useful, leading not to disputation after the manner of the scholastics but to 'the silent contemplation of Nature'. Then, for those who wish to know more, recourse must be had to the study of outward nature by close observation':

So will he observe the nature of things in the heavens, in cloudy and in clear weather, in the plains, on the mountains, in the woods. Hence he will . . . get to know many things from those who inhabit those spots. Let him have recourse, for instance, to gardeners, husbandmen, shepherds and hunters.[30]

From these sources arises the 'first philosophy', an examination of the connections of things, their causes, etc., seeking out generalisations and universals, but always working to simplify: 'Therefore we must always work to simplify matters to their utmost, so that they may be perceived and known by the senses.'[31] The aim is truth, not altercation and the victory of disputation. Thus metaphysical speculation about Nature was deprecated; nature was for use rather than to encourage vain conceptual schemes. This had been the fault of the ancients – they 'introduced into the knowledge of nature opinions and doctrines which even old matrons or little children turn into ridicule'.[32] Vives, indeed, admired the Romans rather than the Greeks – they were more practical. Classical literature was basically considered a source of moral power, not of speculation or style. Again, when rhetoric becomes an essential object of study, it too should be considered not an end in itself but a 'part of practical wisdom'. 'Grace of style is not required predominantly for adornment and the achievement of elaborate composition, but that the art should aptly serve for practical use in life.'[33] Thus the criteria of studies remain truth and practical utility: 'Scholars must make it a practice never to speak against the truth . . . We deride and scorn what is unfelt and unfitted for the practice of life.'[34] And again: 'Let young men declaim, before their teachers, on those matters which may afterwards be useful in life: and not as was the habit of the ancients in the philosophical schools, on matters which never occurred in real life.'[35] It is true that, in characteristic style, Vives still sees that men must be 'formed' and 'imitation' therefore still has a limited place; but even more than Erasmus he stresses that such imitation must be subordinated to the individual natures of the pupils so that 'each may apply himself to that to which he is inclined by his natural impulse'. Differences must be carefully observed and allowed for; some may not be apt to letters at all, but find their fulfilment in the mechanical arts.[36] Nothing should be done 'invita Minerva'.

Even the speculative, superior arts are for use: mathematical studies, for instance, 'should not draw a man to vain and profitless speculation'.[37] The whole orientation of his thought can be summed up in his relative dismissal of the opinions of the ancients concerning nature when he appeals to an 'authority' other than that of historical precedent: 'So the studious will become accustomed to give their assent to reason, rather than to human authority.'[38] This sounds a note which is to become increasingly familiar during the next century.

In general, Vives' view of human nature is optimistic, analogous to Erasmus'. But he appreciates that man is a battleground of better and worse impulses,[39] and asserts the need for the supremacy of reason over the passions, which are the instruments of sin; reason discovers what true justice is and thus aids the political exercise of affairs of state. And so, apart from an appendix which summarises much of what has gone before, Vives concludes his De Tradendis with a consideration of those aspects of practical wisdom – moral philosophy, ethics, economics, politics, the law – which assist judgement and the right ordering of the soul through the predominance of reason over the passions. The whole is sustained by two precepts mentioned in the appendix and summarising usefully the whole direction of his thought: 'This then is the fruit of all studies; this is the goal. Having acquired our knowledge, we must turn it to usefulness, and employ it for the common good.'[40] The second asserts the importance of 'truth' over the products of the orator or poet in these terms:

For the orator . . . gives birth to his speech, the poet to his song; whereas it is not the philosopher or theologian but Nature which gives birth to truth. So the true philosopher interprets a contrary opinion to his own, as an injury to Nature, rather than to himself . . . he who affirms what is true, commits his cause to Nature, Time, God. He who asserts what is false, takes upon himself the defence of himself.[41]

The crux of the matter lies in the next sentence: 'Add to this, words, like the face and bodily form, are external, whilst thought, like health and under-standing, is concerned with the internal.'[42] By 'thought', of course, Vives intends 'thought of things'.

So Vives' general principles of education were partly derived from the humanist tradition and were partly in line with a developing empiricism. The moralistic tendency, a still persisting respect for classical literature, and the basically secular character of education Vives had in common with Agricola and Erasmus, Thomas More and Lily. But more personal to him were the moderation of the Quintilian ideal of eloquent diction, and above all, his insistence on a direct confrontation of mind and nature implying a new standard of 'truth' emerging in new applied sciences and technology serving utilitarian ends.[43] He is thus a precursor of a fundamental shift in educational attention to a more dramatic extent than even Montaigne was to prove; for despite Montaigne's gestures in the direction of an increased autonomous judgement in his appreciation of the importance of 'experience' rather than of books, Montaigne's persuasive practice, as we shall see, indicates the extent to which he is still too enmeshed in the older culture unequivocally to herald the new empiricism. What is ambiguous in Mon-taigne is explicit in the earlier theorist; the utilitarian, experimental tasks of Vives' prescriptions are unmistakable and unambiguous. The emphasis is now explicitly on the authority of reason as formed by contact with nature, not on the verbal authority of the ancients; words are now to be considered subordinate to the 'things' of experience. Vives heralds a whole revolution in educational thinking, where reason, working on the stuff of experience, becomes the court of ultimate appeal rather than a reason ('judgement') which is confined to the assimilation, harmonisation and deployment of past authorities. This is the first unmistakable shift of educational attention which is to culminate in Rousseau's astonishing fable of the pre-adolescent Emile, from whose educational environment all cultural (historical) phenomena are to be banished and the child is to be left in direct confrontation with the 'things' of nature and the consequent exclusive discipline of necessity.

This shift of attention has its implications for the concept of an 'art'. This is no longer to be related to principles and theories derived from, or at least affected by, purely intellectual or even metaphysical speculations – as, for instance, occurred, in the later renaissance conceptions of painting and architecture – but as a result of this direct contact with the 'things' of nature. In this process of evolution there is an acceptance of the validity of the experience of other classes of the community than that of the intellectual elite – 'gardeners, husbandmen, shepherds and hunters' – a group who, together with their social and more technically minded coevals, are increasing-ly to be appealed to as sources of knowledge because of their direct contact with the facts of nature (*natura naturata*). Erasmus had asked what men could learn from trees; Vives points to the experience of gardeners with immediate knowledge of such objects as having a significance beyond ancient classifications. Even poetry is deprecated except in so far as it depicts the actualities of life; one is irresistibly reminded of John Dewey finding in the

Penelope of the *Odyssey* 'a classic in literature because the character is an adequate embodiment of a certain industrial phase of social life',[44] though that is not to suggest that the dissimilarities between the renaissance humanist and the twentieth-century pragmatist are not much more startlingly obvious. Nevertheless, Vives' view of poetry belongs recognisably to the first stages of a tradition which will be noted as this volume proceeds.

NOTES

1 Foster Watson, *Vives: On Education* (Cambridge, Cambridge University Press, 1913), p. 6.
2 ibid., p. 8.
3 ibid., p. 8.
4 ibid., pp. 8–9.
5 ibid., p. 16.
6 ibid., p. 18.
7 ibid., p. 20.
8 ibid., p. 20.
9 ibid., p. 21.
10 ibid., p. 24.
11 ibid., p. 33.
12 ibid., p. 38.
13 ibid., p. 41.
14 ibid., p. 44. cf. also p. 49: 'Unlearned men, however intellectual they may be by nature, cannot be pervaded by so great a vigour of mind as those who are of average intellectual power, when furnished with learning, for they have many others to help them . . .'
15 C. G. Noreña, *Juan Luis Vives* (The Hague, Nijhoff, 1970), p. 183.
16 Watson, op. cit., p. 117.
17 ibid., p. 129.
18 ibid., p. 93.
19 ibid., p. 92.
20 ibid., p. 92.
21 'Copious expression is more useful to the more advanced, that they should be accustomed to express clearly the more abstruse thoughts of their minds' (ibid., p. 104).
22 ibid., p. 127.
23 ibid., p. 138.
24 ibid., p. 145.
25 Quoted T. W. Baldwin, *William Shakspere's 'Small Latine and Lesse Greeke'* (Urbana, University of Illinois Press, 1944), Vol. II, p. 193. Vives admits the power of poetry but fears its moral corruption. At best it supplies ornament rather than substance. This view gradually affected later humanist theorists like Brinsley and Hoole, for whom the literary spirit of Erasmus had little meaning and who returned to the medieval formalism of grammatical study.
26 Watson, op. cit., p. 163.
27 ibid., p. 167.
28 ibid., p. 167.
29 ibid., p. 168.
30 ibid., p. 169.
31 ibid., pp. 174–5.
32 ibid., p. 175.
33 ibid., p. 184.
34 ibid., p. 185.

35 ibid., p. 186.
36 ibid., p. 85.
37 ibid., p. 202.
38 ibid., p. 213.
39 ibid., p. 228. cf. also Vives' assertion that 'The powers of human nature never produce something perfect and complete; there is always something missing to the peak of possible perfection' – so man is basically good but finite – there is always something more to be achieved. Yet history constituted, overall, a progressive movement. Man accumulates knowledge over the ages, but understanding can always be improved.
40 Watson, op. cit., p. 283.
41 ibid., p. 304.
42 ibid., p. 304.
43 cf. Noreña, op. cit., p. 185.
44 cf. J. Dewey, *The School and Society* (Chicago, Phoenix Books, University of Chicago Press, n.d.), p. 90.

CHAPTER 6

'Que Sçais-je?': Montaigne

I

One of the indirect contributions of Michel de Montaigne (1533–92) is to reveal, paradoxically, the convolutions of 'sincerity' and 'naturalness' in the creation of a human being (himself) with obvious implications for his educational theorising. The man who chose to withdraw from public life so as to avoid the lies and untruths he deemed inescapable aspects of the courtier's life found himself adopting the very persuasive devices he affected to despise. His work, considered from one point of view, constitutes an extended exercise in what I have termed artificial natural naturalness – an artifice which attempts to be as little conscious of itself as possible and yet cannot escape the logic of man's need to make.

In any consideration of a developing sense of individuality Montaigne, too, must have a pre-eminent place. His concern is, to a considerable and quite conscious degree, with himself and the relationship of his constantly shifting internal life with the external social and physical world. It is this self-exposure with its claim to honesty which drew a sardonic comment from that other great presenter of self, J. J. Rousseau: 'I have always been amused at Montaigne's false ingenuousness and at his pretence of confessing his faults while taking good care to admit only likeable ones' – and in an introduction to the 1764 manuscript of *The Confessions* Rousseau asserts that 'Je mets Montaigne à la tête de ces faux sincères qui veulent tromper en disant vrai.' This is the pot calling the kettle black with a vengeance.

But of the two Montaigne is subtler and the more ingratiating. Rousseau is simple minded enough to arouse suspicions with the very first sentence of the *Confessions*: 'I am commencing an undertaking hitherto without precedent, and which will never find an imitator' – only a common huckster could be so naïve. But the Frenchman is better bred – though his dedication to the Reader of the *Essays* raises pertinent queries:

This, Reader, is an honest book. It warns you at the outset that my sole purpose in writing it has been a private and domestic one. I have had no thought of serving you or of my own fame; such a plan would be beyond my powers . . .

Had it been my purpose to seek the world's favour, I should have put on finer clothes, and have presented myself in a studied attitude. But I want to appear in my simple, natural, and everyday dress, without strain or artifice; for it is myself that I portray.

The reader of Castiglione will pause at that 'without artifice': is it the artifice that hides artifice, a manifestation of *sprezzatura*, unacknowledged? For after all, this was the man who was capable of writing 'When I play with my cat, who knows whether she is amusing herself with me, or I with her.' Such a capacity for relative, multiple perspective (the influence of the painter as it evolves to encompass, say, Velasquez' *Las Meninas* in the next century, is apparent) implies a high degree of self-consciousness and of one's relationships to others: it is not the remark of a 'simple' man, though it was in line with the sophistication of the age.

And indeed Montaigne's whole position – of which this remark together with the device he had inscribed on his medal: 'Que sçais-je?' – what do I know – may be said to be interestingly symbolic – constitutes a significant retreat from the early renaissance emphasis on pride, *virtu* and self-assertion, its stress on individuality in the post-medieval sense of the word. (I use 'individuality' here to imply self-projection. In the sense of 'interest in self' Montaigne, as I have implied, is without parallel in his own times. Rightly does Ernst Cassirer say that 'Montaigne's *Essais* created a new philosophy of the individual. That the portrayal of a particular man *as* a particular man – with all his peculiarities, accidents and idiosyncrasies – could have a theoretical interest was recognised by no philosophy before the Renaissance.'[1] Before, people had appeared as 'types'. Even the self-assertive individual of the earlier period was, to some extent, a type, for, as I have made clear above, his personality was oriented to a social end – he lacked the inward quality of later romantic individualism.)

Now it is arguable that Montaigne's disclaimer in his Dedication is nothing other than a rhetorical device to attract sympathy. Such 'modesty' was part of the rhetoricians' armoury. But in Montaigne's case I think it goes a little beyond this, for he had early expressed a generalised distaste for mankind's presumption. His father had requested him to translate the *Natural Theology* of Sebond, a work which represented the earlier optimism of the Renaissance concerning man's pre-eminence and the power of his reason. Perhaps bored by his task the son proceeds to launch an elaborate attack on man's vanity and arrogance: he writes an *essai* to make people aware 'of the inanity, the vanity and insignificance of man' – whom he terms 'the frailest and most vulnerable of all creatures'. He denies his superiority to the animals and hence his position in the Chain of Being. He denies, too, any concept of a natural law, for nothing is universally agreed upon: 'Those people amuse me who, to give some certainty to laws, say that there are some that are fixed, perpetual and immutable which they call laws of Nature'; for all such laws are in one place or another 'rejected and disowned, not by one nation, but by many' – destroyed by 'this fine human reason of ours thrusting itself into everything, commanding and domineering, confusing and distorting the face of things, in its vanity and inconsistency'.[2] Similarly our senses are equally subject to deception. Only Revelation can save us. The device 'Que sçais-je?', then, adequately represents a developing scepticism. Yet in his *Essays* he appeals to reason constantly as the truest guide to our affairs. At the same time 'his conception that man is a fluctuating creature subject to the changes which take place in his surroundings, his destiny and his inner impulses'[3] throws doubt on the possibility that the fixed categories implied in a reasoning process can in any profound sense capture the 'reality' of human life. But he is, of course, caught in the quandary on the one hand of the need to act on 'reasonable' grounds – even if only in his writings – and on the other of the appreciation that such action must always falsify the complexity of the life or lives it affects.

To some extent his dilemma reflected one which exercised the more sensitive minds of the age. The earlier humanistic certainties were beginning to come under attack; the new empiricism, applied to human behaviour, challenged the validity in many of its phases of the classical experience – and the classical eloquence – as the ultimate court of appeal in human affairs. The voyages of discovery had revealed different manners and different ethical systems at work in various parts of the extended known world: the Reformation and the wars of religion had finally undermined the medieval ecclesiastical certainties, and in secular matters the discrepancies, in Machiavelli's words, between what was done and what ought to be done had induced a scepticism about man's pretensions which are reflected, for instance, in *Hamlet*. Shakespeare, indeed, is a portent of the profound tensions characterising the later sixteenth- and earlier seventeenth-century consciousness, when change and dissolution were as clearly manifest as stability and construction. Little wonder, then, that there was a feeling discernible that man is not the same person from moment to moment. As Montaigne says: 'Myself now, and my own self, are indeed two.' This is one reason why Proteus and Mercury are such popular mythological figures, why the theme of transformation is so frequently encountered in the literature of the age; man finds himself confronted by the problem of identity just because his personality is no longer stable – but rather needs to be continuously redefined.[4] Thus Montaigne's assumption of modesty is not totally deceptive – the role of simpleton was a mask to hide a greater sophistication than it admitted to, but it was also an escape from forms of assertion which were beginning to be belied by a more complex awareness of the ambiguities of the human situation. A tension had arisen between the old classical personality structure adopted by the earlier humanists and the new awareness of self which revealed an unwonted degree of psychological mobility.

II

This characterisation of Montaigne and his times is highly relevant to his views on the upbringing of children. It explains in part the undogmatic dogmatism of his injunctions; his scepticism is balanced by his confidence. (If he is really as idle and foolish as he says he is, how does he dare to tell us how to bring up children, 'the most difficult and important problem confronting human knowledge'?)[5] But, more crucial, his attitudes to nature and culture become more equivocal than those of his predecessors; he implies less overt admiration for human artefacts, more attention to 'nature' as, in its more primitive sense, a dominant factor in human affairs. He betokens, in fact, a certain disenchantment with the traditional humanistic training in eloquence and style, and recommends a more 'natural and simple' ('naïf') form of communication. It is, however, important to examine this in more detail – for, in fact, the naïvety is itself inescapably a form of artifice.

It is perhaps not altogether to be expected that he should always speak with the same voice; the *Essais* were written over a number of years. And, at first sight, equivocation can to some extent be excused in terms of the nature of his undertaking, which is to reveal the complexities, ambiguities, contradictions of a single human being, himself:

> Now the lines of my portrait are never at fault, although they change and vary. The world is but a perpetual see-saw . . . Constancy itself is nothing but a more sluggish movement. I cannot fix my subject. He is always restless, and reels with a natural intoxication. I catch him here, as he is at the moment when I turn my attention to him. I do not portray his being; I portray his passage; not a passage from one age to another . . . but from day to day, from minute to minute. I must suit my story to the hour, for soon I may change, not only by chance but also by intention. It is . . . an account of thoughts that are unsettled and, as chance will have it, at times contradictory, either because I am then another self, or because I approach my subject under different circumstances and with other considerations. Hence it is that I may well contradict myself but the truth . . . I do not contradict. Could my mind find a firm footing, I should not be making essays [*essais* = attempts].[6]

He indicates that he is attempting to 'present to the world . . . the crude and simple products of nature, and of a weakish nature at that' – and this 'to the world, in which style and artifice receive so much credit and authority'. He wishes to convey his whole being – on which 'he is the most learned man alive'.[7]

So it would seem that the earlier humanistic impulse is wearing itself out through its own 'artificialities' – and there is a desire to get nearer to *nature*, interpreted as simplicity, the more primitive, less humanly formed as an escape from these instabilities – what lies behind the cultural 'artefact'. The 'weakish nature' to which Montaigne admits (or of which he boasts?) provides the necessary excuse for two interesting features of his work, his self-depreciation and his reaction against the sophisticated, the 'artificial', 'art' itself indeed. But then, as hinted, he has his own alternative artifices which imply a refined modification of humanist techniques of persuasion, not the rejection it proclaims itself to be.

Perhaps, however, his concern for ease, his dislike of professionalism, his rejection of artifice is to be taken as an example of *sprezzatura*, of the artifice that hides artifice? – to return to an earlier unanswered question. I think not. As Castiglione uses the term, 'sprezzatura' involved mastery, transcendence, the ease that comes from a perfected artifice; it is not pretended that there is no artifice, just that it is disguised by a superior artfulness.

Montaigne, on the other hand, would like to make it seem that he has no artifice. Castiglione reveals the mechanism of an art that hides art; Montaigne speaks too often against 'art' in its various manifestations to make of his 'natural' the quintessence of artifice. This implies an important change in direction in one who must still rank as a humanist; and I will illustrate it in several fields.

To begin with, he likes simple men – not the simplicity which arises out of mastery but the simplicity of unsophistication – the peasant; and this statement of preference is too pervasive in his work for it to be dismissed simply as a playful manifestation of pastoral:

> The least contemptible sort of man seems to me to be one who, because of his simplicity, stands on the lowest rung; with him, I think, equable relations are most possible. I generally find the behaviour and conversations of peasants more accordant with the rules of true philosophy than those of philosophers.[8]

Elsewhere he admits to being 'drawn towards humble men'.[9] This is accompanied by other criticisms of the 'philosophers' – whose understanding is inferior to that of a 'nature' which they misrepresent.

> As nature has provided us with feet for walking, so she has given us wisdom to guide us through life; a wisdom less subtle, robust, and spectacular than that of the philosopher's invention, but correspondingly easy and salutary, which actually performs very well what the other only promises, for anyone lucky enough to know how to use it plainly and properly, that is to say naturally. The more simply one entrusts oneself to nature, the more wisely one does so.

The next sentence makes the stance quite clear: 'Oh, how soft and pleasant and healthful a pillow, whereon to rest a prudent head, is ignorance and lack of curiosity.'[10]

So the 'nature' that is to be our guide ('whatever accords with it should always be pleasing')[11] is near to the nature of primitive ('uncultured') life. It is true that these injunctions are supported by appeal to the 'Academics and Peripatetics', and the Stoics.[12] But the general position that Montaigne takes up is not in accord with those other lessons of achievement and heroism, of *virtu* and assertion that many of the earlier humanists had derived from the ancients. A middling, unheroic, moderate way is what he advocates:

> It is easier to follow art than nature, but it is also much less noble and commendable. The soul's greatness consists not so much in climbing high and pressing forward as in knowing how to adapt and limit itself. It takes all that is merely sufficient as great, and shows its distinction by preferring what is moderate to what is outstanding.[13]

For nature is good: 'Being herself all good, she has made all things good.'[14] 'Nature', then, still has normative implications – but in the direction of the unsophisticated, the simple and the primitive. Art is no longer the culmination of nature, its highest expression, but is now *contrasted* with the natural: the concept of the 'artificial' is preparing to take on pejorative implications.

For 'art', as will be seen from the penultimate quotation, is suspect. There is especially the 'art' of social life to be examined and rejected: 'The finest lives are . . . those which conform to the common and human model . . . with no marvels and no extravagances.'[15]

There is none of that concern to keep up social appearances we have noted in Elyot and Castiglione. (But then, of course, Montaigne's aim is not political action or rule.) 'I envy those who know how to be familiar with the meanest of their retinue, and to start a conversation among their own domestics.'[16] And again, 'Ease of manner and the ability to unbend are most honourable and fitting qualities in a strong and generous soul.'[17] Plato is rebuked for suggesting that one should use the language of a master to his servants, 'without jests or familiarity', Epaminandas praised for joining the lads of his city in a dance. (Even so, Montaigne finds that he himself seeks intimacy only with 'well-bred and talented men'[18] – there were limits to his desire for intimacy with the commonalty!) It all ties in with his cult of 'sincerity', with appearing to be what one 'really' is. He hates pretence and dissimulation: 'It is a cowardly and servile characteristic, to go about in disguise, concealed behind a mask, without the courage to show oneself as one is.'[19] A generous heart, he comments, 'should never disguise its thoughts, but reveal its inmost depths'.[20] And so he hates 'flatterers and dissemblers'. He speaks of his own outspokenness – to an extent, indeed, that he may be thought tactless and impolite. In a significant piece of self-diagnosis he brings together the two concepts whose relationship and opposition form the main theme of this book: 'It may be that through lack of art, I let my nature have its way.' This alone would be sufficient to point the difference between Montaigne's stated ideal and Castiglione's – for Castiglione assumes that 'art' is an essential defining characteristic of human nature.

So artlessness is praised in various guises. It is 'plain simple fellows' who give 'true testimony' – men of intelligence cannot tell a plain tale 'but twist and disguise them to conform to the point of view from which they have seen them'.[21] Primitive peoples are praised in terms which would seem to deny them consciousness at all, conceiving them to be analogous to the plants and animals: 'These people are wild in the same way as we say that fruits are wild, when nature has produced them by herself and in her ordinary way.'[22] And the remark stimulates further praise of the virtues of naturalness as *opposed* to artifice:

> It is not reasonable that art should win the honours from our great and mighty mother nature. We have so loaded the riches and beauty of her works with our inventions that we have altogether stifled her. Yet, wherever she shines forth in her purity, she makes our vain and trivial enterprises marvellously shameful.[23]

The cult of artlessness is reflected in his image of himself. His attempt (*essai*), he says, is 'simply a trial [*essai*] of my natural faculties, and not of my acquired ones'.[24] He lays no claim to knowledge, he says – 'for though I am a man of some reading, I am one who retains nothing'.[25] He has (pretends to?) a poor opinion of himself and only claims credit for at least knowing his own weaknesses – and so on. His strength lies in his adaptability: 'Not being able to control events, I control myself, and adapt myself to them if they do not adapt themselves to me.'[26] If his whole concern is with himself: 'I have no business but with myself, I unceasingly consider, examine, and analyse myself',[27] he lays claim to a certain objectivity regarding himself: 'I am not so immoderately in love with myself, not so attached to and bound up with myself as to be unable to distinguish and consider myself objectively as I do a neighbour or a tree.'[28] There exists, indeed, a curious tension between his artless attitude to the world and his own talents, and the concentrated effort he applies to his own self-examination. In speech and writing, he says, he cannot imitate. 'As in deeds, so in words, I simply follow my natural way; which is perhaps why I speak better than I write.'[29] Paradoxically, then, this apparently artless man, in effect, concentrates on the delineation of a sole work of art, himself. Things, words themselves, exist in so far as they minister to his own self-image. He represents, for his day and age, the extremes of European self-consciousness and self-awareness – the new awareness and objectivity of self as something independent of traditional models, the beginnings of a free-ranging intellect. Yet, paradoxically, it is clear he retains something of the flexibility of the courtier.

Yet what ultimately is he? Not, certainly, a stream of consciousness, a simple outpouring, though there are times when this is the image of himself he wishes to suggest. He is not as artless (of course) as he wishes to appear. For as we have noted, he sees himself as essentially a rational creature as well as a product of 'fancies', 'constantly' repudiating himself, feeling himself 'wavering and yielding through weakness'.[30] He makes the significant remark 'I have nothing of my own that satisfies my judgement'[31] – 'that satisfies my judgment' makes clear that this 'naturalness' of his is to include reason – and elsewhere he states that 'there is no desire more natural than the desire for knowledge', a well-attested humanist standpoint.

So in Montaigne there is an unresolved conflict between the mutabilities of opinion ('I may be different tomorrow if some new lesson changes me')[32] and the fixities and stabilities of rationality supported by learning:

> Since it has pleased God to endow us with some capacity for reason, so that we may not be, like the beasts, slavishly subject to the general laws, but may adapt ourselves to them by judgement and free-will, we ought indeed to yield a little to the simple authority of nature, but not to let ourselves be tyrannically carried away by her. Reason alone should guide us in our inclinations.
>
> I, for my part, have a strange disgust for those propensities which arise within us without the control and intervention of our judgement.[33]

And so – for instance – he indicates his distaste for newborn babies 'that have neither mental activities nor recognizable body shape by which to make themselves lovable'.[34] Too often are we moved by our children's frolickings and infantile nonsense rather than their mature acts – which is to love them 'as monkeys, not as human beings'. The man who presents himself as the prey to a childish indolence or whimsicality is also the man who repudiates the sentimentalities of childishness. At the core of Montaigne, then, lies a tension between the claims of nature (as artlessness) and culture (as 'rationally' based artifice). Reflection on his own experience convinces him at once of the need for reason and its inadequacy in the face of the ambiguities and complexities of experience (to which his reponse is in danger of appearing a mindless surrender). The very reason that he finds essential at one moment at another he speaks of as being a 'two-edged and dangerous sword'.[35] His difficulty is that 'Reason has so many shapes that we do not know which to take hold of; experience has no fewer.'[36]

And so he represents a retreat from the high consciousness of Castiglione: Castiglione's perfect courtier is consciously and unashamedly the creation of art; the source of Montaigne's self is equivocal. *He* is no longer controlled by culture as manifest in classical or Christian image – instead he is subject to the equivocations of his own psychological instability; by identifying such instability as an essential characteristic of human nature he opens the way to a regression to the more primitive, the less sophisticated. It is a position that so far has only been hinted at in Erasmus' rejection of ecclesiastical ceremonies, his advocacy, in a religious context, of *simplicitas*.

Yet, of course, art plays a major role in this self-presentation, as Dr Margaret McGowan has seen in her penetrating analysis of *Montaigne's Deceits*,[37] a book she symptomatically calls 'The *art* of persuasion in the *Essais*' (my italics). She shows how Montaigne's modesty belongs to a specific literary tradition (a comparison with Erasmus' *The Praise of Folly* is apt), how in fact he developed techniques of persuasion in his writing which copied the very devices of the courtier whose dissembling and flattery he affected to despise: 'On his own admission, he consciously adopted varied stylistic techniques to assault the reader, and to keep him ever on the watch. Modesty is only one type of dissimulation so employed. There are others.'[38] Dr McGowan's book provides the necessary evidence through detailed and meticulous analysis. As she points out, for instance, Montaigne made use of well-turned phrases, and proverbs in a way which aligned him with the practices of courtiers, diplomats and even schoolmen. He used his lawyer's training to assume different styles in order to produce a variety of persuasive effects and showed an intimate acquaintanceship with the 'craftie and secrete methodes' advocated by contemporary writers of books on rhetoric; his modes of argument reveal the habits of writing he derived from his training at school, the elaboration of set themes in the rhetorical tradition. As Dr McGowan concludes: 'The matter could be expressed in terms frequently used by earlier humanists. We have in the *Essais* . . . a blending of eloquence and philosophy . . . Their joining together had become a major subject of discussion for Renaissance writers.'[39]

III

Montaigne, then, made extensive use of 'deceits', a word employed by contemporary rhetoricians to describe oblique and indirect ways of presenting material intended to command a 'greater emotional response from the reader or listener than "natural" or direct ways of presenting ideas'. Yet in line with his self-presentation his educational advice goes entirely contrary to his own practice. He deprecates training in dialectical subtleties and praises those who 'know no rhetoric nor how, by way of preface, to capture the *benevolence of the candid reader'*; instead 'The speech that I love is a simple and natural speech, the same on paper as on a man's lips: a pithy, sinewy, short and concise speech, sharp and forcible . . . rather rough than tedious, void of all affectation, fine irregular and bold . . .'[40] The passage is taken from the essay 'On the Education of Children'. And explicit in that essay are important contrasts between this ideal of 'simple and natural' expression and the conventional scholastic or humanistic models Montaigne repudiates. Part explanation of Montaigne's dilemma lies in the fact that the basically public rhetorical language of the earlier humanists – its words, sentence structure and stylistic devices 'imitated' from the classics – no longer seems to be adequate to the psychological reality and subtlety of what he wants to say – and so in his concern for 'reality' he sketches in the outlines of a new image of the educated man.

Current education, indeed, is condemned by Montaigne for failing to match knowledge with understanding, words with their manifestation in experience, learning with daily existence:

> I readily relapse into my reflections on the uselessness of our education. Its aim has been to make us not good and wise, but learned; and in this it has succeeded. It has not taught us to follow and embrace virtue and wisdom, but has imprinted their derivations and etymologies on our minds. We are able to decline *virtue*, even if we are unable to love it; if we do not know what wisdom is in fact and by experience, we are familiar with it as jargon learned by heart . . . It has chosen for our instruction, not those books which contain the soundest and truest opinions, but those which speak the best Latin and Greek, and along with all its fine words has poured into our minds the idlest fancies of antiquity.[41]

In this famous essay which he wrote for the Comtesse de Gurson, Montaigne has indeed a great deal to say about the relationship between language and substance, words and things: 'A tutor must demand an account not just of the words of his lesson, but of their meaning and substance, and must judge of its benefit to his pupil by the evidence not of the lad's memory but of his life.'[42] Here lies the central core of Montaigne's educational advice and a direct reversal of Erasmus' emphasis on the priority of words over experience. The aim of education is more personal than socio-political; it is to form the private judgement rather than to create the public servant, that judgement which, paradoxically, at other times he repudiates.

Hence what the child learns he must make his own, though in a way which stresses his autonomy to a degree unthought of by Castiglione. Castiglione, too, desired internalisation, but as a matter of absorption through *imitation* of the best models; Montaigne sees it as a matter of autonomous judgement. The pupil must 'sift everything, and take nothing into his head on simple authority or trust'.[43] The words of others must be transformed by his inner consciousness 'to make of them something entirely his own',[44] that is to say, his own judgement, to form which is the aim of his education, his labour and his study. If the pupil is well supplied with *things* 'the *words* will follow only too freely'.[45] Hence 'Knowing by heart is no knowledge.' The study of history, too, will bring him into contact with some of the best minds of the ages; but 'Let him be taught not so much the facts of history as how to judge them.'[46] The focusing point of reality is beginning here to shift from words to their referents, things, from the absorption of others' views to one's own experience. In line with this orientation individuality is allowed to be more idiosyncratic, less 'public'. Education is to be judged by its internal effects, not its social performances; judgement, reason is becoming an internalised, semi-autonomous entity, the rational counterpart of that ability to see oneself in relation to the stream of events which constitutes Montaigne's contribution to the development of human consciousness:

'Que sçais-je?' 'What do I know?' This is the famous question that Montaigne asked in one of his essays. But if he meant, 'What among the many forms of revealed knowledge can best be taken as assured, as absolute and certain?' His answer was, in effect: 'None of them'. Only the knowledge that one gains through personal experience, through inquiring of one's self, through understanding of one's self, can be accounted reasonably certain. To place reliance upon external testimony, upon the bodies of knowledge that are proclaimed as certain throughout the world, is always treacherous for there one finds almost infinite disagreement.[47]

So the aim of this education is to learn how 'to live well and to die well', to know oneself and to learn to regulate morals and behaviour. The self is becoming increasingly isolated, self-dependent rather than the product of acculturation, semi-autonomous in a new, almost 'alienated' sense. The central core of a child's learning must be devoted to philosophy – by which Montaigne means moral philosophy; once his judgement has been formed he can quickly acquire the purpose of logic, physics, geometry and rhetoric.[48] For philosophy, as Montaigne conceives it, teaches us how to live; it makes no use of false subtleties and purposeless erudition: it is, indeed, all very simple.

Away with all these thorny subtleties of dialectics, by which our life cannot be improved; they are wasteful. Take the simple arguments of philosophy, learn how to pick them and make fit use of them; they are easier to understand than a tale by Boccaccio. A newly weaned child is more capable of doing this than of learning to read and write. Philosophy has teachings for man at his birth as well as in his decrepitude.[49]

IV

The regressive side of Montaigne's nature further appears in its recommendations of simplicity and relaxation. The child is not to work too hard, not 'apply himself immoderately to the study of his books . . . How many men have I seen in my time brutalised by this uncontrolled avidity for learning.'[50] One of its disadvantages is that it 'unfits boys for social intercourse'.[51]

Certainly there is a justified reaction against the excesses of humanist and scholastic education; 'our object is . . . not to make a grammarian, or a logician, but a gentleman'.[52] Instead what happens to our 'college Latinists':

> They keep us four or five years learning words and stringing them together in clauses; as many more building up into a long speech, duly divided into four or five parts; and another five, at least, learning to mingle them succinctly and weave them together in some subtle fashion.[53]

In all this there is some truth – any educational ideal in practice tends to ossification, and humanism was no exception. But the reversal of the normal humanist relationship between word and referent becomes too simplistic. He considers that incoherence is the result of imperfect conception, not linguistic deprivation:

> I personally believe – and with Socrates it is axiomatic – that anyone who has a clear idea in his mind will express it, either in rough language, or by gestures if he is dumb . . . He knows no ablative, subjunctive, substantive, or grammar; nor does his servant, or a fishwife on the Petit Pont. Yet they will give you your fill of talk if you will listen, and will very likely make no more mistakes in the linguistic rules than the best Master of Arts in France. He knows no rhetoric, nor how, by way of preface, to *capture the benevolence of the candid reader*; nor has he any wish to do so. In fact, all such fine tricks are easily eclipsed by the light of a simple, artless truth.[54]

There is a deal more to the same effect. The 'sophistical subtlety of some syllogism'[55] is condemned, as are the dialectical subtleties, absurd quibbles, etc., of those who talk for effect or are seduced by a clever phrase to distort their argument so as to bring it in. And so we arrive once more at his praise: 'The speech that I love is a simple and natural speech.' After all, 'Who has ever acquired understanding from logic?'[56]

What exactly did Montaigne mean by such a 'speech'. It is an important question in the history of European culture, in its progress from the elaboration of traditional humanistic rhetoric to the search for 'sincerity' and authenticity of utterance, when the very nature of 'rhetoric' comes under a cloud. Once more its social reference makes it clear that, whatever it is, it is remote from Castiglione's artful artlessness:

> I have been in the habit of copying the careless manner of dress adopted by our young men; the cloak worn negligently with the hood over one shoulder, and the stockings ungartered; which shows a proud contempt for all foreign adornments and a careless neglect of artifice. But I find this carelessness still better applied to the method of speech. All affectation is unbecoming in the courtier, especially in France where we are so gay and so free; and in a monarchy every nobleman ought to model himself on the fashion of the Court. We do well, therefore, to incline a little towards the artless and negligent.[57]

This is sartorial slovenliness, not effortlessness (one recalls Hamlet, 'his stockings foul'd, ungarter'd and down gyved to his ankles'). Montaigne cunningly conflates the two traditions (the 'courtier' and the 'primitive') and veers in the direction of the latter:

> Just as in dress, any attempt to make oneself conspicuous by adopting some peculiar and unusual fashion is the sign of a small mind, so in language, the quest for new-fangled phrases and little-known words springs from a puerile and pedantic pretension. I wish I could limit myself to the language of the Paris markets.[58]

Even allowing for the fact that the passage is directed against false and affected eloquence, the suggestion that the remedy lies in the language of the Paris markets immediately introduces an element quite foreign to anything in the best courtly tradition. A superior art, not a regression to the language of market porters and stall-keepers, would have been the courtly humanist solution in its most sophisticated guise. And whereas one can allow that 'ordinary' people, because of their daily contact with the actualities of existence often preserve a common sense and a largely technical know-how lacking in those who peddle ideas, as a general principle this turning to the simple and the uneducated constitutes an early stage in the *trahison des clercs*. Life is just not simple in that way.

Furthermore, the expressed wish in itself contains elements of a rhetorical pretence. Dr McGowan's analysis has shown impeccably the artifice of Montaigne's own practice. In the world of human culture a wise simplicity emerges – when it does emerge – from a transcendence of effort, an assimilation and subsequent sifting of knowledge, not from a regression to the mentality of servants or fishwives or the denizens of the Paris markets when all too often what is achieved is the simplicity of ignorance in all but the immediate practicalities of life. Yet a whole movement of the European mind culminating in the romantics has tried to persuade itself of the superiority of the primitive. Montaigne moves a step or two in that direction, though he exhibits the scepticism of a refined mind rather than the enthusiasm of a true naïf.

So we have a paradox which repays further investigation, for it constitutes an early appearance of an educational theme which will persist. On the one hand there is the move in the direction of a more personalised judgement, a refusal to depend on the opinions of others and an injunction to test findings against individual experience: this points in the direction of an *extension* of consciousness. On the other hand there is a regressive tendency towards the less sophisticated, the primitive: this points to a *limitation* of consciousness. Does increasing autonomy, the development of an independent reasoning power detached from its traditional acceptances simultaneously foster a regressive element as an escape from the increasing burden of consciousness; or is the scepticism which is implicit in any rejection of traditional authority likely to remove unconsciously accepted supports amidst the infinite complexities of experience and lay the way open to simplistic 'solutions' which are the constant temptation of the unassisted reasoning powers? Above all Montaigne wants to impress us with his independence, his uniqueness. Does this mean that he is forced to identify as problematic what others were content to accept on traditional grounds, and hence to seek refuge in *ab*normal – because primitivistic – outcomes? Is there any necessary connection between his extreme sophistication on one level and his naïvety on another? These are questions worth asking, for Montaigne is not an isolated phenomenon: he provides an early example of a paradox which extends down to our own times – nowhere more forcibly, for instance, than in Tolstoy.

V

In other matters Montaigne is concerned to tempt 'the appetite and the interest of children'; otherwise, he thinks, 'we shall produce only book-laden asses'.[59] He recognised some degree of individual difference but, surprisingly in view of his concern for his own individuality, refused to make much of these differences for educational purposes – largely on the grounds of the problem of diagnosis. Also he remained sceptical of the ability of education to bring about any fundamental change in an individual: 'Natural inclinations are assisted and reinforced by education, but they are hardly ever altered or overcome.'[60] In any case the initial evidence of inclination is slight and obscure; while 'it is difficult to overcome the natural bent' it is also difficult to discover what this is; 'men, falling immediately under the sway of custom, opinion, and law easily change or assume disguises'.[61] So the best thing is to pay little heed to the slight clues afforded by childish behaviour and direct them to the learning of 'what is best and most profitable',[62] a paradoxical outcome for this most paradoxical of men.

Methodologically Montaigne looked to an almost unconscious assimilation as part of an environment rather than to formal training; he particularly recommended the methods his own father used to teach him Latin – by making all around him speak the tongue: 'Without system, without books, without grammar or rules, without whipping, and without tears, I learnt a Latin as pure as my master's own, for I had no way of adulterating or confusing it.'[63] (The reaction against anything redolent of order ('system', 'rules') is worth noting as implying an incipient revolt against classicism.) So was appetite whetted and interest aroused. Greek was taught as an amusement, a game. All should be as easy as possible; thus learning would come to be assimilated almost unconsciously and then made use of; it did not remain inert knowledge but 'indissolubly wedded to the mind'.[64] He hates those who 'appeal from their understanding to their memory'.[65] The classics still remain in some degree the great educators, though with the expected warning that 'I would rather understand myself by self-study than by reading Cicero.' However, once more paradoxically, he 'is not so foolish as to oppose the authority of so many famous minds of antiquity, which it regards as its teachers and masters . . .'[66] But in choice of books he chooses those which speak to him in easy companionship:

> When I meet with difficulties in my reading, I do not bite my nails over them; after making one or two attempts I give them up. If I were to sit down to them, I should be wasting myself and my time; my mind works at the first leap. What I do not see immediately, I see even less by persisting. Without lightness I achieve nothing; application and over-serious effort confuse, depress, and weary my brain . . . If one book bores me, I take up another; and I turn to reading only at such times as I begin to be tired of doing nothing.[67]

Here, quintessentially, is the attitude which informs his educational advice. Its virtue lies in its concern for personal assimilation rather than pedantry; its fault lies in its dilettantism – in the modern pejorative sense. Castiglione represents someone at ease but finely wrought; Montaigne too often de-lineates the ease of relaxation and regression. He finds himself torn between the traditional demands of his role and his preference for self-absorption within the ambiguities of his own nature. Little wonder that he recommends acting as suitable for children: 'Shall I add to the reckoning a certain faculty of my childhood: the power of commanding by expression, and suiting my voice and gestures to any part that I undertook? – Acting does not seem to me an unsuitable pastime for children of good family.'[68] There is no suggestion that such role assumption should serve a politically virtuous purpose.

Indeed, he did not stabilise his educational expectations, as did Castiglione and Elyot, in terms of a specific social role. He distrusted any form of spe-cialised activity, as likely to distort the whole man. (He had himself been a lawyer, soldier and politician; he was mayor of Bordeaux for several years but he never really gave himself to such activities; he remained at leisure not a professional.) Specialised concerns simplified and systematised so that reality in its totality was lost; it was the latter which was his real subject in himself, though hardly in social matters. And because he was always aware of himself in specific concrete situations, always tended to probe the reality of his reactions, he did manage to avoid in certain areas the curse of the disengaged, of those who have no profession with which to anchor themselves into life – abstraction. At the personal level Montaigne retained a constant awareness of the concrete, of the book he had read, the people he met, the customs he approved or disliked. As a man, he found himself in the things of his environment, displaying himself 'embedded in the random contingencies of his life . . . and the fluctuating movements of his consciousness'.[69] Yet it would also be possible to argue that fundamentally he lacked being and that his whimsicality, his contradictoriness, his awareness of change in himself, argues a dissolution of self into those contingencies of his existence. He is in danger of becoming the plaything of his circumstances, the cat's victim rather than its master. Perhaps this, too, is relevant to the paradox of his sophistication and coexisting naïvety.

VI

He wanted, then, in the humanist tradition, to create a gentleman – but not one who found his sole *raison d'être* as the servant of his king. So there was no specific position to keep up, only a generalised air of good breeding and some acquaintance with general culture.

> Even games and exercises will form a good part of his study: running, wrestling; music, dancing, hunting, the management of horses and of weapons . . . I would have the pupil's outward graces, his social behaviour, and his personal demeanour, formed at the same time as his mind. It is not a soul or a body that one is training, but a man; the two must not be separated.[70]

But this comparatively slight reference to these activities takes on an even greater air of casualness in the light of the preceding sentence: '. . . our lessons, occurring as it were accidentally, without being bound to time or place, and mingling with all our other actions, will glide past unnoticed'.[71] Hence the force of '*Even* games and exercises . . .' This is an education for one who, in the end, seeks only to please himself: there is a suggestion here, too, of the *déraciné*, the alienated who, however, is still far too deeply embedded in the tradition of European culture to do more than hint at a sense of disenchantment:[72] 'Is it reasonable . . . that I should present to the world, in which style and artifice receive so much credit and authority, the crude and simple products of nature, and of a weakish nature at that? . . . Musical compositions are the product of skill, mine of chance.'[73] The question, itself, is a piece of artful pleading, of rhetoric. Montaigne cannot escape art, skill – no human can. But it is significant that he should *want* to appear artless – in a world in which, he himself admits, 'style and artifice receive so much credit and authority'.

Essentially he is a transitional figure. Many of his educational recommendations would not have been professed were it not for the humanists – even his interest in himself witnesses to the secularisation and concern for a degree of individuality they fostered. But looking to escape from the often stifling pedantry which, in practice, the ossification of the humanist tradition was beginning to provoke he seeks to check the authority of the eloquence they recommended against what he sees as the realities of individual experience. As he found his own being in the contingencies of his life rather than in the civil busyness of his precursors, so he sought to lighten the burden of his own self-consciousness by an appeal to 'simplicity' and 'naturalness'. He uses all the sophisticated rhetoric of the humanist 'deceit' to suggest that it has all been better said by the ignorant and lowly – though, like many of his trendy successors, he seems to prefer the actual company of his coevals.

Both Vives and Montaigne, then, urge a new, contemporary experiential awareness. They point to a withdrawal from the accumulations of the classical past; Vives looks to the physical environment as a source of enlightenment, Montaigne reveals his personal confusions as increased self-awareness calls into question the old classical personality structure with its commitment to human artifice based on the imitation of former models. Little wonder, then, that the later years of the sixteenth and the earlier ones of the seventeenth centuries found a time of doubts and fears – until men learnt to cope with the new subject–object relationship enforced by the dissolution of the former integration within a purposive universe where traditional culture and 'nature' had fulfilled a common destiny. Montaigne's question 'What do I know?' comes to dominate the new era.

NOTES

1 E. Cassirer, *The Individual and the Cosmos in Renaissance Philosophy*, trans. M. Domandi (New York, Harper Torchbooks, 1964).
2 cf. T. Spencer, *Shakespeare and the Nature of Man* (Cambridge, Cambridge University Press, 1943), pp. 32–40.
3 E. Auerbach, *Mimesis* (New York, Doubleday Anchor Books, 1953), p. 255. The whole chapter is of interest.
4 cf. J. Webber, *The Eloquent 'I'* (Madison, University of Wisconsin Press, 1968), p. 112.
5 Montaigne, *Essays*, trans. J. M. Cohen (Harmondsworth, Penguin, 1958), p. 53.
6 ibid., p. 235.
7 ibid., p. 236.
8 ibid., p. 223.
9 ibid., p. 387.
10 ibid., p. 354.
11 ibid., p. 389.
12 ibid., p. 404.
13 ibid., pp. 399–400.
14 ibid., p. 403.
15 ibid., p. 406.
16 ibid., p. 254.
17 ibid., p. 398.
18 ibid., p. 257.
19 ibid., p. 208.
20 ibid., p. 208.
21 ibid., p. 108.
22 ibid., p. 109.
23 ibid., p. 109.
24 ibid., p. 159.

25 ibid., p. 159.
26 ibid., p. 204.
27 ibid., p. 219.
28 ibid., p. 310.
29 ibid., p. 198.
30 ibid., p. 194.
31 ibid., p. 194.
32 ibid., p. 52.
33 ibid., p. 139.
34 ibid., p. 139.
35 ibid., p. 216.
36 ibid., p. 344. The paradox lies in the fact that all life is flux – but it must be lived as pattern. And the major instrument of pattern is reason.
37 'The word "deceit" is used by contemporary writers on rhetoric to describe those indirect ways of writing or speaking which commanded greater emotional response from the reader or listener than "natural" or direct means of presenting ideas' (cf. McGowan, Introduction, p. vi).
38 M. McGowan, *Montaigne's Deceits* (London, University of London Press, 1974), p. 19.
39 ibid., pp. 162-3.
40 Montaigne, op. cit., pp. 79-80.
41 ibid., p. 222.
42 ibid., p. 55.
43 ibid., p. 56.
44 ibid., p. 56.
45 ibid., p. 76.
46 ibid., p. 62.
47 R. Nisbet, *The Social Philosophers* (London, Paladin, 1974), p. 205.
48 This places Montaigne still in the tradition of those rhetoricians (for so he must be termed) who wished to bolster style with morality.
49 Montaigne, op. cit., p. 70.
50 ibid., p. 71.
51 ibid., p. 72.
52 ibid., p. 76.
53 ibid., p. 76.
54 ibid., p. 77.
55 ibid., p. 79.
56 ibid., p. 291.
57 ibid., p. 80.
58 ibid., p. 80.
59 ibid., p. 86.
60 ibid., p. 242.
61 ibid., p. 53.
62 ibid., p. 53.
63 ibid., p. 82.
64 ibid., p. 86.
65 ibid., p. 292.
66 ibid., p. 162.
67 ibid., p. 161.
68 ibid., p. 85.
69 Auerbach, op. cit., p. 271.
70 Montaigne, op. cit., p. 72.
71 ibid., p. 72.
72 'among all his contemporaries he had the clearest conception of the problem of man's self-orientation; that is, the task of making oneself at home in existence without fixed points of support. In him for the first time, man's life – the random personal life as a whole – becomes problematic in the modern sense' (Auerbach,

op. cit., p. 273). He lacks, however, a sense – such as Shakespeare possessed – of the tragic. He is too evasive for that.

73 ibid., p. 236.

PART TWO

The Empirics: 'Things'

CHAPTER 7

'Heaven Here':
the Coming of Science

I

Just as the humanist movement had its roots deep in the society of the middle ages, so adumbrations of a new approach to knowledge can, as we have seen, certainly be identified in the period when humanism still constituted the recommended educational ideal. 'Nature to be commanded must be obeyed', proclaimed Francis Bacon, the greatest propagandist of the revised episte-mology of the seventeenth century; and before I examine in detail the implications of Bacon's recommendations for education, a rehearsal of those forces which stimulated the one-time Lord Chancellor to trumpet the new age of empirical investigation must begin by examining the changing conception of nature which accompanied it, and the significance of command and obedience which lie behind his terse and paradoxical injunction. We shall need to examine the implications of a changing cosmology, factors leading to an increased desire for a human control, the senses in which this 'nature' was to be 'obeyed', all emerging in a reoriented subject–object relationship which has crucial consequences for human culture and the education intended to transmit it. Persuasive speech and writing were to be gradually but relentlessly replaced by new forms of knowledge as the centre of educational attention – 'experiments for light' and 'experiments for fruit' as Bacon called them, 'truths' and their application: the formation of mind – increasingly a major concern – through direct contact with the world rather than through dependence on the thoughts of others.

During the sixteenth and seventeenth centuries there evolved, gradually but unmistakably, a fundamentally different conception of nature from that which had been accepted for so long – from Greek times, indeed. It accom-panied the emergence of a new form of civilisation in the later seventeenth century, a phenomenon which in Professor Butterfield's view characterises the period as the greatest landmark since the rise of Christianity: 'It repre-sents one of those periods when new things were brought into the world and into history out of men's own creative activity and their own wrestlings with truth.'[1] Briefly, the earlier world conceived of a 'purposeful' nature quali-tatively, the seventeenth century increasingly a mechanical nature quanti-tatively.

The Greek view of nature – which in broad terms prevailed throughout the West until the period under review – was based on the principle that nature, like the human world, was permeated by mind. This was what induced the orderliness and regularity which characterised the workings of nature:

> The Greek view of nature as an intelligent organism was based on an analogy; an analogy between the world of nature and the individual human being, who begins by finding certain characteristics in himself as an individual, and goes on to think of nature as possessed of similar characteristics. By the work of his own self-consciousness he comes to think of himself as a body whose parts are in constant rhythmic motion, these motions being delicately adjusted to each other so as to preserve the vitality of the whole; and at the same time he finds himself to be a mind directing the activity of this body in accordance with its own desires. The world of nature as a whole is then explained as a macrocosm analogous to this microcosm.[2]

To this there succeeded a very different conception – nature as a machine. Collingwood described this view as follows:

> First it is based on the Christian idea of a creative and omnipotent God. Secondly, it is based on the human experience of designing and constructing machines . . . by the sixteenth century the Industrial Revolution was well on the way. The printing-press and the windmill, the lever, the pump, and the pulley, the clock and the wheel-barrow, and a host of machines in use among miners and engineers were established features of daily life. Everyone understood the nature of a machine, and the experience of making and using such things had become part of the general consciousness of European man. It was an easy step to the propositions: as a clockmaker or millwright is to a clock or mill, so is God to Nature.[3]

During the medieval period man's view of nature changed little in fundamentals though it gained considerably in sophistication between the time of Isidore of Seville, who died in 636 and that of Albertus Magnus in the thirteenth century. It was an essentially static world; movement, such as there was, was located within the particular object and was never considered as arising out of any relationship between objects. Thus 'characteristic ways of behaving are attributes; they are part of the fundamental definition of the object';[4] behaviour, action, movement is explained not in terms of relationships but as something adhering in the object concerned. Furthermore, change involved alteration from one unique object into another: changes were transformations and the actions bringing them about unique and unaccountable in generalised terms. As there was no principle of continuity as between one state and another, there could be no general principle of movement governing such changes. 'The universe remained one of discrete and minimally related objects throughout the period.' There was no frame of reference within which individual activities could be understood, no general law binding together individual manifestations; each action appeared governed by unfathomable internal principles, constituting a potentiality of the object in itself and hence unique to it. Discrete objects moved and behaved discretely. The Aristotelian principle of potentiality as explanatory of change constituted a principle which could be guaranteed in advance to explain anything: it merely reinforced the uniqueness of objects and of actions and change by referring back to the inherent nature of the (unique) object.

Any attempt to explain specific events in more general terms tended to be either *ad hoc* or analogic; and even these analogic explanations required unique objects or happenings as their points of departure. Hence the medieval explanatory system was static, not dynamic; it lacked a concept of process so that particular phenomena could be related to the happenings of the physical world as specific examples of universal laws, with the underlying assumption that by nature they provided only a particular example in a world of self-consistent behaviourally regular recurrences. To medieval man fire burned because it was its nature to do so: the explanation was teleological; to post-medieval man the explanation of why fire burned involved relating the specific event to a chemical process universally applicable:

> modern techniques of explanation are, in essence, methods of relating specific events to frameworks of expectation logically prior to any particular event, and these frameworks describe processes . . . a cause in this view is not a property but itself an event, a happening, and causation is a continuous process. Action and interaction comprise the stuff of the universe, and every momentary state is the product of all of the previous relationships within that particular causal process.[5]

The basic requirement which would change what essentially functioned as unique objects into phenomena illustrative of categorisations logically antecedent to any specific manifestation was some sort of unifying structure detectable as inherent in all the individual instances which would provide at once an explanatory framework and afford the opportunity of prediction. During the sixteenth and seventeenth centuries it was realised that mathematics – quantity – could provide such a unifying structure and thus indeed come to constitute the very criterion of the 'real'.

In the medieval setting man was the centre of the universe and the world of nature was considered by many thinkers to be teleologically coextensive with him and his destiny. The universe was assumed to operate lawfully 'according to nature' – and man, too, of course, had the capacity to achieve harmony with his fellows and the environment and also to behave 'according to nature', though he often fell short of this behaviour in practice – the result of his sin. Nevertheless he remained the focal point of the cosmic process, and physical explanation reflected its human orientation; nature existed for man's sake. Thus an explanation in terms of the relation of things to human purpose was accounted just as real as and often more important than an explanation in terms of efficient causality, which expressed their relations to each other. Rain fell because it nourished man's crops as truly as because it was expelled from the clouds. Analogies drawn from purposive activity were freely used. Light bodies, such as fire, tended upward to their proper place; heavy bodies, such as water or earth, tended downward to theirs. Quantitative differences were derived from these teleological distinctions.[6]

Sensory experience – and of course medieval man did use his eyes – was nevertheless limited to the observation of discrete objects and explained in terms of preconceived metaphysical principles – as in his representations in painting where individual people were grouped together in accordance with metaphysical and religious preconceptions, not in accordance with the internal dynamics of an observed relationship. Gradually, however, perspective helped to foster the notion of a structure internal to the persons depicted, as science conceived of the internal dynamics and relationships of objects. What was initially implied was a change in the nature, quality and degree of visualisation.

The new orientation removed man from the centre of the stage, from nature, indeed; and yet paradoxically led him to master the newly objectified workings of the world apart from him to a degree never possible while he regarded himself as coextensive with the natural world. A new metaphysic evolved from the work of people like Copernicus, Kepler and Galileo. Its characteristic features have helped to form the modern world.

Nature, indeed, now came to be regarded as a simple, orderly system. 'Nature . . . doth not that by many things, which may be done by few.' She is 'inexorable' and acts only 'through immutable laws which she never transgresses and cares nothing whether her reasons and methods of operating be or be not understandable by men'.[7] Fundamentally she is mathematical by nature:

> Philosophy is written in that great book which ever lies before our eyes –
> I mean the universe – but we cannot understand it if we do not first
> learn the language and grasp the symbols, in which it is written. This
> book is written in the mathematical language, and the symbols are
> triangles, circles and other geometrical figures, without whose help it
> is impossible to comprehend a single word of it . . .[8]

Mathematics, then, not logic was the key to the universe, the instrument of discovery. Though these discoveries must be checked by 'particular demonstrations, observations and experiments',[9] for it was the senses that offered the world to be explained, Galileo's method moved rapidly from sense experience to the intuition of

> simple, absolute elements in terms of which the phenomenon can be
> most easily and completely translated into mathematical form . . . Have

we performed this step properly, we need the sensible facts no more; the elements thus reached are their real constituents, and deductive demonstrations from them by pure mathematics (second step) must always be true of similar instances of the phenomenon, even though at times it should be impossible to confirm them empirically.[10]

Galileo thus fosters the notion that the world and its functioning are intelligible in terms which transcend ordinary sense experience and are revelatory of God's construction of the universe by way of that rigorous mathematical necessity which we can grasp at least partially by our efforts. 'Nor does God less admirably discover himself to us in Nature's actions, than in Scripture's sacred dictions',[11] for, in Sir Thomas Browne's words: 'Nature is the Art of God.' The notion of a mathematically intelligible world behind the world of fluctuating sense experience has clear affinities with contemporary neo-Platonic views; for implicit in this mathematical meta-physic was a division of the world into primary and secondary qualities; a clear distinction was made between that which is absolute, objective, immut-able and mathematical, and that whose features are relative, subjective, fluctuating and subject to the possible deceits of sense experience. The consequences of this division are fundamental for the emerging world view which has lasted practically to our own times: the focal point of the funda-mental and real has shifted from man to nature. What cannot be measured comes to seem subjective: and the 'real' world is a world of mathematically measurable motions in space and time, even if it is one arising out of a sensory world of observed particulars which forms the initial starting-point. 'The *why* of motion had been the object of study and the study had proceeded in qualitative and substantive terms; with Galileo now it is the *how* of motion that becomes the object of analysis, and that by the method of exact mathe-matics.'[12] A concern for efficient causes replaces the teleological attitudes of the medieval.

Galileo indeed had identified the two factors which needed to coalesce before men could come to a true understanding of nature's workings – obser-vation of empirical 'particulars' which start in sense experience and the formative power of mind exercised through mathematics. The one implies submission to the actualities of fact and behaviour objectively observed, the other hints at a dominating power through its ability to determine regularities and the predictions they enabled. Both elements require further, more detailed investigation, for both have their importance for educational theory and both are connected with specific social manifestations. I will first examine the growing concern for particulars.

II

In his book *The Counter-Renaissance* Professor Haydn has identified a number of intellectual tendencies in reaction against the basic tenets of the classical Renaissance in its initial phase and marked by a spirit of primitivism, empiricism, a contempt for system and a consequent return to 'first principles': the period, in fact,

> is manifested by various kinds of cultural, technological, chronological and religious primitivism . . . in addition, it takes on the large general meanings of an advocacy of simplification and simplicity, and of de-centralised, unsynthesised particular experience – whether in the sense of direct personal contact with the object of knowledge, or the concentration upon some one aspect of possible knowledge (rather than the attempts to fit all aspects together into a coherent and consistent synthesis).[13]

The 'scientists' of this period investigate brute facts: political and historical writers begin to consider man and happenings in terms of actual behaviour. The speculative or universal is rejected in favour of the empirical and particular. The need for simplicity is, indeed, constantly emphasised and one of the most interesting features of these transitional 'loose' empiricists follows from this endorsement of the ideals of simplicity and simplification. They amassed facts and considered the result science; Vives, for instance, stressed the role of 'humble fact' by denuding it of 'importance' – by which he intended to substitute an objective scientific approach for a teleological explanation of phenomena. Then there was their concern for humble witnesses: the superiority of practical men – artisans and the like – over the pride of intellectuals. Vives advises recourse to 'gardeners, husbandmen, shepherds and hunters'. Cartier urges that 'the simple sailors of today . . . have come to know the opposite of the philosophers by true experience'.[14] Greville appealed to 'pure, humble creatures' – experience is opposed to learned theory and speculative knowledge and authority. Montaigne (as we have seen) exalts the humble in a way which turns out to be symptomatic. Liaison between the scientist and the technical skill of the artisan was recommended by men like Dee and Gilbert. Gabriel Harvey listed a number of productive artisans and deprecated an attitude of superiority to 'expert artisans, or any sensible industrious practitioner, howsoever unlectured in schools or unlettered in books'.[15] Walter Raleigh wrote:

> Tell wit how much it wrangles
> In tickle points of niceness;
> Tell wisdom she entangles
> Herself in over-wiseness:
> And when they do reply
> Straight give them both the lie.[16]

Above all, the medieval world vision of a universal law as the *lex aeterna* stemming from the mind of God, rooted in order, displaying design and purpose in every part and hence proclaiming the unqualified rule of Mind, which has thus produced a unity of conception, comes under increasing attacks in the course of a developing belief in relativism. Montaigne deprecates the search for universal man: 'Others fashion man, I repeat him; and represent a particular one . . .' In his concern for his *'peinture de son Moi'* we reach the opposite pole from medieval universalism in a specific concern for the particular: 'Diversity is the most universal quality.'[17] The notion of a universal moral law he considers a fable invented by man to afford some authority to local custom. Even earlier Machievelli had urged individual state rights based on power in place of the organised unity of a common life; and he divorces history, war, the state, justice and law from revelation and divine purpose and unity and thus opens up historical phenomena for empirical investigation.

This new sense of detachment and objectivity implicit in the concentration on the particular was assisted by important technical and social movements. In England especially crucial was the influence of craftsmen and merchants, where technical developments at a more mundane level, a grappling with the hard facts of empirical experience, assisted the development of a more objective spirit. If the new scientific cosmology was to have some of the characteristics of a machine in operation, the tremendous development of technical interest provided a stimulus to some such conception. Socially, as Dr Christopher Hill points out, 'the most obviously *new* social fact in England during the century before 1640' lay in the expansion of 'the middling sort', merchants, artisans and yeomen.[18] To these people humanism had no appeal: 'The urban way of life, pragmatic, utilitarian, and individualistic, where things mattered more than words, experience more than authority, was in harmony with new trends in Protestant and scientific thought.'[19] We are no longer in the theatre but the market-place and the workshop.

The rise of an objective attitude, then, is linked with important social and economic changes – the emergence of the 'middling sort' with its prudential morality and its attachment to the doctrine of work is a highly significant factor in the later sixteenth and early seventeenth centuries. The culture of this new factor in the body politic has been admirably analysed by Professor Louis B. Wright in his *Middle-Class Culture in Elizabethan England.*

A survey of the intellectual interests of the commercial classes in England of the sixteenth and seventeenth centuries shows that the great awakening of the Renaissance was not confined to the learned and the courtly elements in society. On the contrary, the intellectual ferment was particularly active among the groups that were already laying the foundations for a commercial and industrial structure later to have an importance beyond the dreams of any contemporary thinker.[20]

Professor Wright produces a fascinating study of the moral and intellectual interests of these people – their self-confidence, their patriotism, their prudential morality, their practical concerns, their desire for betterment, their concern over learning – and a particular sort of learning, one which stressed utility and the creation of wealth: 'Undoubtedly the educational demands of a large middle class exerted a powerful influence upon pedagogical theorists of the seventeenth century who set out to reform the schools.'[21] Admittedly, the social prestige of the grammar schools and the universities and the desire of the new-made gentlemen to seek the cachet of university training for their children protected the old classical curriculum for a long time to come, practically to our own times. But a developing commercialism in an expanding world created new demands and requirements, and a formidable faith in the power of education itself. The new merchant classes were prominent in the foundations of schools and colleges and supported revised curricula; above all they believed profoundly in the importance of schooling. Here, indeed, is the beginning of the modern bourgeois faith in the efficacy of education. So individual citizens endowed schools and the great trade guilds fostered learning at both elementary and advanced levels. London became an intellectual centre with a diversity of educational facilities comparable to those of Oxford and Cambridge, as Sir George Buck makes clear in *The Third Universitie of England* published in 1615:

> Besides such conventional studies as law, medicine, and theology, Buck describes less orthodox subjects which made up the vast curriculum of his 'third university', where one might study – among a number of other things – writing, bookkeeping, stenography (very useful for taking 'a Sermon, Oration, Play, or any long speech'), modern languages (both European and oriental, useful for merchants), even dancing, self-defense, horsemanship, and artillery tactics. Finally the author adds, 'I must not omit that the Art of Memorie is taught within this Universitie of London.' The general conclusion is that the schools of London make that city the greatest and most useful university in the world for the education of anyone, whether tradesmen or gentlemen.[22]

Gresham's College remains the prototype of the earlier utilitarian college; teaching was in English, not Latin; useful subjects were introduced not then taught in grammar schools, and lectures were aimed at 'merchants and other citizens'.

The thirst for learning among the 'middling sort' appeared insatiable. A moral, puritan urge sought worldly success as an indication of divine favour and conceived of work and godliness as being closely interrelated, for the millenarian faith behind the new enthusiasm must not be forgotten:[23] books were essentially to serve useful ends. The printing presses, now in full flow, poured out a seemingly endless succession of 'technical' handbooks – technical in the modern sense as relating to practical interests, crafts and trade – books of computation, tables of interest, polyglot dictionaries, teachers of languages, handbooks of manners and behaviour intended to assist the aspiring citizen in his quest for social improvement. Such handbooks on an infinite variety of topics, indeed, constituted a powerful means to popular education in Elizabethan times.[24] Domestic relations received the attention of writers; guides to godliness proliferated; lessons derived from history were driven home. The wonders of travel were described, and pride in England's imperial expansion with its opportunities for success in trade praised. Maps, charts and books and descriptions of alien populations encouraged close observation of foreign habits. A literature of popular science – natural history, astronomical, medical – stimulated an unusual curiosity about inventions and revealed a fascination for simple experiments in chemistry and mechanics, and an interest in mechanical devices:

> The State Papers [for Tudor and Stuart times] contain many references to applications for patents for new methods of draining fens, pumping out mines, utilizing coal, and making dyes, glass, steel, clocks, military supplies, and innumerable other products. The literature on the subject is a manifestation of the general interest of a public awakening to the fascination of scientific discovery and mechanical development.[25]

The growing interest in science and technology appears, indeed, to have been specifically an English phenomenon. Thus Dr Hill has calculated that over 10 per cent of the books listed in the *Short Title Catalogue* for the years 1475 to 1640 deal with natural sciences – and nine out of every ten of these were in English.[26] It is not surprising, then, that the great populariser of science, *Buccinator novi temporis*, Francis Bacon, should have been an Englishman. Bacon added social prestige to a movement which had sprung from craftsmen and 'mechanicians' rather than from the universities, from Protestant and Puritan rather than from established religious sources.[27] Tradesmen favoured the new approach, men of traditional learning despised it; and Robert Boyle, later in the seventeenth century telling gentlemen scientists that 'they must converse with tradesmen in their workshops and shops', indicating that it was 'childish . . . and unworthy of a philosopher' to refuse to learn from craftsmen, implied a prejudice against the new ways among the traditionally learned. That a figure of Bacon's importance should have studied and theorised about the achievements of craftsmen – urging that 'The vexations of art are certainly as the bonds and handcuffs of Proteus, which betray the ultimate struggles and efforts of matter' and proclaiming his intention to compile a History of Trades in which scientific reports would be made of successful experiments carried out in the workshops of smiths, watchmakers, carpenters, joiners as well as metal-workers, glass makers, dyers, brewers and many others – gave the scientific approach a tremendous fillip.[28]

So there was a constant interplay between technical developments and scientific thinking:

> It is coming to be realised that the history of technology plays a larger part in the development of the scientific movement than it was once understood to do . . . apart from the transference of ideas and techniques, there must have been an appreciable effect of a subtle kind upon the way in which problems were tackled and upon man's feeling for things, his feeling perhaps even for matter itself . . .
>
> It has been argued that the growing number of mechanical objects in the world at large had induced . . . an interest in the sheer question of the way in which things worked, and a disposition to look upon nature with the same preoccupation . . . Sometimes there seems to be a curious

correspondence between the technical needs of the age and the pre-occupations of scientific enquirers . . . as in the case of ballistics in the sixteenth century and hydraulic problems, perhaps, in the seventeenth. Much of the attention of the Royal Society in its early years was actually directed to problems of practical utility.[29]

Advances in 'experiments for light' and 'experiments for fruit' interacted.[30]

There were, of course, other factors involved during the period which contributed to creating an atmosphere favourable to scientific and technical advance. As Professor J. V. Nef points out in his *Cultural Foundations of Industrial Civilisation*, there was a crucial change in the period 1580–1640 which manifest itself as a rapid increase in concern for the quantitative; and it was during this period that there began to be 'an emphasis on utility as the goal of industrial life – on productivity as a self-justifying end'.[31] Bacon's *New Atlantis* was symptomatic of a changed orientation. Developments in iron metallurgy in England, for instance, induced a concern for quantity and utility rather than quality and elegance and make it possible to speak of an early industrial revolution in the late sixteenth and early seventeenth centuries, manifest in

a concentration of industrial enterprise upon the production of cheap commodities in large quantities. Both in the tastes it generated and the technical problems it raised, the early industrial revolution prepared the way for the later and more celebrated industrial revolution at the juncture of the eighteenth and nineteenth centuries.[32]

The changed attitude involved a shift in values:

It was at this time that men began to attach a *value* that was novel to inventive ideas whose only purpose was to reduce labour costs and to multiply production. This shift in values was at the root of the major inventions which much later brought about the industrial revolution.[33]

It is true that aristocratic tastes and a social structure which encouraged luxury and discrimination in consumer outlook restrained the exploitation of the quantitative on qualitative grounds until the nineteenth century; nevertheless a developing quantitative-mindedness during the early years of the seventeenth century prepared the ground for later industrial developments. As Professor Nef puts it, 'the commitment of the human mind to quantitative values and quantitative methods of reasoning, to tangible, verifiable evidence as the basis for scientific knowledge, and to a more comprehensive mathematics',[34] combined to induce an atmosphere favourable to industrialism and the search for practical benefits, for the relief of man's estate.

Concentration on quantity and quantitative data reinforced a reorientation of attitude from primary to secondary *causes*,[35] teleological to efficient. It implies, in the first place, a this-worldliness, an appreciation of material phenomena as independent causative factors. Numbers come to take on a life of their own as important elements relevant to industrial decisions – sheer quantity becomes a relevant issue in profit and loss calculations influencing the scope and range of manufactories; numbers as such became reasons for doing things, and goals to be attained almost independent of qualitative considerations. They constitute one of several factors which were gradually reorienting men's minds from primary causes, ends sought in relation to essences of being, as manifestations of their (God-given) nature to secondary, efficient causes bound up with function and effectiveness in a chain of causation. Symptomatic of this profound revolution in man's changed attitude to the phenomena of nature was his view of his own historical functioning – and, indeed, of himself in the long run, as a subject for 'educational processing'. As Dr Hill says of Walter Raleigh's *History of the World*, he showed the 'ineluctable working out of cause and effect at the human level';

> Raleigh's emphasis on law looks forward to Boyle and Newton: Raleigh even used the metaphor of winding up a clock to describe God's relation to his universe. Raleigh secularised history not by denying God the first cause, but by concentrating his vision on secondary causes *and insisting that they are sufficient in themselves for historical explanation.*[36]

History, then, is no longer conceived in cyclical terms but derives from changing social and economic circumstances: 'History is *not* just a bran-tub, waiting for us to pick our precedent, nor yet a story of degeneration from a golden past. It is a story of adaptation to change which may be for the better.'[37] In contemplating his own affairs, then, man began to conceive them in terms of social interaction rather than of teleological purposiveness. Just as the natural world could be conquered for the relief of man's estate, so increasingly the social world was open to change on the basis of lessons learned from the past rather than subject to an ineluctable cyclical motion. God is seen to act through human, secondary agents; and so 'Raleigh's and Bacon's view of history, plus the experience of the Revolution, made the idea of *controlled* change conceivable.'[38]

Here again, in the concern for technical change, the element of control is manifest; but it necessitates a submission to the brute irreducible facts of nature; to use a relevant metaphor, technical advance arises out of an ability to work with the grain of the wood and involves a humility in the face of materials and their characteristics. At the same time, this concentration on the technical stimulates only what I have called a 'loose empiricism', an observation for the activity in hand, not a penetration into the inner nature, the internal coherence of the presented facts.

Thus from accepting himself as an integral part of nature very gradually man began to conceive of nature as a collection of things, objects, which as their remoteness grew they could nevertheless learn to control in a piecemeal fashion, arising from technical advances. This gradual evolution of a sense of power over the natural world and hence over his own destiny in it had been in some degree implicit in the secularisation of humanism, with its evolving sense of 'otherness' from the world and the past, and its conception of 'art' and artifice. As the neo-Platonist Ficino had put it, 'Man is not a slave of creative nature . . . rather he is its rival, completing, improving and refining its works.' Man, as we have seen, was to 'make another nature'.[39]

But Bacon makes clear the interrelationship between developments 'for light' and developments 'for fruit'; without advances in what would now be termed fundamental or pure science, advances in technical skill must remain uncertain and haphazard. True, in these early days, the two areas were not clearly defined; but curiosity about the workings of nature was as much a part of the early scientific ethos as the desire for technical advance. How did the notion of a general formative power, necessary to bring order into the chaos of empirical experience, arise and thus foster a genuine science?

III

It arose initially out of the neo-Platonic and magical studies of the later renaissance period when men conceived of the possibility of interfering in the workings of nature. A new metaphysical interest, after the comparative philosophical indifference of the earlier Renaissance, was stimulated by a revival of attention to the medieval cosmology and its 'correspondences' (of lower creation, microcosm, commonwealth, macrocosm and divine and angelic) and was complemented by the developing study of Hermetic and Cabalistic writings with their mystical and magical implications.[40] Conceivably a renewed sense of hierarchy (after the comparative social flexibility of, for instance, Florentine republicanism and the fluidity of the Italian city state) was stimulated by the emergence of the new national societies and the apotheosis of monarchy by which it was accomplished: the new imperial dream (which affected more than the view taken of the Holy Roman Emperor himself) stimulated metaphysical speculations which constituted the political counterpart of the intellectual developments following on the platonising tendencies of the later fifteenth century. Philosophy and magic replaced grammarian 'pedantry' (as Giordano Bruno regarded the earlier humanist obsessive concern for language) and thus stimulated the conception of an ordering power – a conception essential for the development of a true science.

The works of Hermes Tresmegistus were supposedly those of a real person, an Egyptian priest who lived in remote, practically Mosaic times and hence transmitted 'a mysterious and precious account of most ancient Egyptian wisdom, philosophy and magic', writings indeed from which 'Plato and the Greeks had derived the best that they know'.[41] The bibliography of the editions, translations, collections, commentaries on the Hermetic writings in the sixteenth century is long and complicated, testifying to the profound and enthusiastic interest aroused.[42] 'The cosmological framework which they take for granted is always astrological' where 'the material world is under the rule of the stars'.[43] Initiates employed a reformed and learned magic (the medieval magic was an evil, black magic condemned by the church) by which an object relevant to a particular star or planet was thought to be infused with occult powers poured down upon it from the heavenly body on which it depended. Such images (plants, animals, stones, metals, etc.) could store the power derived from the star; and initiates were ones 'who knew how to enter into this system, and use it'.[44] Many of the talismans and procedures were used for specific ends – cures of diseases, overcoming one's enemies – in a word, manipulating the practical world. This manipulation differs from astrology in that astrology determines destiny through study of the stars at birth, whereas this constituted a sort of astral magic intended to escape astrological determinism by gaining power over the stars. It represented an attempt to exercise human will for human benefit, a way of manipulating fortune and chance.

The whole Hermetic-Cabalistic movement, then, implied a further triumphant assertion of the dignity of man and of his power to control his destiny; and there are clear implications for later scientific development implicit in the new stance – Dr Yates assesses the position of Pico della Mirandola as strongly as this:

> The profound significance of Pico della Mirandola in the history of humanity can hardly be overestimated. He it was who first boldly formulated a new position for European man, man as Magus using both Magia and Cabala to act upon the world, to control his destiny by science.[45]

Man became an operator, seeking to draw power from the divine and natural orders in correspondence. The new magic also employed numbers and mathematics in a way not unreminiscent of subsequent scientific utilisation.

In this way, renaissance magic helped to further fundamental changes in human outlook. It confirmed the notion of intervention, interference in the course of nature; it implied a fundamental reorientation of the will:

> It was now dignified and important for man to operate; it was also religious and not contrary to the will of God that man, the great miracle, should exert his powers. It was this basic psychological reorientation towards a direction of the will which was neither Greek nor medieval in spirit, which made all the difference.[46]

Furthermore, it involved the will in a specific sphere – not that of politics but within the broader confines of the universe. Prospero was an unsuccessful ruler, as was his real-life analogue, the Emperor Rudolf II – but both sought to command the elements and discover and exploit the secrets of nature.

The court of the Hapsburg Emperor, indeed, provided one of the major centres for the development of these ideas and provides an indication of their political importance. They had their implications for other national monarchies; but the Holy Roman Emperor himself was profoundly sympathetic to the new metaphysical interests and his court provided a remarkable centre where the political, artistic and philosophical aspects of the movement achieved a unity of organisation which was manifest in the collecting habits of the emperor and his political outlook.

Rudolf's passion for collecting and his habits of patronage, indeed, reflected more than simply aesthetic delight or cultural interest. For Rudolf

> the assembling of many and various items reflected the essential variety in the world, which could nevertheless be converted into unity by a mind which brought them together and divined their internal relations one with another. Once again we see the analogy from microcosm to macrocosm and the search for a 'key' to the harmony of the created universe; in other words *we see an aspect of the pansophic striving* (my italics).[47]

For the collection presented an encyclopaedia of the visible world – and was both animate (gardens, menageries, stables indicated the extent of the emperor's interests) and inanimate – pictures, precious stones, minerals, carvings in marquetry or intaglio, etc. The importance attached to small art objects – in gold, silver, glass, enamel, etc. – bore witness at once to a concern for mannerist virtuosity and an interest in their occult properties.[48]

We begin, indeed, to come to the heart of an understanding of what this revived and transformed belief in the correspondences and their exploitation for magical purposes meant in concrete terms by considering the mentality of the emperor and of many of his confidants and initiates. They showed great interest in the occult, in Hermetism and Cabalism; as we have seen, the occult endeavour attempted to penetrate behind the phenomenal world to a reality which lay beyond it, and which employed symbols and emblems for the purpose. Knowledge was gained, at the lowest level, by sense experience; reasoning led to higher understanding; but the highest of all, normally denied to man, depended on a mode of intellectual intuition of ideas or essences directly apprehended. Visual symbols contributed to this apprehension, for sight was the favoured means by which higher knowledge could be apprehended in a flash, a mode of apprehension superior to that of discursive reason. Hence in artistic creation the symbols used did not 'represent' the truth but in some sense embodied it.[49] Clearly here the concept of 'correspondence' is at work; and indeed in Rudolf's time the 'natural philosophers' of the period 'studied the forces at work in the world around them, not as discretely observed patterns of cause and effect, but as motive spirits acting through a divine scheme of correspondences.'[50] Knowledge was followed by control, a form of power.[51] The Baconian theme was initiated in an unlikely context.

So the cosmology of the sixteenth century formed a tightly-knit coherent system of aprioristic correspondences revived for magical purposes. The study of nature and man must be set against a background where all science, despite its compartments of psychology, medicine, botany, metallurgy and the rest, was intimately linked with the whole cosmic hierarchy. The painter's vision, the poet's insight, the philosopher, the 'scientist' were all communicators whose aim was the revelation of ultimate 'reality'. This artistic attitude can be interpreted as a development of earlier renaissance and humanist notions of 'imitation' as concerned to represent the phenomenal world.

> The new respect for the artist was a recognition of his power, and hence his intellectual responsibility, in possessing private subjective access to great cosmic secrets; while Mannerist expression – its conceits, its imagery, its fantasy – was often a deliberate attempt to communicate profound insights.[52]

Thus 'imitation' more specifically and consciously rejects the notion that it involves simply copying on the grounds that 'the artist must now be true to an inner image which moulds experience and also because nature itself is not a simple objective datum'.[53] The mannerist observed rigid academic rules but they were rules relating to his inner vision of a transcendental reality that only he could capture:

> Mannerist iconography thus became a representation of reality, its image the substance and power of that reality, an essential revelation which was also symbolical since the whole universe could be grasped as a series of correspondences. It was a mythology because the world was mythological.[54]

Hence the whole concept of 'imitation' (and hence the role of mind) had developed further implications since the early Renaissance. What had once been satisfied to represent the surface phenomena of nature (albeit in terms that in the hands of the best practitioners precluded mere copying) was now intended to portray a deeper insight into ultimate reality. The aim was no longer to achieve a *reproduction* of nature but a faithfulness to an anterior 'interior idea' (*disegno interno*) in terms of which nature could be interpreted: as Zuccaro put it:

> By *disegno interno* I mean the conception which is formed in our mind so that we can know something and operate from outside in conformity with the thing understood. Thus we painters, when we want to draw or paint a suitable story . . . first form in our minds the best conception we can of it. At the same time, in using this term of *disegno interno* I do not mean only the conception within the mind of the painter, but also that which any intellect at all may form.[55]

The same process was applied to poetry and its imagery. Whereas previously the 'artificial' had been conceived of in terms involving the reassessment and exploitation of the natural it was now thought of as a revelation of the intelligible 'forms' which constituted the inner essences of nature:

> The poet who imitates not the visible world, but the intelligible as manifested in the visible, will not consider that the use of artifice to emphasise form makes imagery less true to nature . . . The task of

imposing form was not assumed to be easy, but neither was it assumed
to set the poet in opposition to 'nature', the mother of forms within the
poet's mind as without it.[56]

It was in part a withdrawn art, an art which sought peace, from the current
violent world of appearances, within the mind, that sought control over its
own destiny through an apprehension of artistic symbols as manifesting the
calmer world of the intelligible. The process is apparent in the political
manifestation of the court masques and in the books of emblems:

> The emblem reflected in various ways the mentality of the period: . . .
> it was a method of moral instruction through the power of word and
> image; it possessed a hidden message; above all it was a true symbol,
> that is, it meant more than it said and its meaning was a revelation, a
> discovery, not an artistic invention.[57]

Through such symbolism, then, it was possible to reveal the inner truths of
nature; and it was out of this atmosphere of magical symbols – which must
not be thought of as a by-product of the age but central to many of its interests, educational, social, artistic and political – that a specifically scientific
interest grew. At one level the masques, which celebrated in symbolic form
the new monarchical transcendence, contributed, through the elaboration of
their technical devices, to an increased interest in science:

> Though the production of masques, or of musical grottoes, singing
> fountains, or pneumatically controlled speaking statues may not seem
> . . . important applications of science to technology, it was in fact in
> such ways as these that Renaissance science, still involved in a magical
> atmosphere, began to use technical skills on a large scale.[58]

But, more fundamental, was the stimulus to the desire to control – the evocation of the notion, to anticipate Bacon, that knowledge constituted a kind
of power. Attention was directed to the world of 'things' as containing within
it powerful means of magical potency. Above all there was, in the notion of
disegno interno, an emphasis on the creative force of mind, its ability to impose
an intelligible *form* on the natural world, and hence in some degree to bring
it under control. All these factors contribute to a complex scientific and
technical orientation.

Yet magic was not, of course, science, for it was still based on a type of
analogical thinking which had too little to do with a true scientific approach.
The view of nature which prevails is still, in essence, that of the Greeks,
when to 'know' a thing means to become one with it – as in the analogy
between microcosm and macrocosm, the 'correspondences'. For

> this unity is only possible if the subject and object, the knower and the
> known, are of the same nature; they must be members and parts of one
> and the same vital complex. Every sensory perception is an act of fusion
> and reunification. We perceive the object, we grasp it in its proper,

genuine being only when we feel in it the same life, the same kind of movement and animation that is immediately given and present to us in the experiencing of our own Ego.[59]

The analogical method of thinking, which characterised the notion of the correspondences, implies the fundamentally common being of all things: man's conception of nature is still at the stage where he 'can only understand nature by inserting his own *life* into it. The limits of his feeling for life, the barriers to a direct *sympathetic feeling* of nature are at the same time the limits of his *knowledge* of nature.'[60] For a true science to develop, man must come to conceive of nature as in some degree alien, to which he owes obedience and which works according to its own laws, not by analogy with man's.

So, side by side, the two major factors involved in a true scientific development are to be found. The 'magicians' had developed a feeling for 'form', for law binding together phenomena, but are frustrated by their lack of objectivity, so that they produce laws based not on an acceptance of the 'otherness' of the object but on a false analogical model which presumes objects to be of the same basic substance as themselves. The empiricists have accepted the 'otherness' of objects but have failed to detect any manifestation of 'form' which could evolve into a genuine scientific law. Both are concerned with the power of man to control his environment, to intervene between nature and its workings, one through magic, the other through technical know-how. They illustrate, in combination, the curious paradox of submission and domination, a paradox which is come to seem increasingly applicable to the social world during the seventeenth and eighteenth centuries, with crucially important implications for education as itself a formative power. The interesting point is that though the methods and goals of the empiricists and magicians seem so different, in fact there were a number (like John Dee) who contributed to both approaches. In one important respect they are at one: they both, for instance, assisted in a reoriented attitude to nature by finding virtue in the material world, in their refusal to consider matter as undignified or bad: the pre-eminence of 'things' was in process of evolution. Men's attention was directed to the world – and not to what people had, in the past, said about the world. They were beginning to escape from the categorising power of a past culture and accepting a new means of control through their contacts with the natural world: in the process they were to attain a new mastery of experience through the formative power of mind.

IV

What, then, is now needed is a mode of categorisation which will separate the 'necessary' from the 'accidental', discriminate within the world of phenomena itself so that distinctions can be made between what obeys laws and what is fantastic and arbitrary: and this was done, as indicated above, by the intellectualism of mathematics. It was assisted by current theories of art, for

Mathematics and art now agree upon the same fundamental requirement: the requirement of 'form' . . . Here we have a new synthesis
within the world of mind, and together with it a new correlation of
'subject' and 'object'. Reflection on human freedom, on man's original,
creative force, requires as its complement and its confirmation the
concept of the immanent 'necessity' of the natural object.[61]

Thus 'man in his new "free" subjectivity creates, through his art, the reality
of the objective world of nature'. In this development a crucial role was
played by Leonardo da Vinci. As Cassirer puts it:

The decisive point in Leonardo's thought is precisely that a dualism
between the abstract and the concrete, between 'reason' and 'experience',
can no longer exist. Both moments are related and bound to one another; experience completes itself only in mathematics, just as mathematics first 'comes to its fruition' in experience . . . For there is no true
experience without an analysis of phenomena, i.e., without breaking
down into its basic elements that which is given and complex. And the
only way to conduct this analysis is through mathematical demonstration
and mathematical calculation . . .[62]

In this way, 'empirical accidentality' is transformed into 'orderly necessity':

Now, we have found the criterion vainly sought by the Renaissance
philosophy of nature; we have a clearly drawn line of demarcation
between the methodological orientation based on experience and mere
'speculation'. Rules are established for distinguishing the true from the
false and for separating the scientifically feasible from the impossible
and the fantastic. Now, man understands the purpose of his knowledge
as well as its limits.[63]

And so 'Reason is the immanent, unbreakable law, governing nature. Sense,
sensation, or the immediate feeling for life can no longer serve as the means
by which we assimilate nature and discover her secret. Only thought proves
to be truly equal to nature.'[64] This, as we have seen, is what Galileo practised.
He believed that 'philosophy is written in the great book of nature, which lies
constantly before our eyes, but which no one can read unless he has first
learned to understand the ciphers in which it is composed, i.e. the mathematical figures and their necessary relationships'.[65] But whereas Leonardo
saw in painting an organ of understanding of reality analogous to science,
Galileo more symptomatically assigned such art to the world of fiction. In
this he was more typical of the future as literary and artistic experience came
to assume a more subordinate role in the face of a developing scientific
assurance of its monopoly of any access to reality.

Thus became manifest that concern for 'form' which constituted one of
the profoundest motifs of the later Renaissance, developing out of the
increased renaissance preoccupation with theory and speculation and its

increased awareness of the 'things' of practical experience. To summarise, in medieval conceptions nature was assimilated to mind on the basis of analogical thinking; during the later Renaissance it became graspable *through* mind on the basis of mathematical categories. The way is being paved for the *control* of nature through a true assessment of its working, impossible when it was merely thought of as fulfilling a teleological purpose analogous to that of man. Nature had to be accepted for what she was objectively; then she became comprehensible in terms of efficient causes. At the same time men became impressed with their powers of control through reason and cognition. To the developing sense of a capacity for self-formation we have noted in renaissance educational theorising is now added a new conception of the power of knowledge, an encyclopaedic knowledge as an equipment *for* the pupil to acquire through education in his attempt to achieve autonomous self-direction, and knowledge *of* the pupil as a means to his more effective induction into an apprehension of necessity which constitutes a new educational ideal. The conception of reason itself underwent a considerable change. From being the means by which men collated, compared and reconciled intimations of the 'given', whether Christian or classical, reason now becomes a means through which man impresses his capacity for self-determination in the midst of the recalcitrance of circumstances. Hence the changed 'form' of educational knowledge – no longer arising out of an assimilation of past authorities but stemming from the direct confrontation of nature, no longer a means of persuasion through words but of manipulation through cognitive grasp. Hence a new pansophic ideal – salvation through learning – and the education necessary to transmit it.

V

The emphasis on analytical reason and the role assigned to it by so many renaissance thinkers brings to mind an important and symptomatic figure in the history of European education who encapsulates some, at least, of the shifts of attention alluded to in this chapter. Peter Ramus (1515–72) was a university teacher and famous as an author of educational textbooks, some of whose works ran into hundreds of editions and were diffused throughout Europe. Consideration of Ramus will also permit reference to a further crucial factor in the development of a scientific and technical approach and itself a new technology, the development of the printing press. Though in view of his respect for the classics Ramus is normally categorised as a humanist, his emphasis on logic – a logic, however, somewhat different from that of the scholastics – and his curtailing of the scope of his rhetoric provide a factual illustration of a certain shift in humanist attention. He was a humanist, however, in his overt repudiation of the authority of Aristotle (while, incidentally, borrowing quite extensively from the Stagirite) and in his concern – which had been demonstrated by some of the earlier humanists – for mathematics, as well as in his constant appeal to the evidence of the classics. As a logician he seems to have been on a par with Bacon as a practical scientist

– that is to say, limited and incompetent; but pedagogically and culturally he is a crucially important symptom.

The significant elements in Ramism are twofold. It is symptomatic of a new approach to language, characteristic of which is the increasing tendency to treat words as things, at once denotative and, at the same time, objects in space on a printed page, rather than as determinants of meaning in oral–aural contact; in this way they became symptomatic of the new, more sharply defined subject/object relationship. Furthermore, Ramism manifests a developing concern with analysis – in this case in the method and arrangement of knowledge for pedagogic purposes. Its visualist spatial orientation has been analysed with great acuteness by Professor Ong in his pioneer work on *Ramus, Method, and the Decay of Dialogue*, with the stated implication that 'The Visual is the area most proper to science'. As Professor Ong points out,

because of the derivative character of our knowledge through the senses, all intellectual cognition must be treated by analogy with sensory cognition . . . [The] description of mental activity in terms of 'composition' (putting together), or 'implication' (folding up or falling back upon), or 'definition' (setting bounds or limits), or 'division', or even 'description' (drawing a line around or sketching) all exploit . . . an analogy between the field of intellectual activity and a field which involves local motion and is sensorily apprehended in terms of sight.[66]

Humanist culture was essentially one of words and speech – its central discipline rhetoric. Though, as Marcel Proust realised later, utterance constitutes a form of objectification, speech nevertheless, of all forms of communication, carries with it the strongest subjective element – in accent, intonation, 'tone', all those affective and 'interior' concomitants which are inescapable features of the spoken word. Writing, though it continued to carry strongly idiosyncratic features in hand-writing, spatial arrangement of message ('a kind of speech', Castiglione called it), is more objectified; it permits revised structures of thought and expression arising out of the ability to consider, objectively, encoded drafts. Statements in writing, as any author knows, encapsulate what has already been sifted in interior dialogue as alternatives are judged.

When writing is translated into print, a whole new series of processes furthers the development of objectification and, of course, visualisation. Print ensures greater permanence; it necessitates planned reordering, spatially objectified and tied to technical restrictions, of written material. Spatial metaphors are relevant to the 'content' of books – '*on*' the page, '*in*' the book. Standardisation is imposed by the repeatability of the printing process: and the very proliferation of material alters reading habits, so that the medieval habit of reading aloud to oneself became interiorised and silent. The typographical revolution of the later fifteenth century and early sixteenth century had profound repercussions on psychic development and, of course, on education where the printed textbook gradually becomes a major medium of instruction. The proliferation of print was in any case an essential factor in further technological development through its diffusion of technical knowledge and diagrams.

Professor Ong has urged that 'In many ways, the greatest shift in the way of conceiving knowledge between the ancient and the modern world takes place in the movement from a pole where knowledge is conceived of in terms of discourse and hearing and persons to one where it is conceived of in terms of observation and sight and objects.'[67] The process, it hardly needs adding, was prolonged and complex; no one who appreciates medieval technical advances, which it is now realised were greater than was once thought, would argue that medieval man didn't use his eyes. Furthermore, speech – conversation – remained an important medium of intellectual communication in the salons of the eighteenth-century Enlightenment. Yet the shift alluded to makes psychological sense in terms of the gradual objectification of natural phenomena implied, for instance, in the development of perspective by artists and their reorganisation of the interior space of their works, and the reorientation in the attitude to nature from one where natural processes were thought to bear some analogous relationship to man the microcosm, to one where they had to be exteriorised so as to be both accepted in submission and mastered – the burden of this chapter. The printed book encourages – indeed necessitates – a gradual reorientation of psychological attitude, a treatment first of things and then of other persons as objects which changes the whole character of European culture and of the educational prescriptions intended to transmit it.

From this starting-point Professor Ong shows how Ramist logic, like all formal logic, constituted an attempt

> to deal with the activity of minds in terms of these and related visualist analogies. It is interested in the 'structure' of our intellectual activity – a notion which cannot even be conceived except by analogy with some sort of spatial diagram. It does not concern itself with 'tone' or other aural-type phenomena.[68]

The visualist tendency of Ramist logic, its preference for analytic and diagrammatic representation of learned discourse ties in with the new opportunities for spatial display on the pages of books implied by the typographical revolution of the Gutenberg era. The Ramist recategorisation of many of the traditional features of humanist rhetoric as part of dialectic or logic points to a fundamental humanist reorientation which began to conceive of words 'in the mind' analogous to the analytic display of words 'on the page'. Thus, as Ramist textbooks evolve, they become

> more organized for visual, as against auditory, assimilation by the reader. Paragraphs and centred headings appear, tables are utilized more and more until occasionally whole folio editions are put out with every bit of the text worked piecemeal on to bracketed outlines in dichotomized divisions which show diagrammatically how 'specials' are subordinated to 'generals'.[69]

In this way the word gradually moved away from its association with sound and became more and more 'a "thing" in space'. There was, in any case, the tradition that the rhetorician was more concerned with 'words' and the dialectician with 'things': ' "Things" are not constituted in opposition to the mind, but in opposition to the word. The word has an obvious vocal and auditory bearing, which tends to make the whole realm of "things" by contrast that which is apprehended visually and to some extent tactually.'[70] The relationship between this sort of reorientation and the development of theoretical studies in 'artificial perspective' (e.g. by Alberti) for the instruction of painters and artists, so that men became aware of new ordered *relationships* in space transmitted by the new skill on to a two-dimensional canvas, should be obvious. Sight focuses in a way hearing cannot. So typography, the new dialectic with its organisation and methodisation of knowledge, and perspective all played their part in this reorientation as essential concomitant of a developing scientific view. They were accompanied by an increased consciousness of the significance of time which is such a marked characteristic, for instance, of an important phase of the Shakesperian experience.[71]

VI

Any concern with an art must, as consciousness develops, generate an interest in 'method' which obviates the need to acquire skill and knowledge by the hazards of chance or routine; in this way, time could be saved and efficiency assisted. A concern for the conduct of schooling was not a theoretical concern of the Aristotelian tradition, but became one with the humanists:

> Not only do the words *methodus, ordo* and *ratio* appear as nouns in the nominative case in the tables of textbooks, but they also appear in the subtitles, stating that a grammar, for instance, had been written 'in a certain method' or 'by a certain method'. Here we begin to discern a reflection of Humanist dissatisfaction with the method of presentation of traditional disciplines, in which there was no clear order or controlling scheme. The number of school subjects 'brought into order' or 'reduced to art' during the later renaissance is almost unbelievable.[72]

The most methodical, efficient and wide ranging of the humanist reforms was that of the Jesuits – *Ratio Studiorum* – completed in 1586 and ratified in 1599. But a crucial part in the methodising of education was that played by Ramus. Briefly, his view was that the general and universal (in the form, say, of a definition or comprehensive summary) should precede in the order of teaching: the explication of the facts should follow and the illustration by examples should conclude the exposition. This excessively simple sequential structure, in his view, could be applied to all 'subjects'.

His approach, then, was primarily analytical, the breaking down of the general into (usually) dichotomised facts as one moved from the universal to the particular. In terms of classroom procedure, explanation through analysis preceded composition: in this Ramus' approach was quite different from earlier humanist attempts to supply students with examples or arguments – the 'commonplaces' derived from classical sources, as in Erasmus' *De Copia* or his *Colloquies*: the Ramist student depends on his analytical approach to his allotted theme to find something to say. Hence the characteristic amplification of the earlier, rhetorically oriented humanists is replaced by a plainer utterance confined to essentials and relieved only by the one major factor of traditional humanist rhetoric Ramus allowed, ornamentation; and this increasingly came to be conceived of as something applied from the outside. Analysis into plain statement reveals what subject matter is 'really' about: the uniqueness of utterance is lost. This tendency again fixed attention on the written word and hastened the process of translating words into objects, 'things', subjects for analysis rather than aural absorption.

> Secondly, when Ramus and his followers replace the use of collections of *sententiae*, aphorisms, and other sayings of the sort which make their way into commonplace books, with analysis as a device for finding 'matter' for discourse, they shift from a word-wisdom to a kind of classroom-wisdom . . . If an apothegm or a proverb or an aphorism should by any chance come to mind, before one uses it one had best write it down and analyse it – grammatically, rhetorically, logically, mathematically, or 'physically'. What it 'contains' is what comes out of the analysis, not what it actually says before it is analyzed.[73]

To such a mind the poetic aspect of discourse – which arouses resonances beyond that of plain sense – does not exist. All statement is reducible to intellectual content, denotative, otherwise it is deficient as statement. Ramism, indeed, plays a significant part in the decline of Tudor rhetoric and the gradual emergence of the 'plain style' celebrated by Bishop Sprat in 1667. A further point is, of course, that such analytical proceedings and the attitude to discourse fostered by the Ramist methodology reinforces the tendency towards objectification, the conception of discourse as material for analytic treatment as something separate from what, as a totality, it has to say. In these terms, T. S. Eliot's conception of a 'dissociation of sensibility' manifested during the earlier seventeenth century, despite the criticisms to which it has been subjected,[74] begins to take on a certain plausibility: the move from speech to writing and analysis, stimulated by print technology, helps to widen the gap between mind and world, as mind begins to withdraw itself in a developing consciousness. Shakespeare has already celebrated the interior dialogue in soliloquy, a talking *to* oneself. Ramism is symptomatic of a development of an awareness of an *inner* space. Soon Descartes will proclaim that in thought alone is the certainty of existence.

For Ramism, as indicated above, was highly popular – to an extent, indeed, that scholars have been puzzled to explain its wide diffusion unless in certain ways it tied in with some of the scarcely articulated prepossessions of the age; for as a logic its 'single method' was incompetent in the extreme. Its suitability to a developing typographic culture has already been noted. It was also likely to prove attractive to the increasing commercialism and the practicality and 'usefulness' such developments – backed by an enlarged technology – fostered. Whatever its limitations, Ramist logic and rhetoric were intended to be intensely practical in orientation.

Thus it has been said by Dr Hooykaas that Ramist logic *'est donc à la fois une logique d'humaniste et une logique d'empiriste'*.[75] For Ramus it was a principle of nature that use should precede theory, and he stressed use in a manner characteristic of humanists (one recalls Erasmus' 'write, write and then write') but in a range of practical subjects that went beyond earlier humanist ideas. To support him he appealed to the Socrates not of Plato but of Xenophon, the Socrates who urged that to be a sailor, mason or labourer it was not enough to repeat the rules of navigation, masonry, etc. but actually to sail, build and work: *'D'après Ramus les sciences sont contrôleés par l'usage, elles prennent leur source dans l'usage et elles ont leur but dans l'usage.'*[76] And thus, unlike the earlier humanists, Ramus helped to break down the traditional distinction between the liberal and practical or mechanical arts. Similarly, logic was for use, not disputation after the manner of the scholastics: *'L'usage est . . . le parent, le maître et l'arbitre de l'art.'*[77] Ramus is in the tradition of Vives, as humanist, and of the new science and technology in his stress on use and experience. He looks forward to Bentham.

This, nevertheless, was not a scientifically developed empiricism. Despite his mathematical interests – and here also he suggested lines of thought which were to be useful in the future – Ramus had no developed sense of the need to approach nature with some initially conceived hypothetical structure; his empiricism was of the 'loose' variety already noted. But by appealing both to natural reason and to the practice of artisans Ramus united the two traditions out of which a sophisticated science could grow. His physics remained purely descriptive and he had little conception of the need for experimentation; but he brought into collaboration the humanist savant and the cultivated artisan. It was a relationship fraught with significance for the future, and Ramus is an interestingly transitional educationist.

Similarly Ramism made an appeal to the commercial mind which was attracted by the practicality of the *'usuarius'*. As Professor Ong puts it, Ramus helped 'to reduce knowledge to something congenial to the artists' and burghers' commercial views' by tending to regard it as a 'commodity rather than a wisdom'.[78] His view of learning reflected the concern of the commercial world with visible entities, matters moreover which invited itemisation and listing after the Ramist model. Thus Ramism not only sought for its material in the world of practical men, basing its conception of arithmetic, for instance, on the actualities of commercial and industrial practice; the whole orientation of his methodology had a similar objectivity to that of the valuer and dealer in goods: it favoured an attitude which 'made of discourse a kind of thing'[79] and thus became of interest to the artisan and mercantile mind. His notion of method is in itself 'highly reminiscent of printing processes' in that 'it enables one to impose organisation on a subject by imagining it as made up of parts fixed in space much in the way in which words are locked in a printer's form'.[80] (It should not be forgotten that the printing industry itself constituted one of the first examples of comparatively large-scale industrial enterprise.) Such notions have important implications for developments in the theory of education, notably in Comenius' pansophic striving – a search for a 'method of teaching all things to all men', organising knowledge in ways which make his employment of an extended similarity between his new method and the art of printing[81] both illuminating and culturally significant. Comenius was not a Ramist but he had undoubtedly been influenced by the climate of opinion which Ramism had induced; for he too shared the Ramist's view that a boy taught the principles of method could come to control any body of knowledge he might be faced with. Ramism and its method constitutes 'an early step in the procedures which encode knowledge in a neutral levelling format, reducing it to bits of information such as those which will eventually make their way into electronic computers'.[82] They first made their way into children's minds; after all, Comenius specific-ally states that 'knowledge can be impressed on the mind in the same way that its concrete form can be printed on paper'. Does one need a more telling indication of the profound implications of 'method' and the new typographic culture for the future of education derived not from the after-thoughts of historians but by one of the most prominent of seventeenth century educationists himself?

VII

So Ramus is, to some extent, representative of the new educational orientation following the gradual shift from humanistic to scientific perspectives. The emphasis on usefulness, the centrality of cognition reinforced by an analytical methodology all point away from humanistic discourse in the direction of scientific 'knowledge'. Knowledge, from being the understanding derived from a classical literature with its moralistic implication, now encompasses the revised role of mind in its attempts to grasp the objective workings of all external phenomena – and in due course that which arises out of self-scrutiny in the attempt to chart the characteristics of consciousness itself; and it is the power which arises from this grasp of the way 'things' work which is to replace, through technical advance, the persuasions of rhetoric as the focal point of the exercise of human will-power. We are indeed entering on a phase when theoretical considerations – thought – are increasingly conceived of as having the power to direct life, as more and more aspects of existence are brought under the control of deliberation, rational assessment. A new manifestation of reason is based on the ability to foster premeditated ends through analytical procedures unencumbered by traditional ways, prejudices or habits. The appeal is no longer personal in face to face discourse but to impersonal 'evidence', ideally deployed to foster decision making. In the process there is a slow but inevitable gain in personal autonomy as men seek to bring more and more aspects of life under the scrutiny of a rational assess-ment free from what are regarded as the 'prejudices' of the past; the effect, indeed, of this attempt to confront 'things' as they are with the power of intellectual analysis is to remove them from the totalities in which they are embedded in order to manipulate them with due respect for their observed characteristics. Hence the centrality of 'knowledge' and the developing concentration on mind in its cognitive aspect, to the detriment of feeling (in artistic expression, for instance), the assimilation of moral truths, gesture, movement and all those aspects of the total personality provided for by the humanistic education at its most complete. These were important losses as well as gains.

The nature of educational theory itself undergoes a significant change. The humanists had in mind a specific social role; 'words', after all, need to be addressed to persons and humanist education was intended to fit into a variety of defined contexts – legal, administrative, ambassadorial, courtly. The earlier civic humanists, the 'governor', 'the courtier', all had specific political functions; even Erasmus' 'citizen of the world' assumed a context of international scholarship and social usefulness at an appropriate level. Montaigne's concentration on himself is symptomatic of a certain dislocation of accepted mores and customary obligations.

The social reorientation implicit in the concentration on 'things', together with the relative emancipation from classical traditions that it implied, had two consequences for educational theorists. Their aims become more generalised and their theories more fully elaborated. The inability to rely on a specific implied context as the circumstances of their recommendations leads them to widen their range of reference so as to define the social world within which they hope to operate. (After all, the scientific movement was initially anti-elitist and theoretically 'open'.) The ambience of 'things' is wider and more diffuse than that of words tied to classical models, and this is reflected in the increasing generality of their aims. Bacon sought the 'relief of man's estate', Comenius to teach all things to all men, Rousseau to form not even a citizen but 'a man'. Even Locke feels the need to spell out the social context of his gentleman's education more specifically than had been the case of the humanists.

So 'theory' becomes more complex as it draws on a wider range of theorising – about children, about the teacher's role, about social purposes, about psychological development, above all perhaps about methodology. Education, too, becomes more abstract, more remote from the specificities of social action and more widely diffused in its claims and aspirations. After all, the world of 'things' is the universe; and the abstracting and generalising power necessary to deal with it spills over into the conception of education it is intended to subsume. As widening areas of human behaviour and conduct are brought under rational scrutiny, so the pretensions of control widen to take in new classes of the community. Humanity itself was the stated concern of the eighteenth century; it would be surprising if the extension of aims was not reflected in one of the chief means of attaining one's object, education.

Furthermore the development of the printing presses, to which allusion has already been made, encouraged both the diffusion of scientific understanding and the development of scholarly argumentation: 'the printing press encouraged the development of an extensive "scientific" literature written in the vernacular and intended for a mass market . . . Perhaps early printing rendered its most valuable services to what we might call the descriptive sciences – the natural sciences and anatomy – and that mainly by virtue of its ancillary technique of illustration.'[83] The presses had already contributed extensively to the diffusion of more accurate classical texts – in many cases refined versions of works popular in the middle ages – and they furthered humanist scholarly aspirations. But printing as such enabled a more rational form of argumentation in that it enabled the reader to look forwards and backwards, to ponder and repeat. Not only is *thought* more widely diffused – it played an assessable role in the development of the Reformation[84] – its nature changes; it becomes less spontaneous, more the result of consideration, permitted by the ability to re-read as well as to read. The book itself encourages individualisation, for it becomes a private possession and necessitates solitariness for its perusal – a degree of social apartness; furthermore it involves the sequential, linear, and opens the way to a more thorough deployment of theoretical argument as points can be considered and answered no longer in the immediacy of the give and take of dialogue but in the opportunities afforded by what can symptomatically be described as 'turning over in the mind', as if the mind constituted a sort of inner space which could be explored at leisure. Thus the habit of withdrawal encouraged by the study of printed words in rooms (libraries) specially set apart for the purpose, together with the wider intellectual awareness implicit in the abstractions of 'things' – phenomena regarded in the light of certain of their qualities for the purpose of observing universally applicable laws – combined to stimulate theoretical speculation; without the psychic potentialities of print, neither science nor theory could have developed as they did.[85]

But, of course, the process was a long and involved one, accompanied by frequent echoes from an earlier world. Only in Rousseau's projected education of the pre-adolescent Emile do we find the new model in its purest form, when things assume a total tyranny instigated only in the most indirect way by the arrangements of the tutor. Until then we shall note a frequent amalgam of earlier and later characteristics.

Another way of identifying both the gain and the loss involved would be to suggest that, over a long period, the reorientation was from the attempt to encompass all aspects of a few men's experience – rational, behavioural, moral – to a concentration on a single aspect (the cognitive) of all men's; in the process, the cognitive assumed a vast extension of its powers. The development of mind, certainly initiated by the humanists, comes to take priority and ideally, at least, to seek its own autonomy. After all, the time arrives in the nineteenth century when even the classics were valued for their capacity to train the mind; and in the twentieth morality is not 'received' but arrived at through thought, ideally at least.

NOTES

1 H. Butterfield, *The Origin of Modern Science 1300-1800* (London, Bell, 1957), p. 179.
2 R. G. Collingwood, *The Idea of Nature* (London, Oxford University Press, 1965), p. 8.
3 ibid., p. 9.
4 cf. W. J. Brandt, *The Shape of Medieval History* (New York, Schocken Books, 1973), pp. 7-8.
5 ibid., p. 39.
6 E. A. Burtt, *The Metaphysical Foundations of Modern Science* (London, Routledge & Kegan Paul, 1925), p. 5.
7 Galileo, quoted Burtt, op. cit., p. 64.
8 ibid., p. 64.
9 ibid., p. 64.
10 Burtt, op. cit., pp. 70-1.
11 Galileo, quoted Burtt, op. cit., p. 73.
12 Burtt, op. cit., p. 81.
13 H. Haydn, *The Counter-Renaissance* (New York, Scribner, 1950), p. 85.
14 Quoted ibid., pp. 207-8.
15 Quoted ibid., p. 212.
16 Quoted ibid., p. 210.
17 Quoted ibid., pp. 142-3.
18 Christopher Hill, *Intellectual Origins of the English Revolution* (London, Panther, 1972), p. 6. No doubt Professor Hexter would argue that this was one of many such 'expansions' – cf. his essay 'The myth of the middle class in Tudor England' in *Reappraisals in History* (London, Longman, 1961). But this one seemed to be permanent.
19 Hill, op. cit., p. 6.
20 L. B. Wright, *Middle-Class Culture in Elizabethan England* (Chapel Hill, University of North Carolina Press, 1935), p. 655.
21 ibid., p. 43.
22 ibid., p. 63.
23 cf. pp. 185-6 below.
24 cf. Wright, op. cit., p. 169.
25 ibid., p. 598.
26 Hill, op. cit., p. 16.
27 cf. ibid., p. 25.
28 cf. ibid., pp. 73-4 – and below, p. 170.
29 Butterfield, op. cit., pp. 93-4.
30 The phrases are Bacon's – cf. below, p. 168.
31 J. V. Nef, *Cultural Foundations of Industrial Civilisation* (New York, Harper Torchbooks, 1960), p. 60.
32 ibid., p. 59.
33 ibid., pp. 60-1.
34 ibid., p. 64.
35 Not to be confused with primary and secondary *qualities*. It was out of attention to primary *qualities* that interest in second *causes* arose.
36 Hill, op. cit., pp. 180-1.
37 ibid., p. 198.
38 ibid., p. 203.
39 cf. p. 26 above.
40 For a description of the medieval cosmology cf. E. M. W. Tillyard, *The Elizabethan World Picture* (London, Chatto & Windus, 1943). Note, too, the reference to 'the historical fact that many – perhaps most – of those who effected the revolutionary changes in natural knowledge . . . were motivated by a deep conviction of the working of occult forces beyond the range of immediate sensation' (W. P. D. Wightman, *Science in a Renaissance Socetiy*, London, Hutchinson, 1972).

41 F. A. Yates, *Giordano Bruno and the Hermetic Tradition* (London, Routledge & Kegan Paul, 1964), p. 6. (In fact the writings dated probably from between AD 100 and 300 and were produced 'by various unknown authors, all probably Greeks', combining a number of philosophical elements, Greek, Jewish and possibly Persian.) The account that follows owes much to the work of Dr Frances Yates.

42 cf. ibid., p. 17.

43 ibid., p. 22.

44 ibid., p. 45.

45 ibid., p. 116.

46 ibid., p. 156.

47 R. J. W. Evans, *Rudolf II and his World* (London, Oxford University Press, 1973), pp. 176-7. The reference to 'pansophic strivings' should be noted for its relevance to the work of Comenius.

48 cf. ibid., p. 174.

49 A good exposition of the doctrine is to be found in E. H. Gombrich, *Symbolic Images* (London, Phaidon, 1972), especially in the chapter entitled 'Icones Symbolicae'.

50 Evans, op. cit., p. 196.

51 cf. ibid., p. 197. The wording is deliberately chosen to provide a foretaste of the Baconian formula which is explored in the next chapter.

52 ibid., p. 261.

53 ibid., p. 262; cf. the earlier discussion of the concept of imitation, pp. 30-1.

54 ibid., p. 263.

55 Quoted ibid., p. 264.

56 R. Tuve, *Elizabethan and Metaphysical Imagery* (Chicago, University of Chicago Press, 1947), pp. 36-7.

57 Evans, op. cit., p. 269.

58 F. A. Yates, *The Rosicrucian Enlightenment* (London, Routledge & Kegan Paul, 1972), pp. 12-13.

59 E. Cassirer, *The Individual and the Cosmos in Renaissance Philosophy*, trans. M. Domandi (New York, Harper Torchbooks, 1964), p. 148.

60 ibid., p. 154.

61 ibid., pp. 152-3.

62 ibid., pp. 154-5.

63 ibid., p. 155.

64 ibid., p. 156.

65 Quoted ibid., p. 156.

66 W. J. Ong, *Ramus, Method, and the Decay of Dialogue* (Cambridge, Mass., Harvard University Press, 1958), p. 107.

67 W. J. Ong, *The Barbarian Within* (New York, Macmillan, 1962), pp. 69-70.

68 W. J. Ong, *Rhetoric, Romance and Technology* (Ithaca, NY, Cornell University Press, 1971), p. 184.

69 Thus in his analysis of dialectic his tendency was to analyse the categories with dichotomised entities after this fashion:

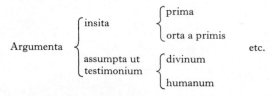

cf. Ong, *Ramus*, pp. 201-2. cf. use of in Bentham: *Chrestomathia*.

70 Ong, *Ramus*, p. 129.

71 cf., for instance, *Troilus and Cressida*.

72 N. W. Gilbert, *Renaissance Concepts of Method* (New York, Columbia University Press, 1963), p. 69.

73 Ong, *Rhetoric*, pp. 162–3.
74 Notably by Professor Kermode: cf. ch. 8 of *Romantic Image* (London, Routledge & Kegan Paul, 1961).
75 R. Hooykaas, *Humanisme, Science et Réforme* (Leyden, Brill, 1958), p. 22.
76 ibid., p. 24.
77 Quoted ibid., p. 26.
78 Ong, *Rhetoric*, p. 173.
79 ibid., p. 180.
80 ibid., p. 180.
81 cf. J. A. Comenius, *The Great Didactic*, ed. and trans. M. W. Keatinge (London, Black, 1896), ch. 32.
82 Ong, *Rhetoric*, p. 189.
83 L. Febvre and H.-J. Martin, *The Coming of the Book*, trans. D. Gerard (London, New Left Books, 1976), pp. 276–7.
84 cf. ibid., pp. 287–319.
85 I have written elsewhere on the implications of a print culture: cf. 'The implications of literacy' reprinted in *Education, Culture and the Emotions* (London, Faber, 1967). Print, of course, is a fundamental necessity for the development of modern schooling – as it is for the development of modern industrialisation. Furthermore, it constitutes a further indication of the developing stress on visualisation which comes to play so important a role in environmental appreciation advocated by Comenius and especially Rousseau through the observation of 'things'. Later theorists (e.g. Pestalozzi) advocate the 'object lesson'. (E. L. Eisenstein, *The Printing Press as an Agent of Change* (2 Vols. New York, Columbia University Press 1978) appeared too late for consideration; but the reader is advised to consult it.)

CHAPTER 8

'Knowledge is Power':
Francis Bacon

I

Bacon was not, of course, in the conventional sense, specifically an educational theorist; yet he was moved by a profound educational ideal, for he wished to change the fundamental orientation of man's attitude to knowledge. Furthermore he had a very great influence on subsequent educationists – stretching from Comenius and his circle in the seventeenth century to John Dewey in the twentieth. A consideration of Bacon's aims, then, of the revolution he charted as propagandist for the new scientific approach constitutes an essential element in the development of educational thought. He, too, proved to be a teacher of educators.

For many of the most sensitive minds of the age, the early seventeenth century was a period of confusion and uncertainty – those like Donne for whom new philosophy 'calls all in doubt'. Despite his personal disappointments, however – and they were severe – Bacon writes with a conviction which stems from a profound belief in man's potential for improvement and betterment. He believes in learning and knowledge – of a certain type. He believes in a method; his great 'instauration', for all its implication of renewal, places the stress on the new, the fresh start. His faith, for all his protestations, is in man and his future rather than in God and history. His frustrations spring from social circumstance, the blindness of his contemporaries, not from any doubts about a capacity to relieve man's estate through his innovations and discoveries. With him, a new sort of simplification receives its early promulgation.

In broad terms the humanists had thought of education, though directed to contemporary social ends, as assimilation into a tradition; hence their stress on imitation, their reliance on the 'commonplaces' or topics as source material, and their general orientation to the classics. Bacon's own writing reveals his debt to the humanist tradition – stylistically it has much in common with forms of rhetorical persuasiveness and his *Essays*, for instance, reveal a characteristic dependence on sentiments culled from the classics, deployed in ways reminiscent of rhetorical 'amplification'.

But he thought of education in terms of the assimilation of knowledge about the contemporary phenomenal world – the world of 'things' – intended to achieve specifically premeditated ends generically included in the notion of the 'relief of man's estate': 'man's estate' he considered in specific terms of ease, comfort, material welfare and bodily health, arising out of the ability first to comprehend and then control the new demythologised nature. With minor exceptions, he repudiated his predecessors, finding them not so much wrong as irrelevant. He was even scornful of Ramus, who was near to him in spirit. He sought Truth – and the benefits of Truth – in faithfulness to empirical fact derived from observation completed by induction.

Bacon's attitude to tradition is indeed to be symptomatic of the new breed of educationists. Frequently he inveighs against the barrenness of previous philosophising – scholastic, humanistic and astral-magical; its effect had been to foster contemplation rather than action and resignation to fate rather than the will to improve human conditions:

> its evasion of problems of experience and reality are reflected in three of its characteristic features: the substitution of verbal for real solutions; the ambition to evolve doctrines in the form of systems that will solve, once and for all, every problem and explain all natural phenomena; the confusion of divine with natural things and of religion with science. This conception of knowledge inevitably leads to sterility and although attempts have, in fact, been made to establish a 'union with things themselves' these have been unmethodical, fragmentary, and uncertain, so that the transition from verbal projects to their realisation has never been accomplished.[1]

In the first book of the *Advancement of Learning* Bacon identified the vices of contemporary culture: 'delicate learning', 'contentious learning' and 'phantastical learning'. He wanted men to see things with fresh eyes and to create understanding – a 'Natural and Experimental history, unencumbered with literature and book learning' – to repair the effects of the Fall. He was a representative of a detached and, to a degree transcending that of the humanists, autonomous mind, in the sense of its emancipation from traditional cultural norms and 'authority'.

The indictment of the schoolmen and of their 'delicate learning' is well known:

> Surely, like as many substances in nature which are solid do putrefy and corrupt into worms, so it is the property of good and sound knowledge to putrefy and dissolve into a number of subtile, idle, unwholesome, and (as I may term them) vermiculate questions, which have indeed a kind of quickness and life of spirit, but no soundness of matter or goodness of quality. This kind of degenerate learning did chiefly reign amongst the schoolmen; who having sharp and strong wits, and abundance of leisure, and small variety of reading; but their wits being shut up in the cells of a few authors (chiefly Aristotle their dictator) as their persons were shut up in the cells of monasteries and colleges; and knowing little history, either of nature or time; did out of no great quantity of matter, and infinite agitation of wit, spin out unto us those laborious webs of learning which are extant in their books. For the wit

and mind of man, if it work upon matter, which is the contemplation of the creatures of God, worketh according to the stuff, and is limited thereby; but if it work upon itself, as the spider worketh his web, then it is endless, and brings forth indeed cobwebs of learning, admirable for the fineness of thread and work, but of no substance or profit.[2]

The criticism of the humanists is almost as notorious: their eloquence was directed to effect, not matter:

the admiration of ancient authors, the hate of the schoolmen, the exact study of languages, and the efficacy of preaching, did bring in an affectionate study of eloquence and copie of speech, which then began to flourish. This grew speedily to an excess; for men began to hunt more after words than matter; and more after the choiceness of the phrase and the round and clear composition of the sentence, and the sweet falling of the clauses, and the varying and illustration of their works with tropes and figures, than after the weight of matter, worth of subject, soundness of argument, life of invention, or depth of judgement.[3]

The schoolmen were worse than the humanists, as 'vain matter is worse than vain words'. But worst of all were the vain imaginations of fantastical learning – the superstitions and miracles of ecclesiastical histories and the imaginings of astrologers, magicians and alchemists. However good their intentions – and Bacon praises their purposes, which were quasi-scientific – their results 'are full of error and vanity'.

In general, the faults of contemporary culture sprang from its too great dependence on authority, 'for disciples do owe unto masters only a temporary belief and a suspension of their own judgement until they be fully instructed, and not an absolute resignation or perpetual captivity'[4]; men, indeed, 'have withdrawn themselves too much from the contemplation of nature and the observations of experience, and have tumbled up and down in their own reason and conceits'.[5] They have above all mistaken the end of learning – which is not entertainment or adornment, a reputation or victory over adversaries in disputation, but 'to give a true account of their gift of reason, to the benefit and use of men . . .' and 'the relief of man's estate'.[6] Reason should no longer be conceived of as the means by which men sought to comprehend God's purpose immanent in the workings of divine nature through the reconciliation of various authoritative texts and precepts but a process by which knowledge, understanding and control could be achieved through the investigation by uncontaminated intellect of the new demythologised nature – demythologised in the sense that God's immanence had been removed even if His ultimate responsibility had not.

II

Now we begin to approach the grand design of Bacon's attempt to reorient the whole direction of contemporary culture. His aims are often interpreted exclusively in terms of utility and the extension of man's powers; but these are themselves dependent on a prior aim – the attainment of truth about the workings of the world as a necessary propaedeutic. As he says in the *New Organon*:[7]

> For I am building in the human understanding a true model of the world, such as it is in fact, not such as a man's own reason would have it to be; a thing which cannot be done without a very diligent dissection and anatomy of the world . . . Truth therefore and utility are here the very same things: and works themselves are of greater value as pledges of truth than as contributing to the comforts of life.[7]

This exalted the role of knowledge – 'For whatever deserves to exist deserves also to be known, for knowledge is the image of existence.'[8] And so, at first, his aim is for 'experiments of light, not for experiments of fruit; following therein . . . the example of the divine creation'.[9] The 'commandment of knowledge', indeed, is 'a commandment over the reason, belief, and understanding of man, which is the highest part of the mind, and giveth law to the will itself'.[10]

It is important, of course, to appreciate the precise terms in which this knowledge was conceived – no longer the knowledge of final but rather of secondary, efficient causes. Current metaphysical preoccupations failed to concern themselves with physical causes and hence failed to stimulate comprehension:

> For the handling of final causes mixed with the rest in physical inquiries, hath intercepted the severe and diligent inquiry of all real and physical causes, and given men the occasion to stay upon these satisfactory and specious causes, to the great arrest and prejudice of further discovery . . . For to say that *the hairs of the eye-lids are for a quickset and fence about the sight* . . . or that *the leaves of trees are for protecting of the fruit*; or that *the clouds are for watering of the earth* . . . and the like, is well enquired and collected in Metaphysics; but in Physic they are impertinent. Nay, they are indeed but remoras and hinderances to stay and slug the ship from further sailing, and have brought this to pass, that the search of the Physical causes hath been neglected and passed in silence.[11]

Bacon is careful to urge that such concern for physical causes does not derogate from divine providence but 'highly confirms and exalts it'. He insists on the compatibility of what he proposes with religion. Whereas a little or superficial knowledge may incline a man to atheism, 'a farther proceeding therein doth bring the mind back again to religion; . . . when a man . . . seeth the dependence of causes and the works of Providence; then . . . he will easily believe that the highest link of nature's chain must needs be tied to the foot of Jupiter's chair'.[12] God, indeed, works by second causes and it is essentially the God-given universe that is being investigated. Bacon's religious affirmation was at least firm enough to make him acceptable to the Puritans; ostensibly, at least, he shared their millenarian aspirations. He saw, too, in scientific power the redemption of mankind and its reinstatement in its pre-lapsarian hegemony over all created things.[13]

Yet his emphasis is on 'The improvement of man's mind and the improvement of his lot' as 'one and the same thing';[14]; and one has the suspicion that Dr Basil Willey is not far out when he urges that Bacon wished to free natural knowledge from any imputation of being forbidden or esoteric and that his prayer that 'things human may not interfere with things divine' (so allowing us to 'give to faith that which is faith's'[15]) was perhaps urged in the interest of science rather than of faith. Certainly the burden of his insistence is on the newly acquired knowledge as Power, for the relief of man's estate, and the benefit and use of life: 'Now the true and lawful goal of the sciences is none other than this: that human life be endowed with new discoveries and powers.'[16] In a period marked by a sense of breakdown and melancholy he continually stresses the human potential of the new understanding: he insists 'that there is hope enough and to spare, not only to make a bold man try, but also to make a sober-minded and wise man believe'.[17]

Thus Bacon fostered a new approach, above all, a new method. He was one of the first great advocates of the fresh start: 'There remains but one course for the recovery of a sound and healthy condition – namely, that the entire work of the understanding be commenced afresh, and the mind itself be from the outset not left to take its own course, but guided at every step; *and the business be done as if by machinery*' (my italics).[18] The final clause has its implications for the new method; but, for the moment, to pursue his emphasis on novelty, he urges: 'We must begin anew from the very foundations',[19] 'my object being to open a new way for the understanding'.[20] He was prepared to make any use of the old (humanist) ways which wouldn't challenge the revised premises from which he worked – they might serve for 'conversation', assist in marshalling arguments and the presentation of new knowledge: but in his analysis of the two approaches, his emphasis was on the 'new and certain paths for the mind to proceed in' in the 'Interpretation of Nature'.

The 'new path' was, in the first place, an Art, in the sense of a method of procedure, directed to a specifically premeditated end, and based on understanding. In criticising the induction of the logicians he blames them for having 'wronged, abused and traduced nature'; instead he urges that 'it is the duty of Art to perfect and exalt Nature'.[21] In saying this he uses the language of the older world. But his procedure was very different – as was his conception of 'nature'.

The characteristics of the Art are revealed in a brief consideration of the shortcomings of a former way of Knowledge and of its instrument, the syllogism: 'The syllogism consists of propositions, propositions consist of words, words are symbols of notions. Therefore if the notions themselves (which is the root of the matter) are confused and over-hastily abstracted from the facts, there can be no firmness in the superstructure. Our only hope therefore lies in a true induction.'[22] *Words* are untrustworthy. Instead, is needed 'the commerce of the mind with *Things*'. I have italicised the two key words because they constitute the burden of a refrain which occurs with monotonous regularity during the whole of the seventeenth and later centuries: 'Things not words' became a major – perhaps the major – cliché of advanced educational thinking for a long time to come.

'Things', of course, were 'particulars'; it was a major indictment of the schoolmen that they 'hastened to their *theories* and *dogmaticals*, and were imperious and scornful towards particulars'.[23] 'One method of delivery alone remains to us; . . . we must lead men to the particulars themselves, and their series and order; while men on their side must force themselves for awhile to lay their notions by and begin to familiarise themselves with facts'.[24]

The link with the mechanical arts, briefly touched on above, is no longer surprising, for these provide precisely the sort of 'particulars', 'facts' that Bacon is concerned about. His world is a technician's delight. Others had already noted a link between technical and scientific advance – notably Agricola in his defence of the art of metallurgy, when he urged that technical and scientific work were inseparable.[25] But Bacon emphasised it constantly. He projected in *The Great Instauration* a natural history which was to include 'much more of nature under constraint and vexed; that is to say, when by art and the hand of man she is forced out of her natural state and squeezed and moulded. Therefore I set down at length all experiments of the mechanical arts . . . [for] the nature of things betrays itself more readily under the vexations of art than in its natural freedom.'[26] Some mechanical arts thrive (albeit a trifle haphazardly) whereas the general understanding of the world has stood still and had done so for nearly 2000 years. 'The remedy for this was to bring learning into relation with industry and invention. His idea was not to discard the wisdom of the learned but to reform it.'[27] He did realise that not all technical developments were necessarily beneficial. Printing, gunpowder and magnetism had transformed human life – yet could be put to bad uses.[28] Normally, however, he sees the technical arts as contributing to the relief of man's estate – and as revealing the real behaviour of nature: 'the history of the arts is of most use . . . It takes off the mask and veil from natural objects. As Proteus did not go through his changes till he was seized and handcuffed, so under the constraint of arts nature puts forth his ultimate efforts and strivings.'[29]

The notion that nature must, to yield up her secrets, be vexed and tortured indicates the curiously ambivalent attitude Bacon took up towards this new objective universe, of which man was simultaneously servant and master. 'Nature to be commanded must be obeyed',[30] for to understand and control nature man must submit to her. His own contribution in advancing knowledge, he says, has been achieved by 'submitting [my] mind to Things'[31] – his personal experience and observation have replaced the authority of books or learned men. In this way paradoxically has been achieved a 'victory of art over nature'.[32] Professor Farrington expresses the essence of the new approach and defines its difference from contemporary Aristotelianism:

Aristotle, in his *History of Animals*, had written very good natural history. His logic was most helpful for the building up of the classificatory sciences for which it was designed. But Bacon wanted to restore to man dominion over nature, to enable him to control and alter and improve on nature, and here Aristotle did not help. It was Bacon's great intuition that in order to effect this purpose the description and classification of nature as she exists free and unconfined should be supplemented by the description and analysis of nature as she has been vexed, imprisoned, bullied, forced, violently interfered with, or in any way affected, by the activity of man . . . The contrast between what he calls *natura libera* and *natura vexata* is fundamental in his thought.

Let us put this in another way. The raw material for the contemplative science of Aristotle could be gathered by the contemplation of nature. The raw material for the active philosophy of Bacon could be gathered only from the examination of man's action on nature. An industrial history in the broadest sense must be the basis for a fresh advance in industry. A scientific industry must be based on the study of man's earlier and less scientific efforts to subdue nature to his own ends. Aristotle's logic was an aid to thinking; its goal was logical consistency. Bacon's logic was a guide to action; its test was whether it worked.[33]

And so 'the relation between man and nature is thought of in a new way';[34] and the life of man has been transformed – by, as just noted, such technologies as those of 'printing, gunpowder and the magnet'. Bacon says that 'no empire, no sect, no star seems to have exerted greater power and influence in human affairs than these mechanical discoveries'.[35] We have reached a period when art can 'change, transmute and fundamentally alter nature'.[36] The dream of the Renaissance – 'to create a second nature' – is about to be fulfilled, in terms, however, different from those anticipated. What is involved is no longer a revelation – of the Intelligible, for instance, after the manner of the neo-Platonists – but a positive manipulation of natural objects to serve human ends.[37]

III

How was it to be done? What was this marvellous new Method of Art which was to transform mankind? Not, as we have seen, by means of the syllogism nor by means of the art of discourse. Instead, by induction which implied dwelling 'duly and orderly' among particulars and rising 'by gradual steps' to achieve understanding rather than floundering amidst 'abstract and useless generalities' achieved as a result of just glancing at 'experiment and particulars in passing'.[38]

It has sometimes been argued that Bacon's doctrine of induction was concerned only with experience, observation of particulars and proceeded simply by collecting examples. This is not altogether true; Bacon appreciated the need for a conceptual scheme within which the chaos of experience could be duly ordered and arranged:

There remains simple experience; which, if taken as it comes, is called accident; if sought for, experiment. But this kind of experience is no better than a broom without its band, as the saying is; – a mere groping, as of men in the dark, that feel all round them for the chance of finding their way; when they had much better wait for daylight, or light a candle, and then go. But the true method of experience on the contrary first lights the candle, and then by means of the candle shows the way; commencing as it does with experience duly ordered and digested, not bungling or erratic, and from it educing axioms, and from established axioms again new experiments; even as it was not without order and method that the divine word operated on the created mass.[39]

A slow and patient process of gathering particulars under headings of increasing generality was needed; by 'a just scale of ascent . . .'

we rise from particulars to lesser axioms; and then to middle axioms, one above the other; and last of all to the most general. For the lowest axioms differ but slightly from bare experience, while the highest and most general (which we have now) are notional and abstract and without solidity: But the middle are the true and solid and living axioms, on which depend the affairs and fortunes of men.[40]

Such axioms limit the abstractness of the most general axioms.

Dr Hill considers that 'Bacon's scientific method is the trial and error of the craftsmen raised to a principle'[41] – but in fact it was more than this, for 'trial and error' omits the fundamental concept of an ordering method, of a formative power, though one strictly subservient to the behaviour it sought to interpret. In this respect scientific and technical arts differed from renaissance artifice, where the formative power was derived from a metaphysical preconception and revealed not an empirical but an orientation fundamentally evaluative. In effect, Bacon attempted to establish 'a true and lawful marriage between the empirical and the rational faculty'. We need to recall his notion, quoted above, that 'the business be done as if by machinery' – and by 'machinery' Bacon intended the work of the 'rational faculty' (aided possibly by instruments) and proceeding according to a prescribed method:

Neither the naked hand nor the understanding left to itself can effect much. It is by instruments and helps that the work is done, which are as much wanted for the understanding as for the hand. And as the instruments of the hand either give motion or guide it, so the instruments of the mind supply either suggestions for the understanding or cautions.[42]

The procedure is clarified in his rejection both of the men of experiment and those of dogmas:

Those who have handled sciences have been either men of experiment or men of dogmas. The men of experiment are like the ant; they only collect and use: the reasoners resemble spiders, who make cobwebs out of their own substance. But the bee takes a middle course, it gathers its material from the flowers of the garden and of the field, but transforms and digests it by a power of its own. Not unlike this is the true business of philosophy; for it neither relies solely or chiefly on the powers of the mind, nor does it take the matter which it gathers from natural history and mechanical experiments and lay it up in the memory whole, as it finds it; but lays it up in the understanding altered and digested. Therefore from a closer and purer league between these two faculties, the experimental and the rational, (such as has never yet been made) much may be hoped.[43]

And so 'another form of induction must be devised', avoiding the 'childishness' of simple enumeration; this new focus will ensure 'that we may not either stick fast in things already known, or loosely grasp at shadows and abstract forms; but at things solid and realised in matter'.[44]

Important psychological factors, however, could interfere with this true attempt to see nature as it was; and one of Bacon's greatest contributions to knowledge lay in his analysis of those features which could prevent man from confronting nature in all its nakedness and apprehending the truth about the world – the Idols: the Idols of the Tribe which 'have their foundation in human nature itself', for 'the human understanding is like a false mirror, which, receiving rays irregularly, distorts and discolours the nature of things by mingling its own nature with it';[45] the Idols of the Cave, which are those of the individual man: 'For every one . . . has a cave or den of his own, which refracts and discolours the light of nature; owing either to his own proper and peculiar nature; or to his education and conversation with others; or to the reading of books, and the authority of those whom he esteems and admires; or to the differences of impressions . . .';[46] the idols of the Marketplace, formed from the associations of men with each other and especially from the distorting power of their common language, for 'the ill and unfit choice of words wonderfully obstructs the understanding'; finally, the Idols of the Theatre, falsities imported by various 'dogmas of philosophies and also from wrong laws of demonstration'.[47] He sums up: 'because in my judgement all the received systems are but so many stage-plays, representing worlds of their own creation after an unreal and scenic fashion'.[48] By implication Bacon raises an issue, which is to exercise philosophers during the next three and a half centuries, concerning the nature and status of knowledge, the problems of epistemology. Now that the attention has been shifted from the revealed or the historical to the 'real', the nature of that reality and the problems involved in coming to understand it move to the centre of the philosophic stage. Bacon's analysis constitutes an important development in the elucidation of the difficulties inherent in understanding the precise relationship of mind and world – and may indeed be said to have contributed, in the long run, to modern relativistic theories of understanding and knowledge. Knowledge is not something received into the hearts of men by intuition or revelation but something to be attained and built up with due regard to precisely those distorting elements of mind Bacon enumerates: 'truth is to be sought for not in the felicity of any age, which is an unstable thing, but in the light of nature and experience, which is eternal'.[49]

Thus, Bacon blamed the mind and its distorting powers for mistaken understanding; instead, he considered that his new inductive method 'leaves but little to the acuteness and strength of wits, but places all wits and understandings nearly on a level',[50] so that 'the entrance into the kingdom of man, founded on the sciences, being not much other than the entrance into the kingdom of heaven, whereinto none may enter except as a little child'.[51] He conceives of himself as having 'purged and swept and levelled the floor of the mind'.[52] Certainly he prepared the way for later explorations of the nature and scope of the understanding.

Professor Farrington does not consider that Bacon intended to suggest that any fool could be a scientist – indeed, the *New Atlantis* makes it apparent that they were to be men of superior understanding and character: but Bacon saw 'the contribution of knowledge that could be made by men of average ability once science had been set upon the right track'.[53] Dr Hill accepts this as a 'noble and all-embracing programme of co-operative action, in which the humblest craftsman had a part to play'.[54] And certainly the implications of 'machinery' quoted above[55] and Bacon's insistence that 'My way of discovering sciences goes far to level men's wits; and leaves but little to individual excellence, because it performs everything by the surest rules and demonstrations'[56] has played its part in that mythology of science which represents it as by nature open, democratic and indeed egalitarian.[57] Thus Dr Hill himself comments:

> Copernicus's theory had 'democratized the universe' by shattering the hierarchical structure of the heavens; Harvey 'democratized' the human body by dethroning the heart . . . The new experimental philosophy . . . made all men equal, as Hobbes was soon to proclaim. One researcher was as good as another, and better than any mere speculative scholar. Every man could be his own expert. In just the same way the radicals used the Protestant doctrine of the priesthood of all believers to justify preaching by laymen, and not merely by university-trained specialists. Bacon was in favour of careers open to the talents, recommending to the youthful Sir George Villiers 'that which I think was never done since I was born . . . which is that you countenance and encourage and advance able men, in all kinds, degrees, and professions'.[58]

Bacon's method, indeed, as has been made clear, implied personal experience and observation rather than the authority of past authors and was in line with the Puritan search for first-hand religious experience rather than reliance on traditional rites. The radical implications – the association with Puritanism, the notion that men's wits are levelled and the idea that 'experience' (as defined in terms of its behavioural characteristics) constitutes an equality of phenomena, each, as expressed within the confines of an hypothesis, to be accepted on equal terms – have undoubted social and political implications for the coming centuries. Renaissance art – here painting is intended – was by nature hierarchical in that the 'reality' it depicted was a metaphysical, divinely derived 'reality' implying value discrimination: so that the phenomenal world within the frame of the picture was rearranged to depict a 'significant' form or an 'idealised' experience (revealing, however, that value *potential* which is the *reality* of human behaviour); science not only is seen to level men's wits but categorises its phenomena ('experience') in terms of the equal significance of individual events and therefore contains (as Dr Hill correctly points out) a 'democratic' (he might have added 'egalitarian') dimension. Thus Bacon's stance involves a fundamental reorientation in man's approach to the world and its particulars. The 'form' of renaissance pictorial art involved value discrimination, that of science uniformity.

Now Bacon conceived of his method as applying to human as well as physical behaviour:

It may also be asked . . . whether I speak of natural philosophy only, or whether I mean that the other sciences, logic, ethics and politics, should be carried on by this method. Now I certainly mean what I have said to be understood of them all; and as the common logic, which governs by the syllogism, extends not only to natural but to all sciences; so does mine also, which proceeds by induction, embrace everything.[59]

This again implied the experiential equality of human behaviour to make it susceptible to generalisation through induction. Thus his 'democratic appeal was an essential part of the Baconian optimism',[60] considers Dr Hill. In view of Bacon's symptomatic importance for this process of levelling and its significance for education it is desirable to examine the nature of his sensibility a little more closely.

IV

There were limits to his 'egalitarian' sympathies. Certain sorts of primitivism are not to be laid at his door:

Again, let a man only consider what a difference there is between the life of men in the most civilised province of Europe, and in the wildest and most barbarous districts of New India; he will feel it to be great enough to justify the saying that 'man is a god to man', not only in regard of aid and benefit, but also by comparison of condition. And this difference comes not from soil, not from climate, not from race, but from the arts.[61]

We must give credit to Bacon for not tolerating certain types of reductionism. He does see that 'arts' – by which he implies a human formative power and artifice – necessitates a degree of civilisation even if his interpretation of these arts induces a levelling of human aspirations and wits.

Yet the monotonal nature of his sense of 'arts' implies a deep and disturbing restriction of viewpoint. Leonardo had seen that, in his terminology, both the creative 'arts' (i.e. in his case painting) and the sciences constituted attempts to define the nature of reality. For this complex approach Bacon substitutes a single way ('method') of defining reality. For the creative 'arts' he has limited respect. His words on poetry are notorious and they convey the essence of his limitation of viewpoint: they are worth quoting at length:

Poesy is a part of learning in measure of words for the most part restrained, but in all other points extremely licensed, and doth truly refer to the Imagination; which, being not tied to the laws of matter, may at pleasure join that which nature hath severed, and sever that which nature hath joined, and so make unlawful matches and divorces of things; *Pictoribus atque poetis*, etc. (Painters and Poets have always been allowed to take what liberties they would.) It is taken in two senses, in respect of words or matter. In the first sense it is but a character of style, and belongeth to arts of speech, and is not pertinent for the present. In the later, it is (as hath been said) one of the principal portions of learning, and is nothing else but Feigned History, which may be styled as well in prose as in verse.

The use of this Feigned History hath been to give some shadow of satisfaction to the mind of man in those points wherein the nature of things doth deny it; the world being in proportion inferior to the soul; by reason whereof there is agreeable to the spirit of man a more ample greatness, a more exact goodness, and a more absolute variety, than can be found in the nature of things. Therefore, because the acts or events of true history have not that magnitude which satisfieth the mind of man, poesy feigneth acts and events greater and more heroical; . . . And therefore it was ever thought to have some participation of divineness, because it doth raise and erect the mind, by submitting the shews of things to the desires of the mind; whereas reason doth buckle and bow the mind unto the nature of things. And we see that by these insinuations and congruities with man's nature and pleasure, joined also with the agreement and consort it hath with music, it hath had access and estimation in rude times and barbarous regions, where other learning stood excluded.[62]

What is essential to this indictment – for this to some extent is what it is in its association with 'rude times' – is the stress on poetry's subjectivity – a source of enlightenment which, to Bacon, must seem inferior to that 'reason' which 'doth buckle and bow the mind unto the nature of things'; his view of the imagination equates it with fantasy rather than with the ability to penetrate into the 'real' world; and he concludes his analysis, after allowing 'poesy' virtue in the expression of 'affections, passions, corruptions and customs', with the implied dismissal: 'But it is not good to stay too long in the theatre.'[63] By quitting the 'theatre' we may be said, symbolically, to be leaving the Renaissance.

So though it would be unjust to say that Bacon has no use for poetry, such use as remains to it is as a supplement to, almost compensation for, 'reason', which now takes the centre of the stage – 'reason' interpreted as investigating the nature of 'things' through the agency of general axioms, at once the servant and manager of nature, working for the relief of man's estate and the discovery of Truth in the terms in which increasingly the seventeenth century was to conceive of it in relation to the behaviour of material particles. To clarify the situation, let me compare how Bacon and a seventeenth-century poet treat of the same theme; the difference in sensibility implied by Bacon's attitude may then become more apparent.

Both Marvell and Bacon write on gardens. Bacon sees his garden[64] as a means of 'vexing' nature to serve his own ends. He provides a handyman's do-it-yourself guide to garden planning. He admits it provides 'the purest of human pleasures' and the 'greatest refreshment to the spirits of man', but he is so busy telling us how to plan one, its size, how it should be ordered, what plants are suitable for what seasons, the role of hedges, fountains – and the like – that we have little time for enjoyment.

Compare his approach to that of Andrew Marvell, to whom the garden is a symbol in terms of which fundamental human problems of retreat, indeed escape, and commitment are worked out. The reason why I have chosen to make this comparison is that it enables us to see at work a very different level of mind from that of Bacon and a very different experiential conception of a garden. Marvell is capable of irony and ambivalence, of seeing at once the charms and delight of the garden and yet bearing in mind always the claims and pressures of society: the ambiguity comes out in the lines

> Society is all but rude
> To this delicious solitude

The mention of the 'industrious bee' and the sense of time passing, the soul preparing 'for longer flight', all introduce elements into the poem which make it, in a final analysis, only equivocally definable as one of retreat. Bacon's busyness is, by implication, glanced at in the 'incessant labours of men' who 'vainly . . . themselves amaze'; Marvell calls into question such single-minded, almost naïve obsession with ordering and arranging and yet simultaneously admits by implication the claims of the larger world, of time and eternity. He sees the ironies of busyness, but he also admits its importance. The finer, more complex, subtler response is that of Marvell; and a dash of his scepticism, his awareness of other values than those of industriousness and officiousness, might have introduced a note of realism into Bacon's optimism. It might have made him less effective as a propagandist – but then propaganda is nearly always based on naïve assumptions and premises.

Bacon, indeed, suffers from the obsessive view of all reformers – their inability to manifest any form of self-criticism, their failure to appreciate any conceivable irony of events which might falsify their predictions. The development of science and technology has conferred immense benefits on mankind – who would be foolish enough to deny them? But for all developments a price has to be paid – and Bacon gives no indication that he is capable even of conceiving of such a price. The Greek attempt, followed largely in medieval and renaissance times, to adjust man to nature, gained metaphysical security and a sense of 'natural' values at the expense of material and medical advances; for Aristotle nature could only be contemplated and classified; no change through knowledge of forms could be effected in a natural body; in any case, contemplative knowledge was superior to practical. It was the aim of Bacon to adjust nature to man by a twin process of sub-servience and 'vexation'. The idea of simple enjoyment – such as forms one strand in Marvell's poem – is foreign to the Great Instaurator, as were these words of Marvell: 'For men may spare their pains when Nature is at work, and the world will not go the faster for our driving.'[65] The poem does not contain a plea for inactivity – but for an activity which, by assessing the trend of events, is content to play a positive but not officious role. Bacon may submit to nature – but only the better to master her; Marvell intuitively realises that natural processes must have their way in certain circumstances. He steers a middle course, sustained by a sense of irony, between the officious-ness of Bacon and the false simplicity of Montaigne, realising both the positive contribution and the limitation of what is 'given' in nature.

V

So if the threat of the humanists' 'Words' was that of a camouflage for hidden motives; that of the scientists' 'Things' is a dehumanised officiousness and Newton's 'single vision'. Bacon gives us an insight into his brave new world (an appropriate designation though he would conceivably not have relished the irony of Huxley's title) in his Utopian fragment, *New Atlantis*. Here is an exposition of the 'arts' by which Bacon hopes to improve on the new objective nature. Here is to be found the 'freedom and humanity' of the ideal state, with its pious customs and the erection and institution of an 'Order or Society which we call Solomon's House: the noblest foundation (as we think) that ever was upon earth; and the lanthorn of this kingdom. It is dedicated to the study of the Works and Creatures of God.'[66] From this state there set forth every twelve years two ships containing Brethren of the House who would search out new 'sciences, arts, manufactures, and inventions of all the world.' In the description of the 'true state of Solomon's House' Bacon realises his dream of a new scientific Utopia – its mechanical arts, its medical advances and its concern for a sort of truth: 'We do hate all impostures and lies: insomuch as we have severely forbidden it to all our fellows, under pain of ignomiy and fines, that they do not show any natural work or thing, adorned as jewellery; but only pure as it is, and without all affectation of strangeness.'[67]

In an interesting comparison between More's *Utopia* and Bacon's *New Atlantis* Dr R. P. Adams[68] contrasts the austerity of the Utopians with the comparative self-indulgence of the inhabitants of the *New Atlantis*: he asserts that in the latter 'the boldest emphasis is laid on the idea that the main purpose of applied science is to bring forth endless, ever-increasing torrents of usable inventions and luxuries or "fruits" . . . we find . . . a notably early appearance of man considered . . . as a "consumer" – as a sort of belly capable of almost infinite distention . . . men's vulgar wants are becoming insatiable . . .' The hatred of lies and adornments indicated as characterising the inhabitants of *New Atlantis* perhaps affords some small measure of caution in accepting Dr Adams's indictment in its entirety; but it is difficult not to agree with his condemnation of Bacon's naïvety on the ground of its failure to afford adequate expression of and protection against human irrationality, and the abuse of power. Bacon seems to have given little consideration to possible abuses in the highly privileged position of the College, which was to decide which of its inventions were to be publicised. And Dr Adams proceeds to quote from Professor Douglas Bush's indictment of Bacon's attitude in his *English Literature in the Earlier 17th Century*:

His separation of the realms of knowledge and faith, and of external and internal morality, was all the more damaging for not being cynical . . . But the whole drift of his scientific and ethical thought was towards empirical, irreligious naturalism . . . To machinery and material progress he sacrificed, in a large and noble way, to be sure, that scale of spiritual and ethical values which the best minds of antiquity, the Middle Ages, and the Renaissance had striven to make prevail.[69]

Clearly there is much to commend in Bacon's attitude: but in its simple and single-mindedness it constitutes both a promise and a *threat* for the future, in ways which its author did not seem able to conceive. And this is not to be put down solely to the naïveties of his times as there were those who, like Jean Bodin, saw sinister possibilities[70] – they were the lacunae of a particular sort of mind, one destined to play a larger role in our affairs with the centuries.

Let Bacon's epitaph be some words by Halifax in his Letter to a Dissenter:

You act very unskilfully against your visible interest, if you throw away the advantages, of which you can hardly fail in the next probable revolution. Things tend naturally to what you would have, if you would let them alone, and not by an unseasonable activity lose the influences of your good star, which promiseth you everything that is prosperous.[71]

Science might have been the wiser to have proceeded piecemeal, out of the particulars of research, rather than under the aegis of an optimistic and often naïve philosophy which paradoxically ignored individual consequences and placed too great a faith in human reasonableness.

For Bacon was very influential; as Dr Charles Webster points out in his recent book, which takes its title from Bacon, *The Great Instauration*:

the vocabulary of Bacon had been assimilated into the millenarian ideology; his philosophical programme, the *Instauratio Magna*, came to be regarded by Beale's generation as the authentic guide to intellectual

regeneration. Accordingly the fragmentary philosophical system be-
queathed by Bacon became for puritan intellectuals both the basis for
their conception of philosophical progress and the framework for their
utopian social planning.[72]

In one way or another he 'educated' subsequent educational theorists both
in the content and methodology (or 'art') of their prescriptions. His views
ushered in a new form of 'art' – still in part a making, but also a submission
to the circumstances of the case (as 'evidence'), in the interests of a view of
truth geared to 'stubborn and irreducible facts' and not to a revelation or any
awareness of value potential within the object of contemplation.

The new position regarding artifice and nature can indeed be summarised
as follows: 'Artifice' as the highest manifestation of renaissance educational
aspiration implied the creation of a being marked by such ease of accomplishment in a wide variety of fields, physical and broadly cultural, that he success-
fully concealed entirely the effort that had gone into his production. In this
way he realised the 'natural' potentialities of his human kind, for man was
part of a wider natural whole, teleologically inclined to the production of his
'best' nature. To be 'natural', therefore, was to be artificially highly wrought,
to achieve the highest values of which man was capable, so that the artifice
itself was entirely hidden. In this way, the courtier achieved the highest
manifestation of his potential. (That man might quarrel as to what precisely
manifested the 'highest' is irrelevant to my argument – what matters is that
they consciously or unconsciously recognised or bore witness to value
discriminations.)

In this Baconian universe artifice was the activity of a mind detached from
nature, observing its behaviour, positing general explanatory theories which
if true would enable man to control phenomena to his own ease and benefit.
His highest aim became not to achieve grace as a manifestation of his ultimate
potential so much as truth concerning efficient causes with a view to mastery
and control, not a Platonic vision of the intelligible and divine but ease and
comfort of living. In this view nature became a neutral external phenomenon
governed by inexorable laws from which God was transcendent only as First
Mover – though initially great stress was laid on the revelatory aspect of the
new knowledge and its confirmation of divine intervention. The 'real' world
was constituted by this matter in motion and many aspects of traditional
culture came to be accepted only as playthings and 'toys', for conversation
and the refinements of exposition, but of no real depth of substance. The
'real' man was a harbinger of economic and technological man, the producer,
who secured health and plenty by vexing and controlling nature for his own
premeditated ends. The man of ease and grace has vanished from our midst –
but the production of technological man could be said to have become an
overriding concern. The former was a total being, for grace was to inform
both mind and body, cultural pursuits and social behaviour. The latter
results almost exclusively from cognition, a mind trained in a certain tradition
of rational appraisal torn between an autonomous detachment from traditional
culture and a pressure to egalitarian conformity implicit in the mythology of

science. It is to his fuller exploration that the subsequent chapters will be largely devoted. His virtue will be in his concern for truth to fact.

There is one further point. Renaissance culture is embedded in the 'creative' arts (in the traditional sense of literature, painting, etc.) and its educational theorising needs to be seen in relation to developments in these fields; ontologically man continued to operate within a largely medieval framework. Scientific, technical culture regards these arts as of secondary importance but raises fundamental epistemological questions regarding the nature and status of claims to knowledge – attention shifts from the arts to philosophy. This must to some extent be reflected in subsequent exposition.

At the same time, the transition occupied a prolonged period stretching from the sixteenth to the nineteenth century. Comenius, for instance, as we shall see, reveals features which point both backwards and forwards – his view of nature, for instance, contains elements that are both medieval and 'modern'.

NOTES

1 P. Rossi, *Francis Bacon: From Magic to Science*, trans. S. Rabinovitch (London, Routledge & Kegan Paul, 1968), p. 44. Yet Bacon was sufficiently child of his age to need some support from the past – in this case a past more remote than that of the humanists' classical antiquity. For in this remote past of the pre-Socratic philosophers he sensed a greater awareness of reality than was to be found in the philosophies of Plato and Aristotle. Again, he accepted the allegorical tradition – the significance of fables, parables and the like which formed so vital a part of contemporary and earlier culture. Scholars have been puzzled why Bacon presented his reforms under the guise of a 'restauration'; in fact Bacon believed that, before the time of Hesiod and Homer, man, as yet untouched by Aristotelian intellectualism and the sterility of Greek philosophy, had partially redeemed his sins which stemmed from the Fall and had recovered some of his original power over nature by the practice of true arts. Greek philosophy had perpetuated Adam's sin of pride and 'with it man fell a second time from power over all creation' (cf. Rossi, op. cit., p. 55). Indeed, in early classical myths he saw a reflection of his new philosophy.
2 M. T. McClure (ed.), *Bacon: Selections* (London, Scribner, 1928), p. 68.
3 ibid., p. 66. At the same time, it should be stressed that not all the early scientists were Protestants – there were a number of Catholics among them.
4 ibid., p. 74.
5 ibid., p. 77. Reason here implies that implicit in scholastic practices – 'authority' and logic.
6 ibid., p. 79. Reason here implies that implicit in scientific and technical understanding.
7 ibid., pp. 365–6 – again scholastic 'reason' is implied.
8 ibid., p. 360. 'Knowledge' is no longer derived from authority but 'experience' of the world.
9 ibid., p. 361.
10 ibid., p. 361.
11 ibid., pp. 140–1.
12 ibid., pp. 45–6.
13 Thus much was made of an early fragment of Bacon's writing 'Valerius Terminus of the Interpretation of Nature' in which he faced the dilemma of the Puritan intellectual challenged by the need to justify the pursuit of knowledge when it was the search for knowledge that had led to the Fall. Bacon concluded that

investigation into nature with utilitarian ends in mind helped to glorify God. Moses and Solomon had provided precedents for these procedures and were regarded by him as inspirations for later times. Indeed, 'God appeared to have sanctioned the rise of experimental science by a special prophecy' (cf. C. Webster, *The Great Instauration*, London, Duckworth, 1975, pp. 22–4).

14 Quoted B. Farrington, *Francis Bacon: Philosopher of Industrial Science* (London, Macmillan, 1973), p. 98.
15 Bacon, *Selections*, p. 15.
16 ibid., p. 323.
17 ibid., p. 355.
18 ibid., p. 273.
19 ibid., p. 286.
20 ibid., p. 274.
21 ibid., p. 173.
22 ibid., p. 282.
23 ibid., p. 174.
24 ibid., p. 287.
25 cf. Rossi, op. cit., pp. 5–6.
26 Bacon, *Selections*, pp. 27–8.
27 Farrington, op. cit., p. 44.
28 cf., ibid., p. 79. A much more usual theme and one in line with Bacon's general optimism occurs in the *Novum Organum*: in answer to arguments that arts and science may be used for wicked purposes he replies: 'Only let the human race recover the right over nature which belongs to it by divine bequest, and let power be given it; the exercise thereof will be governed by sound reason and true religion' (*Bacon*, p. 272).
29 Quoted ibid., p. 136.
30 Bacon, *Selections*, p. 280.
31 ibid., p. 354.
32 ibid., p. 358.
33 Farrington, op. cit., p. 94.
34 ibid., p. 98.
35 Bacon, *Selections*, p. 371.
36 Quoted Farrington, op. cit., p. 95.
37 The 'second nature' of the Renaissance implied the revelation of the potential implicit in the mythologised nature of the pre-scientific era through man's artistic grasp, ultimately, of the transcendental, the intelligible, beyond the grasp of sense; that of the post-scientific era, the workings of the new neutralised nature, is revealed through observation and experiment and exploited for technical purposes.
38 Bacon, *Selections*, p. 284.
39 ibid., pp. 325–6.
40 ibid., p. 347.
41 C. Hill, *Intellectual Origins of the English Revolution* (London, Panther, 1972), p. 110.
42 Bacon, *Selections*, p. 279.
43 ibid., p. 341.
44 ibid., pp. 348–9.
45 ibid., pp. 288–9.
46 ibid., pp. 289–90.
47 ibid., p. 290.
48 ibid., p. 296.
49 ibid., p. 296.
50 ibid., p. 300.
51 ibid., pp. 309–10.
52 ibid., p. 356.
53 Farrington, op. cit., p. 118.
54 Hill, *Intellectual Origins*, p. 88.

55 cf. above, p. 169.

56 Quoted Hill, ibid., p. 88. Rossi (op. cit., p. 33) considers that statements such as these constitute no more than 'a reaction against magical and alchemical methods of research where results were entrusted to mysterious operations'. But this does not 'explain' why Bacon should have adopted his anti-magical stance in quite these terms; clearly in criticising alchemical procedures he is still faithfully reporting on how he sees the role of the scientist in adopting *his* method!

57 Though in fact it has become a quite esoteric set of disciplines, comprehensible in its most sophisticated and advanced forms to only a handful of people.

58 Hill, *Intellectual Origins*, pp. 112–13.

59 Bacon, *Selections*, pp. 367–8.

60 Hill, *Intellectual Origins*, p. 223.

61 Bacon, *Selections*, p. 370.

62 ibid., pp. 122–3.

63 ibid., p. 125. I do not find myself convinced by the arguments of Dr J. L. Harrison in his article 'Bacon's view of rhetoric, poetry, and the imagination' (in *Essential Articles for the Study of Francis Bacon*, ed. B. Vickers, (Connecticut, Archon Books, 1968), that, for instance, Bacon's neglect arises largely because he is dealing with 'deficient arts' in his work (cf. p. 259). True Bacon was much influenced by rhetoric as his writings amply demonstrate; but he seems to me to lack a truly *poetic* sensibility.

64 Bacon, Essay 'Of Gardens'.

65 Quoted C. Hill, *Puritanism and Revolution* (London, Panther, 1969), p. 327.

66 F. Bacon, *The Advancement of Learning and New Atlantis*, ed. A. Johnston (London, Oxford University Press, 1974), p. 230.

67 ibid., p. 245.

68 R. P. Adams, 'The social responsibilities of science in *Utopia*, *New Atlantis* and after', reprinted in *Renaissance Essays*, ed. P. O. Kristeller and P. P. Wiener (New York, Harper Torchbooks, 1968), pp. 137–61.

69 Adams, op. cit., pp. 153–5.

70 He foresaw the implications of the compass, printing and gunpowder; others also saw the implications of gunpowder more fully than Bacon.

71 Quoted Hill, *Puritanism and Revolution*, p. 327.

72 Webster, op. cit., p. 12. John Beale was a clergyman from the West Midlands, one of the group who collaborated with Hartlib in seeking agricultural reform. The reference to social planning constitutes a reminder that Bacon intended his scientific approach to be regarded as relevant to the social and moral as to the physical sciences. His *Essays*, for instance, constituted a means of analysing the behaviour of man in society, in his moral and civil spheres:

> in a sense the term 'scientific' is a misnomer in so far as it suggests a separate category of Bacon's works from the 'literary' productions. The truth is that everything he produced outside his two professional spheres of law and parliament was dedicated to the progress of science (B. Vickers, *Francis Bacon and Renaissance Prose*, Cambridge, Cambridge University Press, 1968, p. 53).

CHAPTER 9

'Celestial Agriculture': Comenius

I

The Baconian philosophy implied, then, another shift in the image of the educated man. Scholasticism survived in the universities, rhetorical humanism remained the inspiration of the aristocracy and of the absolute monarchies of the continent, manifesting itself artistically in the intense theatricality of the baroque.[1] Baconianism, with its emphasis on things not words, its 'vexation' of nature, and its tie-up with artisans and technology appealed to a different public – one of the 'middling sort', puritanically inclined with a concern for 'works' and vocation. Certain features – its millenarian optimism and its commitment to the magic of method – feed later into progressivism, as does a certain implicit egalitarianism and social idealism for the amelioration of man's lot: 'The puritan revolution is recognised as a crucial period in the development of English educational thought. It marked the watershed at which the ideals of humanistic education gave way to the empiricism pioneered by Bacon and Comenius.'[2] Comenius was not an Englishman and though he was much influenced by Francis Bacon his system contained many un-Baconian elements; but the Hartlib–Dury circle of English intellectuals frequently invited the Czech educationist to England, promising him a sympathetic reception by the Parliamentarians; Comenius visited England and stayed for some months, initially under the impression that a formal invitation had been issued to him by the Long Parliament and that England might well set up institutions which might enable him to put some of his pedagogical plans into action. Clearly, then, the Protestant climate of rebellious England provided the sort of environment – the home of the Great Instaurator himself, no less – where Comenianism could be expected to flourish; and a preliminary consideration of developments in England provides an admirable lead-in to a specific consideration of Comenius' theories.

Puritan dissatisfaction with current cultural manifestations mirrored the early Italian humanists' discontent with their inheritance; they were disenchanted with what had gone immediately before them and looked back for renewal to a distant unspoilt age.[3] In both cases, moreover, they looked forward eagerly to a revived and revised culture. This new culture – with its links with Bacon and Comenius – gives the Puritans their representative quality as heralders of a new age. Strands in their thinking are to be of the greatest significance for the future of European culture: a recent study by J. Ben David has concluded that Baconianism played a leading role in making 'revolutionary England, of all the countries in the West . . . the centre of the [scientific] movement during the middle of the seventeenth century'. And Dr Webster glosses the judgement by indicating that 'The Baconianism of the Puritans supplied English science with a valid strategy for conduct and a sense of coherence which was lacking in most scientific groups elsewhere.'[4]

At the same time it is of the utmost importance to grasp the millenarian and eschatological basis of Puritan involvement in the newly developing empiricism, reflected, too, very deeply in Comenius' approach. I have stressed Bacon's emphasis on the fresh start; but his work was assimilated by the Puritans as part of their religious programme of restoring an earlier innocence. And, despite the emphasis on practicality, the starting-point for the seventeenth-century rejuvenation of society was theological, not, as in the nineteenth century, utilitarian. The Puritans, finding the state of man corrupted, felt their efforts of reform to be part of a preordained cosmic plan which would lead to the establishment of the Kingdom of God on earth. Apocalyptic themes and a large output of millennial tracts from the press indicated the popular interest in a providential view of history.[5] (Comenius' own life was much affected by his acceptance of certain prophecies.) Such beliefs penetrated all levels in the Puritan community. But associated were the Puritan doctrines of work, personal endeavour, labour in one's vocation. There was to be no passive waiting on the event of human regeneration but positive effort to achieve it. Hence the dominion of man over nature was seen as an essential element in the eschatological scheme – a scheme in which the promise of Daniel 12: 4, that 'knowledge shall abound as the waters cover the face of the sea' played a fundamental role. (The passage is one to which Comenius also appeals.)[6] Salvation was to be achieved through effort – and a central role in that effort was played by knowledge as newly conceived.

Thus the approach of the Puritan intelligentsia involved an iconoclastic attitude to current cultural norms, a plea for the revival of an ancient, largely biblical wisdom and a new methodology which would increase knowledge and foster improvement. By a process of reassertion and reform a new Golden Age would seem to be at hand: certainly behind their innovatory zeal was an appeal to the Fathers of the early church or the patriarchs of Israel, as the humanists had appealed to the classics; new ideas were, indeed, ostensibly only acceptable if they conformed with certain basic religious premises: 'The language of this movement leaves no doubt that in pushing knowledge forward towards new frontiers, the labourers were convinced that their mission was sanctified by Israel's God.'[7] Yet 'the sciences were employed to add precision to the millennial outline drawn up by theologians; conversely, millennial ideas furnished the natural philosopher with new premises and goals.'[8] Nature would once more 'surrender to man as its appointed governor', in Milton's terms: the whole Puritan social ethic was imbued with these intimations of improvement in man's lot through new discoveries, social welfare proposals, utopian communities and the like: and these were to be manifest in the new 'vexation' of nature recommended by Bacon. Expanding horizons resulting from the voyages of discovery also contributed to a certain optimism. Thus an appeal may still have been made to a past ideal; but in 'renewal' the emphasis gradually shifted to the new.

Bacon's 'philosophical programme, the *Instauratio Magna* came to be regarded . . . as the authentic guide to intellectual regeneration';[9] and Comenius' *pansophia* likewise exercised a potent influence:

> Hence Bacon's writings . . . assumed an almost canonical status. This influence extended, until Bacon became the most important philosophical and scientific authority of the Puritan Revolution. It is therefore only a slight exaggeration to regard Baconianism as the official philosophy of the Revolution . . .
>
> There were of course other philosophical reformers who appealed to the Puritans. It is notable in this context that Comenius, the figure who ranked nearest to Bacon in their estimation, tended to reinforce the religious and millenarian associations of the new philosophy.[10]

The influence of the two Dr Webster sums up in his way:

> Bacon gave precise and systematic philosophical expression to the anti-authoritarianism, inductivism and utilitarianism which were such important factors in the puritan scale of values. The metaphysical aspect of his philosophy avoided the atheistic tendencies which eventually rendered so much of the new philosophy anathema to the protestants.
>
> Bacon's view of nature was substantiated and given a didactic impulse by Comenius, with the result that the Puritans entered the revolutionary decades with a philosophical programme ideally suited to their mood for spiritual, social and intellectual reform.[11]

Bacon's works, then, helped to define the ethics, methodology and organisation of science, as well as to provide a starting-point for specific investigations. The Puritan movement, in turn, afforded a climate of opinion and a social ethos – in terms of mutual assistance and freedom of communication – which helped to define the nature of the new scientific movement. As important, under the Commonwealth, it offered avenues for preferment and employment.

So the initial development of science was clearly geared to extra-scientific purposes; science was not pursued as an end in itself but for its ameliorative and millennial possibilities – including the conquest of disease through medical developments, the production of economic plenty through a revised agriculture and economic reform. The educational implications of Bacon and Comenius fostered a new approach to the upbringing of the young which would be in line with Puritan aspirations.[12]

We find, indeed, as we find in Comenius himself, a curious mixture of utopianism and practicality in the Puritan attitude. Though the millennium was at hand, it was necessary, as has been pointed out above, to work for it. And one of the major ways in which the Puritans expressed their practical bent (which included a concern for manual crafts and technical development) was through education. 'The glorification of God was . . . linked to the idea of the most efficient exploitation of human and material resources.'[13] Hence the teacher was involved in a divine as well as a secular mission. John Dury, employing a common metaphor in likening the task of the teacher to that of a farmer or gardener, regarded the task as a form of 'celestial agriculture'. (Similar metaphors drawn from 'natural' analogies play a large part in Comenius' exposition, also.) In the general reaction against humanism which characterised the Puritan stress on language reform and the use of the vernacular, the reformers were persuaded by those features of Bacon's system which stressed the social role of knowledge and thus confirmed the Puritan view of the benefits of an active life. But if Bacon's *Instauratio Magna* provided guidelines for the reform of education, it was Comenius who evolved a new pedagogy. Paradoxically, Comenius supplied not only the nitty-gritty but the overall utopian justification for Baconian empiricism:

Comenian pansophia provided an explicit biblical sanction for Baconian empiricism, so cementing the integration of Bacon's philosophy into the puritan worldview and underlining the relevance of that philosophy to educational reform. Furthermore, Comenius's work demonstrated that educational reform was an integral element in the eschatological scheme.[14]

Furthermore, Comenius is as explicit and detailed in his condemnation of scholastic and humanistic learning as Bacon:

The third thing whereby Truth is prejudiced, is, as I said, either the carelessnesse, or luxuriance of the stile wherein things are expressed. We call that a luxuriating stile, when in the explication of things, improper, tropicall, hyperbolicall, and allusive words or sentences, and expressions are used: especially when Poets, or Oratours (and sometimes Philosophers and Divines acting their parts) falling upon any subject, which they would amplifie, or extenuate according to their manner, use with their figures, and colours so to alter things, that for the most part they appear not in their native, but in a borrowed, and adventitious forme. Which is nothing else, but a painting, and false glasse, whereas truth ought to be beheld with a pure, and unaltering light.[15]

Elsewhere in the same essay he condemns that 'disease of Schooles, whereby all the time of youth is spent in Grammaticall, Rhetoricall, and Logicall toyes'.[16]

II

Comenius, then, shared the millenarian and eschatological visions of his English fellow Protestants and they exercised a pervasive influence over his educational aims. He spoke in his *Via Lucis* of 'this eventide of the world' when 'wisdom may . . . be happily diffused through all minds and among all people'. The instruments of this wisdom were to be common textbooks, universal schools, a centralised research institution (the analogy with the Baconian view of the *New Atlantis* is clear) and a universal language. Like the Puritans, he looked to education and the diffusion of knowledge as the necessary means to the achievement of the millennium. Indeed, he saw the world itself as nothing other than a great school and all men as learners from the three books which had been placed at their disposal by God – Reason in man, Nature, and the Revelation of the Scriptures. In *The Way of Light* he sees the culmination of a gradual process of human enlightenment in the diffusion of universal learning as the supreme Light leading to man's redemption and harmony with God. He sees in a knowledge of nature and of those human arts which cause nature to reveal her secrets (and serve to increase the amenities of life) ways through which we come to apprehend the spiritual mysteries which constitute our ultimate purpose.[17] Art as defined, Nature, and the Scriptures, then, are mutually enlightening in the ascent to God:

> a true knowledge of the world of Nature will be a key to the mysteries of the Scriptures . . . For as every man is the best interpreter of his own words, so, since the all-wise God is the author of Nature and of Scripture too, the truth which is imprinted upon things cannot possibly fail to harmonise at all points with the truth expressed in his words, or to explain and interpret itself . . . For Nature and Scripture serve each the other as commentator and interpreter, Scripture speaking in more general terms, and Nature in particular instances.[18]

This justification of attention to 'things' because of their being constitutive of 'the all-wise God's' creativity and therefore truly representative of the divine word marks an interesting phase in the shifting focus of attention from words to things. Scientific exploration is vindicated on the grounds that investigations into physical matter simply help to confirm what has been revealed through the scriptures. The 'thing' is not yet regarded as wholly a secular object. Furthermore, in the *Pampaedia* an encyclopaedic understanding is said to be in line with God's gift to Adam of some sort of systematic omniscience: 'Not only did He display before him a theatre of His wisdom with a wondrous variety of things, but gave His express command that he should observe these creatures, divide them into classes, and distinguish them one from another by giving them names.'[19] Knowledge thus was constitutive of that 'form' proper to human beings.

Elsewhere Comenius points out that Art is the image of Nature as Nature is of the Scriptures; 'art', that is to say, becomes manifest through its truth to and understanding of physical fact. A diffusion of universal knowledge constitutes the culmination of a long historical process of gradual enlightenment, from the initial scrutiny of particular objects granted to Adam in his solitary state via oral communications to public assemblies, the invention of writing, the device of printing and the drawing together of mankind through the art of navigation – and thus comes to encompass *all* men. Not that all could achieve equality of understanding but that 'All men are to be taught what belongs to humanity because they are human: all are to be taught the things of God, because they are the image of God: eternal things because they are seekers after eternity.'[20] Such learning is not for its own sake: 'let us teach men . . . to learn not for the sake of learning, but for the sake of knowing; and yet to know not for the sake of knowing but for the sake of exercising themselves in action, and finally to exercise themselves not only for the sake of exercise, but in order to attain the goal of all activities, which is rest and happiness'.[21]

Comenius' stress on Universal Books and Schools and a Universal College and Language by means of which this Universal wisdom can be diffused constitutes his millenarian vision for all mankind. His aim is the total regeneration of all men, the coming of 'Universal Peace over the whole world',[22] the fulfilment of 'Christ's promise concerning the one flock and the one shepherd'.[23] Men, wrought in the same form as the divine likeness' 'achieve through knowledge Panharmony'. A new language, formed from things themselves, permits universal intercommunication.

And so a unified culture will produce a final brotherhood of man. Men shown their highest goal will achieve harmony and peace. To a conscious internationalism there was joined a religious ecumenicity: 'For not the least among the claims of Comenius upon the remembrance of later generations is that he is one of the early prophets of Christian ecumenicity, and that in an age of religious wars, an era notorious for almost incredibly acrimonious denominational rivalry, he worked with zeal and devotion for peace and accord.'[24]

III

The practices of education, then, were directed by this millenarian vision: they could be comprised under the Miltonic formula of 'repair the ruins': 'The most useful thing that the Holy Scriptures teach us in this connection is this, that there is no more certain way under the sun for the raising of sunken humanity than the proper education of the young.'[25] Childhood presents a peculiarly appropriate time for the repair of man's corruption for 'children are simpler and more susceptible to the remedy which the mercy of God grants to the lamentable condition of men . . . From this it necessarily follows that if the corruption of the human race is to be remedied, this must be done by means of the careful education of the young.'[26] Though 'plants of Paradise',[27] it is necessary that such children should 'be . . . imbued with the cleanly precepts of life from [their] very cradle'.[28] Men can be 'most easily formed in early youth'.[29]

That they need to be formed indicates – as does much else in the exposition – that Comenius, despite an overall optimism, was aware of the potential corruption of human nature. There are specific occasions when he asserts that 'the natural man' is depraved: thus when he deprecates the current enthusiasm for the classics he asks, 'Is the natural man not depraved enough, that it is necessary to bring to him and to show to him all manner of wicked-ness, and, as it were, to seek out opportunities to hurl him to destruction?'[30] Virtue, then, had to be inculcated from a very early stage lest vice obtain possession of the mind; children must be protected, for 'our enemy Satan is on the watch'.[31] 'In this corrupt state of the world and of human nature we never make as much progress as we ought, or, if we do advance, are filled with complacency and spiritual pride, through the depravity of our flesh.'[32] For the indulgence of parents hinders 'the natural tendency of children' and 'later on frivolous society leads them into idle ways, while the various occu-pations of city and court life, and the external circumstances which surround them, turn them away from their real inclinations'.[33]

The introduction of the Rousseauesque theme causes us to pause, however. How is it possible to appeal to the 'natural tendency of children' and their 'real inclinations', implying a natural orientation to goodness, as opposed to the corruption of their parents, when in fact Comenius has asserted earlier that the 'natural man' is depraved?

Comenius is, in fact, referring to man's 'nature' in two different senses. There was his pre-lapsarian 'nature' as well as that consequent upon the Fall. Early on, Comenius has proclaimed his intention of using the term to refer to man's *original*, pre-lapsarian being. For the seeds of our redemption through learning, virtue and piety are 'naturally' implanted in us in this sense:

> By the word *nature* we mean, not the corruption which has laid hold of all men since the Fall (on which account we are naturally called the children of wrath, unable of ourselves to have any good thoughts), but our first and original condition, to which, as to a starting-point, we must be recalled. It was in this sense that Ludovicus Vives said, 'What else is a Christian but a man restored to his own nature, and, as it were, brought back to the starting-point from which the devil has thrown him?' (*De Concordia et Discordia*, bk. i)[34]

Such a view of human 'nature' is sustained by a 'natural' force in the universe – 'the voice of nature otherwise the Providence of God' – by which it is helped to actualise its inherent possibilities. Here we are back with the earlier teleological rather than the seventeenth-century empirical view of nature – man achieving harmony with 'natural law' through which God's Providence becomes manifest:

> By the voice of nature we understand the universal Providence of God or the influence of Divine Goodness which never ceases to work all in all things; that is to say, which continually develops each creature for the end to which it has been destined. For it is a sign of the divine wisdom to do nothing in vain, that is to say, without a definite end or without means proportionate to that end.

Whatever exists, therefore, exists for some end, and has been provided with the organs and appliances necessary to attain to it . . . And so it is certain that man also is naturally fitted for the understanding of facts, for existence in harmony with the moral law, and above all things for the love of God (since for these we have already seen that he is destined), and that the roots of these three principles are as firmly planted in him as are the roots of any tree in the earth beneath it.[35]

Despite his avowed objections to accepting truths on authority instead of through first-hand observation, Comenius' statements are constantly supported by analogies drawn from 'nature' as the voice of God (and a means through which God reveals himself) and from the Bible (or revelation, the other source). Even the scheme of Pansophia is protected against criticism by being compared, in its various features, with characteristics of the Temple of Ezekiel and that of Solomon.[36] In effect Comenius reconciles his empiricism and his appeals to biblical authority through the equation: Art imitates Nature; Nature reveals God and neither order of 'truth' can conceivably therefore clash with the truths of revelation. If this were acceptable, Comenius would be consistent:

That which Musicians call harmony, is a sweet consonancie of divers tones the like exact agreement is to be found in the eternall perfections of God, with those which are created in Nature, and those which are expressed in Art: for each of them is harmonious in it selfe, as also in mutuall respect one to another. Nature is the image of divine Harmony, and Art of Nature.[37]

Notions of this sort explain Comenius' belief that 'things' always represent 'truth' – 'But things themselves cannot make another manner of impression in the senses, than as indeed they are.'[38]

So it is within this older teleological framework that Comenius' constant appeal to 'nature' as the guiding principle to his educational system must be understood. It is at once 'natural' in the sense that it abides by the characteristic features of human psychology, takes account of the potential of man's nature and seeks a harmony with that 'natural law' or 'voice of nature' which is God's Providence working to assist man's actualisation of his potential. Ultimately, despite his Baconian enthusiasm, Comenius' overall view of human psychology is derived from man's ontological status: there is a degree of tension possible (at least) between the practical, empirical part of his educational system (its foundation in the supposed facts of human perception and development, its concern for *practical* life and all the implications of man's actual behaviour) and the eschatological metaphysic it is intended to subserve. There is no doubt but that this reveals a fundamental tension implicit in seventeenth-century outlook – that an increasingly empirical concern for actual behaviour and its observation is still for many geared to an authoritarian theological metaphysic which may implicitly contradict or at least inhibit the free play of empirical observation. (Hence the need for the

Enlightenment to free itself from theology and metaphysics.) The victory, of course, lies with empiricism; but the conflict is epitomised – and temporarily concealed – by the violent stresses to which the all-embracing concept of nature is subject. Comenius is comparatively – perhaps completely – unaware of the situation; his empiricism is usually at the service of his metaphysics, as his appeal to 'natural' analogies amply demonstrates. Indeed, his optimism concerning man's educability is derived more from man's ontological status than it is from observation, on the grounds that it is through educability that man realises *his* 'nature' and hence fulfils the law (or 'voice') of Nature. 'It is evident that man is naturally capable of acquiring a knowledge of all things since, in the first place, he is the image of God.'[39] We are back, indeed, with the theory of correspondences: 'Philosophers have called man a Microcosm or Epitome of the Universe, since he inwardly comprehends all the elements that are spread far and wide through the Macrocosm, or world at large.'[40] Thus human potential can even be actualised without external aid: 'It is not necessary . . . that anything be brought to a man from without, but only that that which he possesses rolled up within himself be unfolded and disclosed, and that stress be laid on each separate element.'[41] Here Comenius temporarily forgets that man has corruption also 'rolled up' within himself; there are preliminary hints here that development can be purely endogenous. However, he does make some amends: 'Still it is true that, since the Fall, Reason has become obscure and involved, and does not know how to set itself free; while those who ought to have done so have rather entangled it the more.'[42] So we are coming to be involved in a situation which will become increasingly common in the eighteenth century. To fulfil himself man needs only to unfold from within ('Follow nature'), express himself autonomously, as it were; and yet the unfolding process has complexities about it which seem to need help – the teacher. How does Comenius identify the 'art' of the teacher?

IV

Comenius begins his exploration of the teacher's role with the proposition that man is 'naturally' endowed with psychological aids to learning – organs of sense and – characteristically Puritanical – an appetite for toil, work:

> To the rational soul, that dwells within us, organs of sense have been supplied, which may be compared to emissaries and scouts, and by the aid of these it compasses all that lies without. These are sight, hearing, smell, sound, and touch, and there is nothing whatever that can escape their notice. For, since there is nothing in the visible universe which cannot be seen, heard, smelt, tasted, or touched, and the kind and quality of which cannot in this way be discerned, it follows that there is nothing in the universe which cannot be compassed by a man endowed with sense and reason.
>
> In addition to the desire for knowledge that is implanted in him,

man is imbued not merely with a tolerance of but with an actual appetite for toil. This is evident in earliest childhood, and accompanies us throughout life . . . In a word, the eyes, the ears, the sense of touch, the mind itself, are, in their search for food, even carried beyond themselves; for to an active nature nothing is so intolerable as ease and sloth.[43]

At one moment he seems to imply that the teacher is redundant: 'The examples of those who are self-taught shows us most plainly that man, under the guidance of nature, can penetrate to the knowledge of all things. Many have made greater progress under their own tuition, or . . . with oaks and beeches for their teachers, than others have done under the irksome instruction of tutors.'[44] The unfolding process is in evidence once more. Furthermore the stress laid on the sensationalist basis of human understanding makes a significant epistemological reorientation from the time when Erasmus deprecated learning from trees. Man *can* learn by imbibing from the environment; it has become an active source of tuition unknown to the humanists.

But in general, though man has this 'natural' propensity for learning, 'art' on the part of the teacher plays a necessary part albeit in terms which stress the easy availability of the pupil's mind provided the treatment is right:

Aristotle compared the mind of man to a blank tablet on which nothing was written, but on which all things could be engraved. And, just as a writer can write or a painter paint whatever he wishes on a bare tablet, if he be not ignorant of his art, thus it is easy for one who is not ignorant of the art of teaching to depict all things on the human mind. If the result be not successful, it is more than certain that this is not the fault of the tablet (unless it have some inherent defect), but arises from ignorance on the part of the writer or painter. There is, however, this difference, that on the tablet the writing is limited by space, while, in the case of the mind, you may continually go on writing and engraving without finding any boundary, because, as has already been shown, the mind is without limit.[45]

The stages of the argument are, then, as follows. Ontologically and psychologically – ontologically through the inherent nature of man, psychologically through the gift of the senses and the aptitude for toil – man finds it 'natural' to seek knowledge through education; as 'Nature predisposes matter to become desirous of form', so human nature seeks the 'form' that knowledge supplies. The pre-lapsarian 'nature' reasserts itself as a potential even after the Fall: 'We see, then, that it is more natural, and, through the grace of the Holy Spirit, easier for a man to become wise, honest, and righteous, than for his progress to be hindered by incidental depravity. For everything returns easily to its own nature . . .'[46] Thus the teacher becomes 'the servant and not the lord of nature; his mission is to cultivate and not to transform'.[47] Yet 'our faculties do but exist potentially and need development'. Actual 'knowledge, virtue and piety . . . must be acquired by prayer, by education and by action'.[48]

So the art of 'cultivation' (the agricultural implications should be noted) requires to be 'methodized'. The constant assumption of Comenius is that he has discovered the *one* method which will be successful – to quote the title of his major work: '*The Great Didactic*, Setting forth The Whole Art of Teaching all Things to all Men'. The global aspiration is paralleled by the homogeneity of approach. The overwhelming impression the book gives is that there is an Art which will suit all natures – 'none being excepted', to quote again the title page. (In fact, as we shall see later, there are certain reservations – but the pretension is extensively advertised.)

How then is this 'servant of nature' to proceed with his 'art'? The answer is to some extent implied in the formulaic designation: 'the method employed in teaching should be based on the method of nature'.[49] For 'Nature makes no leap, and neither does art, since it imitates nature.'[50] The connection asserted between 'art' and 'nature' could hardly be closer. What in the context of Comenius' pedagogy is meant by it?

There is, of course, nothing new in the proposition that 'art' imitates 'nature' – it was a renaissance commonplace: any uncertainty arose as to whether imitation implied exact representation or 'idealisation'.[51] But the arts involved were the creative arts – poetry, painting, etc. With Comenius, the nature of the 'art' implied has undergone a marked change – among those implied are the mechanical technical arts, such as are provided by printing presses and the like, as well as those drawn from agriculture, sub-human existence, etc. On the basis of the analogy between his 'art' and 'nature', a similarity between *mechanical* and *organic* processes is implied which is of the deepest interest.

The concept which he finds fundamental to both processes and which clearly helps him to treat them analogously in that of 'order', with its Ramist implications:

We find on investigation that the principle which really holds together the fabric of this world of ours, down to its smallest detail, is none other than order; that is to say, the proper division of what comes before and what comes after, of the superior and the subordinate, of the large and the small, of the similar and dissimilar, according to place, time, number, size and weight, so that each may fulfil its function well. Order, therefore has been called the soul of affairs. For everything that is well ordered preserves its position and its strength as long as it maintains its order; it is when it ceases to do so that it grows weak, totters and falls. This may be seen clearly in instances taken from nature and from art.[52]

He then gives a number of disparate examples drawn from insect and human behaviour, human social arrangements and mechanical processes which are intended to justify his choice of the concept as the key to the setting forth of an adequate pedagogy. The analogies are constructed specifically to illustrate his views on due subordination, inter-relationship and integration. Certain insects have a 'natural talent for harmoniously combining order, number and mass in their constructions' and thus produce work of an admirable fineness. The human body is directed by a single will because of the harmonious ordering of the limbs. A single man rules a nation because law and obedience bring about the subordination of rank upon rank 'down to the meanest serf'. Books can be multiplied by correct type-setting and the placing of paper. Clocks fulfil their time-telling function through a 'well-arranged and well-devised disposition of iron parts'.[53] So, he concludes:

> The art of teaching, therefore, demands nothing more than the skilful arrangement of time, of the subjects taught, and of the method. As soon as we have succeeded in finding the proper method it will be no harder to teach school-boys, in any number desired, than with the help of the printing-press to cover a thousand sheets daily with the neatest writing; or with Archimides' machine to move houses, towers, and immense weights . . . The whole process, too, will be as free from friction as is the movement of a clock whose motive power is supplied by the weights. It will be as pleasant to see education carried out on my plan as to look at an automatic machine of this kind, and the process will be as free from failure as are these mechanical contrivances, when skilfully made.[54]

What then is the function of this series of analogies, drawn from organic, social and mechanical sources, in justifying the notion of order as the basis of an enlightened pedagogy?

In the first place it obviously involves the assimilation of very different types of 'order' as if they were analogous. Such analogical thinking looks back to medieval times when for instance a likeness was drawn between the functioning of a human body and that of the state. The consequences of such forms of argument are disastrous once they are pushed beyond a very superficial level of apparent harmony. Thus we speak of a 'head' of state – but the analogy with a human head in its relation to the rest of the body is of very limited validity. Even in a hierarchical society, the relationship between subjects and ruler is significantly different in many respects from that between head or brain and limbs.

Analogies between the organic life of man and the operation of a machine are similarly unfortunate, though in fact this one has quite a long future before it. Man is not a machine – though Comenius' attempted analogy between the workings of the body and those of a clock would seem to suggest that their behaviour is similarly organised. And a teaching method is not to be identified with either: the concept of 'order' as applied to all three has only a tenuous inter-relationship. A clock operates without choice, in pre-destined ways which are implicit in its manufacture; choice is relevant to the workings of a human body, and hence the relationship between the parts of a body and the mind is different from that between a spring and the parts of a clock. Furthermore, there is a difference between regulating a clock and teaching a skill. In the same way, the relationship of a teacher to a class is not more than superficially analogous to that of the head to the limbs of a body.

Yet time and again Comenius returns to these analogies. From the behaviour of plants, birds and animals a stream of similarities are enunciated in order to justify his stress on order, as if all manifestations of order were of the same type:

> Since this basis [of the art of intellectual discipline] can be properly laid only by assimilating the processes of art to those of nature . . . we will follow the method of nature, taking as our example a bird hatching out its young; and, if we see with what good results gardeners, painters and builders follow in the track of nature, we shall have to recognise that the educator of the young should follow in the same path.[55]

These analogies are followed through in chapter after chapter so that further indication would simply become tedious. All, of course, show similar sorts of shortcomings as does the analogy between the human body and the state analysed above. Such analogies between the educating of children and, say, the behaviour of gardeners *vis-à-vis* their plants persist and become the stock-in-trade of later progressive thinking. By appealing to 'nature' (i.e. the behaviour of organic life) in this way, Comenius justifies his position as one of the earliest progressives – and initiates an appeal to 'natural' and biological/botanical models which persists down to our own time. He utilises, too, the emotive overtones of the 'natural' to gain acceptance of his recommendations in a way which is to become fully familiar.

Just as significant are his analogies drawn from mechanical models; 'art' in this very special sense is assimilated to 'nature'. We have already noted the analogy with clockwork. There is in Chapter XXXII a lengthy analogy between his systems of teaching and the new method of the printing press. Initially a likeness is drawn between the old method of teaching and his own and the old method of reproducing manuscripts by pen and the printing press. In effect he is saying little more than that his method (like that of the printing press) is more efficient and produces better and more rapid results. But then he gets carried away with enthusiasm for the novel reproductive system and its potential productivity, and the analogy is pressed harder, with disconcerting implications: just as it is possible to 'control' and impress paper, so it is possible to fashion minds:

> Pursuing this analogy to the art of printing, we will show, by a more detailed comparison, the true nature of this new method of ours, since it will thus be made evident that knowledge can be impressed on the mind, in the same way that its concrete form can be printed on paper. In fact, we might adapt the term 'typography' and call the new method of teaching 'didachography' . . .
>
> The art of printing involves certain materials and processes. The materials consist of the paper, the type, the ink, and the press. The processes consist of the preparation of the paper, the setting up and inking of the type, the correction of the proof, and the impression and drying of the copies . . .

In didachography (to retain this term) the same elements are present. Instead of paper, we have pupils whose minds have to be impressed with the symbols of knowledge. Instead of type, we have the class-books and the rest of the apparatus devised to facilitate the operation of teaching. The ink is replaced by the voice of the master, since this it is that conveys information from the books to the minds of the listener; while the press is school-discipline, which keeps the pupils up to their work and compels them to learn.[56]

The analogy continues for five more pages, finishing with the indication that he has shown 'that our discovery of didachography, or our universal method, facilitates the multiplication of learned men in precisely the same way that the discovery of printing has facilitated the multiplication of books . . .'[57]

It is perhaps only fair to Comenius to accept that it was the emotional excitement generated by the new inventions that led him thoughtlessly to deploy such analogies; furthermore, as we have seen, he considered such arts 'natural' just as contemporaries regarded the working of the universe in terms analogous to those of clockwork also as 'natural' – descriptive of nature's functioning as well as acceptable and praiseworthy. It does not do to look back to the seventeenth century with minds schooled in the dangers of making category mistakes. Here were two wonders – divine 'nature' and human 'art' (as technical skill) and in his enthusiasm Comenius saw them as functioning in analogous ways. It was simply the effectiveness of *both* that captured his imagination – dependent on his primary assumption that, as nature revealed God, so 'art' imitated nature. His basic error arises out of his desire to assimilate to certain types of human behaviour, 'art', the same sort of perfectionism that is implicit in the divinity of 'nature' and the god-head; human products are always subject to the imperfections, which a putative divinely conceived and ordered nature and God himself necessarily lack. By assimilating the three 'behaviours' of 'art', 'nature' and God, Comenius pre-empts criticism of the human dimension – the one of the three which without a doubt is subject to corruption. His procedure, too, illustrates a mode of reasoning that for a time is to become increasingly common with the progress of science, which proceeds by a process of abstraction from the common sense phenomenal world. To see human beings in terms of botanical or technical models is to reduce them to simpler, less complex entities for the purpose of manipulation in the way in which technical progress had shown to be so successful. Thus children's minds are thought of as sheets of paper, and teachers' activities as similar to the mechanical processes of printing presses. A similar reductionism characterises the famous assimilation of teacher as gardener.

Socially, the printing press analogy points to the attractiveness of the new processes of mass production and to the uniformitarian implications of child minds shaped and moulded to pattern. To the question as to whether a single teacher can teach any number of boys at one time Comenius replies with a strong affirmative – 'it is not only possible for one teacher to teach several hundred scholars at once, but . . . it is also essential'.[58]

In short, as baker makes a large quantity of bread by a simple kneading of the dough and single heating of the oven, as the brick-maker burns many bricks at one time, as a printer prints hundreds of thousands of books from the same set of type, so should a teacher be able to teach a very large number of pupils at once and without the slighest inconvenience.[59]

The analogous image from nature is to conceive of the teacher as the sun, sending forth his rays with equal intensity on all his pupils. This summons up perhaps more acceptable notions of warmth and growth.

Now it is clear that Comenius never intended that his analogies should be analysed to this extent, though to do so is not unrevealing. For what they indicate is a certain rigidity and naïvety of mind which, secure in its promise of the millennium, proceeds with the best of intentions to prepare mankind in accordance with its own vision – of the importance of certain kinds of knowledge, of a single method it has evolved by which the knowledge can be transmitted and of the shaping and moulding which are the pedagogical counterparts of its own visionary certainties. Both 'art' and nature are ransacked for images which will illustrate and justify a preformed eschatological plan. Premature implications of 'unfolding' are rapidly pushed on one side in the fanatical methodological planning by which the 'forms of understanding' are to be impressed, the wax to be moulded, the required shape to be assured:[60] 'The tasks are mapped out for each year, month, day, and hour, and if these divisions are duly observed no class can fail to reach the necessary standard at the end of the session.'[61]

This millenarianism, this certainty of results, this trust in an infallible method, this universalism – for as we shall see, all children, all mankind, are to be involved in the great process of intellectual regeneration – as well as the reductionism implicit in the uniformitarian view of the child as plant or sheet of paper, introduce new notes into educational theorising – ones which from now on will never be altogether absent. Thus, for instance, 'progressivism' has never entirely lost the messianic touch; again, the hint of mass productive methods points to another strand in educational thinking and practice – that which Dickens satirised in his fable of McChoakumchild and Gradgrind busily pouring knowledge into 'the little pitchers'. (Does not Comenius himself use this precise image?)[62] To detect elements of two important traditions, with their very different and highly antagonistic evolution, in the same theorist – one persisting in biological and organic analogies, the other manifesting itself in the mass productive advocacy of the monitorial system – provides an interesting foretaste of theoretical stances yet to come, both of which have left their mark on current practices. Comenius himself advocated a sort of monitorial system in his notion of the Decurion, a pupil charged with the oversight of ten of his fellows. 'It will be as pleasant to see education carried out on my plan as to look at an automatic machine of this kind [e.g. as the movement of a clock], and the process will be as free from failure as are these mechanical contrivances, when skilfully made.'[63] It could hardly be more explicit. Furthermore, the constant stress concerning the *power* of education which informs both 'progressive' and 'mechanical' models is perhaps the element which binds together such apparently disparate images of the teacher as a gardener tending and an entrepreneur impressing. We are beginning to move into a world which sees in its power to take charge of its own destiny through *knowledge* and a particular kind of the use of reason, its most characteristic features. These are perhaps strange words to apply to Comenius who orients all towards the divine: but just as his organic and mechanical models are indiscriminately mixed together, so are his eschatological (implying an other wordly consummation) and his millenarian (referring to a this wordly outcome) aspirations. Furthermore he is essentially a transitional figure, at once pointing back to a medieval cosmogony and forward to a practical empiricism based on the new industrial power of man to *produce*. His naïvety as a man allowed very different levels of experience to coexist in his mind without the need a more critical approach would have felt to reconcile differences between diverse orders of being, human, natural and divine.

In what did this miraculous method further consist? Its basis is order, as noted above – and this has both a logical and a psychological implication. 'Order has been called the soul of affairs.' So 'The basis of school reform must be exact order in all things.'[64]

The first need where subject matter is concerned is gradation: 'That all studies should be carefully graduated throughout the various classes, in such a way that those that come first may prepare the way for and throw light on those that come after',[65] and, he added a little later, so that 'those which come first may be fixed in the mind of those that follow'. This is to exist within an organisational framework where there is a 'proper division of work and of rest ... disposition of studies, intervals to relieve strain, and recreation'.[66]

These unexceptionable (though in some senses hardly 'natural') principles must be understood in relation to the haphazard approach in contemporary schools when 'Grammars are diffuse, complicated, and overburdened with unnecessary matter. Phrase-books are haphazard compilations often ill-suited to the end in view.'[67] Method in this sense is not our primary concern; one merely needs to note that Comenius translated his recommendations into a series of practical textbooks illustrative of his principles – the *Vestibulum*, the *Janua*, etc., which had a fantastic success when they were first published, were translated into many European languages as well as Arabic, Turkish, Persian and Mongolian. His books were used for many years and frequent attempts were made to lure him to write more. Clearly, in relation to their times they constituted an almost revolutionary improvement.

V

The stress on sense experience as the basis of human knowledge, on which alone the intellect can work, has important implications for the Comenian curriculum and for its order of presentation:

And since nothing exists in the mind that has not previously existed in the senses, the intellect takes the material of all its thoughts from the senses, and performs the operations of thought in a manner that may be termed 'inner sensation', that is to say, by acting on the images of things that are brought before it.[68]

Thus 'instruction should be given through the senses, that it may be retained in the memory with less effort',[69] especially in the case of the very young. A major aid to teaching in the Mother-School, the first school, is the picture book: 'At this age instruction should mainly be carried on through the medium of sense-perception, and, as sight is the chiefest of the senses, our object will be attained if we give the children pictures of the most important objects in physics, optics, astronomy, geometry etc.'[70] Hence the appearance of *Orbis Pictus*, one of the first picture books ever devised for teaching children. Also it is 'desirable to represent pictorially, on the walls of the classroom, everything that is treated of in the class, by putting up either precepts and rules or pictures and diagrams illustrative of the subjects taught.'[71] This emphasis on things seen, this visualist introduction to the world of 'things' involved a criticism of the humanists and the scholastics who depended on authority and the words of others. Such people

have not shown [children] the objective world as it exists in itself, but only what this, that, or the other author has written or thought about this or that object, so that he is considered the most learned who best knows the contradictory opinions which many men have held about many things. The result is that most men possess no information but the quotations, sentences, and opinions that they have collected by rummaging about in various authors, and thus piece their knowledge together like a patchwork quilt.[72]

In the schools, indeed, 'Scarcely anyone teaches physics by ocular demonstration and by experiment, but only by quoting the works of Aristotle and of others.'[73] This situation must be rectified: 'men must, as far as is possible, be taught to become wise by studying the heavens, the earth, oaks and beeches, but not by studying books; that is to say, they must learn to know and investigate the things themselves and not the observations that other people have made about things'.[74] Otherwise pupils are only able to 'repeat the technical terms and the rules of the arts, but do not know how to apply them practically'.[75] So 'Everything should, as far as is possible, be placed before the senses'[76] – such is the 'golden rule for teachers'.

There are three 'cogent reasons' for this mode of procedure:

Firstly, the commencement of knowledge must always come from the senses (for the understanding possesses nothing that it has not first derived from the senses). Surely, then, the beginning of wisdom should consist, not in the mere learning the names of things, but in the actual perception of things themselves . . .

Secondly, the truth and certainty of science depend more on the witness of the senses than on anything else. For things impress themselves directly on the senses, but on the understanding only mediately and through the senses. This is evident from the fact that belief is at once accorded to knowledge derived from the senses, while an appeal is always made to them from *a priori* reasoning and from the testimony of others . . . Science, then, increases in certainty in proportion as it depends on sensuous perception . . .

Thirdly, since the senses are the most trusty servants of the memory, this method of sensuous perception, if universally applied, will lead to the permanent retention of knowledge that has once been acquired.[77]

As it was, in schools currently 'The classification of objects is unnaturally made to precede a knowledge of the objects themselves, although it is impossible to classify, before the matter to be classified is there.'[78] So the notion of order has a psychological as well as a logical dimension: sense experience should precede any form of verbalism; the Erasmian formula concerning the priority of language is firmly reversed. The psychological principle that experience should precede instruction receives one of its first definitive formulations; and the order of schooling is based on this psychological notion – the Mother (1–6), Vernacular (6–12), Latin (12–18) and University (18–24):

The difference between these schools is threefold. Firstly, in the earlier schools everything is taught in a general and undefined manner, while in those that follow the information is particularised and exact; just as a tree puts forth more branches and shoots each successive year, and grows stronger and more fruitful.

Secondly, in the Mother-School the external senses should be exercised and taught to distinguish the objects that surround them. In the Vernacular-School, the internal senses, the imagination and the memory, in combination with their cognate organs, should be trained, and this by reading, writing, painting, singing, counting, measuring, weighing, and committing various things to memory. In the Latin-School the pupil should be trained to understand and pass judgement on the information collected by the senses, and this by means of dialectic, grammar, rhetoric, and the other sciences and arts that are based on principles of causation. Finally, to the University belong those subjects that have special relation to the will, namely, the faculties, of which theology teaches us to restore harmony to the soul; philosophy, to the mind; medicine, to the vital functions of the body; and jurisprudence, to our external affairs.

Our faculties are best developed in the following manner. The objects should first be placed before the organs of sense on which they act. Then the internal senses should acquire the habit of expressing in their turn the images that result from the external sensation, both internally by means of the faculty of recollection, and externally with the hand and tongue. At this stage the mind can begin to operate, and, by the processes of exact thought, can compare and estimate all objects of knowledge. In this way an acquaintance with nature and a sound judgement may be obtained . . . Let our maxim be to follow the lead of nature in all things, to observe how the faculties develop one after the other, and to base our method on this principle of succession.[79]

Thus the logical order of presentation is geared to psychological principles of development. Verbal training is not to be neglected – but 'as words are but the husks and coverings of things' it is to be closely related to the experiences of the 'real' world: 'instruction in language goes hand in hand with instruction in facts':

The scholar should be trained to express everything that he sees in words, and should be taught the meaning of all the words that he uses. No one should be allowed to talk about anything that he does not understand, or to understand anything without at the same time being able to express his knowledge in words . . . From this it follows that we ought to exclude from our schools all books that merely teach words and do not at the same time lead to a knowledge of useful objects.[80]

An anti-humanist bias is clearly implied; exercises intended only to train style, which pay little or no attention to the objects of knowledge are to be avoided:

As a rule, no care is shown in the choice of the subjects that are given as exercises in style, and there is no connection between the successive subjects. The result is that they are exercises in style and nothing else, and have very little influence on the reasoning powers . . . Literary taste should therefore be taught by means of the subject matter of the science or art on which the reasoning powers of the class are being exercised.[81]

This is very near to Thomas Sprat's rejection, in his *History of the Royal Society*, of 'amplifications, digressions and swellings of style'. Style is to be subordinate to matter, reversing the humanist emphasis on words as the determinants of things. 'Things' now constituted the reality – and so words geared to things would be unambiguous and straightforward in meaning: 'It is necessary, that the true signification of words (especially such as are of more general use) be fully agreed upon, that homonymies, and ambiguous expressions breed no more dissensions; and this will be effected by accurate definitions of things, such as Mathematicians usually premise before their demonstrations.'[82] Comenius – like many of his contemporaries – considered that mathematics (especially deductive Euclidean geometry) constituted an ideal form of knowledge because it gave 'solid demonstration by which assent is wrested'.[83]

All these admonitions are related to the very same ends the humanists has educed in disputing the educational priorities of the scholastics – the needs of active, practical life. The coincidence of stated aim simply indicates what very different actual procedures and undertakings can be subsumed under the same admonition: what was practical life to the humanist was very different in content from that which Comenius was concerned to promote, and it was geared to very different social purposes.

Both, it is true, emphasised morality; but practical life to one meant the political or juristic persuasiveness of the orator while to the other it implied the commonsense world of practical utility. 'Whatever is taught should be taught as being of practical application in every day life and of some definite use.'[84] Many aspects of the classics were thus deprecated as being 'productive neither of piety nor of morality nor essential for the cultivation of the mind'. 'Such are the names of heathen deities, the myths connected with them, and the religious observances of the ancients, as well as the productions of scurrilous and indecent poets and dramatists.'[85]

Comenius' pansophic strivings, his stress on *universal* knowledge, entailed a wide-ranging curriculum which covered both traditional grammar, dialectic and rhetoric and more modern subjects. But at the centre of his concern is useful knowledge – the classical languages were to be learned because of their usefulness as the agencies of European scholarship without which no fully educated man could maintain adequate relationships with his peers rather than as repositories of human wisdom. Even the children's spare-time, leisure occupations were to maintain the serious practical concern of their formal education:

Finally it will be of immense use, if the amusements that are provided to relax the strain on the minds of the scholars be of such a kind as to lay stress on the more serious side of life, in order that a definite impression may be made on them even in their hours of recreation. For instance, they may be given tools, and allowed to imitate the different handicrafts, by playing at farming, at politics, at being soldiers or architects, etc. In spring they may be taken into the garden or into the country, and may be taught the various species of plants, vying with one another to see who can recognise the greater number. In this way they will be introduced to the rudiments of medicine, and not only will it be evident which of them has a natural bent towards that science, but in many the inclination will be created.[86]

These injunctions are justified on the grounds that, followed through, 'for the first time would schools be a real prelude to practical life'.[87] 'Wisdom' is taken care of by Revelation through the Scriptures: knowledge is for practical life – the Baconian relief of man's estate. A third of the *Orbis Pictus* is devoted to descriptions of practical crafts of which Comenius had a considerable knowledge.

The emphasis, too, is on learning by doing, practice; in this he was like Erasmus, though it is relevant to remember that Erasmus' emphasis on learning to write was built out of a prior assimilation of both concept and content, not on the direct confrontation of experience:

> Artisans do not detain their apprentices with theories, but set them to do practical work at an early stage; thus they learn to forge by forging, to carve by carving, to paint by painting, and to dance by dancing. In schools, therefore, let the students learn to write by writing, to talk by talking, to sing by singing, and to reason by reasoning. In this way schools will become work-shops humming with work . . .[88]

Comenius was not against the use of books but favoured books which contained epitomes of knowledge after the Ramist pattern: 'For every school, therefore, books . . . should be written . . . and should constitute a complete, thorough, and accurate epitome of all the subjects of instruction.'[89]

In this way human knowledge and understanding could be encapsulated in a series of textbooks – simplified and pared down to essentials in a way which contrasted strongly with the amplifications characteristic of the 'rhetorical' age. 'Matter', as with Ramus, is now a question of content, what discourse could be said to be 'about' irrespective of expression.

VI

In this emphasis on orderly development from the concrete to the more abstract the importance of an early start is as strongly stressed as in Erasmus – for then the 'seeds of all the knowledge' necessary for the journey through life are to be planted. The rudiments of a wide variety of subjects are to be acquired – physics, optics, astronomy, geography, time, history, geometry, arithmetic, statics, mechanics, economics, household affairs, as well as certain basic concepts of identity and comparison and some element of grammar, rhetoric and dialectic. As Comenius summed it up in the *School of Infancy*, children were to *know* some things, to *do* some things, and to *say* some things. Where the last are concerned, the emphasis is on practical usage and learning through listening and imitation. Indeed early concept formation in this wide variety of linguistic and practical learning is bound up with observation and practice. A not untypical example relates to mechanics: 'They will receive a training in mechanics if they are permitted or are actually taught to employ their hands continually; for instance to move something from one place to another . . . to construct something, or to pull something to pieces . . .; the very things children of this age love to do.'[90] For, 'Mechanics do not begin by drumming rules into their apprentices. They take them into the workshop and bid them look at the work . . . produced.'[91]

Following the mother-school for the infants comes the Vernacular-School. Here the emphasis is on the mother tongue. The learning of the younger children is not to be pre-empted by Latin, 'that nymph on whom such unbounded admiration is generally wasted',[92] as Comenius calls it. To teach a foreign tongue before that of the homeland is 'as irrational as to teach a

boy to ride before he can walk'.[93] Furthermore, the sort of education proposed, that 'in the objects that surround us . . . can be best obtained from
books written in the mother-tongue, which embody a list of the things that
exist in the external world'.[94] The later study of Latin will be eased because
what the words refer to will be known.

So the curriculum of the vernacular-school constitutes a continuation of
the education of sense-experience of the mother-school – including such
practical subjects as the mechanical arts – as well as instruction in reading
and writing and some elementary introduction to biblical studies, the cate-
chism and the rules of morality. Learning by heart is necessitated for the
acquisition of religious understanding – but moral principles should be
learned and put into practice.

So far the concern has been for universal education – and in the vernacular-
school 'We are . . . seeking a way by which the common people may be led
to understand and take an interest in the liberal arts and sciences.'[95] All
should be educated together – for 'it is undesirable to create class distinction
at such an early age'[96] – girls as well as boys.

Broadly speaking the mother-school is concerned with the external senses
of sight recognition, the vernacular-school with the internal senses of memory,
imagination and the like. Now the work of the Latin-School begins – to
which admission should not be reserved 'for the sons of rich men, nobles,
and magistrates . . . The wind blows where it will, and does not always begin
to blow at a fixed time.'[97] Hence the traditional seven liberal arts are to be
taught, together with further instruction in the more empirical subjects –
physics and some of the 'mechanical arts' such as agriculture and medicine,
geography, chronology and history; finally there is a concern for morality
and theology. Indeed 'real studies' are to precede dialectic and ethics, again
on the grounds that study of facts must precede that of language:

> Things exist in themselves and are quite independent of their relation
> to thought and to speech. But thought and speech have no meaning
> apart from things, and depend entirely upon them. Unless it refers to
> definite objects, speech is nothing but sound without sense, and it is
> therefore absolutely necessary to give our pupils a thorough preliminary
> training in real studies.[98]

Thinking accurately must precede speaking well – hence rhetoric is left to
the end. It is clear that style is to remain always subordinate to accuracy of
content – accuracy, that is, defined in relation to 'real studies' – the world
of things. Finally, the most important subject is history: 'An acquaintance
with history is the most important element in a man's education, and is, as
it were, the eye of his whole life.'[99] Included is biblical history, natural
history, the history of art and inventions, of morals and customs and a
general history of the world, with special reference to the pupils' native land.

The method was not really applicable to university studies, the fourth
stage of the grand design – for such studies were only relevant to 'select
intellects, the flower of mankind. The rest had better turn their attention

to more suitable occupations, such as agriculture, mechanics or trade.'[100] Most students should specialise in a particular field – but those of quite exceptional talent should be urged to pursue all branches of study, a pansophic ideal. Interestingly, this ideal should be pursued not necessarily by reading original writings but through epitomes – interestingly because Comenius clearly (perhaps again under Ramist influences) thinks that the flavour and content of a great writer can be conveyed through summaries – writers of the calibre of Cicero, Plato, Aristotle, Augustine, etc. This is in line with his general approach which, as we have noted, sees discourse as content; he defines words as the masks of things and his model language is that of mathematics. Language is to convey information – its subtler, emotional content is lost.

Comenius himself was a man of wide if superficial knowledge; and in taking all knowledge (*pansophia*) as his ideal, he desired to emulate for man the omniscience of God. He was not, of course, the only man to urge the importance of encyclopaedic learning, yet it is a mistake to define *pansophia* simply as an encyclopaedic knowledge without stressing the importance of its internal coherence. Indeed, Comenius explicitly complains of the dangers of specialisms, especially as manifest in existing textbooks:

> Metaphysicians sing to themselves alone, natural philosophers chant their own praises, astronomers dance by themselves, ethical thinkers make their laws for themselves, politicians lay their own foundations, mathematicians rejoice over their own triumphs, and theologians rule for their own benefit. Yea, men introduce even into the same field of knowledge and science contradictory principles whereby they build and defend whatever pleases them, without much troubling themselves about the conclusions derived from the premises by other men.[101]

Unity and co-ordination in cultural and scientific studies were needed. Comenius believed that human knowledge came from the senses, reason (the intellect), and divine revelation. The reconciliation of these three sources enabled a unified conception of all things known to be arrived at. By seeking knowledge of God, nature and the arts through the apprehension of their essences – God revealing Himself so as to produce an apprehensible image of himself and of His 'ideas' concerning the world of nature and the arts of man – man was able to harmonise the various aspects of his understanding and thus arrive at a fundamentally rational conception of all things and of the modes of their differentiation. Hence can be constructed 'an accurate anatomy of the universe, dissecting the veins and limbs of all things in such a way that there shall be nothing that is not seen, and that each part shall appear in its proper place and without confusion'.[102] Thus *pansophia* constituted an attempt to produce a coherent view of 'reality': '*Pansophia*: This book will be nothing else than a transcript duly arranged of the books of God – of Nature, of Scripture and of the Notions innate in the mind; so that whoever shall read and understand this book shall at the same time read and understand himself, the nature of the world and God.'[103]

To convey this understanding there must be a language perfectly attuned to
correspond to the reality of things:

> As in the realm of concepts no being can be without that which exists,
> nor no place without something which is in place, nor persistence without
> something that persists . . . and just as in nature there is no matter without
> something that is material – so there must be in the new language no
> thing without a name, no designation without characteristic, no sound
> or characteristic without a thing be designated. The number of things,
> distinguished by form from each other, must tally with that of words,
> no more and no less.[104]

Even Comenius himself saw this as, in some respects, a vast process of
simplification:

> by a true Anatomy of the universe, all things that can be thought of
> may be reduced to their generall kinds and species: and so, that what-
> soever is to be said of any thing, may at once be said of all things,
> whereof it can be said. By this means we shall find all things both better
> grounded and more contracted, even beyond our hopes: because the
> understanding being by a few rules freed from an infinite number of
> hops and barres, will runne through and dive into all things of its owne
> accord.[105]

Characteristically, as a Protestant bishop, he worked to dispense with
'ceremonialism' – what Scripture and the patristic writings *said* was enough.
He did not see that ritualistic participation was itself a way of learning, an
introduction through agencies other than rational into a mystery. So he
attempted to reconcile empiricism and theology – as Dr V. Jelinck puts it
in his introduction to his translation of Comenius' *Analytical Didactic*, he
'cherished the medieval dream of harmonizing biblical revelation with all
worldly science'.[106] Certainly he believed in the role of sensory knowledge
as the means to virtue; it is through art and knowledge that man is offered
the opportunity of realising his 'real', pre-lapsarian nature. Though society
can be 'frivolous' and men are, in their fallen state, liable to corruption,
Comenius believes, despite all his own personal frustrations and disappointments, in the importance of this 'celestial agriculture' – an infallible method
geared to the redemption of mankind through a close study of natural and
human reality and expressed in an unambiguous language from which all
rhetorical excesses have been purged in the interests of a perfect accord
between word and external reality, concept and sensuous experience.

The way was not even hard. The object of his *Didactic* Comenius summarised as follows:

> To seek and to find a method of instruction, by which teachers may
> teach less, but learners learn more; by which schools may be the scene
> of less noise, aversion, and useless labour, but of more leisure, enjoy-

ment, and solid progress; and through which the Christian community may have less darkness, perplexity, and dissension, but on the other hand more light, orderliness, peace and rest.[107]

It is here, indeed, that Comenius did show awareness of the importance of feelings which 'are half our being'. In his classroom he allowed emulation, geared to mutual assistance.[108] The 'school itself should be a pleasant place, and attractive to the eye both within and without'.[109] Rooms should be bright and clean, ornamented by pictures (if of an improving kind!); there should be a place to play and a garden, so that children will go to school 'with as much pleasure as to fairs'. Studies should arouse liking not distaste; they must be pursued actively – through dramatic representation if feasible: children have an 'urge for activity' and play. Harsh discipline should be avoided. In sum, through his method, schools will become 'places of amusement, houses of delights and attractions'. No one will, in deference to the rest of Comenius' work, qualify 'amusements' as frivolous: he wished for humanity, not brutality, enjoyment, not grind, willing co-operation through natural inclination, not forced attention. We can salute these aspirations within their context of serious study and religious purposes even while finding his whole system utopian and naïvely idealistic. It is perhaps odd that a man who had a keen sense of the 'real' world should gear his insights to a scheme so unrealistic in practice – though, in fact, he shares such aspirations with many of his age. The first great empiricist in education is also an idealistic visionary: it is a combination we shall encounter again, if in modified form. But it raises the profound question – why should the birth – and development – of empiricism – of science and positivism – be so frequently geared to millenarian aspirations so hopelessly out of tune with the realities of human behaviour? It is a question raised with varying degrees of sharpness in educational writings from Comenius to Tolstoy – and beyond.

Perhaps part of the answer is that literature is a better guide to 'reality' – human reality – than science. And indeed, if we compare the empiricists with the humanists, we see that the humanists, in their use of language, are geared to certain of the actualities of human behaviour. They derive their education from a literature which is itself revelatory of human conduct – in political and social matters especially. Their use of language is oriented towards people – for the purpose of persuasion. Their prototype is the orator – the man geared to the moving of human heads and hearts. They appreciate the central role, in human affairs, of power – and address themselves to the problem of its virtuous exercise.

The great image of humanist education is the theatre, that of the empiricists the workshop. A theatre affords opportunities for insincerities and posturings – but it is essentially a place of human interaction. The new empiricists are geared to things and their behaviour; they conceive of power in a technical guise, of language in terms of a one-to-one correspondence with the 'real' world. Inevitably the temptation gradually comes to treat human beings as if their conduct could be regulated and predicted with much the same assurance as that of the material world; human problems are thought to be susceptible to that same process of analysis and isolation which had worked so well in the world of things. In their case knowledge, not persuasion, was power. The way of 'persuasion' takes account of the irrational element in mankind; the way of knowledge anticipates unfailing rationality, persuasion according to the *evidence*. The humanists assumed that men were men of feeling as well as of reason and taught their pupils – ideally at least – to behave accordingly, with due awareness of human susceptibility to emotion as well as argument. The empiricists assumed that men were men of reason who would be moved by knowledge – positive knowledge of things as they are: 'For there will be no ground for dissenting, when all men have the same Truths clearly presented to their eyes.'[110]

The humanists saw the need for their persuasive powers to be geared to a moral philosophy; there was an assumption of the possibilities of counter-persuasion, of dialogue. The empiricists came to assume that Truth was its own morality and could self-evidently imply conduct. Now it is true that men have sexual urges; it is not true that they should always be expressed. Truth (as truth to fact) contains no necessary dimension of moral injunction – the worlds of fact and value are distinct, and from the truth of a proposition no necessary moral obligation follows. A humanist education was open to grave abuses in human manipulation but it remained within a human dimension; the new science drew its prestige from the manipulation of the non-human universe and sought to repeat its success within the moral world.

For the moment, however, the situation was disguised because of the assumption of the analogical workings of 'art' (implying knowledge), nature and revelation – an assumption explicitly stated as forming the basis of Comenius' whole pedagogic scheme. This meant that technical advance was sustained by the implication of moral purposiveness inside the millenarian and eschatological framework within which Comenius conceived his undertaking. If 'art' worked like nature and nature functioned in accordance with divine revelation, 'art' was sustained by God's purposiveness. As I have insisted above, 'things' were not yet purely secular objects and the discoveries through 'art' of the laws which ordered their inter-relationships and permitted their exploitation for technical purposes were considered to be in harmony with the workings of a divinely ordered nature and the revelations of Scripture. The whole technological undertaking was therefore underpinned by a putative moral purposiveness sustained by divine approval. It contributed, after all, to the 'relief of man's estate', employed the God-given potential of human beings within a structure still conceived of in quasi-teleological terms. Bacon had paid lip-service at least to a view of nature which conceived of it as revelatory of the divine purposiveness; about Comenius' sincerity there could be no doubts. The problems of justification would arise only when the full implications of the de-mythologised universe were appreciated and men must seek other justifications for their revised 'arts' than accordance with divine will.

In terms of developing individualism there is a growing tension between the autonomy implicit in the appeal to individual sense experience and the imposition of an overall pattern of development. On the one hand, there is encouragement to an emancipated confrontation of the sensory world – 'emancipated', that is, from what people have previously said about it; on the other hand there remains the certainty – implicit, for instance, in both the biological and mechanical models analysed above – that what is allowed to grow, or is imprinted constitutes the correct mode of development, is in accord with pre-established norms. This points to a developing dilemma in which theorists – first unconsciously – increasingly find themselves. Release from the constraints of historical culture poses the question of the positive positions to be adopted other than those implicit in a purely material necessity, derived from scientific and technological 'law'. The question does not arise in any acute form for Comenius, for despite his 'modernity' he remains tied resolutely to a traditional, fundamentally religious outcome. 'Art', 'nature' and divine purpose are sufficiently in harmony in their workings to obviate any need to face fundamental questions. The tension remains, as yet, an unconscious one – at least in the mind of the Czech educator. The ambiguities of the teacher's position as 'the *servant* of nature' are, at present, held in suspension.

Yet Montaigne's question 'What do I know?' remains in the theorists so far considered, in large measure unexamined. Bacon had thrown doubts, in his analysis of the Idols, on the ability of the human mind to arrive at 'truth', though this had barely affected his optimism. Comenius had disposed of the matter on the grounds that man was 'naturally capable of acquiring a knowledge of all things since . . . he is the image of God'. But there were dubious propositions implicit in the emphasis on sense experience – could the senses never deceive? Furthermore, what is the relationship between language and world – are 'words . . . but the husks and coverings of things'? Clearly, conceptions of the nature of language and 'reality' – and the connection between the two – have important implications for education. Furthermore, important epistemological issues had already been raised by Descartes – and were to be considered by Locke.

NOTES

1 cf. Germain Bazin, *The Baroque* (London, Thames & Hudson, 1968), p. 40.
2 C. Webster (ed.), *Samuel Hartlib and the Advancement of Learning* (Cambridge, Cambridge University Press, 1970), p. vii.
3 cf. C. Webster, *The Great Instauration* (London, Duckworth, 1975), p. 15.
4 ibid., p. 515.
5 cf. ibid., p. 5.
6 cf. J. A. Comenius, *A Reformation of Schools*, trans. Samuel Hartlib, 1642 and reproduced by the Scolar Press, 1969, p. 29.
7 C. Webster, *The Great Instauration* (London, Duckworth, 1975), p. 15.
8 ibid., p. xvi.
9 ibid., p. 12.
10 ibid., p. 25.
11 ibid., p. 514.
12 cf. ibid., p. 30.
13 ibid., pp. 505–6.
14 ibid., pp. 113–14.

15 Comenius, *Reformation of Schools*, p. 19.
16 ibid., p. 20.
17 J. A. Comenius, *The Way of Light*, trans. E. T. Campagnac (Liverpool, Liverpool University Press, 1938), p. 122.
18 ibid., p. 118.
19 J. A. Comenius, *On Education*, ed. J. Piaget (New York, Teachers College Press, Columbia University, 1967), pp. 139-40.
20 Comenius, *Way of Light*, p. 128.
21 ibid., pp. 132-3.
22 ibid., p. 202.
23 ibid., p. 203.
24 M. Spinka, *John Amos Comenius* (Chicago, University of Chicago Press, 1943), p. 56.
25 J. A. Comenius, *The Great Didactic*, ed. and trans. M. W. Keatinge (London, Black, 1896), p. 166.
26 ibid., p. 167.
27 ibid., p. 213.
28 ibid., p. 212.
29 ibid., p. 209.
30 ibid., p. 394.
31 ibid., p. 368.
32 ibid., p. 381.
33 ibid., p. 239.
34 ibid., p. 192.
35 ibid., pp. 192-3.
36 Comenius, *Reformation of Schools*, pp. 80-9.
37 ibid., p. 39.
38 ibid., p. 18.
39 Comenius, *Didactic*, p. 193. It is this millenarian vision which protects Comenius from the melancholy and sense of disruption which afflicted many of his contemporaries.
40 ibid., p. 194.
41 ibid., p. 194.
42 ibid., p. 194.
43 ibid., p. 195.
44 ibid., p. 195.
45 ibid., p. 196.
46 ibid., p. 203.
47 ibid., p. 333.
48 ibid., p. 204.
49 ibid., p. 342.
50 ibid., p. 357.
51 cf. p. 33 above.
52 Comenius, *Didactic*, p. 245.
53 ibid., pp. 246-7.
54 ibid., pp. 248-9.
55 ibid., p. 264.
56 ibid., p. 441.
57 ibid., p. 446.
58 ibid., p. 316.
59 ibid., p. 317.
60 If it is pointed out that Erasmus and other humanists employed much the same imagery (cf. p. 62 above) the mass implication of Comenius' context introduces a somewhat different dimension in its implication of uniformity. When, however, Comenius stresses the notion of 'formation' he is, of course, in the humanist tradition.
61 Comenius, *Didactic*, p. 444.

62 ibid., p. 440 – he asserts that even people without teaching competence can take suitably arranged material and 'pour it into their pupils'.
63 ibid., p. 249.
64 ibid., p. 245.
65 ibid., p. 276.
66 ibid., p. 261.
67 ibid., p. 124.
68 ibid., p. 258.
69 ibid., p. 291.
70 ibid., p. 416.
71 ibid., p. 291. cf. Bentham's suggested practice later.
72 ibid., p. 300.
73 ibid., p. 301.
74 ibid., p. 302.
75 ibid., p. 301.
76 ibid., p. 336.
77 ibid., p. 337. In actual fact, the role of sense experience in scientific development is a limited one.
78 ibid., p. 267.
79 ibid., pp. 408–9. Note the influence of Ramism in the initial move from the general to the particular.
80 ibid., p. 329.
81 ibid., pp. 330–1.
82 Comenius, *Reformation of Schools*, p. 42.
83 J. Sadler (ed.), *Comenius* (London, Collier Macmillan, 1969).
84 Comenius, *Didactic*, p. 341. At the same time, the teleological framework within which this 'busyness' was thought to operate should not be forgotten.
85 ibid., p. 332.
86 ibid., p. 331.
87 ibid., p. 332.
88 ibid., p. 347.
89 ibid., p. 324.
90 ibid., pp. 412–13.
91 ibid., p. 348.
92 ibid., p. 419.
93 ibid., p. 419.
94 ibid., p. 419.
95 ibid., pp. 423–4.
96 ibid., p. 418.
97 ibid., p. 419.
98 ibid., p. 428.
99 ibid., p. 432.
100 ibid., pp. 433–4. There is an interesting discrepancy here between the claim to teach 'all things to all men' and Comenius' actual acceptance of a hierarchy of talent. He believed in any case that the general welfare depended on every man safeguarding himself in his own proper status, neither leaving it nor thrusting in advance of others (*The Way of Light*, p. 131). For

> A vast difference will remain between men who are learned in the popular and elementary sense, and those who are professionally learned – such a difference as God indicated when he foretold that the light of the moon should be as in the light of the sun, but yet that the light of the sun should be seven times greater.

Elsewhere he indicates, despite the claim on the title page, that 'the same method cannot be applied to all alike' on the grounds of individual differences between scholars (*Didactic*, p. 333).
101 'Introduction to Pansophy' – quoted Spinka, op. cit., p. 66.

102 Quoted *Didactic*, p. 34.
103 *Way of Light*, p. 148. *Pansophia* was to contain 'the very marrow of eternal truth' in its overall structure and generality and in *The Way of Light* was distinguished as such from *panhistoria* (concerned with the 'variety of particular things') and *pandogmatia*, which 'reviewed various theories and opinions . . . about things' (cf. *Way of Light*, pp. 145-6). The aim of *pansophia* was 'not so much to make men learned as to make them wise', and so it contains universal truths set forth in the strictest order and perfectly arranged – in unbroken gradation from first to last, so that it 'can be apprehended by simple people whoever they may be' (*Way of Light*, p. 150). The other works are subordinate to this general treatment – and the treatment itself involved a hierarchy from the immediacies of sense to the knowledge of God.
104 Quoted Sadler, op. cit., p. 27.
105 Comenius, *Reformation of Schools*, p. 13.
106 J. A. Comenius, *Analytical Didactic*, trans. V. Jelinck (Chicago, University of Chicago Press, 1953), p. 8.
107 Comenius, *Didactic*, p. 156.
108 ibid., p. 317.
109 ibid., p. 283.
110 Comenius, *Way of Light*, p. 202.

CHAPTER 10

'The Under-labourer'
in Courtly Clothes: Locke

I

It will by now be becoming apparent that the new ideal of an educated man was beginning to differ significantly and extensively from that favoured by the humanists. Comenius to some extent is atypical in that he is a representative of a revolutionary section in a turbulent and intellectually transitional age, an age where, temporarily at least, the normal hierarchies of class are overturned: in this respect the welcome he received in England is especially significant. The notion of all things to *all men* departs significantly from the frankly elitist line which the humanists had pursued in their concern for the education of a restricted and powerful class. Formal education, after all, was still largely a matter for the comparative few, the leaders in central and local government; even Comenius himself, despite his universalistic aspirations, implies in his writings a hierarchical society though, like his master, Bacon, he accepted artisans and craftsmen as sources of enlightenment in a way which would have seemed strange to a traditional humanist. With Locke we seem to be on course again – back to the gentleman. The Restoration has taken place and the king is once more on his throne. But the world has changed; though it is arguable – it has been argued – that Locke's gentleman belongs to the Courtier tradition, in fact, despite the likeness, there are also profound differences in the curricular recommendations: a different sort of practicality takes the place of the combined chivalric and literary education thought central to the education of the Courtier. The social ambience was, in any case, somewhat different, though still restricted.

But before Locke's specific educational recommendations are considered it is necessary to examine the changed philosophical climate which so deeply affected the new orientation. To do this it will be necessary to consider some of the crucial features of the new epistemology which formed the central philosophical problem of the age. The problem of knowledge, as I have indicated at the end of the last chapter, had been raised, in an acute manner, by the work of people like Bacon with their reaction against the traditionally known and accepted and their emphasis on the discovery of new knowledge. What, then, constituted knowledge, how was it arrived at? What marked its limits? This new knowledge furthermore implied power. The humanists had trained men for power in the exercise of government: in what sense did the new found power differ from the political power manifest in the older tradition?

To explore current preoccupations with the problem of knowledge it will be necessary to examine briefly the philosophical position of Locke himself, but also to say a little about the other great influence on the seventeenth-century thinking on the matter, Descartes, who died when Locke was 18, and was therefore much his senior contemporary. The former certainties based on revelation and a traditional cosmology were yielding to the new empiricism which indicated that behavioural problems could be solved in ontological terms. Pre-seventeenth-century attention in general had been focused on the nature of being; and physical questions had been answered in terms of the actualisation of potentiality as a basic characteristic of an existence which was in essence teleological. With the realisation that questions relating to behaviour were not being answered by assuming that things behaved as they did because it was their 'nature' to do so, psychological and epistemological queries were necessarily raised as to what constituted knowledge and how it was to be established. This emphasis on the nature of knowledge places the act of knowing in the centre of the human stage. As Professor Gellner has pointed out, before Descartes knowing was a process in the world, one of the many aspects of living; after Descartes, the world became an event within knowledge.

II

René Descartes (1596–1650) had attempted a solution to the problems – and his rationalism modified latterly by an increasing realisation of the importance of empirical investigation constituted the counterpart to Locke's later empiricism modified by indications of rationalism. Together they profoundly influenced all subsequent developments.

Method was central to Descartes' wish to attain *certain* knowledge and at the same time, to *advance* knowledge: he sought 'a method that gives [him] the means . . . of gradually augmenting [his] knowledge'.[1] It was to be one of universal application within the unity of the body of sciences; he began from his interest in creating a new Geometry and graduated to a belief in his power to evolve a Method which would, in view of the unity of the sciences, enable him to solve all problems.

This famous Method started with doubt and the avoidance of 'precipitancy and prejudice'; it involved analysis as a means to the solution of problems, encompassed an orderly presentation from the simple to the more complex, and avoided the omission of relevant material. Geometrical demonstration remained the guiding principle in this enunciation of the various stages of method.

> The long chains of simple and easy reasonings by means of which geometers are accustomed to reach the conclusions of their most difficult demonstrations, had led me to imagine that all things, to the knowledge

of which man is competent, are mutually connected in the same way, and that there is nothing so far removed from us as to be beyond our reach, or so hidden that we cannot discover it, provided only we abstain from accepting the false for the true, and always preserve in our thoughts the order necessary for the deduction of one truth from another.[2]

Hence his special emphasis on the necessity for Order. It is, as Professor Kemp Smith notes, 'in the *orderly* handling of the data . . . that "the whole secret of method consists" '. And he quotes from the *Regulae*: 'In this one requirement [that of due order] we have the sum of all human endeavour; whoever enters on the pursuit of knowledge must rely on this as implicitly as he who entered the labyrinth had to rely on the thread that guided Theseus.'[3] This order, Descartes urges, is something inherent in the things themselves; also it is an order inherent in the sequence in which we tackle the various sciences. We need to start from what is simple and indubitable and advance by orderly steps which are themselves indubitable so that progress is made, as in the case of geometry: 'it is for the things themselves to disclose their order to us, never for us to impose an order of our own devising'.[4]

But perhaps even more important was his initial emphasis on the need for doubt – for it implied a search for a new principle on which what constituted knowledge could be based. He found this principle in the famous *Cogito ergo sum*, 'being' becoming dependent on thought. Positively this tends to make mind more important than matter and has therefore subjectivist tendencies; but negatively it implied the clearing away of an immense area of the past, of inherited notions, traditional ways: it asserted the authority of the individual ego against the accumulations of social experience, it obliterated the nuances and half tones of traditional wisdom in favour of clarity and distinctness, the two virtues Descartes assigned to what was to be considered indubitably worthy of the appellation 'Knowledge', and which resulted from certain intuitions of the mind rather than from the evidence of the senses, which he considered subject to deception.

Both Descartes' emphasis on the centrality of knowledge and his definition of his Method have certain interesting implications for the general orientation of the intellectual world in which we are now moving. To begin with, it is perfectionist in intent – his first projected sub-title for the *Discourse* ran as follows: 'The Project for a universal science which can elevate our nature to its highest pitch of perfection'. There are hints of puritan millenarianism here. Even more explicit is its anti-authoritarianism. Such *a priori* features as remained were of a very different dimension from those large helpings of historically unchallenged assumptions which constituted previous attempts at explaining the physical universe, just as a mode of reasoning based on a geometrical model differed greatly from the traditional syllogistic approach or the 'judgement' relevant to a rhetorical exercise. It must be remembered that Descartes' conception of knowledge, though deductive, was deductive from intuited truths, not through the syllogism. The syllogism, in fact, he considered simply an instrument for explaining what was already known; it was useless in the discovery of new truths, for the conclusion was already

implicit in the premises: 'In using the syllogism the mind is taught not itself
to *see* truth but to *believe* it on the authority of the syllogistic rules.'[5] In this
way the clever deceive themselves, for all their learning, in disregarding the
simple and self-evident intuitions from which true knowledge can be built
up; and of which 'the rustic is never ignorant'.[6]

Indeed, as with Comenius and Bacon, the Method was conceived of as a
sort of tool which did much to level differences of ability: 'For to be possessed
of a vigorous mind is not enough; the prime requisite is rightly to apply it.
The greatest minds, as they are capable of the highest excellences, are open
likewise to the greatest aberrations; and those who travel very slowly may
yet make far greater progress, provided they keep always to the straight road,
than those who, while they run, forsake it.'[7]

Descartes believed, indeed, that there was in all men the same *lumen
naturale* (natural light of reason or cognitive awareness): 'Good sense is, of
all things among men, the most equally distributed.' Diversity of opinion
sprang not from unequal endowment but 'solely from this, that we conduct
our thoughts along different ways, and so do not fix our attention on the same
objects'.[8] In general, any inequality of 'esprit' was manifest in superiority
of inventive power – for 'esprit' included memory and imagination as well
as reason. Thus Descartes believed in an equality where the recognition of
truth was concerned but an inequality where the discovery of new truths was
involved; the latter required a superiority of 'esprit'.

This belief in equality of reason in power of apprehension involved, as
corollaries, a trust in individual reason and a distrust of traditional authority
as found in books: 'I thought that the sciences contained in books . . . composed as they are of the opinions of many different individuals massed together,
are farther removed from truth than the simple inferences which a man of
good sense using his natural and unprejudiced judgement draws respecting
the matters of his experience.'[9] One of the things, then, that Descartes
emphasises is the need for 'self-instruction'. For, as he continues:

> since God has endowed each of us with some light of reason by which
> to distinguish truth from error, I could not have believed that I ought
> for a single moment to rest satisfied with the opinions of another, unless
> I had resolved to exercise my own judgement in examining these whenever
> I should be duly qualified for the task.[10]

Unless we were rationally convinced we should never be persuaded of the
correctness of anything. Descartes, then, is also an advocate of the fresh
start, the evolution of intuited truths from a basis of scepticism.[11] Indeed,
one reason for writing as he did in the vernacular instead of in Latin was to
appeal to minds hitherto uncorrupted by the authority of the Schools: 'those
who make use of their unprejudiced natural reason will be better judges of
my opinions than those who give heed to the writings of the ancients only'.[12]
In this way he represents that belief in cognitive autonomy when, as Dr
Anthony Quinton puts it: 'The individual knower or subject is represented
as setting out on his cognitive career with nothing more than the senses and

the reason that he stands up in!'[13] – a view which has exercised a profound influence on modern European thought as it has provided a deeply influential educational model current among contemporary educational philosophers. The tension between traditional belief and autonomy, already commented on in relation to Descartes' contemporary, Comenius, is resolved largely in favour of the latter in the Cartesian view.

III

So Descartes evolved a method which as a tool of thought would obviate that loading of the memory with past authorities in favour of the rational deduction of certain knowledge from intuited 'just causes and true principles': *'En choisissant les mathématiques comme type de la science, Descartes fait passer la science de la mémoire à la raison.'*[14] Custom and example were to be abandoned; his preference for the work of a single mind rather than the traditions built up by many, points to a plea for rational planning rather than haphazard growth:

> one of the very first [thoughts] that occurred to me was, that there is seldom so much perfection in works composed of many separate parts, upon which different hands had been employed, as in those completed by a single master. Thus it is observable that the buildings which a single architect has planned and executed, are generally more elegant and commodious than those which several have attempted to improve . . . In the same way I fancied that those nations which, starting from a semi-barbarous state and advancing to civilisation by slow degrees, have had their laws successively determined, and, as it were, forced upon them simply by experience of the hurtfulness of particular crimes and disputes would by this process come to be possessed of less perfect institutions than those which, from the commencement of their association as communities, have followed the appointments of some wise legislator.[15]

Here, incipiently, we have the preference for rational planning over 'growth'.

The purely formal system of Mathematics supplied the most certain knowledge. Descartes often asserts that he has always reckoned 'among the number of the most certain truths those I clearly conceived relating to figures, numbers, and other matters that pertain to arithmetic and geometry, and in general to the pure mathematics'.[16] Gilson goes as far as to say that Descartes' decision to reserve the name of truth to the *'seul et unique genre de connaissances qui appartiennent au type mathématique'* represents the *'véritable révolution cartesienne dans l'ordre de la pensée'*.[17] Mathematics had the great virtue of being unambiguous; for error arose often because 'the majority attend to words rather than things; and thus frequently assent to terms without attaching to them any meaning'.[18] Furthermore, its rationalistic pattern of deduction from assumed axioms constituted the Cartesian paradigm of how to proceed in fields other than the mathematical and hence constituted Descartes' major contribution to the new thought.

Descartes' aim, in fact, was fundamentally, not metaphysical and abstract but 'practical, even utilitarian'.[19]

> For by [some general notions respecting physics] I perceived it to be possible to arrive at knowledge highly useful in life; and in room of the speculative philosophy usually taught in the schools, to discover a practical, by means of which, knowing the force and action of fire, water, air, the stars, the heavens, and all the other bodies that surround us, as distinctly as we know the various crafts of our artisans, we might also apply them in the same way to all the uses to which they are adapted, and thus render ourselves the lords and possessors of nature.[20]

He considers that practical consequences provide an important spur to the discovery of truth, when the outcome 'must presently punish him if he has judged amiss', and therefore are more likely to foster truth than those speculations 'conducted by a man of letters in his study'.[21] We know that Descartes studied Flemish in order to enter into relations with artisans ignorant of Latin and French; that he concerned himself with painting ('*sans doute la Perspective*',[22] as Gilson opines), military architecture, the art of navigation, and, of course, medicine, mostly matters of immediate utility.

Clearly revealed, then, is a profoundly anti-historical element in Descartes' work. Methodical doubt is necessary that we shall overcome the prejudices and unwarranted assumptions of childhood; both individually and in terms of social tradition it was necessary to begin anew by the process of *doubt*.[23] Even language, as we have seen, was a source of error. What was sought was 'certain knowledge', not that due to 'custom and example'.[24] 'The over curious in the customs of the past are generally ignorant of those of the present.'[25] As noted earlier, an aspect of this anti-historicism was its anti-bookishness. He mentions in the *Discourse* his resolution to abandon the study of letters and 'resolved no longer to seek any other science than the knowledge of myself, or of the great book of the world'.[26] As Gilson comments: '*Descartes sait desormais par expérience personelle que la science ne se trouve pas dans les livres; il renonce donc, non pas nécessairement à lire, mais à croire que la lecture soit une methode efficace pour découvrir la verité.*'[27] He sought a tool to think with rather than a memory overloaded; for the science of the Renaissance '*est donc affaire de pure mémoire*'.[28] And so Descartes helps to set a pattern for the future. So often from now on two characteristic features of philosophical ideologies – ideologies which fed into the related theories of education – will be the pronouncement of an initial repudiation, a rejection, in various terms, of the past – or to be more accurate, of aspects of the past, for the past in some form or other must always remain with us – followed by the intellectual formulation of some new approach, Method, way, which will reorient thought, the society, the educational system in some more desirable direction. Thought is beginning to direct life to practical ends – thought working from intuited truths which are within the natural capacities of all men and to which inherited conceptions constitute a hindrance rather than a help.

IV

'A tool to think with' rather than a repository of traditional wisdom – the formula provides a not inapt introduction to Locke's survey of the Understanding, its nature and limitations. 'The Commonwealth of learning is not at this time without master-builders', he wrote in his Epistle to the Reader of his *Essay Concerning Human Understanding*:

> but every one must not hope to be a Boyle or a Sydenham; and in an age that produces such masters as the great Huygenius and the incomparable Mr. Newton, with some others of that strain, it is ambition enough to be employed as an under-labourer in clearing the ground a little, and removing some of the rubbish that lies in the way to knowledge.[29]

The modesty of the undertaking fulfils something of the same dismissive function as Descartes' method of doubt. Hindrances to true knowledge have included a propensity for 'Vague and insignificant forms of speech, and abuse of language', which 'have so long passed for mysteries of science';[30] the use of wrong methods, such as the recourse to fundamental principles or 'maxims', which are innate, known prior to all experience, or too strong a reliance on the use of the syllogism as the one true means to knowledge[31] ('The search for the proper method of procedure was one whose importance all the thinkers of the seventeenth century agreed in emphasising.');[32] or the refusal to accept the inherent limitations of the human mind. Hence we 'let loose our thoughts into the vast ocean of Being; as if all that boundless extent were the natural and undoubted possession of our understanding'.[33] Thus, the solution is 'to take a survey of our own understandings, examine our own powers, and see to what things they were adapted'.[34] In this way we may 'learn to content ourselves with what is attainable by us in this state'.[35] Hence the aim was both practical and utilitarian: 'to inquire into the original, certainty, and extent of human knowledge, together with the grounds and degrees of belief, opinion, and assent';[36] and behind this inquiry lay the concern for the improvement of mankind: as he expressed it in a note on study which he wrote into his journal for the year 1677: 'That which seems to me to be best suited to the end of man, and lie level to his understanding, is the improvement of natural experiments for the convenience of this life and the way of ordering himself so as to attain happiness in the other – i.e. moral philosophy, which in my sense comprehends religion too, or man's whole duty'[37] – a view which is essentially Baconian.[38]

Locke's philosophy was rooted in epistemology, the study of man's processes of gaining knowledge, the kinds, nature and limits of this knowledge, and the distinction between knowledge and belief; he set out to 'examine our own abilities, and see what *objects* our understandings were, or were not, fitted to deal with'.[39] In so far as the book was concerned with *how* we gained our knowledge, it raised psychological problems; in so far as it was concerned with *what* the mind could be said to know, the nature and extent of human knowledge, it was properly philosophical. The greater part of the book was concerned to answer the latter type of question; but it remains true that, as one of the chief experts on Locke of our time has it, Locke 'is rightly regarded as the father of English psychology'.[40]

In either case, his views are clearly matters of great interest to the educationist.

The first part of Locke's *Essay* is concerned to refute one possible source of our knowledge, a view of which had commonly been held even if not in quite the naïve form that Locke expressed it; Locke denied that man possessed in the understanding 'certain *innate principles*; some primary notions, κοιναι ϵννοιαι, characters, as it were stamped upon the mind of man; which the soul receives in its very first being, and brings into the world with it'.[41] By this he did not mean to deny that men possessed innate inclinations or potentialities or dispositions; for example, he admits that 'Nature, I confess, has put into man a desire of happiness and an aversion to misery; these indeed are innate practical principles which (as practical principles ought) do continue constantly to operate and influence all our actions without ceasing': but, he concludes, 'these are inclinations of the appetite to good, not impressions of truth on the understanding',[42] with reference to the latter. 'The scholastic method of basing all knowledge upon maxims which were supposed to be intuitively known as certain was dangerous because it led us to be uncritical of the basic axioms of knowledge.'[43] Thus, he denied the innateness of any rules of morality and speculative principles, or self-evident logical propositions or 'maxims', as they were called. (The sorts of 'maxims' Locke had in mind were that 'what is, is'; that 'it is impossible for the same thing to be and not to be'; that 'the whole is greater than its parts'; and the like.) That such principles do not exist innately Locke shows from the experience of children: 'Hath a child an idea of impossibility and identity, before it has of white or black, sweet or bitter? . . . The names *impossibility* and *identity* stand for two ideas, so far from being innate, or born with us, that I think it requires great care and attention to form them right in our understandings.'[44]

Locke was denying that there was any universally acceptable *a priori* knowledge on which our understanding of the world could be built, if by *a priori* knowledge we imply 'a knowing of principles whereby we order experience, a knowing which is logically prior to that experience itself'.[45] It is important to realise, as Dr John W. Yolton has very clearly brought out, that this disagreement over innateness was very relevant to seventeenth-century controversies, and no dry matter for academic dispute:

In the minds of these critics of Locke's polemic against innate knowledge, the alternative was clear; innate ideas and principles, or relativity of morals. This alternative haunted all the men who read Locke's polemic in the seventeenth century . . . The vital issue between Locke and his critics on this question was the grounds and foundations of morality and religion. The epistemological question concerning the genesis of our ideas was not an isolated theoretical problem for Locke or for his contemporaries. It was a question integral to the practical problems of life.[46]

'Religion and morality had been shaken, tradition questioned', concludes Dr Yolton; for the principles which are regarded as being 'innate', at least in its 'naïve' form, 'are always formulations of the existing values of the society'.[47] By thus questioning the whole notion of 'innate' ideas, in any of the forms in which it appeared (and it appeared in several), Locke seemed to be opening the way to scepticism and atheism; he was at the same time freeing the individual from the constraint of his past; even the rules of morality, far from being innate or self-evident, were such that *'there cannot any one moral rule be proposed whereof a man may not justly demand a reason'*.[48]

The denial of innateness – which has profound educational implications – prefaced the revelation of the experiential basis of all our knowledge. Locke, in fact, accepted the representative theory of perception and knowledge; that is to say, he posited the presence of an intermediary object between the perceiving mind and the ultimate object, an intermediary which he termed an 'idea'. Physical entities could be known only through the mediation of ideas: 'It is evident the mind knows not things immediately, but only by the intervention of the ideas it has of them. Our knowledge, therefore, is real only so far as there is a *conformity* between our ideas and the reality of things.'[49] How, then, does the mind acquire these ideas?

Let us then suppose the mind to be, as we say, white paper void of all characters, without any ideas. How comes it to be furnished? Whence comes it by that vast store which the busy and boundless fancy of man has painted on it with an almost endless variety? Whence has it all the *materials* of reason and knowledge? To this I answer, in one word, from EXPERIENCE. In that all our knowledge is founded; and from that it ultimately derives itself. Our observation, employed either about *external sensible objects, or about the internal operations of our minds, perceived and reflected on by ourselves, is that which supplies our understandings with all the materials of thinking.* These two are the fountains of knowledge, from whence all the ideas we have, or can naturally have, do spring.

First, our Senses, conversant about particular sensible objects, do convey into the mind several distinct perceptions of things, according to those various ways wherein those objects do affect them [i.e. the senses] . . . This great source of most of the ideas we have, depending wholly upon our senses, and derived by them to the understanding, I call SENSATION.

Secondly, the other fountain from which experience furnisheth the understanding with ideas, is the perception of the operations of our own mind within us, as it is employed about the ideas it has got; which operations when the soul comes to reflect on and consider, do furnish the understanding with another set of ideas, which could not be had from things without; and such are *perception, thinking, doubting, believing, reasoning, knowing, willing,* and all the different actings of our own minds; which we being conscious of, and observing in ourselves, do from these receive into our understandings as distinct ideas, as we do from bodies affecting our senses. This source of ideas every man has wholly in himself; and though it be not sense, as having nothing to do with external objects, yet it is very like it, and might properly enough be called *internal sense.* But as I call the other Sensation, so I call this REFLECTION.[50]

The understanding, however, not only required 'ideas'; it was also responsible for the creation of general and universal notions: 'All things that exist being particulars . . . the sorting of them under names is the workmanship of the understanding, taking occasion, from the similitude it observes amongst them, to make abstract general ideas.'[51] Hence it follows that '*general* and *universal* belong not to the real existence of things, but are the inventions and creations of the understanding, made by it for its own use, and concern only signs, whether words or ideas'.[52] Thus 'they are made by the mind, not by nature'. With similar implications he distinguishes between primary and secondary qualities. The primary qualities – solidity, extension, figure, motion or rest, and number – are those which are 'utterly inseparable from the body, in what state so ever it be'.[53] The secondary qualities – colours, smells, tastes and sounds 'and other the like sensible qualities' – are 'nothing in the objects themselves but powers to produce various sensations in us'.[54] This distinction between primary and secondary qualities is an old one; but whereas to the scholastic both were objective, in Locke the secondary qualities are being regarded – like the 'generals' – as subjective, dependent upon mind. (It is relevant to note that 'these primary qualities are just the concepts which the scientist of the seventeenth century found it necessary to presuppose if his science was to be possible'.)[55]

One important aspect of Locke, then, tended to idealism and a certain epistemological scepticism. As a contemporary pointed out, 'The "ideal" principles of Locke lead to scepticism "because they will neither allow us to suppose, nor can prove the real Existence of things without us"'.[56] Also, by making the universal into a meaning, a character or group of characters shared by particulars of the same sort,[57] he made universals dependent on complex ideas which had been formed of a number of particulars. Admittedly 'Men, observing certain qualities always joined and existing together, therein copied nature'; for 'Nobody joins the voice of a sheep with the shape of a horse, nor the colour of lead with the weight and fixedness of gold.'[58] Nevertheless it is the mind which selects the qualities and frames from them an essence. Thus in this respect the tendency was to remove importance from the external world to the viewing mind, from object to subject. As Professor Aaron puts it:

the fixity of the universal is determined from within rather than from without. Whereas for the orthodox Aristotelian standpoint we apprehend *abc* to be essential features of real objects external to and independent of us, so that our universal depends entirely on the nature of the objects outside us and is *discovered* by us, for Locke the universal is 'a creature of our own making'. It is we who decide that *abc* together frame what *we* mean by the general term.[59]

Hence Locke reacted against the universal of both the Aristotelian and the Platonic type, for both

> give the universal a kind of objectivity which, if his view of the universal is sound, it cannot possibly possess. If the term *objectivity* connotes fixity and permanency in meaning, then Locke has room for such objectivity . . . But . . . he never has room for objectivity in the further sense, as meaning what is not created by the mind but is merely apprehended and discovered, and pertains to a world of realities wholly independent of the mind. The universal cannot possess such objectivity, because, in Locke's view, it is I myself who frame the universal . . .[60]

There seems, therefore, in Locke nothing to correspond to the real essence of the Aristotelians as forming 'the very being of anything whereby it is what it is'. It is true that from Locke's point of view, much of the talk about substance was irrelevant. His aims were largely practical and his scepticism theoretical. Though the issue was important because of its theological implications, and hence attracted the outraged comments of contemporaries, Locke was too concerned with the practical implications of his epistemological interests to be seriously worried by theoretical objections.

Nevertheless, Locke's ambivalent position on the subjective–objective continuum has its important educational implications which justify a fairly lengthy exposition. For one thing, it reinforces the subjectivist implications of this 'Crusonian story of initially solitary knowers'[61] based on sense-perception, memory and inference or reflection. But simultaneously it encouraged a more thorough concern for the nature of the external world and its sense data than the world had ever seen previously. Educationally speaking, Locke stressed both the importance of individual psychology and subjective 'bent' ('nature') and the fact that man was, in considerable measure, formed by his environment – those particulars – objective 'things' – of which his 'sensations' made him aware, and formed the basis of his understanding. Where children especially were concerned, sensation was foremost:

> The first years are usually employed and diverted in looking abroad. Men's business in them is to acquaint themselves with what is to be found without; and so growing up in a constant attention to outward sensations, seldom make any considerable reflection on what passes within them, till they come to be of riper years; and some scarce ever at all.[62]

Here surely we have intimations of both subjectivist – later appearing as self-expressive – notions and objective environmentalist theories of educational development. The dilemma can be illustrated by a further brief consideration of his views on language which are complicated by the relation of words to 'ideas' rather than to things in themselves: 'it is perverting the use of words, and brings unavoidable obscurity and confusion into their signification, whenever we make them stand for anything but those ideas we have in our own minds;' instead, a 'great abuse of words is, the *taking them for things*'.[63] Where simple ideas are concerned, there is little problem: 'Whoever . . . mistook the ordinary meaning of *seven* or a *triangle*?';[64] more abstract terms, such as 'justice' or 'glory', dependent on the voluntary collection of simple ideas, the products of individual minds, are more difficult to establish.

This has its relevance to the way in which the meanings of complex terms are first acquired:

If we will observe how children learn languages, we shall find that, to make them understand what the names of simple ideas or substances stand for, people ordinarily show them the thing whereof they would have them have the idea; and then repeat to them the name that stands for it; as *white, sweet, milk, sugar, cat, dog*. But as for mixed modes, especially the most material of them, *moral* words, the sounds are usually learned first; and then, to know what complex ideas they stand for, they are either beholden to the explication of others, or (which happens for the most part) are left to their own observation and industry; which being little laid out in the search of the true and precise meaning of names, these moral words are in most men's mouths little more than bare sounds; or when they have any, it is for the most part but a very loose and undetermined, and, consequently, obscure and confused signification.[65]

Where simple ideas are concerned, 'the only sure way of making known the signification of the name of any simple idea, is *by presenting to his senses that subject which may produce it in his mind*, and make him actually have the idea that word stands for'.[66] It is obvious that Locke's views on language played an important part in his belief that direct experience is *ultimately* the only way to grasp either simple or complex ideas – hence the impetus given to the development of situational education within the world of 'things' so marked in Rousseau.[67] And yet the subjectivist implications of 'natural bent' and of its representation through 'ideas' (so that words relate to 'ideas' and not necessarily to things in themselves) persist as a threat to those who would posit too easy a connection between mind and the stimulus of 'things' in the world. Locke raises the profound issue of the precise relationship between mind and world and produces an ambiguous answer which is to exercise later epistemologists profoundly. Now that the problem of knowledge is moving to the centre of the philosophical scene its resolution in diverse form is found to have important implications for educational theorists for whom knowledge in its post-renaissance form constitutes so central a concern.

V

Locke, then, marked a tendency which

> led to a movement away from metaphysics towards empiricism; from
> scholastic reliance upon definitions and predetermined schemes of
> thought, to an impartial phenomenological analysis of knowledge; from
> a simple, direct form of realism to a complex, representative position
> embodied in the generally accepted way of ideas; from making theory
> of knowledge harmonize with the requirements of religious beliefs and
> theological dogma, to the reverse: to making theology keep in step with
> the demands of the phenomenological analysis of knowledge.[68]

In the process he makes education of the utmost importance; for his denial
of innateness fosters a tendency to look to human formation and education
as the vital element in the development of human beings, even beyond what
the humanists – who certainly realised that men were 'fashioned not born' –
had considered. Perhaps the most famous words Locke ever penned on
education were those which appeared in the first section of the *Thoughts*:
'I think I may say that of all the men we meet with, nine parts of ten are
what they are, good or evil, useful or not, by their education. 'Tis that which
makes the great difference in mankind.' Though there are elements elsewhere in the *Thoughts* which indicate some inconsistency with this position,
it was a statement which was later to feed into the uniformitarian tendencies
of the next century.

Yet his work marks a certain limitation, even a desiccation, of sensibility
which emerges in his curricular prescriptions. What I mean can be gleaned
initially from his remarks contrasting 'wit' with 'judgement' to the advantage
of the latter:

> For *wit* lying most in the assemblage of ideas, and putting those to-
> gether with quickness and variety, wherein can be found any resemblance
> or congruity, thereby to make up pleasant pictures and agreeable visions
> in the fancy; *judgement*, on the contrary, lies quite on the other side, in
> separating carefully one from another, ideas wherein can be found the
> least difference, thereby to avoid being misled by similitude, and by
> affinity to take one thing for another. This is a way of proceeding quite
> contrary to metaphor and allusion.[69]

This reinforces the impression gained from Bacon's coolness on the subject
of poetry; analysis replaces 'creativity' and meaning is to be found primarily
and most fruitfully in an attempted congruence of mind and world arrived
at through 'sense experience', through the similitude of ideas and 'things'.
The very definitive flatness of Locke's style reinforces the note of sobriety
inherent in Bishop Sprat's 'mathematical plainness', his inability to detect
in metaphor, for instance, an alternative mode of exploring 'reality', of
revealing complexities which are beyond the plain statement of 'clear and
distinct' ideas. Locke may have opened up 'a whole new subject for philoso-

phical enquiry', epistemology, and had a fertilising influence on philosophical thinking which even today is not exhausted. Perhaps, however, it is as well to conclude this survey of his philosophical views with a warning from Santayana. The modernness of Locke, he discovers, lies in his tendency to deny his own presuppositions in line with that tendency, characteristic of both Descartes and Locke, to foster a fresh start and repudiate the past. Such procedures of denial we take for granted as desirable, ignorant as we are of the 'natural causes which have imposed them on the animal mind'. He proceeds:

> But this critical assurance in its turn seems to rely on a dubious presupposition, namely, that human opinion must always evolve in a single line, dialectically, providentially, and irresistibly. It is at least conceivable that the opposite should sometimes be the case. Some of the primitive presuppositions of human reason might have been correct and inevitable, whilst the tendency to deny them might have sprung from a plausible misunderstanding, or the exaggeration of a half-truth; so that the critical opinion itself, after destroying the spontaneous assumptions on which it rested, might be incapable of subsisting.[70]

VI

I have already referred to Locke's apparent relevance, educationally speaking, to the aristocratic tradition. He had read *The Courtier* and had been much influenced by what was still essentially the aristocratic ideal of Montaigne. His central stress on conduct as much as – indeed rather than – learning, his desire to form a total, rounded personality, and the similarity of the core of his recommendations – implying an emphasis on 'gracefulness' and on 'an habitual and becoming easiness', strongly critical of any manifestations of affectation – echoes Castiglione's concern for 'grace' and his evocation of *sprezzatura*. There is much, too, in his concern for the centrality of 'artifice' – associated with his general view of child nature – which is reminiscent of the humanists. Philosophically advanced, Locke himself proves to be educationally conservative in many matters apart from the role assigned to the understanding and its objects and its implied cognitive autonomy, where there is a decisive break with traditional models.

His specific epistemological interests in themselves indicate what is to prove a certain reorientation of curricular interest. Certainly he was concerned with the education of the sons of gentlemen – those below the rank of baron – and his is essentially a class society, so that 'a prince, a nobleman, and an ordinary gentleman's son, should have different ways of breeding'.[71] Yet it is clear that Locke belongs to the world of 'things' which has now entered the gentleman's purview to an extent unthinkable in the sixteenth century. His stress on scientific and technical pursuits as relevant to a gentleman's activities reflects the influence of Bacon and contemporary scientists like his friends Richard Boyle and Isaac Newton. This is the 'doctrine of courtesy' –

clearly still manifest – becoming useful in a quite different sense from that intended by Castiglione. Furthermore Locke's concern with the nature and functioning of mind has implications for his educational views. It witnesses to that psychological awareness which constitutes one of his chief additions to educational theory. His subjectivism contributed to that dissolution of the objective world of the ancients and the scholastics and, by making world in some degree at least dependent on mind, encouraged an increasing emphasis on the pupil and an attention to his psychological characteristics.

Locke's denial of innate ideas had important consequences.[72] For the effect was to place great stress not only on the importance of education but also on the development of autonomous reasoning powers. And indeed, he speaks in one place of the child as 'white paper, or wax, to be moulded and fashioned as one pleases'.[73] The humanists, too, had spoken of 'moulding' but they had not assumed quite so virgin a field for their endeavours. Nevertheless, like the humanists, Locke holds two somewhat inconsistent views of the role of the educator, an inconsistency which stems from a certain traditional ambivalence towards child nature. Lurking in Locke's advice, indeed, are three different views of 'nature' all of which are broadly familiar from humanist times: two relate to innate disposition (for it will be remembered that although Locke denied the presence of innate *ideas*, he admitted the presence of innate *propensities* or *inclinations*). Sometimes he speaks as if such 'natural' characteristics (manifest largely in psychological terms) are matters to be encouraged, sometimes he writes as if 'nature' is something to be overcome in the course of human education. Finally he seems to indicate that what is achieved as a result of education, nurture, is itself 'natural'. So 'nature' referring to origins, can provide characteristics which are both desirable and to be resisted; and it is also used to refer to outcomes which he regards as desirable – a harking back to the older view, shared with the humanists, of man's 'natural' potential for good. Its use is therefore both descriptive and normative. There may be a somewhat different emphasis here – but also much that belongs still to the humanist tradition.

In *The Conduct of the Understanding*, Locke stresses the richness of 'natural' endowment, almost as if with the right sort of education – and the emphasis is placed on upbringing (as artifice) as the essential component in the actualising of this potential – there were few limits to human capacity.

We are born with faculties and powers capable almost of anything . . . but it is only the exercise of those powers which gives us ability and skill in anything, and leads us towards perfection . . .

As it is in the body, so it is in the mind: practice makes it what it is; and most even of those excellencies which are looked on as natural endowments, will be found, when examined into more narrowly, to be the product of exercise, and to be raised to that pitch only by repeated actions.

To what purpose all this but to show that the difference so observable in men's understandings and parts does not arise so much from their natural faculties as acquired habits.[74]

There are strong hints of uniformitarian tendencies here – 'naturally' men have similar potentialities and differences arise as a result of education. But elsewhere this view is modified on the grounds that 'natural dispositions' turn a child's mind one way rather than another, and represent a check to the complete ability of the educator to fashion as he pleases. Such differences of 'natural parts' are quite frequently referred to, sometimes in terms very different from the implied homogeneity of the previous reference:

> There is . . . great variety in men's understandings, and their natural constitutions put so wide a difference between some men in this respect, that art and industry would never be able to master, and their very natures seem to want a foundation to raise on it that which other men easily attain unto. Amongst men of equal education there is great inequality of parts.[75]

Thus 'strength of memory is owing to a happy constitution, and not to any habitual improvement got by exercise'.[76] The apprehension of this original difference in endowment makes Locke urge the educator to observe the child, in order to find out 'which way the natural make of his mind inclines him':

> Begin therefore betimes nicely to observe your son's temper, and that, when he is under least restraint. See what are his predominant passions and prevailing inclinations . . . For as these are different in him, so are your methods to be different, and your authority must hence take measures to apply itself [in] different ways to him . . . But of this be sure, after all is done, the bias will always hang on that side that nature first placed it.[77]

Locke's appreciation of individual differences is much more detailed than that of the humanists. It involves careful psychological observation of behaviour in order to discover what each child is 'naturally' best fitted for; the child is coming to be seen as an objective entity:

> By this method we shall see, whether what is required of him be adapted to his capacity, and any way suited to the child's natural genius and constitution: for that too must be considered in a right education. We must not hope wholly to change their original tempers, nor make the gay pensive and grave; nor the melancholy sportive, without spoiling them. God has stamped certain characters upon men's minds, which, like their shapes, may perhaps be a little mended; but can hardly be totally altered and transformed into the contrary.
>
> He, therefore, that is about children, should well study their natures and aptitudes, and see, by often trials, what turn they easily take, and what becomes them; observe what their native stock is, how it may be improved, and what it is fit for; he should consider what they want, whether they be capable of having it wrought into them by industry,

and incorporated there by practice; and whether it be worth while to endeavour it. For, in many cases, all that we can do, or should aim at, is, to make the best of what nature has given, to prevent the vices and faults to which such a constitution is most inclined, and give it all the advantages it is capable of. Every one's natural genius should be carried as far as it could; but to attempt the putting another upon him, will be but labour in vain; and what is so plastered on, will at best sit but untowardly, and have always hanging to it the ungracefulness of constraint and affectation.[78]

We have preliminary intimations of child-centredness here. Are, then, children to be regarded as blank pages or as bundles of propensities? Is it the job of the educator to fight or to follow 'nature'? In certain respects it was necessary to combat natural tendencies; thus children lack reason and judgement: 'their want of judgement makes them stand in need of restraint and discipline'.[79] Again, they have a 'natural propensity to indulge corporal and present pleasure';[80] furthermore, 'The natural temper of children disposes their minds to wander.' These features must be taken into account, and must guide the behaviour of the educator accordingly. In these cases, his job is to overcome 'natural' propensities, and induce changes of attitude which involve definite intervention; it is necessary to offset 'unguided nature' in teaching children to resist their 'inclinations', for instance.

Often, however, it is the job of the educator to go along with 'natural' disposition. Thus

What they do cheerfully of themselves, do they not presently grow sick of, and can no more endure, as soon as they find it is expected of them as a duty? . . .

As a consequence of this, they should seldom be put upon doing even those things you have got an inclination in them to, but when they have a mind and disposition to it.[81]

They like their freedom and should be subtly encouraged to seek instruction rather than have it imposed: 'the chief art is make all that they have to do sport and play'.[82] Again, where some of the minor accomplishments are concerned, like drawing, the tutor is to consider natural talent in deciding whether it is worth bothering about them at all. The child may, says Locke, soon acquire the necessary skill in drawing 'especially if he have a genius to it: but where that is wanting, unless it be in the things absolutely necessary, it is better to let him pass them by quietly, than to vex him about them to no purpose: and therefore in this, as in all other things not absolutely necessary, the rule holds, "*Nihil invita Minerva*" '.[83]

VII

It is, however, but a comparatively small step from concern with 'nature' in these psychological respects to the erection of 'nature' as a principle superior in some ways to human intervention. Thus, in arguing against tight clothing Locke urges: 'Let Nature have scope to fashion the body as she thinks best. She works of herself a great deal better and exacter, than we can direct her.'[84] Professor J. L. Axtell, in a footnote to section 108, even extends the range of Locke's recommendations: 'In all his philosophy – educational, medical and epistemological Locke recommended that "Nature have scope"[85] etc. [cf. above]. In the *Essay*, his emphasis was on the natural limitations of the human understanding; in medicine, on natural cures, such as rest, fresh air, and proper foods.'[86] There is an occasional hint that the social world – parents, social custom – can corrupt and pervert: 'parents, by humouring and cockering them when little, corrupt the principles of nature in their children . . .'[87] Again, Locke suggests that social customs can plant 'unnatural appetites' by introducing children to cruelty and the idea of killing. To find pleasure in pain 'I cannot persuade myself to be any other than a foreign and introduced disposition, an habit borrowed from custom and conversation . . . Thus, by fashion and opinion, that comes to be a pleasure, which in itself neither is, nor can be any.'[88] This ought to be guarded against 'so as to settle and cherish the contrary, and more natural temper of benignity and compassion in the room of it'.[89] Yet in general Locke is too much at home in his society to favour unassisted 'nature'; the responsibilities of choice are usually placed explicitly in the hands of the adult; he has to choose which to encourage among the observable psychological potentialities of the child – only rarely is the suggestion of the superiority of human abdication made on the grounds that nature (as a normative principle) 'knows' best.

So overall the aim remains a cultural ideal still much in the humanist tradition – for by a legerdemain so typical in the use of this word 'nature', Locke finds that the outcomes of *guided* nature are also 'natural': rightly so, of course, because – I have noted the point earlier – it is 'natural' to human beings to be the products of artifice, and without sorting out the semantic confusions Locke implicitly recognises this fact. Thus while at one moment we are enjoined to make 'the best of what nature has given', we are the next recommended to 'wipe off all that plainness of nature, which the *à-la-mode* people call clownishness'.[90] Such changes as are to be made must themselves become 'natural': 'what he is to receive from education . . . must be something put into him betimes, habits woven into the very principles of his nature'.[91] It is not, that is to say, to be regarded as something assumed externally, as a 'counterfeit carriage, and dissembled outside'.[92] In this way what is formed becomes 'natural' in this other sense – in line with an ideal of conduct which in turn is in harmony with what can be regarded as the 'natural' inclinations of human beings to achieve a high degree of artifice 'by repeating the same action, till it be grown habitual in them, the performance will not depend on memory, or reflection . . . but will be *natural* in them. Thus, bowing to a gentleman when he salutes him, and looking in his face when he speaks to him, is by constant use as *natural* to a well-bred man as breathing.'[93] Here, what is 'natural' is what has been acquired, after the process described as the 'weeding' out of faults, and the 'planting' of habits more pleasing. Thus we return once more to the paradox of *The Courtier* – the artificial can become the natural by manifesting itself as an art which hides art by a process of inner assimilation. We encounter similar objections to 'affectation' as the product of an art which reveals itself in a lack of ease:

> *Affectation* is not, I confess, an early Fault of Childhood, or the Product of untaught Nature; it is of that sort of Weeds, which grow not in the wild uncultivated Waste, but in Garden-Plots, under the Negligent Hand, or Unskilful Care of a Gardner. For this Reason it is the more carefully to be watched, because it is the proper Fault of Education; a perverted Education indeed, but such as young People often fall into, either, by their own Mistake, or the ill Conduct of those about them.[94]

In its place is to be substituted, again in the courtier tradition, 'Gracefulness'; as defined by Locke it is evocative of that 'sprezzatura' emphasised by Castiglione: that art which so hides art as to have become 'natural,' so 'easy' as to 'flow' from a 'well turn'd disposition', with a mind free, in an effortless 'unconstrained' way:

> He that will examine, wherein that Gracefulness lies, which always pleases, will find it arises from that Natural Coherence, which appears between the Thing done, and such a Temper of Mind, as cannot but be approved of, as suitable to the Occasion . . . A mind free not low and narrow, not haughty and insolent, not blemished with any great Defect, is what every one is taken with. The Actions, which naturally flow from such a well-formed Mind, please us also, as the genuine Marks of it; and being as it were natural Emanations from the Spirit and Disposition within, cannot but be easy and unconstrain'd. This seems to me to be that Beauty, which shines through some Men's Actions . . .; when by a constant Practice, they have fashion'd their Carriage, and made all those little Expressions of Civility and Respect, which Nature or Custom has established in Conversation so easy to themselves, that they seem not Artificial or Studied, but naturally to flow from a Sweetness of Mind, and a well turn'd Disposition.[95]

So 'the carriage [i.e. deportment] is not as it should be, till it is become natural in every part; falling, as skilful musicians' fingers do, into harmonious order without care and without thought'.[96] Habit and example are the sources of this easy grace in the renaissance 'imitative' tradition: style of deportment, precepts, rules are of little use:

> let them have what instruction you will, and ever so learned lectures on breeding daily inculcated into them, that which will influence their carriage, will be the company they converse with and the fashion of those about them. Children (nay, and men too) do most by example. We are all a sort of cameleons, that still take a tincture from things near us.[97]

Hence the injunction to keep children away from the example and 'flatteries' of servants. 'Imitation' clearly plays an analogous role to that assigned to it in *The Courtier* in this area of education – and a sort of 'freedom' is its outcome – a positive freedom to behave gracefully.

VIII

Behaviour, then, in terms of manners, social relationships, is in the Courtier tradition. (And, of course, the tradition persists, as the *Letters* of Lord Chesterfield make clear.)[98] The radical departure from that tradition lies in the role assigned to conscious understanding and reason with implications for the nature of the recommended curriculum. The Courtier-Governors were to become literate and well read in humanist acquired learning; but the role assigned to the rational powers of the mind takes on a different complexion in Locke and operates in a very different context. The exercise of the rational judgement in deploying the moral authority of the ancients, manifest in a persuasive eloquence as the driving force behind political decision making, is to be replaced by the examination of relevant phenomena, social or natural, and the arrival at rational conclusions on the basis of the acquired evidence.

In his *Conduct of the Understanding*, Locke urges the fundamental importance of the understanding in the conduct of a man's affairs (and of course his aim was to produce a man of affairs, of business): action should always be supported by reasons: 'No man ever sets himself about anything but upon some view or other, which serves him for a reason for what he does: and whatsoever faculties he employs, the understanding, with such light as it has, well or ill formed, constantly leads; and by that light, true or false, all his operative powers are directed.'[99] In considering his views on education, then, it is of fundamental importance – and incidentally highly revealing of his view of reason and its functioning, its relation to authority and to 'particulars' characteristic of the new empiricism – to consider how the 'understanding' should be formed. For Locke considered it to be of the highest importance that the understanding should be rightly conducted in its search for knowledge and the judgement it makes.

So he sets out in the *Conduct* to refute contemporary methods of logical training of the intellect in the scholastic tradition and to advance a better method of education, adducing 'the great Lord Verulam's' authority for his innovatory zeal. He begins by listing current defects. There are those who trust tradition and example; those who 'put passion in the place of reason' and content themselves with 'words which have no distinct ideas to them'; and those who although they use reason, do not see sufficiently round a question because of failure to correct personal impressions by the wider experience of others.

As example Locke compares the religious bigot and the man who 'surveys our differences in religion with an equitable and fair indifference'[100] and asks which is the more likely to judge rightly of new religious controversies? Obviously the latter is intended, assuming, as Locke makes clear he does, that the two men start with equal endowments, and 'all the odds between them has been the different scope that has been given to their understandings to range in, for the gathering up of information and furnishing their heads with ideas and notions and observations, whereon to employ their mind and form their understandings'.[101] Only in thus ranging far and wide, exercising the freedom of his intellect within the whole field, will the understanding be improved and a 'logical chicaner [be distinguished from] a man of reason'.[102] Width of knowledge through observation is thus an important component of reason.

The free ranging intellect serves as a protection against 'prejudice'. Prejudice may always be recognised by considering the nature of the evidence on which conclusions are founded, for assent should be 'no greater than what the evidence of the truth he holds forces him to'.[103] A man must therefore always be willing to examine the grounds of his beliefs and realise the need to consider arguments for and against them. Yet 'Men are fond of certain tenets upon no other evidence but respect and custom, and think they must maintain them or all is gone.'[104] Instead they must show an indifferency (i.e. impartiality) for all truth, in the sense of loving it simply because it is truth and for no other reason. The appeal is to observation, not authority; the model of reasoning is become a scientific one.

And so Locke goes on to consider the nature of the procedures which might lead to the acceptance of the truth of a proposition. He mentions some erroneous criteria of beliefs (e.g. 'it hath been long received in the world, therefore it is true; or, it is new, and therefore false').[105] Instead it is necessary to get 'clear and determined ideas' for 'particular matters of fact are the undoubted foundations on which our civil and natural knowledge is built'. Then comes the need to acquire the 'notion of a long train of consequences from sure foundations'. He considers practice essential: 'would you have a man reason well, you must use him to it betimes, exercise his mind in observing the connexion of ideas and following them in train'.[106]

Stressing the need for 'industry and application', he recommends mathematical reasoning as a model of how to proceed in many types of argumentation: 'For in all sorts of reasoning every single argument should be managed as a mathematical demonstration.'[107] The value of mathematics in training lies in its revelation of 'the necessity there is in reasoning, to separate all the distinct ideas, and see the habitudes [i.e. relations] that all those concerned in the present enquiry have to one another, and to lay by those which relate not to the proposition in hand, and wholly to leave them out of the reckoning'.[108] He is concerned, therefore, that reason should proceed on a basis of right *fact* and also that it should observe in more complex and abstract argumentation those rules which depend on the distinctness and clarity of the ideas employed and their relevance to the question in hand.

What matters, however, is not exclusively the acquiring of knowledge, but the acquisition of the means by which learning may be both fostered and deployed:

The business [of education] in respect of knowledge, is not, as I think, to perfect a learner in all or any one of the sciences, but to give his mind that freedom, that disposition, and those habits that may enable him to attain any part of knowledge he shall apply himself to, or stand in need of, in the future course of his life.[109]

This intellectual psychic mobility, and not 'the instilling a reverence and veneration for certain dogmas under the specious title of principles' is the business of education.

In considering the defects to which the understanding is prone the same criteria are apparent. Certainly understanding must be based on correct knowledge of the facts; but some fail to draw conclusions from their knowledge; others fly to axioms all too quickly, 'from every particular they meet with'.[110] Some allow themselves to be biased, forgetting that 'To think of everything just as it is in itself, is the proper business of the understanding.'[111] Again, some learn up arguments of others on which to base their beliefs, whereas

The sure and only way to get true knowledge, is to form in our minds clear settled notions of things, with names annexed to those determined ideas . . . It is in the perception of the habitudes and respects our ideas have one to another that real knowledge consists, and when a man once perceives how far they agree or disagree one with another, he will be able to judge of what other people say, and will not need to be led by the arguments of others.[112]

Flexibility of mind comes from width of experience in a variety of fields: 'But I do not propose it as a variety and stock of knowledge, but a variety and freedom of thinking; as an increase of the powers and activity of the mind, not as an enlargement of its possessions.'[113]

In other words, the emphasis is on learning how to learn, application, rather than simply on accumulating facts, though a clear factual basis is important. The whole implied relationship to the tradition is quite different from that of the humanists – we have the self-activated knower learning to confront experience equipped only with relevant reasoning powers rather than the product of 'imitation'. Thus, reading does not necessarily lead to understanding: 'Reading furnishes the mind only with materials of knowledge, it is thinking makes what we read ours.'[114] The partiality to particular studies that men happen to be skilled in, except in the case when theology is the subject,[115] often leads to arrogance or the application of techniques learnt in one field to fields where they do not apply. Again, it leads to the attribution of all knowledge to the ancients or moderns; or to truth as dependent on popularity; or to truth as dependent on authority, especially that in books: books, indeed, are 'great helps of the understanding and instruments of knowledge', but can keep men 'from attaining to solid and true knowledge. This I think I may be permitted to say, that there is no part wherein the understanding needs a more careful and wary conduct than in the use of books.'[116] Thus Locke supports that reaction against traditional knowledge which Bacon had early publicised, knowledge relying on 'citations' and 'authorities'.

The handling of language, it will be inferred, can be a frequent source of error, when (the familiar theme) 'words' are mistaken for 'things': 'They who would advance in knowledge, and not deceive and swell themselves with a little articulated air, should lay down this as a fundamental rule, not to take words for things, not suppose that names in books signify real entities in nature, till they can frame clear and distinct ideas of those entities.'[117] A word needs to evoke a distinct idea in the mind of a reader. All too often empty terms have misled people, so that 'the supposing of some realities in nature answering those and the like words, have much perplexed some and quite misled others in the study of nature'.[118] Our conceptions are made up of ideas, so that if people 'cannot give us the ideas their words stand for it is plain they have none'; for 'Words are not made to conceal, but to declare and show something.'[119] He reveals a specific distaste for the humanists when he asserts that 'eloquence, like the fair sex, involves a pleasurable deceit'. (Those with a humanist training, as has been noted, were not unaware of the possibility.)

Locke attacks the scholastics for the 'distinctions' which their philosophy has led them to observe, in contrast with that apprehension of true divisions which nature really has placed in things. Distinctions are

> to be taken only from a due contemplation of things, to which there is nothing more opposite than the art of verbal distinctions made at pleasure in learned and arbitrarily invented terms . . . It is not therefore the right way to knowledge to hunt after and fill the head with abundance of artificial and scholastic distinctions . . . knowledge consists only in perceiving the habitudes and relations of ideas one to another, which is done without words . . . he that will conduct his understanding right must not look for [distinctions] in the acuteness of invention nor the authority of writers, but will find only in the consideration of things themselves, whether he is led into it by his own meditations or the information of books.[120]

Thus Locke aligns himself with those – like Bacon – who consider that the mind should 'buckle' itself to the nature of things as they are in themselves, and that 'Evidence . . . is that by which alone every man is (and should be) taught to regulate his assent . . .'[121] Indeed 'ignorance with an indifferency for truth is nearer to it than opinion with ungrounded inclination, which is the great source of error'.[122] To inhibit the formation of bad verbal habits Locke points to the value of visual aids for children learning to read:

> If his Aesop has pictures in it, it will entertain him much the better, and encourage him to read when it carries the increase of knowledge with it: for such visible objects children hear talked of in vain . . . whilst they have no ideas of them; those ideas not to be had from sounds, but from the things themselves, or their pictures.[123]

This emphasis on 'real' or positive knowledge acquired through the senses should accompany the subsequent learning of Latin: 'the learning of Latin being nothing but the learning of words, a very unpleasant business both to young and old, join as much other real knowledge with it as you can, beginning still with that which lies most obvious to the senses; such . . . as is the knowledge of minerals, plants, and animals . . .'[124] Children, indeed, 'may be taught anything that falls under their senses, especially their sight';[125] but 'the art and formality of disputing' should be avoided lest the pupil becomes 'an insignificant wrangler'.[126] Experiment and inquiry are what bring us to true knowledge, and the mind should range at will free from all passion: 'it is best that it should be always at liberty, and under the free disposal of the man, and to act how and upon what he directs'.[127] Dogmatism, authority, ancient categorisations imprison the mind.

And so the main characteristics of Locke's view of reason become apparent. The mind is to be freed from ancient authority and to exercise itself in an understanding of the 'real' world of things and 'particulars' of which it is to form true ideas. It must be bound by the 'evidence' – and 'evidence' is derived from both the world of things and from the agreement of clear and distinct ideas one with another. There is truth to 'fact' and truth to the rules of reasoning based on truth to fact and the relevance of distinct ideas one to another. His aim is partly iconoclastic in the Baconian tradition and partly to reconstruct a surer basis for knowledge and understanding than that implicit in ancient authority. And that basis must be truth – truth to 'particulars' and truth to the laws of evidence; so that from sensation and reflection men be better equipped to pursue their social lives, more tolerant and less dogmatic; relieved in their daily existence by the discoveries that the new, unpretentious philosophy has enabled men to make. It constitutes the claim of the individual intellect against the claims of custom, tradition and dogma; it appeals, in the scientific manner, to the actuality of observation.

In this he was at one with his age: 'At the outset of Locke's intellectual career, we notice the same determination to strike out an independent line, the same desire to begin again *de novo*, the same anxiety to be intellectually free and self-sufficient, which was working like leaven in the spirit of the age.'[128] He was against mystery, against metaphysics – like the philosophers of the eighteenth century whom he so profoundly influenced: 'Our business here is not to know all things, but those which concern our conduct. If we can find out those measures whereby a rational creature, put in that state which man is in this world, may and ought to govern his opinions and actions depending thereon, we need not be troubled that some others things escape our knowledge.'[129]

The importance of this new image of how men should conduct themselves (for it is essentially decision oriented) in their practical life can hardly be overstressed; in essentials it defines the ideal of rational behaviour with which many of us still hope to manage our affairs. The two key words I have emphasised are 'indifferency' and 'evidence'. The rational man, in Locke's view, is one who has conquered passion or premature commitment to a specific standpoint in favour of impartial investigation; and in coming to a decision he must be bound not by inclination or personal feeling on the one hand or the authority of others on the other but by the 'evidence' which he can make available. Persuasion to action is no longer the prerogative of the personalised appeals of oratory but awaits the impersonal implacability of knowledge.

For certain important types of decision making it clearly provides a relevant model – though it underplays, as Professor Oakshott has pointed out, the need to operate from inside the tradition of procedure relevant to the category of decisions to be taken. There is much even here that must simply be accepted on the authority of predecessors as constituting the correct habits of use and wont. The ability even to search for evidence assumes at least a prior capacity to recognise what is to count as relevant; and this presumes some previous unquestioned – though not unquestionable – initiation into the form of understanding as a prerequisite to the acceptance of what is to count as sufficient reason.

But its emphasis on impartiality is clearly inappropriate in certain forms of decision making. Would it help one to decide whom to marry, for instance? Furthermore, does it not evidence an undue degree of scepticism by demanding 'evidence' in contexts where faith could be thought to have as important a part to play as rational appraisal? In attempting to banish mystery it exceeds, paradoxically, the terms of its own licence to operate in a manner which is not altogether unreasonable – for if one thing is certain it is that life is a mystery. The emphasis on clarity and distinctness which characterises its 'way of ideas' implies an initial analytical undertaking and a consequent restriction of focus which may very well omit vital elements in the issue at stake; at the least it places an undue strain on the capacity to recognise relevance. In this connection its concern for the fresh start, the banishment of previous authorities in a spirit of initiation constitute procedures potentially at least as dictatorial as the submission to precedent, habit, custom or tradition it seeks to replace.

IX

Certainly it betokens the early appearance of an educational model which has become popular among the philosophers of our own day – that of autonomous man – man freed in his intellect from the tyrannies of the past to come to his own decisions. It is then the more interesting to re-emphasise that Locke in effect absolves certain areas of behaviour from the scrutiny of the understanding in a way which would seem highly reprehensible to later advocates. For instance, the traditional habits of a gentleman are not called into question – under the guise of 'breeding' they are accepted from the aristocratic tradition and passed on in all their intangibility as essential characteristics of this practical member of the upper classes. Even the pre-eminence of the need for Virtue is not argued or supported on any grounds of 'evidence'.

And indeed Locke does not put the education of the understanding first among his educational aims, but prefers to draw on the accumulated capital

of a specific mode of behaviour for his major purposes, placing learning last
on his list: 'That which every gentleman . . . desires for his son . . . is contained I suppose in these four things, Virtue, Wisdom, Breeding and Learning.'[130] As with Castiglione, then, this constitutes the education of a complete
human being – morals, manners, behaviour as well as learning. Virtue is
placed first – and in terms which would seem to suggest little opportunity for
personal decision taking or the exercise of understanding. It is, Locke asserts,
something 'harder to be got than a knowledge of the world'. And so 'That
which requires most time, pain, and assiduity, is to *work into them* the principles and practice of virtue and good breeding' (my italics).[131] Modern
notions of the development of moral autonomy are out of place; indeed, it
is advised that the young shall be removed from social contact with their
fellows for fear of contamination. Thus the usual argument used to justify
sending boys to school, that they will learn a certain ease and confidence
among their fellows, is refuted: 'it is not the waggeries or cheats practised
among school boys . . . that make an able man; but the principles of justice,
generosity and sobriety, joined with observation and industry, qualities
which I judge schoolboys do not learn much of one another'.[132] Vice is
acquired so easily. Hence segregation, not the opportunities to develop
moral insight, constitutes the approved method.

To promote Virtue, children should learn to tell the truth; and they
should acquire a true knowledge of God. It is, however, inadvisable to go
too far in attempting to explain the nature of God to a child, lest his head be
'filled with false, or perplexed with unintelligible notions of Him'. All it is
necessary for the child to know is that God is the maker and doer of good to
all who love and obey him. 'I think it would be better, if men generally
rested in such an idea of God, without being too curious in their notions
about a being, which all must acknowledge incomprehensible; whereby
many . . . run themselves into superstition or atheism . . .'[133] One notes simultaneously both an unwillingness to pursue mystery and an element of
indoctrination.

Wisdom, Locke's second desideratum, is in the main not a thing that
children can acquire; it refers to 'a man's managing his business ably and
with foresight in this world. This is the product of a good natural temper,
application of mind and experience together, and not to be taught children.'[134]
Children can only be taught to 'have true notions of things . . . to raise [their]
minds to great and worthy thoughts; and to keep [them] at a distance from
falsehood'[135] in preparation for what, at their age, is beyond their grasp.

For a gentleman, Breeding, his third requisite, is obviously vitally important. 'Knowledge of the world' takes priority over knowledge: 'A great part
of the learning now in fashion in the schools of Europe, and that goes ordinarily
into the round of education, a gentleman may, in a good measure, be un-
furnished with, without any great disparagement to himself, or prejudice to
his affairs.'[136] What are needed instead are 'prudence and good breeding . . .
the knowledge of a man of business, a carriage suitable to his rank, and to be
eminent and useful in his country, according to his station'. If he wants
learning, he can acquire it for himself later:

The great work of a governor is to fashion the carriage, and form the mind: to settle in his pupil good habits, and the principles of virtue and wisdom; to give him, by little and little, a view of mankind; and work him into a love and imitation of what is excellent and praiseworthy; and in the prosecution of it, to give him vigour, activity, and industry.[137]

In the acquiring of these social virtues, dancing plays an important part:

And since nothing appears to me to give children so much becoming confidence and behaviour, and so to raise them to conversation of those above their age, as dancing, I think they should be taught to dance, as soon as they are capable of learning it. For, though this consist only in outward gracefulness of motion, yet, I know not how, it gives children manly thoughts and carriage, more than any thing.[138]

At the same time, Locke warns that he would 'not have children much tormented about punctilious, or niceties of breeding'.[139] These can be acquired later. Furthermore, he warns against the learning of 'apish, affected postures'; a 'natural unfashionableness' is much to be preferred; 'And I think it much more passable to put off the hat, and make a leg, like an honest country gentleman, than like an ill-fashioned dancing-master.'[140]

One of the requirements of social life is a willingness to share what one has with one's friends. Covetousness, 'being the root of all evil, should be early and carefully weeded out; and the contrary quality, of a readiness to impart to others, implanted'.[141] Furthermore, children should become inured to small hurts: 'They should be hardened against all sufferings, especially of the body, and have a tenderness only of shame and for reputation. The many inconveniences this life is exposed to, require we should not be too sensible to every little hurt.'[142]

There are, then, whole areas of human behaviour which must be 'implanted', 'fashioned', 'worked into', made habitual, derived from 'imitation', acquired without that questioning that Locke seems to consider the essential function of the understanding. Like many pioneers, he is only partially able to transcend what his later followers would come to regard as the 'prejudices' of his times and social ambience. 'Autonomy' is to be confined to the area of the understanding – it is not appropriate to certain vital areas of conduct.

Learning has been placed last, and indeed, Locke considers it of least importance: 'I imagine you would think him a very foolish fellow, that should not value a virtuous or a wise man infinitely before a great scholar. Not but that I think learning a great help to both, in well-disposed minds; but yet it must be confessed also, that in others not so disposed, it helps them only to be the more foolish or worse men.'[143] And he has some scornful remarks to make on those who think that Latin and Greek are of such fundamental importance; they are inferior to 'virtue, and a well-tempered soul'[144] – and yet 'Latin and learning make all the noise'.[145] His whole orientation, indeed, is in this respect profoundly anti-humanist and anti-scholastic. He deprecates specifically the humanist practice of writing 'themes' and verses.

A 'taste' of the sciences and of scholarship is what is necessary and a capacity for application 'to keep him from sauntering and idleness': 'For who expects, that under a tutor a young gentleman should be an accomplished critic, orator, or logician? Go to the bottom of metaphysics, natural philosophy or mathematics? Or be a master in history or chronology?' All that is necessary is 'to open the door, that he may look in'.[146] Once more, the stress is on learning how to learn; the mind is to become an instrument for, rather than a repository of, learning: 'his tutor should remember that his business is not so much to teach him all that is knowable, as to raise in him a love and esteem of knowledge; and to put him in the right way of knowing and improving himself, when he has a mind to it'.[147]

What a boy needs to be taught is that 'which will be of most and frequentest use to him in the world';[148] and he must begin by learning to read and write and 'to express himself well in his own tongue'.[149] Then he should learn French, followed by Latin. Latin, though 'absolutely necessary to a gentleman', is a waste for anyone who is going to enter upon a trade, where 'he fails not to forget that little which he brought from school'.[150] When learnt, it is to be acquired by the direct method, for usage: 'I know not why any one should waste his time, and beat his head about the Latin grammar, who does not intend to be a critic, or make speeches, and write dispatches in it';[151] the Latin learnt is to assist reading, not for the writing of themes and verses. Greek is only necessary for a scholar.

Drawing is to be encouraged, because of its utility during foreign travel; moreover, some skill in perspective and drawing has its uses.[152] Locke indeed is against the arts except insofar as they administer to utility. He objected to children learning to write Latin verses as he objected to verses and poetry in general, thus repudiating what had had an important place in the humanist curriculum. Poetry and gaming he thought often went together; there were clearly limits beyond which it might be undesirable to follow the natural bent of children:

> and if he have a poetic vein, it is to me the strangest thing in the world, that the father should desire or suffer it to be cherished or improved. Methinks the parents should labour to have it stifled and suppressed as much as may be; and I know not what reason a father can have to wish his son a poet, who does not desire to have him bid defiance to all other callings and business: which is not yet the worst of the case; for if he proves a successful rhymer, and gets once the reputation of a wit, I desire it may be considered what company and places he is likely to spend his time in, nay, and estate too. For, it is very seldom seen that any one discovers mines of gold or silver in Parnassus. 'Tis a pleasant air, but a barren soil; and there are very few instances of those who have added to their patrimony by anything they have reaped from thence.[135]

Again, he objected to authors being got by heart; occasional good passages may be learnt; but too many scraps of authors acquired may well form a pedant 'than which there is nothing less becoming a gentleman'.[154]

Music, too, he thought could be a waste of time: 'it wastes so much of a young man's time, to gain but a moderate skill in it, and engages often in such odd company, that many think it much better spared'.[155] He was equally unfriendly to painting. Ill painting is a poor thing; 'and to attain a tolerable degree of skill in it requires too much of a man's time. If he has a natural inclination to it, it will endanger the neglect of all other more useful studies'; if he has no inclination, of course, he is just wasting his time. Moreover, as a sedentary occupation it uses up a man's mind which should be kept for serious study; in his time of relaxation he should seek some 'exercise of the body, which unbends the thought and confirms the health and strength'.[156] The stress on utility and the implied concentration on certain aspects of 'experience' as alone bearing the stamp of reality are beginning to involve curriculum restrictions of great significance for the future.

The sciences, such as geography, astronomy, chronology, anatomy, some history and 'all other parts of knowledge of things that fall under the senses, and require little more than memory' should, however, receive attention. Here, indeed, 'if we would take the true way, our knowledge should begin and in those things be laid the foundation; and not in the abstract notions of logic and metaphysics, which are fitter to amuse than inform the understanding in its first setting out towards knowledge'.[157] Arithmetic, too, is important, as the 'first sort of abstract reasoning . . . and is of so general use in all parts of life and business, that scarce anything is to be done without it'.[158] Geometry is recommended, as much as may be 'necessary or useful' to a man of business.[159] History, 'the great mistress of prudence, and civil knowledge',[160] is also advocated. Some knowledge of the law would be advisable for an English gentleman. Rhetoric and logic, as usually taught, are a waste of time: children are to learn to express themselves in plain easy sense in English by practice, not by learning rules and figures as in the conventional courses.

One concession beyond immediate utility, however, Locke does make. Where natural philosophy is concerned, he recommends its division into two parts, one of Spirits and the other of Bodies. The former, of which metaphysics treats, should come first 'not as a science that can be methodised into a system, and treated of upon principles of knowledge; but as an enlargement of our minds towards a truer and fuller comprehension of the intellectual world, to which we are led both by reason and revelation'.[161] Thus a history of the Bible is to be studied. One reason why this study is to be taken before the study of bodies is because the physical world lies so open to our senses that all else is liable to be excluded unless a particular effort be made to study the immaterial parts; this is important because 'it is evident, that by mere matter and motion, none of the great phenomena of nature can be resolved: to instance but in that common one of gravity; which I think impossible to be explained by any natural operation of matter, or any other law of motion, but the positive will of a superior Being so ordering it'.[162] Though no system of natural philosophy will afford a 'comprehensive, scientific, and satisfactory knowledge of the works of nature', yet some of the systems are to be studied by a gentleman 'to fit himself for conversation'. It is clear even here, however, that Locke thinks more highly of those who conduct experiments than of metaphysicians: he prefers the study of such 'writers as have employed themselves in making rational experiments and observations, than in starting barely speculative systems'.[163] Thus he recommends a study of Boyle and 'the incomparable Mr. Newton'; the latter has shown 'how far mathematics, applied to some parts of nature, may, upon principles that matter of fact justify, carry us in the knowledge of some, as I may so call them, particular provinces of the incomprehensible universe'.[164]

Finally, Locke urges the necessity of learning a manual trade. Often such a skill is worth having for its own sake, as in 'painting, turning, gardening, tempering and working in iron, and all other useful arts'.[165] Many times, however, it is important because it conduces to health; thus 'gardening and working in wood' are recommended 'as being fit and healthy recreations for a man of study or business'.[166] (Locke has already, of course, in the early pages of his book stressed the need for health education; children were to be exposed to the air, and thus become accustomed to 'heat and cold, shine and rain'.[167] Locke himself was a doctor.)

His idea of recreation, then, was change of occupation: 'for recreation is not being idle . . . but easing the wearied part by change of business'.[168] Whatever is done should be profitable and useful; youth can thus be weaned from 'that sauntering humour, wherein some, out of custom, let a good part of their lives run uselessly away'.[169] Other manual arts, like 'perfuming, varnishing, graving, and several sorts of working in iron, brass, and silver',[170] the cutting of precious stones or optical glasses, are also recommended. For a man of business it is necessary to learn to keep accounts, not least as a check on his own expenditure. Travel is recommended, but not as currently employed; the pupil should go either when he is younger, to learn the language, when he can be kept under control; or be sent when he is older, when he has some sense; adolescence is just the wrong time.

Locke stresses the importance of method in learning. There is the method inherent in the subject matter; also there is that inherent in the mind, 'from the knowledge it stands possessed of already, to that which lies next, and is coherent to it, and so on to what it aims at, by the simplest and most un-compounded parts it can divide the matter into'. Thus it will be of great use if the pupil can learn to have 'distinct notions, wherever the mind can find any real difference'; but 'distinction in terms' is to be avoided where there are no 'distinct and different clear ideas'.[171]

Utility and profit in the Baconian sense are stressed time and again: 'he should make the child comprehend . . . the usefulness of what he teaches him; and let him see, by what he has learned, that he can do something which he could not do before, something which gives him some power and real advantage above others who are ignorant of it'.[172] 'Improvements', 'use and consequences', 'profit',[173] these are the words which constantly reappear.

In this orientation we begin to see the cultural significance of a man like Locke, in so many respects at one with his age. His interests are scientific rather than literary or artistic – he belongs emphatically to the world of 'things' and 'the relief of man's estate'. He became, in 1668, a member of the newly formed Royal Society – and as Professor Axtell puts it 'never failed to share the working *ideals* of the new scientific movement with its advocates. For half his life he rubbed elbows and exchanged ideas with most of the leading English and European scientists of his day.'[174] An enemy of system building and cosmic speculation as resulting only in 'imaginings', 'fancies' and 'fine but useless speculations', he considered it 'no absurdity to think that this great and curious fabric of the world, the workmanship of the almighty, cannot be perfectly comprehended by any understanding but his that made it . . .'[175] Scientifically he gradually came to recognise the superiority of the mathematico-experimental work of his great friend Newton over the Baconian inductive model. But he never ceased to see in social usefulness the real test of scientific endeavour – as he stressed utility as the criterion for his educational recommendations. He urged the importance of scientific subjects in the education of the young, and though he later came to recommend 'the study of spirits' even before the 'study of bodies'[176] lest the latter pre-empt the whole attention of men and lead to a materialism which would threaten religion,[177] he remained convinced that, studied properly, the investigation of phenomena could only aid religion: 'I readily agree the contemplation of his works gives us occasion to admire, revere, and glorify the Author.'[178]

In these curricular respects, then, there is also a marked break with the courtier tradition – the courtier-adviser is replaced by the man of business. Paul Hazard, writing with the French social order in mind, finds his image of the educated man replicates that of the new bourgeois rather than that of the aristocrat. In England the distinction between the two orders was nothing like so marked; and Locke's ideology fits very well Mr Spectator's questioning: 'Ought a man to be always thinking about polite letters and the fine arts? Good honest work, business, trade, serving, those useful arts that tend to make life easier – things like that should occupy us as much and more.'[179] Pierre Coste, Locke's French translator, considers that Locke had in mind, not the nobility but those who in France would be termed '*de bons bourgeois*, the upper middle class'.[180] The humanists had stressed social usefulness too – but in a different ideological context; Locke emphasises breeding, moral virtue – but practicality as understood in the world of things. Hence his preference for practical, even artisan-like pastimes and his low estimation of the arts, poetry and music. Metaphysically he is an 'under-labourer' and rejects fancies and imaginings; socially he wants a man who, while setting a certain social tone and pursuing a career of virtue, will himself participate in those useful activities (intellectual, political, commercial and industrial) which will help to relieve man's estate: an interest in the new science, a bulwark of the countryside as magistrate, lord-lieutenant and even perhaps parliamentarian, a worker and craftsman on his own estate, a polite and well-bred conversationalist in society. Such was the new ideal, courtier still in manners and morals but an updated man of business in his capacity for thinking and innovation rather than for relying on the accumulated 'common-places' of a past culture, in his willingness to investigate the immediate sensuous world and observe its functioning, and in acquiring the habits of sceptical questioning and reliance on evidence rather than trusting to past authority and the opinions of the ancients, in learning through doing rather than through precept. And the philosophy that sustained this point of view? One which

> purposely restricts itself to what can be directly apprehended in the human mind. An idea of nature which hesitates to recognise it as wholly good, but which regards it as powerful, regulated, and consonant with reason: whence a natural religion, natural law, natural freedom and natural equality. A morality subdivided into a number of constituent moralities; recourse to social usefulness in order to know which one to choose . . . Science, which will ensure the boundless progress of man, and therefore his happiness. Philosophy, the guide of life.[181]

We are surely entering upon a critical, rationalistic age rather than a mythico-poetic one – the Enlightenment.[182]

Yet even in Locke there were hints – the merest hints, no more – of a different condition. Did he not derive knowledge from the senses – instruments of a more varied application than he altogether conceived of? And did he not, in speaking of pleasure and pain, unveil the psychology of desire? These aspects of man's nature were to be kept in check by reason; but even in education all was not to be worked out and planned – we are enjoined to take advantage of the humour or disposition of the moment – a passing curiosity, a hint of spontaneity. And it should be remembered that 'Plain and rough nature' is found superior to affectation or 'an artificial ungracefulness'. We are moving out of the high renaissance world when art improved on nature into the plainer, more mundane environment of the Dutch genre painters of the seventeenth century – with their faithful reproduction of bourgeois settings or scenes of low life – or of *things* (flowers, still lifes) lovingly delineated; truth to a metaphysical vision is being replaced by 'truth' to fact and observation. But in the process we are also concerned to deny in some measure our heritage; what is to replace it need not necessarily be rational stability; for to question is to unsettle. And Locke himself in his appreciation of the importance of desire linked it with 'uneasiness', 'where, by the by, it may be of some use to remark, that the chief, if not the only spur to human industry and action is uneasiness'.[183]

So Locke remains a slightly more ambivalent figure than he is often presented. But before the romantic progressives seized on his hints of spontaneity and psychological unease, the subjectivist aspect of his view of 'ideas', the other, greater ambiguity in Locke – the tension between his humanist views of conduct and manners and his new 'scientific' conception of understanding and utility – had to be worked out. The definitive break comes with Rousseau, heir to the further challenge posed by the Enlightenment to the traditional order. For Rousseau at once repudiates Locke's stress on the centrality of formation in the upbringing of a creature with varied predispositions to work on while he welcomes a theory where 'experience' based on sensation plays a prominent role – and where the differences between people are being thought of increasingly as arising from environmental stimuli, and hence crucially, education. Furthermore, in Rousseau with his emphasis on 'things' and their utility, the old humanist form of liberalisation – still vestigial in Locke's concept of the morals and manners of the gentleman – practically disappears. Certainly it plays no part in the education of the young Emile – whose freedom is not that of mastery but of a limited ignorance; and whose discipline is not that of a transcending art – but 'necessity'.

NOTES

1 R. Descartes, *A Discourse on Method*, trans. J. Veitch (London, Everyman, 1957), p. 4.
2 ibid., pp. 15–16.
3 N. Kemp Smith, *New Studies in the Philosophy of Descartes* (London, Macmillan, 1952), p. 63.
4 ibid., p. 89.
5 ibid., p. 68.
6 Quoted ibid., p. 69.
7 Descartes, op. cit., p. 3.
8 ibid., p. 3.
9 ibid., p. 11.
10 ibid., p. 22.
11 cf. ibid., p. 12.
12 ibid., p. 61. He did, however, warn that 'the single design to strip one's self of all past beliefs is one that ought not to be taken by everyone' and warned against 'restless and busy meddlers who . . . are yet always projecting reforms'; there is indeed a difference, he points out, between those who thus seek to innovate in intellectual matters and those who have the urge to in public affairs. In the latter custom has often made things tolerable, and 'the defects are almost always more tolerable than the change necessary for their removal' (ibid., pp. 12–13).
13 A. Quinton, 'Authority and autonomy in knowledge', *Proceedings of the Philosophy of Education Society of Great Britain*, Vol. V, no. 2 (July 1971), p. 201.
14 E. Gilson (ed.), *R. Descartes: Discours de la Méthode: texte et commentaire* (Paris, Vrin, 1947).
15 Descartes, *Discourse*, pp. 10–11.
16 ibid., p. 121.
17 Gilson, op. cit., p. 201.
18 Descartes, *Discourse*, p. 197.
19 Ian Roth, 'Cartesian studies', *The Cambridge Journal*, May 1954, p. 469.
20 Descartes, *Discourse*, p. 49.
21 ibid., p. 9.
22 Gilson, op. cit., p. 146.
23 For the nature of Cartesian doubt as against renaissance scepticism, note Gilson, op. cit., pp. 267–8, 269. 'Not that I imitated the sceptics who doubt only that they may doubt, and seek nothing beyond uncertainty itself; for, on the contrary, my design was simply to find ground of assurance . . .' (*Discourse*, p. 23).

24 *Discourse*, p. 14.
25 ibid., p. 6.
26 ibid., p. 8.
27 Gilson, op. cit., p. 94.
28 ibid., p. 94.
29 J. Locke, *An Essay Concerning Human Understanding*, ed. R. Wilburn (London, Everyman, 1947), p. xxiii: subsequently referred to as *Essay*.
30 ibid., p. xxiii.
31 'We must, if we will proceed as reason advises, adapt our methods of inquiry to *the nature of the ideas we examine* and the truth we search after' (*Essay*, IV.xii.7).
32 R. I. Aaron, *John Locke* (London, Oxford University Press, 1971), p. 62.
33 Locke, *Essay*, I.i.7. To facilitate the finding of references in different editions, quotations from Locke will usually be identified in terms of section numbers, i.e. Book I, Chapter i, section 7.
34 ibid., I.i.7. The very process of the examination would, of course, be guided by the assumptions in terms of which the undertaking was initiated.
35 ibid., I.i.4.
36 ibid., I.i.4.
37 Quoted Aaron, op. cit., pp. 68–9.
38 cf. above, p. 167.
39 Locke, *Essay*, p. xx.
40 Aaron, op. cit., p. 119.
41 Locke, *Essay*, I.ii.1.
42 ibid., I.iii.3.
43 J. W. Yolton, *John Locke and the Way of Ideas* (London, Oxford University Press, 1968), p. 26.
44 Locke, *Essay*, I.iv.3.
45 Aaron, op. cit., p. 86.
46 Yolton, op. cit., pp. 64 and 68.
47 ibid., p. 29.
48 Locke, *Essay*, I.iii.4.
49 ibid., IV.iv.3.
50 ibid., II.i.2–4.
51 ibid., III.iii.1 and 13.
52 ibid., III.iii.11.
53 ibid., II.viii.9.
54 ibid., II.viii.10.
55 Aaron, op. cit., p. 116.
56 Henry Lee quoted in Yolton, op. cit., p. 101.
57 Aaron, op. cit., p. 199.
58 Locke, *Essay*, III.vi.28.
59 Aaron, op. cit., p. 201.
60 ibid., pp. 203–4.
61 Quinton, op. cit., p. 203.
62 Locke, *Essay*, II.i.8.
63 ibid., III.x.14.
64 ibid., III.ix.19.
65 ibid., III.ix.9.
66 ibid., III.xi.14.
67 cf. below, pp. 268–9.
68 Yolton, op. cit., p. 205.
69 *Essay*, II.xi.2.
70 G. Santayana, *Some Turns of Thought in Modern Philosophy* (Cambridge, Cambridge University Press, 1933), p. 5.
71 J. Locke, *Some Thoughts Concerning Education*, s. 216. Again, references will be given to sections to facilitate reference to various texts, e.g. those of J. W. Adamson (Cambridge, Cambridge University Press, 1922) and J. L. Axtell (Cambridge,

Cambridge University Press, 1968) of the latest editions. Subsequently referred to as *Thoughts*.

72 Though J. A. Passmore ('The malleability of man in 18th century thought' in E. R. Wasserman (ed.), *Aspects of the 18th Century*, Baltimore, Johns Hopkins Press, 1965, p. 22) considers that 'The crucial importance of Locke's *Some Thoughts Concerning Education* is not so much in its rejection of innate ideas as in its rejection of original sin.' The humanists had, however, consistently underplayed the notion of original sin.

73 *Thoughts*, s. 216.

74 J. Locke, *Of the Conduct of the Understanding* in *The Educational Writings of John Locke*, ed. J. W. Adamson (Cambridge, Cambridge University Press, 1922), s. 4.

75 ibid., s. 2.

76 Locke, *Thoughts*, s. 176.

77 ibid., ss. 101-2.

78 ibid., s. 66.

79 ibid., s. 40.

80 ibid., s. 48.

81 ibid., ss. 73-4.

82 ibid., s. 63.

83 ibid., s. 161. This repeats later humanist injunctions – for instance, those of Erasmus; cf. p. 67 above.

84 ibid., s. 11.

85 Axtell, op. cit. (cf. note 71 above).

86 ibid.

87 ibid., s. 35.

88 ibid., s. 116.

89 ibid., s. 116.

90 ibid., s. 67.

91 ibid., s. 42.

92 ibid., s. 42.

93 ibid., s. 64 (my italics).

94 ibid., s. 66, Axtell edition (which preserves original capital letters) only.

95 ibid., s. 66.

96 ibid., s. 93, Axtell edition.

97 ibid., s. 67, Axtell edition.

98 Indeed, Professor Root, who writes an Introduction to the Everyman edition of the *Letters*, speaks of the father's 'creative passion, trying to model . . . a perfect work of art'. The persistence of the renaissance conception is interesting.

99 *Of the Conduct of the Understanding*, s. 1. Adamson speaks of the *Conduct* as 'complementary to *Some Thoughts* and – therefore indispensable to an understanding of Locke's ideas respecting education' – how best to cultivate the rational element in man. It is published in his edition of *The Educational Writings of John Locke*.

100 ibid., s. 3.

101 ibid., s. 3.

102 ibid., s. 3.

103 ibid., s. 10.

104 ibid., s. 11. It is interesting to note the criticisms Locke makes of those who live a confined existence, cut off from sources of intellectual life: 'The day-labourer in a country-village has commonly but a small pittance of knowledge, because his ideas and notions have been confined to the narrow bounds of a poor conversation and employment.' This constitutes a significant contrast with later 'progressive' notions, for example in Rousseau. In Locke one is aware of a relationship to international intellectual circles, very different from the isolated self-centred position of Rousseau; Locke is an 'insider', Rousseau an 'outsider'.

105 ibid., s. 13.

106 ibid., s. 6.

107 ibid., s. 7.
108 ibid., s. 7.
109 ibid., s. 12.
110 ibid., s. 13.
111 ibid., s. 14.
112 ibid., s. 15.
113 ibid., s. 19.
114 ibid., s. 20.
115 ibid., s. 20.
116 ibid., s. 24.
117 ibid., s. 29.
118 ibid., s. 29.
119 ibid., s. 29.
120 ibid., s. 31.
121 ibid., s. 34.
122 ibid., s. 35.
123 *Thoughts*, s. 156.
124 ibid., s. 169.
125 ibid., s. 181.
126 ibid., s. 189.
127 *Conduct*, s. 45.
128 P. Hazard, *The European Mind 1680–1715*, trans. J. L. May (Harmondsworth, Penguin, 1973), p. 280.
129 Foreword to Pierre Coste's translation of Locke's *Essay*, quoted Hazard, op. cit., p. 283.
130 Locke, *Thoughts*, s. 134.
131 ibid., s. 70.
132 ibid., s. 70.
133 ibid., s. 136.
134 ibid., s. 140.
135 ibid., s. 140.
136 ibid., s. 94.
137 ibid., s. 94.
138 ibid., s. 67.
139 ibid., s. 67.
140 ibid., s. 196.
141 ibid., s. 110.
142 ibid., s. 113.
143 ibid., s. 147.
144 ibid., s. 177.
145 ibid., s. 177.
146 ibid., s. 94.
147 ibid., s. 195.
148 ibid., s. 94.
149 ibid., s. 189.
150 ibid., s. 164.
151 ibid., s. 168.
152 ibid., s. 161.
153 ibid., s. 174. It should perhaps be added that Locke regrets, in the *Conduct*, that 'Many a good poetic vein is buried under a trade, and never produces any thing for want of improvement' (*Conduct*, s. 4).
154 ibid., s. 175.
155 ibid., s. 197.
156 cf. ibid., ss. 2–3.
157 ibid., s. 166.
158 ibid., s. 180.
159 ibid., s. 181.

160 ibid., s. 182.
161 ibid., s. 190.
162 ibid., s. 192.
163 ibid., s. 193.
164 ibid., s. 194.
165 ibid., s. 202.
166 ibid., s. 204.
167 ibid., s. 9.
168 ibid., s. 206.
169 ibid., s. 208.
170 ibid., s. 209.
171 ibid., s. 195.
172 ibid., s. 167.
173 cf. ibid., s. 197.
174 Axtell, op. cit., p. 70.
175 Quoted Axtell, op. cit., pp. 72-3.
176 cf. above, p. 242.
177 cf. Axtell, op. cit., pp. 78-9.
178 Quoted Axtell, op. cit., p. 79.
179 Quoted Hazard, op. cit., p. 376.
180 ibid., p. 376.
181 ibid., p. 378.
182 The concepts are taken from E. Cassirer, *The Philosophy of the Enlightenment* (Boston, Mass., Beacon Press, 1955).
183 cf. *Essay*, II.xx *passim*.

CHAPTER 11

'The Disenchantment of the European Mind': the Enlightenment

I

The philosophers of the eighteenth century continued the attack on the old cultural order which had been initiated by the most prominent seventeenth-century writers and at the same time sought to construct a new, specifically intellectual order based on reason and observation – with a certain range of 'feelings' playing an increasingly important role as the century proceeded. These philosophers were pre-eminently educationists in the broader sense (and often in the narrower one relevant to the upbringing of the young) for they had, essentially, a didactic purpose, the production of a new society and a new cultural order: their 'patron saints and pioneers were British: Bacon, Newton, and Locke'.[1]

But first I must revise briefly what they were against and sought to do away with. If periods of human history can be defined in terms of the pre-dominance of the mythopoeic or the spirit of critical realism they manifested without a doubt the urge towards critical scrutiny. They reacted against myth, which they regarded as superstition, metaphysics which some dismissed as nonsense, revelation which they considered revealed only 'the tainted sources of the Christian religion' and 'the vices of the Chosen People':[2] 'everything was subject to the sovereign power of criticism; nothing in the past was sacred, least of all sacred things'.[3] In this, of course, they only continued what men like Bacon, Descartes and indeed Locke had initiated, though these had not attacked Christianity. Now, however, 'Everything must be examined', Diderot reiterated in the *Encyclopédie*, 'everything must be shaken up, without exception and without circumspection'.[4] Such destruction laid the way open for a powerful redeployment of human effort, albeit in positive theoretical terms – the product of *thought* – which mirrored their rationally argued rejections;

> To be disenchanted is not to give way to jaded, supercilious skepticism, but to shift canons of proof and direction of worship. What is at work in the incredulity of philosophes is not the shrinking of experience to the hard, the measurable, the prosaic, the surface of events; it is, on the contrary, an expansion of the natural. The disenchanted universe of the Enlightenment is a natural universe.[5]

The 'natural' universe was, of course, the neutralised nature of mechanical necessity that had, in Bacon's terms, to be both submitted to and 'vex'd'. The miraculous no longer implied an interference with the order of nature – it was, in fact, that order itself: 'the only miracle was the miracle not of irregularity but of regularity'.[6] The enunciation of these regularities constituted one of the great theoretical reconstructions of the Enlightenment.

Something of their spirit can be defined in their attitude to history. They fostered, paradoxically, a history which in a profound sense was anti-historical. The true historian submits himself to the past, seeks to comprehend it in its own terms before he asseses. (The renaissance historians had made a tentative move in that direction.) History must posit some function behind even the seeming grossest superstition or irrationality and it is the historian's task to ferret this out; what he achieves constitutes at least some check to the provincialism and arrogance of the present. But what the historians of the Enlightenment sought – and they found it in the classics – was a reassuring reflection of their own image, a reinforcement of their preferences. In any profounder sense they were anti-historical. They did not seek to learn from the differences of history – they only sought their own image as a didactic confirmation of their moral stance. 'It was the affinity of one literary elite for another. Despite the vast distance in time and the obvious difference in concerns and status, the two belonged to a single family, allied by their tastes, their strategies, their aims, their styles, and above all, their view of the world.'[7] Antiquity, indeed, 'gave the philosophers models of analytical penetration, and ancient life that was a museum of striking examples'.[8] It assisted them in their attempts to free the world from enchantment – to 'chase the sacred from its privileged sanctuary and [treat] it as a fact . . .' They no longer saw history as tied to tradition but, after the analogy of science, as revelatory of law. Their identification with their Roman precursors continued the process begun during the Renaissance, which was, of course, similarly classically oriented: indeed 'the philosophers saw the Renaissance as the first act of a great drama in which the Enlightenment itself was the last – the great drama of the disenchantment of the European mind'.[10] But whereas the humanists had sought to model the present on the example of the classical past, the philosophers interpret the classical past in terms of their predetermined preoccupation with modernity. In other respects they saw the past largely as the barbarous precursor of their own state of enlightened superiority.

II

By 'freeing' man *from* the constraints of his past, the philosophers were faced with the prospect of defining what man was then free *to* become. They were, in fact, now involved in the antinomies of freedom, presented with a task of reconstruction – and the century as a whole produced two separate and in some respects antagonistic solutions to the problem. One might be said to derive from the centrifugal implications of Locke's stress on individuation –

that notion of the individual consciousness set in a specific time and space;
the other sprang from the centripetal implications of his attempt to define
the nature of the human understanding – as that which constitutes the general
and uniform condition of mankind in its search for knowledge. The one
implies an incipient heterogeneity, relativism, the other (initially the stronger)
a homogenising force. The split had been initiated by the dualism implicit
in the work of Descartes which split subject from object, mind from world,
and thus encouraged on the one hand a tendency to solipsism and on the
other the attempt to bridge the gap through the objective scrutiny of scientific
observation. Admiration for the new scientific and mathematical advances
indeed had disposed the philosophers to accept the uniformity of the understanding and of human nature generally.

For, impressed with the success of empirical investigation into the material
world, and considering man to be as much part of the world of nature as
any other living or non-living creations, they had attempted to derive their
view of man from scientific observation. Locke had sought to define the
potential of the human understanding from a comprehension of its workings.
His successors studied the various social manifestations and patterns of belief
which voyages of discovery had revealed to their scientific gaze and, though
impressed by their diversity, considered that they could induce a uniform
'human nature' out of the accidents of time and place:

'It is universally acknowledged', David Hume wrote in a famous passage,
'that there is a great uniformity among the actions of men, in all nations
and ages, and that human nature remains still the same, in its principles
and operations. The same motives always produce the same actions.'
Indeed, 'Mankind are so much the same, in all times and places, that
history informs us of nothing new or strange in this particular.'[11]

The reference to history is symptomatic: variation sprang out of differences
of environment, not the basic patterns of growth or behaviour. For it is not
to be suggested that, in very human fashion, the philosophers did not in some
degree differ among themselves as to how this human nature manifested itself.
But the implication of uniformity was implicit in their empiricism – science
demands regularities as the prime necessity of its functioning. The very
attempt to apply science to society enforced a conception of uniformity on
the units of which it was comprised.

The scene of these manifestations of regularity was 'nature' – 'nature' as
the empirically observable, of which human nature was thought to form a
part. In the hands of the philosophers regularity implied a fundamental
similarity of behaviour: 'Uniformitarianism', as Arthur Lovejoy says in his
essay on 'The Parallel of Deism and Classicism',[12] is 'the just and fundamental principle of [the] general and pervasive philosophy of the Enlightenment.' Differences in taste or judgement were manifestations of error and
universality of appeal a mark of truth. The moral, social or educational
reformer aimed to standardise men and their beliefs, likings and institutions:

Typical is a remark of Spinoza's, reported by one of his early biographers:
'The purpose of Nature is to make men uniform, as children of a common
mother.' . . . [Hence] 'according to nature' meant, first and foremost,
that which corresponds to this assumption of uniformity; it is perhaps
still necessary to repeat that in the most frequent of the normative uses
of the term 'nature' in the Enlightenment, the principal element in the
signification of the word *is* uniformity. Despite its sixty-odd other
senses, it was primarily and chiefly because of *this* connotation that
'nature' was the sacred word of the Enlightenment.[13]

And indeed, the attack upon distinctions between men and their views and
the eventual reaction in favour of uniqueness and individuality was the
'actual and dominating fact in the intellectual history of Europe for two
hundred years'.[14]

This homogeneity of human nature was the psychological and ontological
counterpart of the 'commonness' of the world of things which constituted
man's 'natural' habitat. The two-world view (at once 'natural' and transcendental) of the middle ages and the Renaissance was disappearing: in its
place was instituted a common world – common in the sense that its interpretation was open to all unconstrained by the intervention of priest or magus,
common, too, in the sense that it was constituted by a collocation of phenomena whose behaviour was ordered by natural laws the discovery of which
depended on common observation. The approach of the philosophers was
fundamentally in line with that initiated by Bacon and Newton. Hence the
move we have noted so often, from the theatre to the market place, from the
creation of metaphysical systems to the study of actuality. Thus Diderot
wrote in his *Prospectus for the Encyclopédie*, in preparing his articles on craft
and industry:

> We addressed ourselves to the ablest craftsmen of Paris and the kingdom,
> we took the trouble of going to their workshops, interrogating them,
> taking down their dictation, developing their thoughts, eliciting from
> them the terms appropriate to their profession, constructing lists from
> them, defining them, talking with those from whom we had obtained
> memoranda, and (an almost indispensable precaution) rectifying, in long
> and frequent conversations with some, what others had imperfectly,
> obscurely, and sometimes incorrectly expressed.[15]

As Professor Gay comments: 'Hand and intellect, technology and philosophy,
separated since the Greeks, were now finding common ground in the utiliza-
tion of science for the sake of improving man's lot.'[16] What he goes on to call
'this disciplined aggression against concrete problems' does indeed mark 'an
epoch in the human will'.[17] 'Man is unhappy because he did not know
nature', urges Holbach in the opening to his *Système de la Nature*. This
'disciplined aggression' had already achieved great successes in the material
world both of understanding and control; why should it not be equally
successful in application to the world of man? Science, indeed, it was that

made progress; Turgot pointed out that the arts were limited and had reached their apogee in the time of Augustus; science was for ever advancing.[18]

The philosophers, furthermore, following Locke, accepted the need to proceed on the basis of evidence; thus the Abbé Yvon approvingly told how the Greeks had 'invented that critical philosophy which defies all authority, and which, in its search for the truth, wishes to be guided by the glimmer of evidence alone'.[19] This evidence could only be discovered by applying the same techniques of investigation, a similar instrumental application of the understanding, to men as to things: as Volney in his book *The Ruins* put it:

> Man is governed, like the world of which he forms a part, by natural laws, regular in their operation, consequent in their effects, immutable in their essence; and these laws, the common source of good and evil, are neither written in the distant stars, nor concealed in mysterious codes; inherent in the nature of all terrestrial beings, identified with their existence, they are at all times, and in all places, present to the human mind; they act upon the senses, inform the intellect, and annex to every action its punishment and its reward. Let man study these laws, let him understand his own nature, and the nature of the beings that surround him, and he will know the springs of his destiny, the causes of his evils, and the remedies to be applied.[20]

But in fact this assimilation of man to the world of things constituted the fundamental error of their philosophy, for it involves two very different conceptions of the laws of nature being treated as if they were the same. The effect of the scientific revolution has been, in the physical, material sphere, to replace teleological explanations by empirical. Aristotelian explanations in the middle ages, as we have seen, had subserved physical phenomena under the aegis of general teleological explanations which pervaded all the phenomena of nature. The scientific revolution substituted explanations in terms of *how* phenomena behaved for such ultimate attempts to explain *why* they behaved in the way they did. Scientific explanations depended on the observation of regularities from which predictions could be made. In the first case what was central to humanity, its involvement in a search for purpose, was inappropriately attributed to physical phenomena; in the second, the neutrality implicit in the behaviour of material phenomena became analogically inappropriately attributed to human beings.

For 'explanations' of many aspects of human behaviour remain obstinately teleological. To confuse the two sorts of relevant laws of nature is to confuse fact and value. 'Natural law' in the scientific sense refers to regularities observed and predicted in the behaviour of material phenomena; 'natural law' with reference to human beings in many of their activities implies purposive behaviour thought to be in line with 'nature' as a teleological concept. The idea of purpose or end cannot be avoided where human beings are concerned as it can where material phenomena are involved simply because human beings have a conception of themselves entirely lacking where the physical world is concerned. It always makes sense to ask people *why* they are acting as they are; it makes no sense to ask a stone why it falls – it simply makes sense to measure at what speed it drops. Another way of putting it would be to say that human beings inhabit a world of values – where notions of choice are relevant and indeed unavoidable – whereas a stone is simply subject to observable physical laws. It may be 'natural' to man to be artificial – but that makes it a different sort of naturalness from that of material particles.

The attempt, then, to apply scientific approaches to human behaviour has always been bedevilled by this confusion of these two sorts of the laws of nature – the one empirical and the other normative. And the Enlightenment, which inherited the ambiguity scientific advance had propounded, failed, in general, to avoid the trap: 'nature' was the scene of man's investigations and could be used purely in a descriptive sense to refer to 'natural phenomena'. But 'nature' also carried, in so many contexts, evaluative overtones; and 'natural law' has historically constituted that ideal state of affairs – propounded in many versions by God himself – against which human law and institutions could be measured.

Thus in the psychological field there was an attempt to make morals a branch of psychology. Many of the philosophers assumed that since psychology

is the discipline which gives us knowledge of human desires and wants, it is by this feature also distinguished by its capacity to solve all value problems . . . Because *desires* happen to be facts of mental life, they concluded that *values* were likewise facts of mental life, and accordingly that the solution of moral problems was a task with which the science of psychology was by itself competent to deal.

Since they believed further that human nature was a given constant; that the elemental, constituent desires and wants as opposed to the channels of expression into which those wants happened to run, were permanent characteristics of human nature, they concluded that there was a rationally determinable system of values of enduring validity. Consequently, progress was for them the term used to signify a process whereby man approached ever more closely to the realization of a system of values, whose eternal validity was taken for granted. The theory of progress, implicit in all their thinking, was a teleological one. The end was given; it remained constant, and the criterion of progress was the evidence of upward movement towards this given, fixed goal, which represented the satisfaction of all existing human wants.[21]

So appeals to the 'natural man', man in general, or the 'essentials' in human nature implied apparently factual generalisations but in effect expressed ideal, normative conceptions of man; and attempts, for instance, to write the history of this being were vitiated as history, by the selective process which chose those elements, from the millions of possible historical events, which would reveal how this 'essential' being had (or would) come about. So much eighteenth-century history was written from this standpoint that it provides a further indication of a fundamentally anti-historical bent. History as what actually happened was subsumed under a developmental description supporting, for instance, concepts of human progress which inevitably should have raised value-questions relating to the norm implicit in the assumption of 'progress', a word with undoubted value overtones in terms of 'betterment'.

And indeed Condorcet, on the analogy of the natural sciences, wished to use the historical 'sciences' for predictive purposes:

> If man can predict, with an assurance almost complete, the phenomena of which he knows the laws; if, even when they are unknown to him, he can, according to the experience of the past, foresee, with great probability, the events of the future; why would one regard as a chimerical enterprise, that of tracing, with some verisimilitude, the picture of the future destinies of the human species, according to the results of its history? The only foundation of belief in the natural sciences, is this idea, that the general laws, known or not known, which regulate the phenomena of the universe, are necessary and constant; and by what reason would this principle be less true for the intellectual and moral faculties of man, than for the other operations of nature?[22]

Only on the basis of a *selective* view of the past and the assumption that the selection so chosen would be projected into the future could such an assertion be made; and the 'selection' inevitably involved a value orientation.

The fact of the matter was that the philosophers, despite themselves, had inherited the Christian teleology and had reinterpreted the concept of the 'heavenly city' to be achieved in Christian eschatology in earthly terms. They were, as Professor Carl Becker has indicated, 'engaged in that nefarious medieval enterprise of reconciling the facts of human experience with truths already, in some fashion, revealed to them'.[23] The emphasis on scientific fact was ultimately bogus: their views of history, society and man were tailored to the support of their teleological vision.

> Alas yes, that is, indeed, the fact! The eighteenth-century Philosophers, like the medieval scholastics, held fast to a revealed body of knowledge, and they were unwilling or unable to learn anything from history which could not, by some ingenious trick played on the dead, be reconciled with their faith . . . The essential articles of the religion of the Enlightenment may be stated thus: (1) man is not natively depraved; (2) the end of life is life itself, the good life on earth instead of the beatific life after death; (3) man is capable, guided solely by the light of reason and experience, of perfecting the good life on earth; and (4) the first and essential condition of the good life on earth is the freeing of men's minds from the bonds of ignorance and superstition, and of their bodies from the arbitrary oppression of the constituted social authorities. With this creed the 'constant and universal principles of human nature', which Hume tells us are to be discovered by a study of history, must

be in accord, and 'man in general' must be a creature who would conveniently illustrate these principles.[24]

It is interesting to note that, although the philosophers clearly stood for the autonomy of the individual (as we have seen) in urging release from traditional habits and sanctions, liberty played a comparatively minor role in their stated progressive aspirations. It is as if the emphasis had shifted from disentanglement to a consideration of its implications and consequences. An examination of the various pictures of the end state of humanity aimed at in their writings, as Dr Sampson points out, indicates that behind the many variations in their aspirations

> there is a fairly clearly defined pattern, common to them all, which gradually emerges. I refer to a common passion for the principle of equality and probably as a corollary to this, for a rigorous regulation of the life of the community, down to the minutest detail. Although the principle of liberty receives occasional honourable mention, it is for the most part left to take care of itself in the anxiety to ensure that human nature, still apparently suspected of being wayward, shall be kept securely on the path of equality.[25]

As man cannot live in a vacuum, disengagement rapidly necessitated some sort of positive commitment. And so they were much more concerned with the problem of privilege than with that of power. 'They too easily assumed that with equality and enlightenment, the problem of power could be safely left to take care of itself. The major social evils of their time were universally ascribed to the twin vices of acquisitiveness and ignorance . . .'[26] Hence their concern with human rights, as a result of which all men merited equal consideration in terms of their common humanity. Hence, too, their faith in the power of institutions to make men good – institutions among which must be included the school – and their neglect of the need, recognised by the humanists, to educate men for the exercise of power in *human* affairs. The ideal of the Enlightenment is essentially related to notions of the perfectibility of man – a perfectibility related not to older notions of a cataclysmic conversion but to ideas of gradual moral improvement such as education could provide. Education could induce that equality of outcome which was the logical result of subjecting beings of a similar original nature to an identity of influences: as Hartley put in his *Observations on Man*:

> If beings of the same nature, but whose affections and passions are, at present, in different proportions to each other, be exposed for an indefinite time to the same impressions and associations, all their particular differences will, at last, be overruled, and they will become perfectly similar, or even equal. They may also be made perfectly similar, in a finite time, by a proper adjustment of the impressions and associations.[27]

Enlightened by a methodology derived from scientific observation, their education could gradually achieve perfection for all human beings; that it could fall into evil hands did not seem to strike the philosophers.

The stress on uniformity and hence equality is not, indeed, surprising, considering their scientific orientation. Science begins in freedom – that of observation and detached assessment, unhampered by dogma or belief; but it ends in law and uniformity. All observed phenomena, once freely classified as belonging to a specific 'category', follow a uniform pattern of behaviour it is the very purpose of the method to discover. By a similar paradox, as Bacon noted, men obey only to master; they respect the independence of the evidence simply in order to bring it under control. In one very fundamental way concern for the world of things, its regularities and predictive possibilities within it, reflected back on the way human beings unconsciously began to conceive of and organise themselves. The hierarchical differentiation implicit in the old cosmology began to give way to the uniformitarian tendencies implicit in the new. It is possible to suggest that, for some at least, power was not a problem because to consider it as such was to introduce an element of arbitrariness absent from their predominantly scientific orientation. It was power in the human sense of *unpredictable* interference that was lacking in their scientific teleology – such unpredictableness, could, almost by definition, play no part in their laws of human nature. It was precisely this unpredictability that the persuasiveness of humanistic discourse allowed for, was indeed intended to cope with, through the flexibility of 'words', discourse and dialogue. Implicit in the assimilation of the world of things to that of men was a certain simplification of human politics and a potential for cultural homogenisation: 'The Enlightenment was . . . an age devoted, at least in its dominant tendency, to the simplification and the standardization of thought and life – to their standardization by means of their simplification.'[28] Certainly, as we shall see, there were other tendencies – but this remains a potential legacy of the period.

This dilemma – barely articulated as such at the time but easily apparent to later analysis – of the consequences of the prolonged process of disengagement from traditional habits and sanctions, clearly deeply affects the notion of educational artifice in the deliberate action of the teacher. The implication that men, like material particles, behave and develop 'naturally' permits the lifting of traditional human restraints: children can be left to follow the 'laws' of their own 'nature'. But the inescapable purposiveness implicit in human affairs necessitates a laying down of a 'right' order of progression. Hence the two unresolved and conflicting conceptions of 'natural law' produce a problem for the teacher as artificer which has consequences of the utmost importance for contemporary and later 'progressive' theorising. Education as pedagogy faces the dilemma of either being totally unimportant (it all happens 'naturally'), or in the face of the vacuum produced by the repudiation of the historical culture, of the most overwhelming significance – 'l'éducation peut *tout*', as Helvetius put it (my italics). One way out of the dilemma, of course, is that education itself should follow 'natural' lines – the effect of which is to smuggle in prescription in the guise of 'natural' development. Much of this is clearly manifest in Rousseau.

III

Yet, even in the world of common experience, there were also profound forces which were encouraging a pluralism of outlook, individuality, a stress on the uniqueness of subjectivity, even eccentricity. The opening up of a common world can stimulate the tendency to see similarity at the basis of what previously had been divided off – a common human nature underlying all the differences of 'forms' – or reveal an unsuspected diversity and differentiation; potentially, a 'loose' empiricism reveals an immense heterogeneity. The eighteenth century found their world among ordinary things; the mixture of styles in their novels and plays reflected their view, common to their seventeenth-century forebears, that reality belonged to workshops as well as salons, in trade as well as in the abstractions of political theorists, in participation in specific happenings as well as in thought. 'Their literature . . . is the imaginative transfiguration of the real.'[29] This, after all, was the period of the rise of the novel, with its concern for truth to individual experience and its reaction against the classical preference for the universal and the general. Locke's view of personal identity as that of an existence at a particular locus in space and time, maintaining itself in a continuity of consciousness through duration and involving causal connections with past experience, involves a new principle of individuation as the product of a spatio-temporal environment. The novelist, as Professor Ian Watt points out, is concerned with 'an authentic account of the actual experiences of individuals'[30] – the human counterpart of the clear and lucid pictorial representation of things in space which marked so much of Dutch *genre* painting, with its frequent hints of a casual, momentary collocation in time. A man's very personality was seen to be represented by the 'things' by which he surrounded himself. Pope, for instance, was fully conscious as to how what a man chose to hang on his walls expressed his personality: 'A man not only shows his taste but his virtue, in the choice of such ornaments.'[31]

Here we see 'things' in a different light – not as representing that necessity from the understanding of which alone men can gain their freedom, but as chosen offshoots of specific personalities, not representative of an inexorable regularity, but expressive, conceivably, of whim or idiosyncratic choice, part of a world which men have *created* around themselves rather than sought to assimilate themselves to. After all, the identity crisis initiated by the rejections of the philosophers had to be expressed in individual terms. The agony of the young Hume is the potential fate of all such rebels:

In the end, Hume proclaims that he no longer knows who he is; his stable self-image has dissolved in a sea of doubt and despair . . . And he is driven to ask: 'Where am I, or what? From what causes do I derive my existence, and to what condition shall I return? Whose favour shall

I court, and whose anger must I dread? What beings surround me? . . .'
Such insistent questions are a precious indication of the price that
rebellion exacted from the philosophers.[32]

So emerged the movement towards diversity. It had been preparing, in a
subterranean sort of way, for a surprisingly long time. After all, it was implicit in that notion of plenitude which characterised the idea of the Great
Chain of Being – fullness, richness, diversity, not uniformity. And, for all
the egalitarian implications of the writings of the philosophers, it is interesting
to note that in no century was the notion of the Great Chain more pervasive
than in the eighteenth. The principles of plenitude and continuity had been
evoked, paradoxically, to support the essential logicality, rationality of the
world; but 'they were at heart ideas profoundly antipathetic to the simple
rationalism of the Enlightenment'.[33] There were incipient protests against
the prevailing spirit of rationalism, the notion that the paradigm of human
decision making was to be found in the analytic approach of the geometrician.
Thus the Abbé Dubos in his *Critical Reflections on Poetry and Painting*
expatiates on the logic of the philosophers:

> This philosophical spirit, which transforms men into such reasonable,
> such logical beings, bids fair to turn a large part of Europe into what
> the Goths and Vandals made of it in days gone by. I see the essential
> arts neglected; customs that contributed most usefully to the preser-
> vation of society done away with and speculative reasoning taking the
> place of practical work.[34]

Dubos had been influenced by Locke – that Locke who had indicated that
'the chief if not the only spur to human industry and action is uneasiness',[35]
whose concern in education was for the individual. Dubos saw that Genius
transcended all rules and conventions – as, for that matter, did Pope: 'There
is a happiness beyond the reach of art.' Reasoning should be transcended in
the passionate engagement of outstanding ability.

So passion, sentiment, feeling, leading to various forms of eccentricity,
whether of a primitive or sophisticated kind, gradually came to lead men
away from logicality, rationality, the homogenising effects of reason and the
spirit of geometry into a diversified world which stressed individuality
rather than uniformity, and the uniqueness of feelings and sentiments rather
than the similarity of reason:

> There have, in the entire history of thought, been few changes in
> standards of value more profound and more momentous than that which
> took place when . . . it came to be believed not only that in many, or in
> all, phases of human life there are diverse excellences, but that diversity
> itself is of the essence of excellence; and that of art, in particular, the
> objective is neither the attainment of some single ideal perfection of
> form in a small number of fixed *genres* nor the gratification of that least
> common denominator of aesthetic susceptibility which is shared by all

mankind in all ages, but rather the fullest possible expression of the abundance of differentness that there is, actually or potentially, in nature and human nature . . .[36]

Such expression, to which history has assigned the term 'romantic', stressed the unusual, the grotesque, the particular (in landscape, for instance), the distinctness of peoples in other ages or other places, the ephemeral, the local and diverse – in a word, the original.

So came about 'the substitution of what may be called diversitarianism for uniformitarianism as the ruling preconception in most of the normative provinces of thought'.[37] It was linked with notions of fecundity and indeed creativity. It led to the conscious pursuit of idiosyncrasy: 'It is precisely individuality', wrote Friedrich Schlegel in the *Atheneum*, 'that is the original and eternal thing in men.'[38] It had, as Lovejoy points out, its dangers: 'To say "Yes" to everything and everybody is manifestly to have no character at all';[39] man needs to renounce as well as to affirm for he cannot express everything within him. To overcome the constrictions of reason, it is not necessary to fall into the trap of total amorphousness; but, of course, given the pluralism of the coming age the problems of limitations, renunciations become crucial – certainly for the educationist, who is faced with the necessity for action, the application of his art on a human 'nature' which is beginning to resist the human necessity for boundaries.

IV

And so, paradoxically, even 'diversity' was forced to become the subject of theoretical consideration. 'Diversity' did not develop as an escape from the abstract articulation of uniformitarian sentiments but as an alternative enunciation, supported by arguments – for example, in the political form of 'liberalism' as defined by J. S. Mill. The philosophical speculations of the uniformitarians were seen to demand an alternative, analogously theoretical reply. And so the character of educational theory developed to assimilate the new pervasive spirit of abstract thought – which now penetrated very much more deeply and into more aspects of human life than ever before. 'Theoretical man', against whom Nietzsche reacted a hundred years later, becomes much more of an actuality than he had been in previous centuries – and this was due partly to the changed role of philosophy: no longer did it simply underpin a theological system; instead, it penetrated into many aspects of human life. The process – and 'process' is now an operative word – has been brilliantly described by Ernst Cassirer in *The Philosophy of the Enlightenment*:

the Enlightenment produced a completely original form of philosophic thought . . . For nothing less than the universal process of philosophizing is now seen in a new light. In England and France, the Enlightenment begins by breaking down the older form of philosophic knowledge, the

metaphysical systems. It has lost faith in the 'spirit of systems' . . .
Instead of confining philosophy within the limits of a systematic doctrinal structure . . . the Enlightenment wants philosophy to move freely
and in this immanent activity to discover the fundamental form of
reality, the form of all natural and spiritual being. Philosophy, according
to this interpretation, is no special field of knowledge situated beside
or above the principles of natural science, of law and government, etc.,
but rather the all-comprehensive medium in which such principles are
formulated, developed, and founded. Philosophy is no longer to be
separated from science, history, jurisprudence and politics; it is rather
to be the atmosphere in which they can exist and be effective.[40]

And, indeed, Cassirer continues to make a point of the most fundamental
significance for the future of our cultural life and, hence, for education.
For, while it penetrated into so many aspects of life, it did not confine itself
merely to reflection on what it observed: Instead

This philosophy believes rather in an original spontaneity of thought;
it attributes to thought not merely an imitative function but the power
and task of shaping life itself. Thought consists not only in analyzing
and dissecting, but in actually bringing about that order of things which
it conceives as necessary, so that by this act of fulfilment it may demonstrate its own reality and truth.[41]

Hence, in educational terms, the changed role of cognition, its gradual pre-
dominance in the curriculum of our own times, and its emergence as a tool.
It betokens the time when the curriculum was to be conceived of as a process
rather than as a body of truths, an activity rather than as knowledge stored;
its early stirrings have already been noted in Locke:

Reason is now looked upon rather as an acquisition than as a heritage.
It is not the treasury of the mind in which the truth like a minted coin
lies stored; it is rather the original intellectual force which guides the
discovery and determination of truth . . . The whole eighteenth century
understands reason in this sense; not as a sound body of knowledge,
principles and truths, but as a kind of energy, a force which is fully
comprehensible only in its agency and effects.[42]

To live is to *think* – to see problems is to seek 'solutions'. It is specifically
the new form consciousness is to take – no longer an articulation of a unified
interplay of feeling and cognition as in the world of words, of rhetoric, but
a creative ordering of the world of things in largely cognitive terms: this
becomes the new paradigm. Philosophy takes its energy from the analogy
of science and it comes to seek a similar control. Hence life itself becomes
increasingly a matter of intellectual scrutiny, rational appraisal, theoretical
articulation, conscious planning and attempted control. A philosophical,
critical, cognitive spirit replaces what was basically a literary one, marrying

intellect and affect. Affect itself becomes the province of romantic revolt, not a central characteristic of man's functioning; and even it becomes subject to theory – in progressivism. We approach the age of ideologies.

The nature of educational theorising itself changes: in the past, men had been content to record their recommendations without seeking justification in other than very general terms of religious obligation or social utility. Now, educational theorising comes embedded in a much more extensive view and analysis of the general human condition. The development is forecast in the work of Comenius with his *pansophia* and its implications for human improvements, and Locke, with his general study of the human understanding, at once psychological and epistemological. The new generation of theorists have views on man, knowledge and society – not only did Locke and Rousseau, for instance, write works of political as well as educational theory, but their specifically educational work articulates social, epistemological, political and ontological theories.

And, indeed, the whole rejection of traditional outlooks and values implied a much more fundamental assessment of the educational undertaking than had been necessary when there was much that it could be assumed would be implicitly acceptable. The courtier, for instance, existed within a specific and accepted social context which needed – indeed, perhaps brooked – little discussion: he *inherited* a social order that was, in part, traditional, but, in any case, ultimately unquestionable; the terms of his existence were reasonably fixed, the framework given; it was part of his formation to accept past models. But the new critical spirit, 'calling all in doubt' (to quote an early expression of the felt dilemma, that of Donne), implied a much more intense search for justification ('evidence') before recommendation could become acceptable.

Furthermore, the end-product was much more in question and admitted, overall, a wider range of possibilities. To propound a social purpose, for instance, or even a practical one was now to require a definition of what sort of society or of practicality was intended. The result of criticism emerged as an extended range of new possibilities even while it narrowed educational objectives more exclusively on mind. Locke, as we have seen, depended on the accumulated capital of hierarchical Europe for his purpose of forming the morals and manners of a gentleman; but when Rousseau rejected the old order (symbolised in his objections to the concept of 'Citizen') and proclaimed his intention of forming simply 'a Man' he was entering deeper waters than perhaps he had anticipated. He marks in that attempt both the repudiation of an inherited conception and the new dilemmas enforced by emancipation, and thus in the history of educational theory marks both an end and a beginning.

NOTES

1 Peter Gay, *The Enlightenment*, Vol. I: *The Rise of Modern Paganism* (London, Weidenfeld & Nicolson, 1967), p. 11.
2 ibid., p. 87.

3 ibid., p. 86.
4 Quoted ibid., p. 142.
5 ibid., p. 148.
6 ibid., p. 149.
7 ibid., p. 97. cf. also on the whole question of enlightenment historiography, R. G. Collingwood, *The Idea of History* (London, Oxford University Press, 1946), pp. 76–85.
8 Gay, op. cit., p. 150.
9 ibid., p. 149.
10 ibid., p. 279. Professor Gay provides an interesting comparison of the renaissance and enlightenment periods, cf. pp. 257–79. In general the Renaissance was much less secular in outlook, though the process of secularisation had begun.
11 Quoted Gay, op. cit., Vol. II: *The Science of Freedom* (London, Wildwood House, 1973), p. 169.
12 Reprinted in *Essays in the History of Ideas* (Braziller, New York, 1955), pp. 78–98.
13 ibid., p. 80.
14 ibid., p. 81.
15 Quoted Gay, op. cit., Vol. I, p. 183.
16 ibid., p. 183.
17 ibid., p. 183.
18 cf. Gay, op. cit., Vol. II, p. 164
19 Gay, op. cit., Vol. I, p. 73.
20 Quoted R. V. Sampson, *Progress in the Age of Reason* (London, Heinemann, 1956), p. 139.
21 ibid., pp. 64–5.
22 Quoted ibid., p. 123.
23 C. L. Becker, *The Heavenly City of the Eighteenth-Century Philosophers* (New Haven, Conn., Yale University Press, 1959), p. 102.
24 ibid., pp. 102–3.
25 Sampson, op. cit., p. 131.
26 ibid., pp. 133–4.
27 Quoted J. A. Passmore, *The Perfectibility of Man* (London, Duckworth, 1972), p. 166.
28 A. O. Lovejoy, *The Great Chain of Being* (Cambridge, Mass., Harvard University Press, 1942), p. 292.
29 Gay, op. cit., Vol. I, p. 179.
30 Ian Watt, *The Rise of the Novel* (London, Chatto & Windus, 1957), p. 27.
31 Letter to Richard Allen (1736), quoted M. Mack, *The Garden and the City* (London, Oxford University Press, 1969), p. 32.
32 Gay, op. cit., Vol. I, p. 66.
33 Lovejoy, *The Great Chain*, p. 288.
34 Quoted Hazard, *The European Mind 1680–1715*, trans. J. L. May (Harmondsworth, Penguin, 1973), p. 456.
35 Locke, *Essay*, II.xx.6.
36 Lovejoy, *The Great Chain*, p. 293.
37 ibid., p. 294.
38 Quoted ibid., p. 307. Lovejoy goes on to identify 'the first and great commandment' of the romantic ideal as 'Be yourself, which is to say, be unique'.
39 ibid., p. 312.
40 E. Cassirer, *The Philosophy of the Enlightenment* (Boston, Mass., Beacon Press, 1955), pp. vi–vii.
41 ibid., p. viii.
42 ibid., p. 13.

CHAPTER 12

'The Mountain Goat, not the Ballet Dancer': Rousseau

I

I have written on Rousseau before.[1] There I drew attention to the instability of his personality and to the split in his consciousness between, on the one hand, the tendency to equate 'real life' with facts of a technical or scientific nature and, on the other, his propensity for fantasy – a dichotomy which goes far to explain the curious blend of logicality and dream which characterises his *Emile*, its recognition of the processes of orderly psychological development with its unreal idealisation of childish and simplified forms of behaviour. I also provided an extended analysis of his use of the concept of 'nature' – an analysis it is unnecessary to repeat here in detail other than to note that for Rousseau it constitutes his major approval word and that, while spanning the usual gamut between descriptive and prescriptive uses, its orientation is towards the more primitive, as providing a standard by which to judge the inadequacies of civilised existence. 'Nature' constitutes the scene of man's attempts at technical mastery, affords examples of superior treatment by which to judge the inadequacies of contemporary upbringing, and provides a norm, in the 'natural man', at which to aim, by discovering the 'real' human being beneath the accretions of a perverted socialisation. But all these matters will be sufficiently illustrated in this further study both of his methodology and of his aims and of the curricular means through which he seeks to achieve them. For Rousseau as much as anyone poses the problem of what man, in his new-found emancipation, is to become; he theorises about all phases of children's development – as he sees them – in a social context within which nothing is to be taken for granted as it currently exists.

II

Emile's education takes place in two broad phases: pre- and post-adolescence. The first three books are taken up with the earlier phase and are concerned largely with the world of 'things' which constitute both his first objects of knowledge and the ambience within which he forms his first tentative social relationships. In the fourth Emile is allowed to enter the moral world of man; his original innocence having been preserved during his early up-

266

bringing, he can now do so without too much risk. But much of the fundamental significance of Rousseau lies in the first three sections of the work.

'His original innocence': here in a sense lies the impetus behind the whole
of *Emile*. Thus, in a letter to Cramer, Rousseau writes: 'You say very truly
that it is impossible to form an Emile: but can you believe that *that* was my
aim, and that the book which bears this title is a treatise on education? It is
a philosophical enough work on this principle, put forward by the author in
other works, that man is naturally good.' Hence the significance of the
opening words, 'God makes all things good; man meddles with them and
they become evil.' How, then, does one so bring up a child that he preserves
this original innocence? Education 'comes to us from nature, from men, or
from things'.[2] In the period of pre-adolescence it is from men that Emile is
to be protected; in order to preserve the 'natural' (i.e. innocent and pre-
sumably pre-lapsarian) man it is necessary that he should encounter only the
discipline of 'things': 'When children only experience resistance in things
and never in the will of man, they do not become rebellious or passionate,
and their health is better.'[3] For indeed

> There are two kinds of dependence; dependence on things, which is the
> work of nature; and dependence on men, which is the work of society.
> Dependence on things, being non-moral, does no injury to liberty and
> begets no vices; dependence on men, being out of order, gives rise to
> every kind of vice, and through this master and slave become mutually
> depraved. If there is any cure for this social evil, it is to be found in the
> substitution of law for the individual; in arming the general will with a
> real strength beyond the power of any individual will. If the laws of
> nations, like the laws of nature, could never be broken by any human
> power, dependence on men would become dependence on things; all
> the advantages of a state of nature would be combined with all the
> advantages of social life in the commonwealth. The liberty which pre-
> serves a man from vice would be united with the morality which raises
> him to virtue.
>
> Keep the child dependent on things only. By this course of education
> you will have followed the order of nature. Let his unreasonable wishes
> meet with physical obstacles only, or the punishment which results
> from his own actions, lessons which will be recalled when the same
> circumstances occur again. It is enough to prevent him from wrong
> doing without forbidding him to do wrong.[4]

The child, in fact, must learn to succumb to necessity, the necessity implicit
in the laws binding physical phenomena; to be subjected to the will of man
is to risk infection with those evil ways which men have developed in society.
The brief reference to the 'general will', evocative of the *Contrat Social*,
indicates the sole way in which the action of humans can become like that
of things, in its need to observe law. Being subjected to the same kind of
inexorable law as are things he regards as leading to an ideal form of existence,
where the advantages of nature and of social life would be combined. Ad-

mitting that this is an impossible ideal (he seems unaware of its politically despotic implications), he chooses as the next best route of escape from dependence on men the attainment of a sort of autonomy – 'self help', which mirrors Bacon's insistence on obedience to physical 'law' as the means to control. One can note in this early education of Emile a most significant revelation of the extreme consequences of the Enlightenment's disengagement from the traditional culture and its acceptance of scientific law as constituting the genuine 'reality'.

So until adolescence the child is to be kept dependent on 'things' – as the means to discipline and as the objects of study with a view to basic competence. An explicit contrast is made with 'words': 'I do not like verbal explanations . . . Things! Things! I cannot repeat it too often. We lay too much stress on words; we teachers babble, and our scholars follow our example.'[5] So 'I would have the first words he hears few in number, distinctly and often repeated, while the words themselves should be related to things which can first be shown to the child.'[6] Though children can reason about 'things that affect their actual and sensible well-being', they would appear to be incapable of the sort of abstract reasoning which demands judgement of a moral kind:

> The very words *obey* and *command* will be excluded from his vocabulary, still more those of *duty* and *obligation*; but the words strength, necessity, weakness, and constraint must have a large place in it. Before the age of reason it is impossible to form any idea of moral beings or social relations; so avoid, as far as may be, the use of words which express these ideas, lest the child at an early age should attach wrong ideas to them, ideas which you cannot or will not destroy when he is older.[7]

Let him, in fact, find 'necessity in things, not in the caprices of man; let the curb be force not authority . . . for it is in man's nature to bear patiently with the nature of things, but not with the ill-will of another'.[8] Above all, let there be no learning of useless symbols when children have no idea what the words signify: 'The first meaningless phrase, the first thing taken for granted on the word of another person without seeing its use for himself, this is the beginning of the ruin of the child's judgement.'[9]

This dependence on the physical world has a number of implications and consequences, psychological and social. Emile, in order to be so confined, is to be abstracted from the conventional social world of his parents and from the historical circumstances of his birth. If he comes from a good family so much the better: 'He will be another victim snatched from prejudice.'[10] Within the natural order all men are equal and thus Emile becomes a representative human figure – representative, that is, of the unavoidable basic requirements for living in a world which makes at least physical demands: 'We must therefore look at the general rather than the particular, and consider our scholar as a man in the abstract, man exposed to all the changes and chances of mortal life.'[11] In this way, the reality of man's being will be exposed beneath the accretions of civilisation, the false posturings demanded by social life. (The homogenising implications of this 'man in the abstract' are worth noting – they tie in with the uniformitarian tendencies of the Enlightenment.) Rousseau expatiates on the disadvantages of a social training for a conventional society:

In the social order where each has his own place a man must be educated for it. If such a one leaves his own station he is fit for nothing else. His education is only useful when fate agrees with his parents' choice; if not, education harms the scholar, if only by the prejudices it has created . . .

In the natural order men are all equal and their common calling is that of manhood, so that a well-educated man cannot fail to do well in that calling and those related to it. It matters little to me whether my pupil is intended for the army, the church, or the law. Before his parents chose a calling for him nature called him to be a man. Life is the trade I would teach him.[12]

Emile's education at this stage marks a deliberate repudiation of the humanist concern for linguistic development as the prime factor in acculturation; for the complexities of personal speech are substituted the limited possibilities of impersonal law.

III

How, then, is this 'man' to develop, for Rousseau cannot leave him simply *dependent* on things, desirable though initially he finds the situation. How does he conceive what basically appertains to humanity, in face of the inexorable demands of necessity and physical law?

Rousseau accepts Locke's views on innate ideas: 'We are born capable of learning, but knowing nothing, perceiving nothing.'[13] So the initial prolonged phase of disengagement from cultural and social institutions which constitutes a state of independence and autonomy from human interference poses the problem of how Emile is to find his way around this 'natural' habitat. There are suggestions that development should remain endogenous: 'The mind should be left undisturbed till the faculties have developed.'[14] Education, it is urged, should be 'negative': 'Do not save time, but lose it' [15]– the injunction is the opposite to Erasmus' stress on the need for immediate intervention. 'Let him not be taught science, let him discover it.'[16] It would seem that Emile is to acquire an education from contact with the environment: 'His sense experiences are the raw material of thought . . . He wants to touch and handle everything; do not check these movements which teach him invaluable lessons. Thus he learns to perceive the heat, cold, hardness, softness, weight or lightness of bodies, to judge their size and shape and all their physical properties.'[17]

The fable, indeed, which reveals the whole orientation of this development is that of Robinson Crusoe. Earlier in the book one of Aesop's fables had been rejected on the grounds that its factual inaccuracies made it unsuitable for youthful minds: 'The cheese was held in his beak by a crow perched on a tree; it must indeed have smelt strong if the fox, in his thicket or his earth, could smell it. This is the way you train your pupil in that spirit of right judgement . . .'[18] ('Judgement' works within a quite different context from what it did in humanist theory.) There is much more to the same effect, as the fable of the fox and the crow is analysed remorselessly in terms of criteria it was never intended to meet. But *Robinson Crusoe* is the one book Emile is encouraged to read – for it is 'the best treatise of an education according to nature'.[19] *Crusoe*, after all, is every man's *vade mecum* in self-help in the acquiring of a basic technical competence: 'The surest way to raise him above prejudice and to base his judgement on the true relations of things, is to put him in the place of a solitary man, and to judge all things as they would be judged by such a man in relation to their own utility.'[20] Identification with Crusoe provides at once motivation and a concern for the fundamental necessities of life and their production as the hoped for outcome of this development according to the laws of nature:

> What a motive will this infatuation supply . . . The child who wants to build a storehouse on his desert island will be more eager to learn than the master to teach. He will want to know all sorts of useful things and nothing else; you will need the curb as well as the spur.[21]

Indeed, so enthusiastic is Rousseau for this new world of a limited technical mastery that he allows the workshop to provide Emile's first steps in social and moral understanding: 'Your main object should be to keep out of your scholar's way all idea of such social relations as he cannot understand, but when the development of knowledge compels you to show him the mutual dependence of mankind, instead of showing him its moral side, turn all his attention at first towards industry and the mechanical arts which make men useful to one another.'[22] Characteristically, the world of the workman is considered superior to that of the sophisticated and cultivated, whose artefacts are dismissed as trifles:

> The value set by the general public on the various arts is in diverse ratio to their real utility. They are even valued directly according to their uselessness. This might be expected. The most useful arts are the worst paid, for the number of workmen is regulated by the demand, and the work which everybody requires must necessarily be paid at a rate which puts it within the reach of the poor. On the other hand, those great people who are called artists, not artisans, who labour only for the rich and idle, put a fancy price on their trifles . . .
> What idea will they form of the true worth of the arts and the real value of things when they see, on the one hand, a fancy price and, on the other, the price of real utility, and that the more a thing costs the less it is worth.[23]

Crusoe is approved of because he prefers the work of the artisan to that of the artist, the toolmaker to the jeweller.

So the world of 'things' fulfils a double purpose: it exercises a necessary if limited control, the inescapable minimum of constraint, and introduces to the approved social milieux. There is a retreat from full participation in a sophisticated society to 'autonomy' (within certain physical limitations), and isolation broken by approved contact with peasants and the labouring classes; Emile is to 'emulate the mountain goat, not the ballet dancer'.[24]

All this is accompanied by a number of indications of resentment against the current cultural order. Human institutions 'are one mass of folly and contradiction';[25] the morals of the town are 'vile'.[26] Reading is the 'curse of childhood'. 'Books, what dull food for a child of his age!'[27] Direct contact and manual work are praised, on the grounds that they would afford the basic competences to enable a child to earn his living in uncertain times. For 'of all the pursuits by which a man may earn his living, the nearest to a state of nature is manual labour; of all stations that of the artisan is least dependent on Fortune'.[28] Thus to pursue the education of 'nature' is no longer to betoken a reference to a teleological universe seeking to actualise man in his full potentiality, but in line with the new nature of mechanical necessity implies a regression to a limited, mechanistic order of restricted competence. It is not surprising to find Rousseau urging that 'Ignorance never did any one any harm' or deprecating the traditionally learned:

Who can deny that a vast number of things are known to the learned, which the unlearned will never know? Are the learned any nearer truth? ... Everyone knows that the learned societies of Europe are mere schools of falsehood, and there are assuredly more mistaken notions in the Academy of Sciences than in a whole tribe of American Indians.[29]

By contrast Emile

is ready for anything. He can handle the spade and hoe, he can use the lathe, hammer, plane, or file; he is already familiar with these tools which are common to many trades ... Moreover his senses are acute and well-practised, he knows the principles of the various trades; to work like a master of his craft he only needs experience, and experience comes with practice.[30]

The ideal role of this early education is no longer that of the courtier or gentleman – it is that of the workman, the one who combines technical know-how with an imagined freedom.

And in what does this 'freedom' consist? Certainly, freedom *from* the constraints of a complex civilisation, once a basic sufficiency has been secured; but freedom *to* do what, once released from the inhibitions of normal social convention? We find that the discipline of things is to be offset by an affective freedom of self-expression. Emile gives way as he wishes to impulse: 'He does not know the meaning of habit, routine and custom, what he did yesterday has no control over what he is doing to-day; he follows no rule, submits to no authority, copies no pattern, and only acts or speaks as he pleases.'[31] So he becomes 'keen, eager, and full of life . . . absorbed in this present state, and delighting in a fullness of life'.[32] He runs, jumps and shouts to his heart's content,[33] unconstrained by 'civilised' behavioural standards. Outside the constraints of physical necessity he is undeterred by the affective controls of civilisation. If on the one hand he would seem to provide an early prototype of technological man, on the other he constitutes a model for romantic impulse release and manifestations of individual whim.

IV

But 'fullness of life'? Surely this impulse release constitutes, in fact, the enslavement of an undisciplined discharge of energy which vents itself not in the freedom of mastery, of achievement, of moving with greater confidence within even the physical world as we know it, but in futile 'jumps and shouts', ebullitions of feeling which waste themselves in manifestations without meaning and therefore without humane consequence. 'Fullness of life' is not to be equated with mere energy release, even if one allows that such rather than an enervated boredom would be the outcome of Emile's enforced isolation.

In Emile, indeed, we can judge some of the implications of the Enlightenment's desire to set men free from traditional restraints. Emile's 'autonomy' is assured by removing him from the influence of men; his 'well-regulated liberty' is to be subject only to the discipline of things – that which arises from the new knowledge of mechanical necessity. Rousseau obviously must face up to the need to reintroduce him to society – this is to be his adolescent training. But what alternative 'culture' does he inhabit as an autonomous human being? For culture, of a kind, he does inhabit, of course. To call Rousseau anti-historical, anti-cultural is to indicate his distaste for the historically evolved society of his times, with its characteristic stresses and strains – an 'environment' which, in actual fact, no one can avoid. Yet Rousseau, the prime enemy of the 'artificial', produces at least as synthetic a youngster as those he criticises: paradoxically, the great advocate of freedom in effect manipulates his pupil into demonstrating those characteristics he admires much more ruthlessly than any pedagogue of the old school; for instance, he removes him from any possibility of rebellion: 'No doubt [Emile] ought only to do what he wants, but he ought to want to do nothing but what you want him to do.'[34] Nothing is to be *told* Emile and he is not to read books; but Rousseau cannot escape the moral dilemmas implicit in the very notion of education; so desire is equated with morality: 'When he only does what he wants, he will soon only do what he ought . . .'[35] The emphasis may seem to be on motivation and 'present interest' – but interests are in effect subject to a selective process. Rousseau has avoided the initial possibility of unsavoury interests by positing a child of 'natural goodness'; provided that the tutor makes no errors in the environment he provides (a large assumption), the boy can only pursue healthy 'interests' as Rousseau conceives them. By ensuring that desire is geared to the tutor's moral insight – for it is, after all, a very specific environment Emile is to inhabit – Emile, by escaping the vices of men, is anaesthetised from any tendency to argue. He may have no moral insight; but at the end of the day he is dependent on that of his tutor.

The point is that Emile is not simply to learn from any environment, but from an *arranged* environment; Rousseau's advice runs as follows: 'Remember you must be a man before you try to train a man: you yourself must set the pattern he shall copy. While the child is still unconscious there is time to prepare his surroundings so that nothing shall strike his eye but what is fit for his sight.'[36] Sense experiences must be presented to him 'in fitting order'; the phrase implies a very specific purposive intervention.

Rousseau, indeed, cannot escape the implications of the dilemma that ultimately, only man can educate man; he is subject to the dynamics of what it means to be human. Order needs to be imposed on the chaos of nature. Emile cannot be left to an uninterrupted 'natural' development, despite the suggestions of endogenous possibilities. There is no law in the development of human beings analogous to that implicit in the physical world. Its very structure implies a sequence: 'every concrete example suggests another and always points to the next in the series. This succession . . . is the order followed by most men, and it is the right order for all children.'[37] Only as a manifestation of sophisticated insight is it possible to detect that sequence.

For the injunction is: 'Teach your scholar to observe the phenomena of nature; you will soon rouse his curiosity . . . Let him not be taught *science*, let him discover it' (my italics).[38] And here, of course, a re-reading of the second sentence induces a fuller realisation of implication. To refer to 'science' is to refer to a humanly categorised world based on an accumulation of observations and their being brought together under hypotheses and laws – an alternative culture to the humanist world of words and texts. And indeed, in various ways it is clear that Rousseau wishes to foster very specific if limited cultural competences in Emile. He is to learn about the motion of the earth and sun during his walks; a visit to a fair is to provide an opportunity to learn about the properties of the magnet ('The study of physics is begun.'). There may be psychological support behind this: 'Undoubtedly the notions of things thus acquired for oneself are clearer and much more convincing than those acquired from the teaching of others; and not only is our reason not accustomed to a slavish submission to authority, but we develop greater ingenuity in discovering relations, connecting ideas and inventing apparatus . . .'[39] But the process involves inescapably the need for Emile to add 'art to nature':[40] 'If instead of making a child stick to his books I employ him in a workshop, his hands work for the development of his mind.'[41] The art is the technical art of instrument making; the criterion of utility is introduced: 'The objects of real utility may be introduced into his studies.'[42] Evaluative implications are manifest.

So Emile, this 'natural' child, is clearly both the product of human artifice through the arranged and ordered presentation of data and himself become artificer. He is simply to exchange a more limited for a more sophisticated cultivation. That uniform 'nature' which is explicit in Rousseau's view of the 'natural' man is manifested through proximity with artisans and craftsmen, peasants and labourers;[43] it becomes part of romantic mythology that such people are more 'real' than the more sophisticated, reveal in some way the 'essentials' of human nature, its uniformity:

> Hitherto I have made no distinction of condition, rank, station, or fortune; nor shall I distinguish between them in the future, since man is the same in every station; the rich man's stomach is no bigger than the poor man's, nor is his digestion any better; . . . and indeed the natural needs are the same to all, and the means of satisfying them should be equally within the reach of all. Fit a man's education to his real self, not to what is no part of him.[44]

Part of Rousseau's problem, of course, arises out of his desire to preserve notions of the natural goodness of man – pervasively present, in a much modified form, in the humanist view, as we have seen – in the demythologised world of the Enlightenment philosopher and the early scientist. The humanist could argue the (relative) goodness of man because his world-view allowed him to harmonise man's potential with the God-given natural law. Neutralise the universe, demythologise nature's laws so that they function purpose*lessly* (in human terms) driven by their own morally neutral internal momentum, and it is only possible for him to reintroduce the inescapable moral dimension in the education of human beings by literally making a virtue of necessity. This is precisely what initially Rousseau attempts. 'Things' now provide the disciplinary force previously exercised by man and at the same time help preserve the pristine goodness of his birth. But of course it is impossible to maintain this pedagogic abdication; and what is fostered is an alternative culture stimulated by the indirect intervention of the tutor. For 'things,' viewed from a *human* standpoint, have their own if restricted cultural order – and need to be presented in that order to make sense.

What, then, is to be the nature of this alternative culture, built on man's putatively uniform wants and needs, and stimulating the mind through observation and activity within the common world of 'things', where 'bodily exercise and manual work unconsciously arouse thought and reflexion'.[45] Let us see how Rousseau defines the Emile whom, willy-nilly, he has 'formed', in this earlier stage of his training.

The attempt is to 'form' him at two levels – those of will and understanding. Emile must not be checked by word or the actions of men and yet he must learn that there are grave limits to his powers; furthermore his passions must not be aroused. So he must be disciplined and his will curbed by the inertia and responsiveness of natural phenomena: from them he will learn submission to necessity, and in this way he will be able to achieve that 'perfect equilibrium between the power and the will' which is the mark of 'true happiness'.[46] He will, that is to say, become attuned to his physical environment; it will afford him stability, and a norm by which to judge his later human education.

But – as has been briefly noted – the very means of control that Rousseau opts for this pre-adolescent child become themselves ways by which Emile himself learns, in his turn, to control. The paradox is that implicit in Bacon's insight that in order to master nature it is necessary to obey her. The control involved is partly one of understanding and partly one of technical mastery. Emile must be stimulated to exercise his senses and to derive from them the understanding his observation has afforded him; he has to learn to correlate the phenomena he has encountered and through a combination of experiment and induction to acquire some insight into their behaviour. In this way he learns to reason in the manner Rousseau considers appropriate for the older but still pre-adolescent child. 'After exercising his body and his senses you have exercised his mind and his judgement . . . At first our pupil had merely sensations, now he has ideas.'[47]

Indeed, Emile is to be a 'natural man living in society' and must know how to live in it and earn his living; so '*he must reason whether he wants to or no*' (my italics).[48] He has come to understand 'reality' as a young scientist comes to understand that concept; what he knows he knows by first-hand contact and not on the authority but through the guidance of others. Furthermore, he has acquired no great store of factual knowledge 'but the means of getting it when required'.[49] Let Rousseau reveal how he sees the position as Emile stands on the brink of his entry into society:

> Emile's knowledge is confined to nature and things. The very name of history is unknown to him, along with metaphysics and morals. He knows the essential relations between men and things, but nothing of the moral relations between man and man. He has little power of generalisation, he has no skill in abstraction. He perceives that certain qualities are common to certain things, without reasoning about these qualities themselves. He is acquainted with the abstract ideas of space by the help of his geometrical figures; he is acquainted with the abstract idea of quantity by the help of his algebraical symbols. These figures and signs are the supports on which these ideas may be said to rest; the supports on which his senses repose. He does not attempt to know the nature of things, but only to know things in so far as they affect himself. He only judges what is outside himself in relation to himself, and his judgement is exact and certain. Caprice and prejudice have no part in it. He values most the things which are of use to himself, and as he never departs from this standard of values, he owes nothing to prejudice.[50]

The foregoing analysis should have made quite clear the fact that the deployment of the notion of 'natural man' is merely a move in a game to foster an alternative artificiality – that involved in the manipulation of things rather than of words, in technical mastery rather than verbal persuasiveness, in manifesting only his own subjective desires rather than in acquiring the need to consider others. Certainly it has been accomplished by a process of depriving Emile of much of his humanity in the moral and aesthetic fields. It fails entirely to grasp the need for even young children to adopt social roles as a preliminary means to discovering themselves. Such a process, it has been noted, is fraught with dangers, for it can mask egotism and sycophancy – that is not in question. Castiglione's solution was to advocate working through role adoption by means of imitation and observation of the best models until what inevitably began as artificiality ended as effortlessness, *sprezzatura* – the creation of a *second* nature. Only in this way can moral probity and sincerity be achieved – the moral sincerity of a virtuous man integrated into society as the adviser of his prince. Rousseau thinks such sincerity can only come through the preservation of an *original* nature, through what turns out to be an equally artificial form of education which shields Emile from all possibility of moral transgression by removing him from the ethical and aesthetic worlds in a way impossible to operate in practice. He fails to see that working through, testing roles and opinions in a social context, is the only possible way to maturity, that the only hope of curbing those particular artifices of morals and manners he so dislikes is not to attempt to shun them but to foster discrimination and to assist the internalisation of those acceptable until they become an integral part of the personality. Rousseau's evasive action constitutes a historically important moment in the history of European culture; it encourages the fiction that the 'natural' is to be equated with the socially limited working at little more than subsistence level (the 'useful') – and thus denies potentialities of a human 'nature' which constituted the 'natural' in a teleologically conceived universe where a much fuller range of human attributes sought actualisation. In either case, it is inevitably artificial man who is formed, for artifice, as has been so often emphasised, is inextricably bound up with human development. What Castiglione seeks is the total human being shaped and formed through its cultural, social and intellectual contacts to achieve a consummation; what Rousseau proposes is a fixation at the limited level implied by contact with the facts of 'nature' ('things') in the naïve faith that this will provide a protection against the temptations which arise out of the inevitable introduction into the social order which even he admits must take place at adolescence. It marks the beginning of the romantics' desire to alter the rules of the game in a way which it is beyond the capacity of humans to do. The only way to a full human maturity (and many fall by the wayside) is through the process of working through; one cannot retreat into a simplified world and then hope to cope with the complexities of the real one.

Furthermore, the growing emphasis – it has been noted in Comenius and Locke, to the former of whom words were but the 'husks and coverings of things' – on a restricted view of language, the attempt to limit it to a denotative usage, along with Locke's deprecation of the poetic sensibility constitutes an implied circumscription of human experience, an implication sustained by Rousseau's ruthless banishment of 'fancy' characterising Aesop's fable of the fox and the crow. That words can deceive is both the charge laid against them by Locke and the admitted weakness of the humanist approach which has been constantly referred to in this book; but

this is the price one pays for human freedom and the ability to speculate,
to pass beyond the immediacies of sense experience and practical activities
to the creation of 'fictions' which may, nevertheless, be deeply revelatory of
a human reality. Unequivocal meaning, which seems to be the growing ideal,
constitutes a threat to human speculative possibilities, which requires ambiguities and ironies reflected in equivocal discourse as part of its very freedom
to operate. To control language, to purge it of its uncertainties, its essentially
poetic and metaphoric possibilities, constitutes one more piece of evidence
of the growing dominance of the technical – and mathematical – model as
coming to pre-empt, almost unconsciously, the formation of the human
mind, to the detriment of its freedom in speculation, its refusal to be tied
to the contingencies of time and place.

V

But is it fair to criticise Rousseau before the full implications of his later
educational scheme have been considered? In fact, the real meat of Rousseau
is in these earlier books – the last two largely indicate, where they depart
from the initial impetus, the incoherencies of a personality deeply at odds
with his society and unable to evolve a coherent *social* view of his protégé.
However, this later phase reveals other facets of its author.

For Rousseau, the passions are only aroused at adolescence; and, with its
arrival, the whole nature of his educational scheme alters. The aim is still
the same – to foster a 'natural' development (in this case accepting that it is
'natural' to man to live in society) which will, nevertheless, avoid the normal
processes of socialisation and thus avoid the corruptions of conventional
social life. So, from being kept dependent on things only, Emile has now to
enter, and learn how to cope with, the world of men. The passions, stimulated by his contact with his fellows, now manifest themselves: 'We have
reached the moral order at last.'[51] How is this situation to be handled?

Of course, already much is thought to have been achieved in the first
phase: 'As for Emile, if in childhood he was distinguished by simplicity and
good sense, in his youth he will show a warm and tender heart; for the
reality of the feelings depends to a great extent on the accuracy of the ideas.'[52]
This accuracy, it is thought, has been secured during his probationary period
which has induced the correct linguistic cohesion of word and thing. Nevertheless, the tutor has now to play a more direct role by controlling and
directing the impulses of the growing youth. There are, in fact, two main
strategies – one is to slow down the development of the passions, the other
is to preserve from contact with the corruptions of the world by means
other than isolation.

The passions are accepted as fundamental to men – they are a means to
self-preservation and to destroy them would be 'to overcome nature, to re-
shape God's handiwork'.[53] But they are, 'naturally', few in number. Modifications result from 'external influences, without which they would never
occur, and such modifications, far from being advantageous to us, are harmful.

They change the original purpose and work against its end; then it is that man finds himself outside nature and at strife with himself.'[54] So 'amour de soi' (self-love), essential for our preservation, becomes 'amour-propre' (pride and selfishness). How is the growing youth to be protected from this development?

One of the solutions is predictable – to live amongst rude and simple people, and thus preserve the 'realities' already achieved:

> By nature men are neither kings, nobles, courtiers, nor millionaires. All men are born poor and naked, all are liable to the sorrows of life, its disappointments, its ills, its needs, its suffering of every kind; and all are condemned at length to die. This is what it really means to be a man, this is what no mortal can escape. Begin then with the study of the essentials of humanity, that which really constitutes mankind ... Remove [adolescents] from great cities, where the flaunting attire and the boldness of the women hasten and anticipate the teaching of nature. Bring them back to their early home, where rural simplicity allows the passions of their age to develop more slowly.[55]

The other solution is to slow down the development of the emotions: 'Do you wish to establish law and order among the rising passions, prolong the period of their development, so that they may have time to find their proper place as they arise. Then they are controlled by nature herself, not by man; your task is merely to leave it in her hands.'[56]

To achieve this retardation, however, the method of approach must now drastically alter: 'we must take the opposite way from that hitherto followed and instruct the youth rather through the experience of others than through his own'.[57] This is the time for history, so that he can acquire an understanding of the corruptions of men without necessarily having to suffer from their depredations. Furthermore, an overt and highly active intervention on the part of the tutor is sanctioned: 'When he is carried away by the flood of existing customs and I draw him in the opposite direction by means of other customs, this is not to remove him from his place, but to keep him in it.'[58] So Rousseau becomes quite explicit in his willingness to reveal his own authority. 'Must I abdicate my authority when most I need it?'[59] In pursuit of 'the one art absolutely necessary to a civilised man, the art of living among his fellow-men', Rousseau admits to his absolute mastery over Emile's will:

> It is true I allow him a show of freedom, but he was never more completely under control, because he obeys his own free will. So long as I could not get the mastery over his will, I retained control over his person; I never left him for a moment. Now I sometimes leave him to himself because I control him continually.[60]

Certainly, this control is to be supplemented by ties of affection, gratitude and an awakened reason. But Rousseau now explicitly accepts that: '*Much art is required in order to prevent man in society from being altogether artificial*' (my italics).[61] The pretence that Emile can be left to his own devices, that education should be 'negative', that development can be endogenous, though never convincingly maintained even in the world of things, is now finally and quite overtly abandoned. Authority, disguised as the authority implicit in arranged situations in the upbringing of the young Emile, is now fully admitted. What accounts for this frankness?

The fact of the matter is that Rousseau has always indicated that he fears the influence of men more than he fears the necessity of things. The latter participate in the putative benevolence of primitive nature; their laws of behaviour can be learned and mastered. The former constitute, to his mind, a constant threat to the desired equilibrium of the self, manifest as 'sincerity'. Only the poorer classes, partly because they, too, inhabit the world of things and, therefore, live closer to primitive nature, can be trusted; the learned, the sophisticated, the leaders in society offer the menace of personal corruption; no one was more disenchanted with the European mind than Rousseau. To show the significance of Rousseau it is necessary to ask why. It is the more desirable to do so in that, though neither a stable personality nor an especially wise man, he is deeply revealing and symptomatic of forces which have profoundly affected our own times. Nothing could be more artificial nor contrived than the education he provides Emile – and yet his conscious 'art' is directed only against the 'artificial', by which he intends *all* manifestations of sophisticated society.

One explanation is that Rousseau was neurotic and the reason why he found people especially threatening lay in his persecution mania. No doubt there is a limited truth in this, but if it had been the total explanation, Rousseau would hardly have become the significant figure he has.

Then it is arguable that the French society of his time was in a bad way and the ruling classes demonstrated precisely the corruptions he assigned to them. Again, there is some truth in this, but it would still not explain the persistence of Rousseau's attitude once the social cause had been removed in the Revolution of 1789.

Perhaps Rousseau's concern for the natural man and his turning to the less sophisticated members of society constitutes simply one more version of the perennial concern for pastoral which plays so important a role, for instance, even in the classical experience. Again, there is something in this – to an extent, indeed, that it is worth pursuing a little further by drawing attention to how far Rousseau's reductionism reflects a typical pastoral situation and how far it departs from it.

Dr Bolgar has drawn attention to the fact that, by the end of the Renaissance, men

> turned to the ancient literatures not so much to learn a necessary lesson as to enjoy a salutary contrast. The republican virtues of Rome, the good life of the Athenian heyday became myths which served as a rallying point for spiritual discontents, providing glimpses of a culture that was now pictured as essentially different from the pattern of contemporary Europe.[62]

If one wants to class Rousseau's *Emile* as a 'rallying point for spiritual discontent', it must be realised that many similar expressions indicated a very different qualitative response to an endemic situation. Pope, for instance, manifested a sophisticated rusticity which Professor Mack has analysed in *The Garden and the City*;[63] but the alternative Pope offered to the Walpole ethos demonstrates a very different proposition from Rousseau's cult of the labouring classes. What has come to be called the retirement myth was pervasive in the seventeenth and eighteenth centuries and induced, at various times, a Christian search for self-purification, an impetus towards scientific research and the cult of landscape gardening. As E. M. W. Tillyard put it, drawing on Maren-Sofie Røstvig's monumental study *The Happy Man: Studies in Metamorphoses of a Classical Ideal*: 'It was not mere evasion but the setting of life in another direction.'[64]

But the outcome of Rousseau's protest is overtly regressive. It pretends, for part of the time, to be artless when, indeed, it is clearly highly artificial – this has been sufficiently demonstrated not to need further illustration. When it comes to admit 'art', it aims not at the transcendence of 'artificiality' but at its removal. It seeks not the reform of contemporary social values but their reversal, on the grounds that 'Man is the same in every station of life: if that be so, those ranks to which most men belong deserve most honour.' Humanist education faced up to the realities of social power and differentiation and strove to purify its exercise by making it persuasive and virtuous; Rousseau, as far as possible, ignores its necessity, and substitutes naïvety (at best) for renaissance *virtu*. He deprecates learning and artistry of any sophistication, Emile's tastes and reading being always oriented in the direction of simplicity and 'nature'. It is small wonder that Sir Isaiah Berlin, in a radio talk some years ago, identified Rousseau as the 'first militant low-brow in history'. His 'pastoralism', furthermore, is unrelieved by any sense of irony; it is not intended as a temporary retreat within which to recoup one's forces, but as a permanent regressive state.

For Rousseau's rejection of his times, in fact, goes deeper than the normal 'civilised' reaction against the inevitable imperfections of social life; it reveals a profound resentment against the existing social order as such, a sense of alienation which has persisted into our own times as a 'counter-culture'. Young Emile's impulse release, the relaxed nature of Rousseau's own rusticity, imply a protest against the very notion of civilised creative endeavour; Emile's 'equilibrium', his balance of power and will, arise out of restrictions involving retardations and unrealistic segregations rather than a positive contention with the challenges, opportunities and temptations of social life. It didn't even work, as Richard Edgeworth, who brought up his first-born according to Rousseau's precepts and methodology and has inscribed his regrets for the instruction of posterity, discovered.

VI

When we do examine how this elaborately brought up young man is to manifest himself in society – as it is admitted that he must – the answer turns out to be highly ambiguous. Emile's conduct is marked both by humility and arrogance. He seeks to be a man of the people, yet in his attitude to them he is insufferably superior: 'Although Emile has no very high opinion of people in general, he does not show any scorn of them, because he pities them and is sorry for them.'[65] He loves 'liberty above all things', and yet he is at pains to conform so as not to attract attention:

> Far from disregarding the ways of other people, Emile conforms to them readily enough; not that he may appear to know all about them, nor yet to affect the airs of a man of fashion, but on the contrary for fear lest he should attract attention, and in order to pass unnoticed; he is most at his ease when no one pays any attention to him.[66]

Yet though he is most at ease when ignored, this curiously intangible young man 'scarcely troubles himself at all about what people think of him'.[67] He has grasped those basic simple ideas which Rousseau regards as the most useful:

> I have convinced him that all wholesome ideas, ideas which are really useful to mankind, were among the earliest known, that at all times they have formed the true bonds of society, and that there is nothing left for ambitious minds but to seek distinction for themselves by means of ideas which are injurious and fatal to mankind.[68]

Naturally our paragon deprecates such forwardness – but is not averse to a certain thrustingness on his own account: 'He will have pride enough to wish to do well in everything that he undertakes, and even to wish to do it better than others; he will want to be the swiftest runner, the strongest wrestler, the cleverest workman, the readiest in games of skill . . .'[69] He is to keep his taste 'pure and wholesome' on pleasant books and, despite the fact that he 'sets so small a value upon words', becomes an acute connoisseur of literary styles. He dismisses 'the chatter of the academics' and only glances (in order to dismiss) the work of 'modern compilers, journals, translations, dictionaries',[70] but becomes a discriminating appraiser of the classics where is to be found 'a certain simplicity of taste which goes straight to the heart'.[71] (The ancients, indeed, are permitted – because they 'are nearer to nature'[72] than the authors of his own day.) It is all a little puzzling.

The description of Emile's adolescent development closes in a typical romantic dream of the simple, rustic life where 'pleasure is ours when we want it; it is only social prejudice which makes everything hard to obtain and drives pleasure before us'.[73] Once he is married to Sophy, the young couple will revive the Golden Age: 'In fancy I see the population increasing, the land coming under cultivation, the earth clothed with fresh beauty.' Emile may even be called to 'sterner duties': 'If the prince or the state calls you to the service of your country, leave all to fulfil the honourable duties of a citizen in the post assigned to you.'[74]

How does one explain the extraordinary range of inconsistencies, this amorphousness of social role? The ambiguities arise because Rousseau's egalitarian commitments, pervasive throughout the book, forbid the presentation of any defined social order and, hence, fail to achieve definition of social role. Within the simplified economy that he permits (tastes being always oriented to the 'natural' fail to register marked discriminations; there is, indeed, something anomalous in the very admission of 'tastes' into this simplified existence) it is not possible to give a coherent picture of the end product of his system because clarity and definition is dependent upon opportunities and refinements – and these Rousseau is determined to eradicate as representative of the traditional order. Apart from the limitations implicit in physical nature, he is concerned to abandon, as far as possible, discrimination and qualitative distinction. Little wonder that his artificial 'natural man' lacks clarity of form.

Furthermore, a great deal of this education, as indicated, is preventative, 'negative' in a sense other than that attributed by Rousseau himself. It is explicitly non-formative, for it rejects historical forms and models and seeks only to preserve a highly dubious 'natural' goodness, the lineaments of which defy close articulation. In these circumstances, amorphousness is hardly surprising. But, in effect, 'natural goodness' constitutes simply a rallying point for the disengagement from the traditional culture thought necessary by the Enlightenment. It provides a reason for abstraction from current social pressures; it constitutes the most telling argument in favour of the fresh start.

If one now tries to define the place of Rousseau, specifically, in the historical development charted in this book, one sees that he represents a line of protest already implicit, to some extent, in the reaction of the empirics against the humanist. They accept an alternative culture of scientific pursuits which will feed into the later eighteenth-century theorising of men like Priestley and that of nineteenth-century educationists like Spencer, Huxley and other advocates of a scientific orientation. Initially, Rousseau would seem to be one of them, for the young Emile is brought up as a young scientist learning to categorise and manipulate the world of things. But, in Rousseau, there is a more fundamental discontent which rejects all contemporary 'forms', humanistic and, in the end, scientific. What he seeks is some quintessential being, some dream image balancing will and power, achieving the equilibrium of reason and feeling and finding it only among the uneducated and more primitive – the 'natural', a manifestation, ideally, of a first, unspotted nature.

And, indeed, in Rousseau, the artisan, labourer, peasant, from being regarded by Bacon, Descartes and others of the seventeenth century simply as sources of technical know-how, come to be considered as representing desirable life-styles, simpler and more sincere than that man of the world who 'almost always wears a mask. He is scarcely ever himself and is almost a stranger to himself . . . Not what he is, but what he seems, is all he cares about.'[75] The repetition, almost word for word, of the dichotomy between 'being' and 'seeming' enunciated by Petrarch almost four-and-a-half centuries previously reminds one of the extent to which, over the centuries, the dilemma has haunted the European consciousness – and of the very different solutions which have been proposed for the problem. Rousseau's preference for the simpler, more primitive life-styles as affording the ambience within which we can discover our 'true' selves is at once utopian and regressive. It is utopian in its perfectionism and regressive in its implicit denial of the sheer range of human potentiality; all are to be reduced to similar levels of competence. Paradoxically, humanist elitism nevertheless made explicit allowance for human diversity and urged the observation of children so that their tendencies could be allowed for; no tag appears more frequently than the injunction '*Nihil Minerva invita*'. But Rousseau arrogantly assumes that he has defined a quintessential human nature that is the same for all; his call for the observation of Emile only cloaks an underlying prescriptive certainty as to what will be found. Diversification plays no part in his prescriptions. Only when he is forced to indicate how this essential nature should manifest itself amidst the inescapable diversities of social life does his model reveal its inconsistencies – for, as Rousseau is the first to claim, his paragon is 'man in the abstract', and such an abstraction lacks coherence within the ineluctable demands of the real world.[76]

Rousseau's book achieved a *succès* de *scandale* in its own day; few educational theorists of his times – and theory now began to proliferate – ignored him. Some, like David Williams, largely welcomed his influence, some, like Edgeworth, assessed him critically, others, like Vicesimus Knox, excoriated him. His influence until our own times was largely confined to what might be termed an emerging liberal intelligentsia some of whom, influenced by a climate of opinion to which he contributed much, set up 'progressive' schools of their own. At a more popular level, his central notion which he shares with the romantics, that the human being is most truly 'himself' outside the conventional social order, has deeply affected our postwar world. It is embodied in such diverse manifestations as the current idealisation of the working classes, often by those with no first-hand knowledge of them, the phenomenon of the 'drop-out', the deep revulsion against any suggestion of 'artificiality' and the corresponding acceptance of all forms of 'naturalness', however repellent, the cult of 'sincerity' and 'authenticity'. The renaissance ideals of achievement and transcendence, a confidence in 'forms' of civilised behaviour, an eager identification with sophisticated values based on historical models, a sense of the vitality of the past and of the role it had to play through creative imitation, all these are currently in eclipse. In contrast to the effort and discipline clearly implied by renaissance theory, Rousseau would seem to offer an indulgent relaxation which would simultaneously reveal the central core of being.

Emile, then, both signals an end and heralds a beginning. In Roussea's own time, the old culture was still strong enough to warrant considerable emphasis on disengagement, a process which exercised in so many contexts the tutor's ingenuity – so that in fact we are always somewhat clearer in the book about what Rousseau is against than what he is for – required the initial isolation of the pupil and his subsequent careful manipulation. A new formless, 'democratic' and specifically egalitarian ambience is foreshadowed in the pluralistic incoherence of Emile's social identity, with no settled role in the historical setting, at once distinguished and indistinguishable. *Emile* never forms part of the central tradition of educational theorising; but it plays a part in the gradual attenuation of the classical humanist tradition and, in due course, encourages a line of thinking which is to afford a powerful challenge to the dominant emphasis on mind and the assimilation of knowledge (with its socially divisive implications) as the prime function of education. There were, in that challenge, strengths as well as weaknesses, and the former will receive due attention in the next volume as part of the evolution of progressive thought it will attempt to chart. What has been incipiently revealed in the present work is the initiation of a line of thought which seeks to substitute an 'expressionist' theory of education for a 'formative' one reflected in an attempted readjustment of the interplay of 'art' and 'nature'.

NOTES

1 cf. my *Education and Values*, ch. 3 (London, Faber, 1965).
2 J. J. Rousseau, *Emile*, trans. B. Foxley (London, Everyman, 1943), p. 6.
3 ibid., p. 33.
4 ibid., p. 49.
5 ibid., p. 143.
6 ibid., p. 37.
7 ibid., p. 53.
8 ibid., p. 55.
9 ibid., p. 76.
10 ibid., p. 20.
11 ibid., p. 10.
12 ibid., p. 9.
13 ibid., p. 28.
14 ibid., p. 57.
15 ibid., p. 57.
16 ibid., p. 131.
17 ibid., p. 31.
18 ibid., p. 78.
19 ibid., p. 147.
20 ibid., p. 147.
21 ibid., p. 148.
22 ibid., p. 148.
23 ibid., pp. 148-9.
24 ibid., p. 104. (There is a lingering concern for 'gracefulness' in the passage which leads up to this distinction: Emile is to acquire agility and to hold himself 'easily and steadily', for 'An easy carriage is always graceful, and the steadiest positions are the most elegant.' But the stage tricks of dancing masters are to be studiously avoided. Even Rousseau wants it both ways.)
25 ibid., p. 46.
26 ibid., p. 59.
27 ibid., p. 123.
28 ibid., p. 158.
29 ibid., p. 167.
30 ibid., p. 162.
31 ibid., p. 125.
32 ibid., p. 123.

33 ibid., p. 50.
34 ibid., p. 85.
35 ibid., p. 85.
36 ibid., p. 59.
37 ibid., p. 135.
38 ibid., p. 131.
39 ibid., p. 139.
40 ibid., p. 140.
41 ibid., p. 140.
42 ibid., p. 140.
43 Though actually he is against repetitive work (cf. p. 163) – he wants productive work which needs at least some intelligence, and concedes that it may be reasonably clean: 'he must work like a peasant and think like a philosopher' (p. 165).
44 ibid., pp. 156–7.
45 ibid., p. 165.
46 ibid., p. 44.
47 ibid., p. 165.
48 ibid., p. 167.
49 ibid., p. 167.
50 ibid., p. 170.
51 ibid., p. 196.
52 ibid., p. 188.
53 ibid., p. 173.
54 ibid., p. 173.
55 ibid., pp. 183 and 192.
56 ibid., p. 180.
57 ibid., p. 198.
58 ibid., pp. 280–1.
59 ibid., p. 281.
60 ibid., p. 298.
61 ibid., p. 282.
62 R. R. Bolgar, *The Classical Heritage and its Beneficiaries* (Cambridge, Cambridge University Press, 1954), p. 3.
63 M. Mack, *The Garden and the City* (London, Oxford University Press, 1969).
64 E. M. W. Tillyard, *Some Mythical Elements in English Literature* (London, Chatto & Windus, 1961), p. 79.
65 *Emile*, p. 301.
66 ibid., p. 301.
67 ibid., p. 302.
68 ibid., p. 304.
69 ibid., p. 304.
70 ibid., p. 309.
71 ibid., p. 308.
72 ibid., p. 309. This is a view of the classics which would no doubt have bewildered some of the humanists, who looked on the writings of the ancients as models with which to correct the barbarism of the middle ages.
73 ibid., p. 320.
74 ibid., pp. 438–9.
75 ibid., p. 191.
76 It should not be thought that the purpose of this analysis of what I have called Rousseau's 'reductionism' is to imply the inherent and necessary superiority of the sophisticated over the 'simple'. For one thing, the 'simple' or ordinary (or whatever term one uses to designate them) people, because of their close contact with certain of the material actualities of daily living, develop a sense of reality which is denied our emancipated 'liberal' intelligentsia, who live in terms of abstractions (rather, in fact, like Rousseau – he is an early example of the breed). Furthermore, I have, on many occasions, expressed admiration for the 'culture'

of the folk in pre-industrial times. Why, then, do I criticise Rousseau's appeal to such people unreservedly? Part of the answers lies in my realisation that Rousseau has made no realistic assessment of the strengths and weaknesses of folk existence. His picture of them constitutes a pure indulgence on his part, failing to recognise that they, too, reveal complexities; for him, they constitute pure abstractions, ready to offer solace for his own social inadequacies, an alternative milieu to which he can appeal in a dream of resolution of his own problems. It's not that recognition of the folk *necessarily* implies a reductionist outlook – but of Rousseau's folk it certainly does.

At the same time, it should also be said that, whatever the very real virtues of folk culture, I could never be so foolish as to think that it offered the range of satisfactions, the sheer awareness of human possibility, the complexity of achievement that has been afforded by 'high' or sophisticated culture (think of the stupendous manifestations of the renaissance culture itself). And I would argue this in the full realisation that the sophisticated often incorporated elements of folk culture in their own productions.

Emile, indeed, is symptomatic of the beginnings of a profound cultural crisis – the challenge of mass egalitarian men to traditional humanistic culture – which will be explored in the next volume.

Conclusion

During the period covered by this volume, then, the notions of art and nature have undergone significant changes in their relationship one to the other. Nature, once the scene of a teleological striving and therefore value oriented, has become a neutral setting, observing its own laws which men may discover but only master by obeying. When 'art' was manifested within a teleological framework, it made sense to speak of different levels of achievement – and one way to signalise 'art' at its best was to speak of the art that hides art; for in such a setting aesthetic and moral considerations come into play as man may be said to reveal a 'higher' or 'lower' manifestation of his accepted potential. To operate within such a world of value at all – however in detail those values may be said to manifest themselves, a matter, usually, for dispute – is to regularise concepts like 'better' or 'worse'. The phrase 'the art that hides art' is simply a way of signalling a certain consummation of artistry, of indicating that this is a 'better' art.

When, however, 'art' (in this respect as what we have come to call 'science') is manifest within a neutralised nature, it is subject not to the criteria of 'better' or 'worse' but of 'truth' to objective fact; it is effective only if it fits the facts of the case and is controlled not by a metaphysical vision but behaviour quite independent of human volition. 'Truth' to objective fact becomes the sole criterion of achievement. Hence talk of *levels* of art become irrelevant – all that matters is accuracy and efficiency.

'Art', then, has ceased to operate typically within the world of values (though the tendency persists because to be human is to inhabit a world necessitating value discrimination) and instead operates within the neutralised nature where the 'fit' with the actualities of behaviour is all that matters. But where humans are concerned, what *are* these actualities? Any attempt to assimilate human development to the 'truths' of human nature turns out to be a more ambiguous occupation than at first thought. The cult of 'sincerity' – which has hovered behind the evolution with which this book is concerned – faces the ineluctable necessity imposed on human beings of *choice*. The actualities of human behaviour are not defined with the rigour with which the actualities of the behaviour of material particles are – man has a range of possibilities which constitute, for him, the moral world of value with which he has to come to terms. To be sincere to oneself is to necessitate a search for what that self, among various possibilities, entails. It is, in any case, always in some degree to be true to an *image* of oneself – for consciousness inevitably plays a role in the definition.

Now the humanists mitigated the harshnesses of Christian sinfulness, but still saw human nature as a scene of conflict – hence their emphasis on 'formation', 'moulding' and their concern for artifice, a formative power which would help transcend 'primitive' nature through the evolution of a 'second nature' in line with metaphysically conceived possibilities. But once blur the necessity for any self-transcendence, as Rousseau blurs it through his emphasis on primitive *goodness*, and the status of the primitive becomes equivocal. Rousseau seeks mastery within the natural world – but within the moral world he seeks only to preserve what has initially been given. Yet to equate 'sincerity', the 'real self' with the primitive self, which is what, in effect, he does, is as inadequate as to equate it with the more debased 'artificialities' of a courtly existence. For man is neither purely the 'primitive' nor purely the 'artificial' but a complex amalgam of the two; something of him is *given*, but much is *made* – this the humanists explicitly realised. This is how Castiglione can found his 'art' on 'nature' and produce a 'second nature' of traits assimilated to a higher power than that of the primitive, yet become 'natural', 'spontaneous', 'effortless' in the process.

The development in this volume can be seen from a variety of perspectives. It charts the problems arising as one moves from a more traditional to a more 'open' society; it is characterised by the growing predominance of a scientific, neutral over a mythologised, teleological, concept of nature and its implication for notions of *human* nature. It indicates what happens as more and more aspects of life are brought into the area of conscious decision making and come to be directed by thought and theoretical considerations. It records the gradual evolution of a belief in formation and education rather than in the less conscious assimilation of historical models. Paradoxically, as life becomes more complex, more the function of thought, an increasingly important strand of *thought* looks to 'artificially' primitive solutions, as if in compensation. Above all, it poses for the next volume the problems of an increasingly complex possibility of role assumption and therefore of educational models, stretching from the romantic endeavour to discover the 'realities' of human nature under the accretions of history at one extreme, and the growing demands on mind in an increasingly complex society, complex technically, socially, at the other, with a still persisting but attenuating classical humanist model under attack by both in differing ways. The position is exacerbated by the spread of formal education to new classes of the community and the problems of assimilation to traditional models they pose. Hence education in general is tempted to become something increasingly abstracted from any specific social function, for it must encompass, in the name of fairness, all possibilities within it. And this movement is forecast, too, in this volume – in the change from an education specifically directed at a social and political elite – and concerned, therefore, with the realities of social power – to one which comes to direct itself increasingly to the uniformities thought to exist underneath the conventional social differences and explicit in Rousseau's repudiation of the Citizen in favour of the Man. It is a change encouraged by the altered focus of attention from Words which imply individual contexts to Things which operate according to universal law. It becomes manifest in a changed orientation to language and its functioning – from the full affective-cognitive range implicit in the rhetorical discourse of the humanists to the increasingly denotative emphasis of the empirics, and its accompanying 'plainness' and neglect of – indeed, hostility to – affect (except as part of romantic protest). The new culture becomes rich in an understanding affiiliated to mathematical and scientific models and the control of natural phenomena these permit; but it loses the richness and 'copiousness' of humanistic experience defined through the range of its rhetorical linguistic usage. The socially inferior status of feeling, implied in romantic protest and the sense of the alienation which accompanied it on the one hand, and the triumph of a particular type of rationalism geared to the abstractions of thought, from which affect was deliberately excluded after the scientific model, on the other, has profound implications for our culture and the theorising about education intended to sustain it which will be explored in the next volume.

Short Biographies of the Main Theorists

Francis Bacon, Lord Verulam
Francis Bacon was born in 1561, the younger son of Sir Nicholas Bacon, Lord Keeper of the Great Seal. At the age of 12 he was sent to Trinity College, Cambridge, leaving after three years 'with a profound contempt for the course of study pursued there' and 'a fixed conviction that the system of academic education in England was radically vicious', as Macaulay put it. In 1576 he was admitted to Gray's Inn and shortly after began his training in diplomacy in the suite of the English ambassador to Paris. He had already been introduced to court life but when his father died suddenly, the ill will of the Cecils, to whom he was related, prevented his preferment. In 1582, however, he was called to the Bar and two years later entered Parliament. He became Queen's Counsel and associated himself with the Earl of Essex, the then favourite of the queen, though this did not prevent his participation in the prosecution of Essex when the latter fell from favour. After the death of Elizabeth he became a persistent suitor for the favour of the new king, who knighted him. He had previously published a few of his essays, and in 1605 issued *The Advancement of Learning*. He married in 1606 and a year later was made Solicitor-General. Subsequently he became Attorney-General, a Privy Councillor and Keeper of the Great Seal and finally, in 1618, Lord Chancellor of England. He gained favour by his support for the doctrine of the Divine Right of Kings and by his shifting allegiances to those great nobles who found favour with James I. In 1620 he published *Novum Organum*. But in 1621 he was accused by Parliament of accepting bribes – a practice usually condoned, but in this case relentlessly pursued by the former Chief Justice, Coke, whose dismissal Bacon had secured. Bacon was sentenced to imprisonment, a heavy fine, and declared incapable of holding office in the state. The king was able to mitigate the fine and the imprisonment and Bacon was allowed to retire to his estate near St Albans. Here he devoted himself to further writing, published in 1623 the *New Atlantis* and revised his *Essays*. He died in 1626.

Baldassare Castiglione
Castiglione was born in 1478 at Casatico, his father's estate in Mantua. He thus grew up in aristocratic surroundings and was friendly with the Gonzaga princes of his native state. After a period at Milan University he worked in the service of the dukes of Milan and Mantua. It was in Mantua that he became known to the exiled Duke of Urbino; and when Guidobaldo and his wife, Elizabetta, were restored, Castiglione entered their service in 1504. For the next twelve years he continued to serve first Guidobaldo and then, after the duke's death in 1508 when Urbino became a papal fief, Francesco Maria della Rovere, nephew of Pope Julius II. On the deposition of the 'Lord Prefect' (Francesco), Castiglione fled to Mantua where he married and settled down as one of the close friends of the Gonzagas. In 1519 he was employed in diplomatic missions and finally became Mantuan ambassador to Rome. There, in 1524, Pope Clement VII made him papal nuncio to Spain, and in Spain he

lived the rest of his life, dying in Toledo in 1529. He spent many years of his life on his book *The Courtier*, completing the first draft while living in Urbino and ceaselessly adding to it and polishing it. Friends urged its publication, and in 1527, after the death of the duchess Elizabetta, Castiglione sent the manuscript to the Aldine press in Venice. It appeared in 1528 and rapidly went through a number of editions and translations, appearing in Sir Thomas Hoby's translation in England in 1561.

John Amos Comenius

The offspring of a prosperous miller who belonged to a religious body known as the Moravian Brethren, Comenius was born in Moravia in 1592. He became an orphan at an early age. He attended a village school, and then, in his sixteenth year, was sent to a Latin school where he became one of many whose youth was wasted in what he termed the 'slaughter-houses' of the young. It was this experience, however, which led him to devise new pedagogic methods. He desired to become a minister of the Moravian Brethren and studied at Herborn, Heidelberg and Amsterdam during which time he came under the influence of one of the most remarkable men of his time, Alsted, who had himself an encyclopaedic knowledge and indeed published an *Encyclopaedia Scientiarum Omnium*, a work which exercised a considerable influence on *The Great Didactic*. After returning to his own people Comenius became rector of two schools and married. But the outbreak of the Thirty Years' War and the invasion of Fulneck, where he was stationed, by Spanish troops led him to flee after losing much of his library and some of his manuscripts. In 1622, also, his wife and two children died of an epidemic. He married again and was sent by the Brethren to Poland to report on the advisability of their moving to that country as a refuge from persecution. In fact, Comenius moved to Lissa in 1628, where, in 1636, he became rector of the gymnasium. It was here that he composed most of his didactic works, including the *Didactic* itself; he also became a bishop of the exiled Moravian Brethren. His work as a teacher encouraged him to write suitable textbooks for his school, books which became famous throughout Europe, including the *Janua Linguarum Reserata*, an introduction to the Latin language. *The Great Didactic*, though probably finished in 1632, remained in manuscript until 1849, though a Latin version was published in Amsterdam in 1657.

In 1641 he was invited to England with a view to assisting in the reform of education under Parliament; little came of this at the time and he then went to Sweden where he undertook the writing of textbooks for that country's Latin schools. After six years he accepted an invitation to establish a school in Hungary. Finally in 1654 he settled in Amsterdam where he devoted his time to his pansophic writings. In 1658 he published his famous *Orbis Sensualium Pictus*, one of the first children's picture books. He died in 1670.

Sir Thomas Elyot

Elyot was born during the 1490s, the offspring of a long line of country gentry. His father, who had served as a justice in the Western Assizes and later on the King's Bench, provided him with a good education at home, at one of the Inns of Court, and at Oxford, where he took first his Bachelor's degree and then one in Civil Law. The most formative influence on his life, however, was his association with the humanistic circle of Sir Thomas More, where he met Thomas Linacre who taught him Greek and medicine, Hans Holbein and probably men like Erasmus, Colet and Vives. Thomas Elyot soon began to participate in the business of government. He became Clerk to the Justices of Assize for the Western Circuit in 1511; twelve years later Wolsey made him Chief Clerk of the King's Council. On Wolsey's fall in 1530 he retired to his manor of Carlton near Cambridge to write *The Governor*. To this book he owed his appointment as ambassador to the Emperor Charles V. Subsequently he wrote or translated a number of other works concerned with politics and government, and thus helped to popularise the classics in England. He died in 1546.

Desiderius Erasmus

The illegitimate son of a priest and a widow, Erasmus was born about 1466 in Rotterdam. Educated first in Gouda and then at Deventer where 'an occult force of nature drove [me] to the humanities', he nevertheless acquired an antipathy to the methods of instruction, which were still medieval. In 1486 he became a member of the Augustinian Canons at Steyn and in 1492 ordained priest. During his monastic period he wrote the tract *Antibarbari*, justifying pagan learning. In 1495 he attended the University of Paris where he made the acquaintanceship of Lord Mountjoy who invited him to England in 1499. There he developed a firm friendship with Sir Thomas More and John Colet who stimulated further his developing interest in humanism and education. In 1500 the *Adages* appeared, the first of a number of editions which were used as school texts throughout Europe. In 1501 he published *Enchiridion Militis Christiani* (*Handbook of the Militant Christian*) in which he deployed his strategy for the maintenance of a Christian outlook. Between 1506 and 1509 he travelled extensively in Italy, returning to England in 1509 where he composed the Greek-entitled *Moriae Enkomion* (*Praise of Folly*), employing a pun on his host's name (Sir Thomas More). In 1511 he moved to Cambridge where he lectured in Greek, and published his first major treatise *De Ratione Studii* (*On the Correct Method of Instruction*) in 1511 and a new school textbook, *De Copia Verborum* (*Concerning Verbal Amplification*) in 1512, a book he dedicated to Colet for use in his newly established school at St Paul's. In 1514 he resumed his continental wanderings and published in 1516 *Institutio Principis Christiani* (*The Education of a Christian Prince*). In the same year came his highly, acclaimed version of the New Testament in a carefully edited Greek text accompanied by a Latin translation. Two years later, another of his most famous textbooks, the *Colloquies*, intended to assist in the teaching of Latin conversation, achieved wide acclaim. He became somewhat reluctantly involved in the Lutheran debate, attacking Luther but equivocal in his attitude to the Catholic church. His ideal was the cultivated man, not the narrow partisan. By now widely known, though a centre of controversy, he received many invitations to visit a wide variety of countries and spent time in a number of European centres, including towns in the Low Countries, Basle and Freiburg. He finally returned to Basle in 1535 where he died in 1536. His last important work on education *De Pueris Instituendis* (*On the Education of Boys*) he first published in 1529.

John Locke

Locke was born in 1632 of a middle-class Puritan family. He was educated at Westminster school and then, in 1652, went to Christ Church, Oxford, where subsequently he became tutor, lecturer in Greek and reader in rhetoric. In about 1664 he began the study of medicine and developed a growing interest in natural sciences, an interest which led to his election to the Royal Society in 1668. For a time he considered a political or diplomatic career. A chance meeting at Oxford with Lord Ashley (later the first Earl of Shaftesbury and one of the most prominent political figures of the age) resulted in an invitation to join Ashley's household as family physician and family adviser. Locke thus moved to London where he became closely involved with the political career of his master, who became Lord High Chancellor; he also became tutor to Shaftesbury's son. In 1675, however, Shaftesbury (as by then he had become) fell from power and Locke retired to France, partly because of ill health brought about by over-work and partly as a means of retiring temporarily from active political involvement. When Shaftesbury returned to power in 1678 Locke, who had been spending his time on philosophical writings during his sojourn in France, re-entered his service. Once more Shaftesbury, who greatly desired to prevent the succession of the king's brother James, fell from favour and Locke retired to Holland, officially in exile after 1685. There he continued to write, producing his *Two Treatises of Civil Government* and part of the *Essay Concerning Human Understanding*. After the Revolution of 1688 Locke was free to return and did so early in 1689. He now became a permanent resident at Oates, the home of Sir Francis Masham, and except for a period between 1695 and 1700, as commissioner of the Board of Trade and Plantations, continued to live there as a private citizen until his death in 1704. In 1690 he published *An Essay Concerning Human Understanding* followed in three years' time by *Some Thoughts Concerning Education*, a book which went through several revised editions. His work *Of the Conduct of the Understanding* was published posthumously in 1706 in *The Works of Mr. John Locke*. In addition to his writings on education he acted as tutor and educational adviser to several other families; and indeed some of the letters of advice he wrote became incorporated in his educational writings.

Michel de Montaigne

Montaigne was born in 1533, the son of a landowner in the Dordogne valley. He was sent to the Collège de Guienne at the age of 6. He read philosophy at the universities of Bordeaux and Toulouse. In 1554 he obtained a legal position in Périgueux and transferred in 1557 to Bordeaux, where his father had been elected mayor. Bordeaux became the scene of much disorder owing to conflicts which broke out between the Catholics and the Huguenots, culminating in the execution of a prominent Huguenot, and Montaigne received an early lesson in the need for toleration. Some time at the French court followed, but he returned to Bordeaux in 1563. Two years later he married Françoise de la Chassagne, who brought him a considerable dowry. On the death of his father in 1568 he inherited the estates at Montaigne. Next year he published a translation of the *Natural Theology* of Sebond, a work undertaken initially at his father's request. In 1571 he abandoned the law and his public positions and retired to his estate. His peaceful application to the writing of the *Essais* was interrupted by civil war but once more he retired to his library in 1576. Shortly after he had handed two volumes of his works to the printer in 1580 he travelled extensively in Germany and Italy, seeking a cure for the stone. During the remaining twelve years of his life – he died in 1592 – he acted as mayor of Bordeaux for two years; but he had abandoned all political ambitions and despite attempts by Henry of Navarre who thought highly of him, to engage him in a political post he preferred his life on his estates, expanding and revising his *Essais*, of which further editions were published at frequent intervals.

Jean-Jacques Rousseau

Rousseau's father was a watchmaker; Jean Jacques was born in 1712 in Geneva, his mother dying when he was only a week old. He was brought up by his father for the first ten years of his life and then by an uncle. After two years at school, to which he was sent by his uncle, he became apprentice first to a notary and then to an engraver. Both employments proved unsatisfactory and he left Geneva at the age of 16. During the next twenty years he tried a number of vocations – he acted as servant, studied for the priesthood (having been converted to Catholicism), practised music, worked as a secretary and tutor; but all his efforts ended in failure. His various adventures brought him into contact with Madame de Warens, a wealthy widow, whose lover he became for a time. During the latter part of this period he spent some time in Paris, where he came to be introduced into literary circles through his temporary friendship with Diderot and contributed to the *Encyclopédie*. He was 37 before he showed real signs of intellectual ability; in 1749 he entered an essay, a *Discourse on the Arts and Sciences*, for a prize at the Academy of Dijon and won. Its publication the following year brought him fame. From this time on he published extensively. In 1755 his *Discourse upon Inequality* attracted some attention. In 1762 he published *La Novelle Héloise*, *Emile* and *The Social Contract*, all of which brought him both fame and notoriety. He had in 1754 returned to Geneva, forsworn Catholicism and become Protestant again. He returned to Paris in 1756 and when his books were published they were considered anti-clerical and dangerous to public order. The Parlement of Paris condemned *Emile*, and Rousseau fled to Switzerland; he was, however, forced to leave there when Geneva joined Paris in condemnation of his work. For a number of years he moved round from country to country, living for short periods in Switzerland, England, France and Prussia; in England he was a guest of David Hume. He became increasingly unbalanced and quarrelled with many of his former acquaintances, including Hume. He had formed a liaison with a woman of the lower classes, Thérèse Le Vasseur, by whom he had five children all of whom he is reported to have sent to orphanages. He finally returned to France in 1770 where he completed his autobiography, the famous *Confessions*. He died in 1778.

Juan Luis Vives

Vives was born in Valencia in 1492. In 1509 he attended the University of Paris and continued there for the next five years; during this period he became friendly with Erasmus. Following his years at the university he became a teacher, first as a private tutor to William de Croy and then at the University of Louvain. In 1523 he was invited by Wolsey to occupy a chair at Oxford, at Corpus Christi College which had been founded a few years previously. In 1528 he found it necessary to leave England, for he had become involved in the dispute over Henry VIII's divorce from a fellow Spaniard, Catherine of Aragon; he moved to Bruges, where he lived until his death in 1540. Whilst in England, however, he maintained his friendship with Erasmus and formed others with English humanists such as Sir Thomas More; these relationships he continued to enjoy during the later years of his life, and in 1531 he published his major educational work *De Tradendis Disciplinis* (*On the Transmission of Learning*). Previously he had written against scholasticism – where his debt to Erasmus and other humanist authors is clear – and, at the request of Queen Catherine, a short treatise on the education of women.

Select Bibliography

Aaron, R. I., *John Locke* (Oxford University Press, 1971).

Adams, J., *The Evolution of Educational Theory* (Macmillan, 1912).

Ariès, P., *Centuries of Childhoood* (Penguin, 1973).

Ascham, R., *The Schoolmaster*, ed. L. V. Ryan (Cornell University Press, 1967).

Auerbach, E., *Mimesis* (Doubleday Anchor Books, 1953).

Bacon, F., *The Advancement of Learning and New Atlantis*, ed. A. Johnston (Oxford University Press, 1974).

Bacon, F., *Selections*, ed. M. T. McClure (Scribner, 1928).

Bainton, R. H., *Erasmus of Christendom* (Collins, 1972).

Baldwin, T. W., *William Shakspere's 'Small Latine and Lesse Greeke'*, 2 Vols (University of Illinois Press, 1944).

Bantock, G. H., *Education and Values* (Faber, 1965).

Baron, H., *The Crisis of the Early Italian Renaissance* (Princeton University Press, 1966).

Baxandall, M., *Painting and Experience in Fifteenth Century Italy* (Oxford University Press, 1972).

Baxandall, M., *Giotto and the Orators* (Oxford University Press, 1971).

Bazin, G., *The Baroque* (Thames & Hudson, 1968).

Becker, C. L., *The Heavenly City of the Eighteenth-Century Philosophers* (Yale University Press, 1959).

Bietenholz, P. G., *History and Biography in the Work of Erasmus of Rotterdam* (Geneva, Librairie Droz, 1966).

Blunt, A., *Artistic Theory in Italy 1450–1600* (Oxford University Press, 1962).

Bolgar, R. R., *The Classical Heritage and its Beneficiaries* (Cambridge University Press, 1954).

Bowen, J., *A History of Western Education*, Vol. II (Methuen, 1975).

Boyd, William and King, E. J., *The History of Western Education*, 10th edn (Black, 1972).

Bradbrook, M. C., *The School of Night* (Cambridge University Press, 1936).

Brandt, W. J., *The Shape of Medieval History* (Schocken Books, 1973).

Bryson, G., *Man and Society* (Princeton University Press, 1945).

Burckhardt, J., *The Civilisation of the Renaissance in Italy* (Phaidon, 1944).

Burke, P., *Popular Culture in Early Modern Europe* (Temple Smith, 1978).

Burtt, E. A., *The Metaphysical Foundations of Modern Science* (Routledge & Kegan Paul, 1925).

Butterfield, H., *The Origin of Modern Science 1300–1800* (Bell, 1957).

Cartwright, J., *Baldassare Castiglione: His Life and Letters*, 2 Vols (Murray, 1908).

Caspari, F., *Humanism and the Social Order in Tudor England* (Teachers College Press, Columbia University, 1968).

Cassirer, E., *The Individual and the Cosmos in Renaissance Philosophy*, trans. M. Domandi (Harper Torchbooks, 1964).

Cassirer, E., *The Philosophy of the Enlightenment* (Beacon Press, 1955).

Cassirer, E. et al., *The Renaissance Philosophy of Man* (University of Chicago Press, 1948).

Castiglione, B., *The Book of the Courtier*, trans. G. Bull (Penguin, 1967).

Charlton, K., *Education in Renaissance England* (Routledge & Kegan Paul, 1965).

Chastel, A., *The Studios and Styles of the Renaissance* (Thames & Hudson, 1966).

Chaytor, H. J., *From Script to Print* (Cambridge University Press, 1945).

Clarke, M. L., *Classical Education in Britain (1500–1900)* (Cambridge University Press, 1959).

Collingwood, R. G., *The Idea of Nature* (Oxford University Press, 1965).

Comenius, J. A., *A Reformation of Schools*, trans. S. Hartlib 1642 (Scolar Press, 1969).

Comenius, J. A., *The Way of Light*, trans. E. T. Campagnac (Liverpool University Press, 1938).

Comenius, J. A., *The Great Didactic*, ed. and trans. M. W. Keatinge (Black, 1896).

Comenius, J. A., *Analytical Didactic*, trans. V. Jelinck (University of Chicago Press, 1953).

Craig, Hardin, *The Enchanted Glass* (Blackwell, 1950).

Danby, J., *Shakespeare's Doctrine of Nature: A Study of 'King Lear'* (Faber, 1949).

Dannenfeldt, K. H. (ed.), *The Renaissance: Basic Interpretations* (Heath, 1974).

Descartes, R., *A Discourse on Method*, trans. J. Veitch (Everyman, 1957).

Durkheim, E., *The Evolution of Educational Thought*, trans. P. Collins (Routledge & Kegan Paul, 1977).

Elias, N., *The Civilising Process*, trans. E. Jephcott (Blackwell, 1977).

Elyot, Sir Thomas, *The Book named The Governor*, ed. S. E. Lehmberg (Everyman, 1962).

Erasmus, D., *The Education of a Christian Prince*, trans. L. K. Born (Columbia University Press, 1936).

Erasmus, D., *Praise of Folly*, trans. B. Radice (Penguin, 1975).

Evans, R. J. W., *Rudolf II and his World* (Oxford University Press, 1973).

Farrington, B., *Francis Bacon: Philosopher of Industrial Science* (Macmillan, 1973).

Febvre, L. and Martin, H.-J., *The Coming of the Book*, trans. D. Gerard (New Left Books, 1976).

Ferguson, W. K., *The Renaissance in Historical Thought* (Harvard University Press, 1948).

Fletcher, H. F., *The Intellectual Development of John Milton*, Vol. 1: *From the Beginnings through Grammar School* (University of Illinois Press, 1956).

Garin, E., *Italian Humanism*, trans. P. Munz (Blackwell, 1965).

Gay, P., *The Enlightenment*, Vol. I: *The Rise of Modern Paganism* (Weidenfeld & Nicolson, 1967).

Gay, P., *The Enlightenment*, Vol. II: *The Science of Freedom* (Wildwood House, 1973).

Gilbert, N. W., *Renaissance Concepts of Method* (Columbia University Press, 1963).

Gilmore, M. P., *The World of Humanism 1453–1517* (Harper Torchbooks, 1962).

Gilson, E. (ed.), *R. Descartes: Discours de la Méthode: texte et commentaire* (Paris, Vrin, 1947).

Goffman, I., *The Presentation of Self in Everyday Life* (Penguin, 1969).

Gombrich, E. H., *Art and Illusion* (Phaidon, 1962).

Gombrich, E. H., *Norm and Form: Studies in the Art of the Renaissance* (Phaidon, 1966).

Gombrich, E. H., *The Story of Art* (Phaidon, 1967).

Gombrich, E. H., *Symbolic Images* (Phaidon, 1972).

Greenblatt, S. J., *Sir Walter Raleigh: The Renaissance Man and his Roles* (Yale University Press, 1973).

Gwynn, A., *Roman Education from Cicero to Quintilian* (Columbia University Press, n.d.).

Haskell, F., *Patrons and Painters: A Study in the Relations between Italian Art and Society in the Age of the Baroque* (Chatto & Windus, 1963).

Haydn, H., *The Counter-Renaissance* (Scribner, 1950).

Hazard, P., *The European Mind 1680–1715*, trans. J. L. May (Penguin, 1973).

Hexter, J. H., *Reappraisals in History* (Longman, 1961).

Hill, C., *Intellectual Origins of the English Revolution* (Panther, 1972).

Hill, C., *Puritanism and Revolution* (Panther, 1969).

Holmes, G., *The Florentine Enlightenment* (Weidenfeld & Nicolson, 1969).

Hooykaas, R., *Humanisme, Science et Réform* (Leyden, Brill, 1958).

Howells, W. S., *Logic and Rhetoric in England (1500–1700)* (Princeton University Press, 1956).

Huizinga, J., *The Waning of the Middle Ages* (Penguin, 1965).

Isham, T., *The Diary of Thomas Isham of Lamport (1658–81) kept by him in Latin*, trans. N. Marlow (Greg International Publishers, 1971).

Javitch, D., *Poetry and Courtliness in Renaissance England* (Princeton University Press, 1978).

Joseph, Sister Miriam, *Shakespeare's Use of the Arts of Language* (Columbia University Press, 1949).

Kearney, H., *Scholars and Gentlemen: Universities and Society in Pre-Industrial Britain* (Faber, 1970).

Kelso, R., *Doctrine of the English Gentleman* (University of Illinois Press, 1929).

Knowles, D., *The Evolution of Medieval Thought* (Longman, 1962).

Kristeller, P. O., *Renaissance Concepts of Man* (Harper Torchbooks, 1972).

Kristeller, P. O. and Wiener, P. P. (eds), *Renaissance Essays* (Harper Torchbooks, 1968).

Larner, J., *Culture and Society in Italy 1290–1420* (Batsford, 1972).

Lechner, J. M., *Renaissance Concepts of the Commonplaces* (Pageant Press, 1962).

Lee, R. W., *Ut Pictura Poesis: The Humanistic Theory of Painting* (Norton, 1967).

Levey, M., *Early Renaissance* (Penguin, 1967).

Levey, M., *High Renaissance* (Penguin, 1975).

Locke, J., *The Educational Writings of John Locke*, ed. J. W. Adamson (Cambridge University Press, 1922).

Locke, J., *An Essay Concerning Human Understanding*, ed. R. Wilburn (Everyman, 1947).

Locke, J., *Some Thoughts Concerning Education*, ed. J. L. Axtell (Oxford University Press, 1968).

Lovejoy, A. O. *Essays in the History of Ideas* (Braziller, 1955).

Lovejoy, A. O., *The Great Chain of Being* (Harvard University Press, 1942).

Lovejoy, A. O. and Boas, A., *Primitivism and Related Ideas in Antiquity* (Octagon Books, 1965).

McGowan, M., *Montaigne's Deceits* (University of London Press, 1974).

Machiavelli, N., *The Prince*, trans. W. K. Marriott (Dent, 1931).

Mack, M., *The Garden and the City* (Oxford University Press, 1969).

Major, J. M., *Sir Thomas Elyot and Renaissance Humanism* (University of Nebraska Press, 1964).

Mandrou, R., *From Humanism to Science (1480–1700)* (Penguin, 1978).

Margolin, J.-C., *Erasmus: Declamatio de Pueris Statim ac Liberaliter Instituendis* (Geneva, Librairie Droz, 1966).

Mathew, G., *The Court of Richard II* (Murray, 1968).

Meiss, M., *Painting in Florence and Siena after the Black Death* (Harper & Row, 1964).

Montaigne, M. de, *Essays*, trans. J. M. Cohen (Penguin, 1958).

Montaigne, M. de, *Essays*, 3 Vols, trans. J. Florio (Everyman, 1910).

Mumford, L., *The Culture of Cities* (Secker & Warburg, 1940).

Nash, P., Kazamias, A. M. and Perkinson, H. J. (eds), *The Educated Man* (Wiley, 1965).

Nef, J. V., *Cultural Foundations of Industrial Civilisation* (Harper Torchbooks, 1960).

Nelson, W., *Fact or Fiction: The Dilemma of the Renaissance Storyteller* (Harvard University Press, 1973).

Nisbet, R., *The Social Philosophers* (Paladin, 1974).

Noreña, C. G., *Juan Luis Vives* (The Hague, Nijhoff, 1970).

O'Kelly, B. (ed.), *The Renaissance Image of Man and the World* (Ohio State University Press, 1966).

Ong, W. J., *The Barbarian Within* (New York, Macmillan, 1962).

Ong, W. J., *Ramus, Method, and the Decay of Dialogue* (Harvard University Press, 1958).

Ong, W. J., *Rhetoric, Romance and Technology* (Cornell University Press, 1971).

Orme, N., *English Schools in the Middle Ages* (Methuen, 1973).

Panofsky, E., *Meaning in the Visual Arts* (Penguin, 1970).

Panofsky, E., *Renaissance and Renascences in Western Art* (Harper & Row, 1972).

Parkes, H. B., *The Divine Order* (Gollancz, 1970).

Passmore, J. A., *The Perfectibility of Man* (Duckworth, 1972).

Pocock, J. G. A., *The Machiavellian Moment* (Princeton University Press, 1973).

Pope-Hennessy, J., *The Portrait in the Renaissance* (Phaidon, 1966).

Price, K., *Education and Philosophical Thought*, 2nd edn (Allyn & Bacon, 1967).

Reti, L. (ed.), *The Unknown Leonardo* (Hutchinson, 1974).

Rice, E. F., *The Renaissance Idea of Wisdom* (Harvard University Press, 1958).

Rossi, P., *Francis Bacon: From Magic to Science*, trans. S. Rabinovitch (Routledge & Kegan Paul, 1968).

Rousseau, J. J., *Emile*, trans. B. Foxley (Everyman, 1943).

Rowse, A. L., *The Elizabethan Renaissance: The Cultural Achievement* (Macmillan, 1972).

Russell, B., *History of Western Philosophy* (Allen & Unwin, 1946).

Sampson, R. V., *Progress in the Age of Reason* (Heinemann, 1956).

Seigel, J. E., *Rhetoric and Philosophy in Renaissance Humanism* (Princeton University Press, 1968).

Shearman, J., *Mannerism* (Penguin, 1967).

Sheavyn, P., *The Literary Profession in the Elizabethan Age*, 2nd edn revised by J. W. Saunders (Manchester University Press, 1967).

Simon, J., *Education and Society in Tudor England* (Cambridge University Press, 1967).

Smith, N. Kemp, *New Studies in the Philosophy of Descartes* (Macmillan, 1952).

Spencer, T., *Shakespeare and the Nature of Man* (Cambridge University Press, 1943).

Stone, L., *The Crisis of the Aristocracy 1558–1641* (Oxford University Press, 1965).

Strong, R., *Splendour at Court* (Weidenfeld & Nicolson, 1973).

Struever, N. S., *The Language of History in the Renaissance* (Princeton University Press, 1970).

Tillyard, E. M. W., *The Elizabethan World Picture* (Chatto & Windus, 1943).

Tracy, J. D., *Erasmus: The Growth of a Mind* (Geneva, Librairie Droz, 1972).

Trinkaus, C., *'In Our Image and Likeness'*, 2 Vols (Constable, 1970).

Tuve, R., *Elizabethan and Metaphysical Imagery* (University of Chicago Press, 1947).

Ullmann, W., *Medieval Foundations of Renaissance Humanism* (Elek, 1977).

Vasari, G., *The Lives of the Artists*, trans. G. Bull (Penguin, 1975).

Vickers, B. (ed.), *Essential Articles for the Study of Francis Bacon* (Connecticut, Archon Books, 1968).

Vickers, B., *Francis Bacon and Renaissance Prose* (Cambridge University Press, 1968).

Watson, Foster, *Vives: On Education* (Cambridge University Press, 1913).

Watt, Ian, *The Rise of the Novel* (Chatto & Windus, 1957).

Webber, J., *The Eloquent 'I'* (University of Wisconsin Press, 1968).

Webster, C., *The Great Instauration* (Duckworth, 1975).

Webster, C. (ed.), *Samuel Hartlib and the Advancement of Learning* (Cambridge University Press, 1970).

Weiss, R., *The Renaissance Discovery of Classical Antiquity* (Blackwell, 1973).

Wightman, W. P. D., *Science in a Renaissance Society* (Hutchinson, 1972).

Willey, B., *The Seventeenth Century Background* (Chatto & Windus, 1934).

Willey, B., *The Eighteenth Century Background* (Chatto & Windus, 1940).

Williams, D., *Trousered Apes* (Churchill Press, 1971).

Wittkower, R., *Architectural Principles in the Age of Humanism* (Academy Editions, 1973).

Woodward, W. H., *Desiderius Erasmus Concerning the Aim and Method of Education* (Teachers College Press, Columbia University, 1964).

Woodward, W. H., *Studies in Education during the Age of the Renaissance 1400–1600* (Teachers College Press, Columbia University, 1967).

Woodward, W. H., *Vittorino da Feltre and Other Humanist Educators* (Teachers College Press, Columbia University, 1963).

Wright, L. B., *Middle-Class Culture in Elizabethan England* (University of North Carolina Press, 1935).

Yates, F. A., *The Art of Memory* (Penguin, 1969).

Yates, F. A., *Astraea* (Routledge & Kegan Paul, 1975).

Yates, F. A., *Giordano Bruno and the Hermetic Tradition* (Routledge & Kegan Paul, 1964).

Yates, F. A., *The Rosicrucian Enlightenment* (Routledge & Kegan Paul, 1972).

Yates, F. A., *The Theatre of the World* (Routledge & Kegan Paul, 1969).

Yolton, J. W., *John Locke and the Way of Ideas* (Oxford University Press, 1968).

Index

Works by the main theorists are indexed throughout except within the chapters devoted to these authors. Here, only the first mention of each of their writings is indexed, other references being cited in the notes at the ends of the relevant chapters.